PLAYING BRITANNIA

Also by Juliet Campbell and her father Wilfred d'A Collings.

One Small Island and Two World Wars

PLAYING BRITANNIA

HOW I BECAME HER EXCELLENCY

Juliet Campbell

First published 2023 by Holywell Press

Published by
Holywell Press
16–17 Kings Meadow
Ferry Hinksey Road
Oxford
OX2 0DP

A catalogue record for this book is available from the British Library.

ISBN: 978-1-916929-00-5

Designed and typeset by Holywell Press, Ltd., Oxford.
Printed in Great Britain by Holywell Press, Ltd., Oxford.

Contents

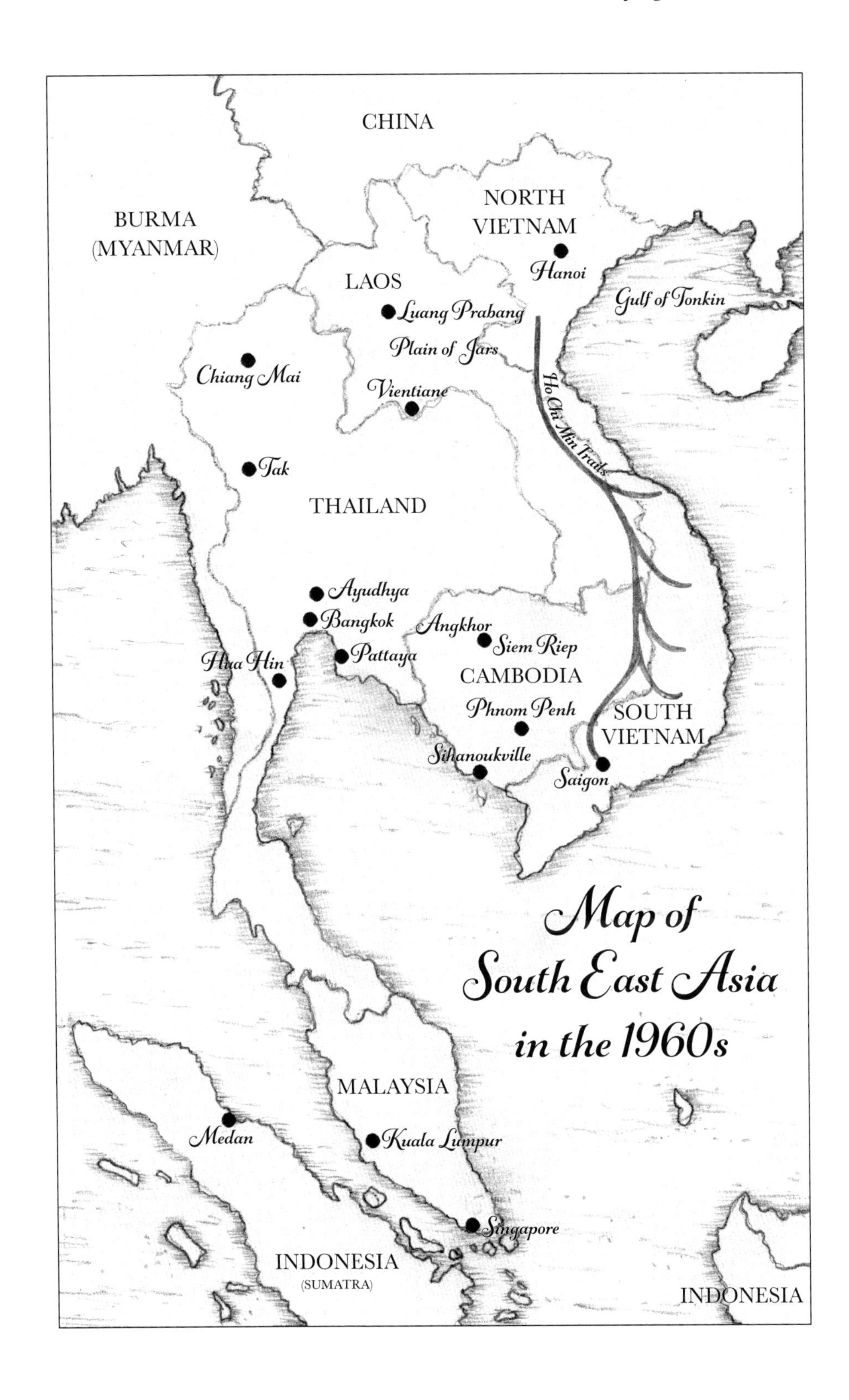
CHINA
BURMA (MYANMAR)
NORTH VIETNAM
Hanoi
Gulf of Tonkin
LAOS
Luang Prabang
Plain of Jars
Chiang Mai
Vientiane
Ho Chi Min Trails
Tak
THAILAND
Ayudhya
Bangkok
Angkhor
Siem Riep
Hua Hin
Pattaya
CAMBODIA
Phnom Penh
SOUTH VIETNAM
Sihanoukville
Saigon
Map of South East Asia in the 1960s
MALAYSIA
Medan
Kuala Lumpur
Singapore
INDONESIA
(SUMATRA)
INDONESIA

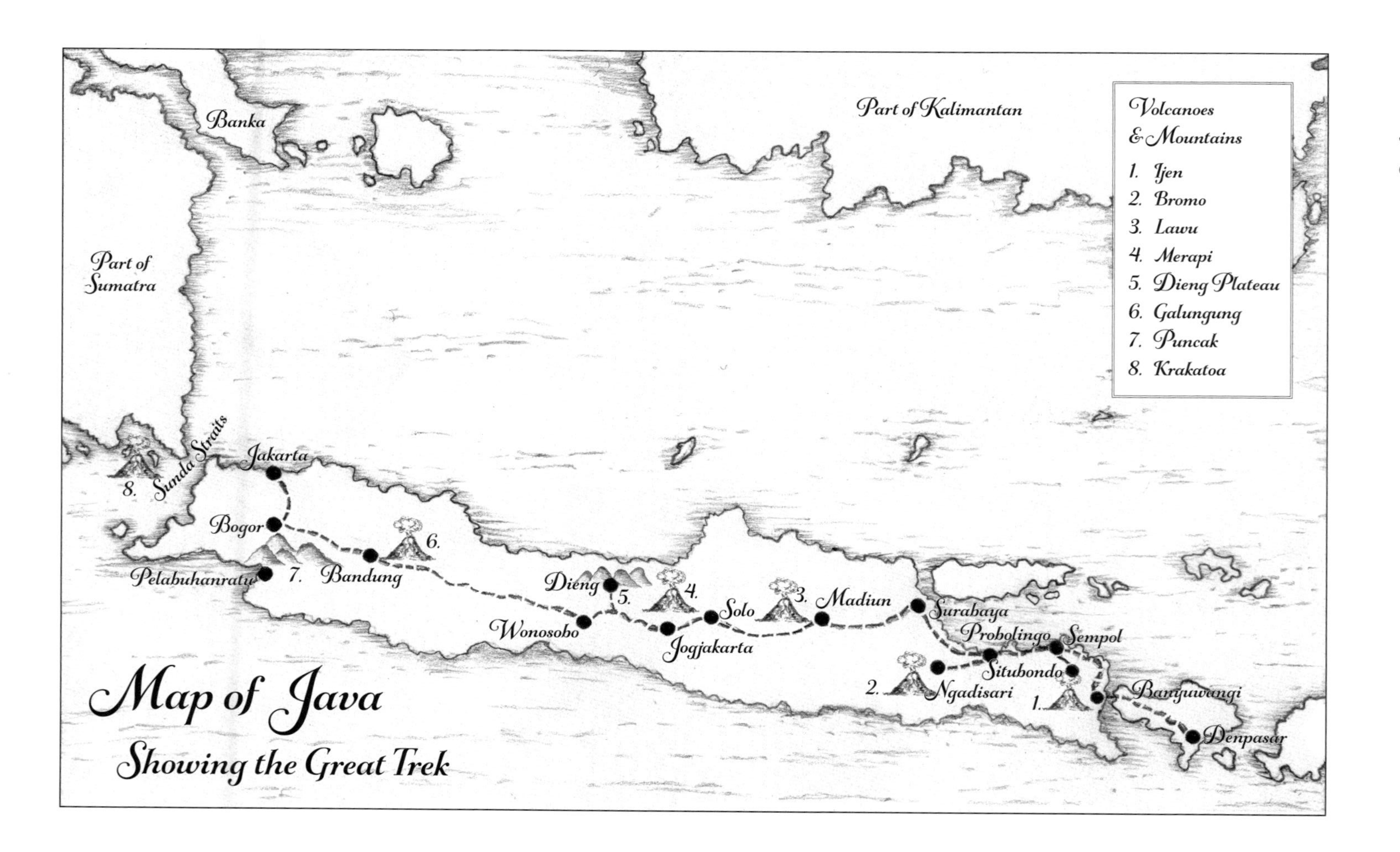
Map of Java
Showing the Great Trek
Volcanoes & Mountains
1. Ijen
2. Bromo
3. Lawu
4. Merapi
5. Dieng Plateau
6. Galunggung
7. Puncak
8. Krakatoa
Part of Kalimantan
Part of Sumatra
Banka
Sunda Straits
Jakarta
Bogor
Pelabuhanratu
Bandung
Wonosobo
Dieng
Jogjakarta
Solo
Madiun
Surabaya
Probolingo
Ngadisari
Situbondo
Sempol
Banyuwangi
Denpasar

INTRODUCTION

Letters are going out of fashion, more's the pity. I used to await the post with a touch of excitement, never knowing what treats the day would bring. Writing a letter is a pleasant pastime too if one lets oneself go. Best of all is a regular correspondence, especially when one is writing to someone one cares about. Today most of what I receive goes straight into the bin, but every now and then I still have the thrill of opening a real letter, and what a pleasure that is. Every Sunday while I was at boarding school the girls were required to write a letter to their parents. Thus started a habit that stayed with me when I went to Oxford and my parents were living in Beirut. When I joined the Diplomatic Service and was sent to South East Asia in the 1960s the letters took on a new significance in the absence of other means of communication. They were the all-important link to my distant home and family and they also became a sort of diary as I recorded the strange world in which I found myself. Somewhere along the way my mother started to keep my letters, and when my parents died I found them in their hundreds, a daunting pile that I put aside to be dealt with – someday, maybe. I doubt if I would have done anything with them without the help of my granddaughter Elizabeth who typed them all onto a computer, a mammoth task for which I am immensely grateful.

As I gradually read the letters through and put them into some sort of order the past came alive for me and I felt the urge to put them into a book. But there was a problem. There was a lot of material, too much, about certain phases of my life – Oxford, Bangkok, Jakarta – but little if anything at all about other long periods. Perhaps I wasn't writing home. Perhaps my mother didn't think the letters interesting enough to keep. Perhaps they simply got lost. Anyhow I realized with sinking heart that I needed to edit the letters down to manageable proportions and to write, more or less from scratch, about the other periods of my life which were at least as interesting. I also reread old diaries. The result is a story at two speeds with chapters of unequal length. It is also a story told by two voices: the Juliet (or Jen, as my parents called me) of long ago and the woman of advancing years who looks back on her younger self. Alas, I do not have the letters from my parents which I so eagerly awaited.

Before going any further I should introduce the parents to whom my letters were addressed. I loved them both dearly. My father, Maj Gen Wilfred d'Auvergne Collings, was a Guernseyman, the sixth of the eight children of a local doctor. He was born in 1893 and hardly left his beloved island until he went to Sandhurst in 1912. Not having the funds needed for a smart regiment, he joined the Royal Army Service Corps (later RASC) and spent most of the First World War in the hellholes of Gallipoli and Mesopotamia. The Second World War saw him back in the Middle East and North Africa, where he performed great feats in organizing the transport of supplies to troops on the move in the featureless Western Desert, and finally as Director of Supplies and Transport to Field Marshal Montgomery during the liberation of Western Europe. On leaving the army he spent a number of years as Director of Supply in UNRWA, the arm of the UN set up to deal with the wave of Palestinian refugees resulting from the creation of Israel. This is what took the family to Beirut while I was growing up.

My mother, Nancy Bishop, was also the child of a doctor. Indeed, she was the daughter of two doctors: her own mother Mary Sinclair was one of the first women to graduate in medicine from Edinburgh University. My mother's parents separated when she was quite young – a shameful matter in those days – and she grew up shuttling between the two and various kind friends and relatives. An intelligent and witty woman with a gift for friendship, she had a patchwork education. When she was about nineteen she spent a year in a sanatorium with TB, and got engaged to a man who died. She was very knowledgeable about antiques having worked for some years for the antiques department of Peter Jones. She met my father while in Guernsey visiting her own father who was the Island's Officer of Health. Wilfred was home on leave from Khartoum where he was on secondment to the Sudanese Army. They married in the Town Church in Guernsey and had two sons, Francis and Philip, before I was born in 1935.

They were very different personalities. My father was a man of great common sense and quiet humour who got on with things and with everyone. My mother was high-spirited, quick witted and critical, a very elegant woman with many friends. She was wonderful in a crisis, such as evacuation with small children in wartime, but she could be very sharp when bored or frustrated. When my father to his great relief inherited family property in Guernsey – they had sold their house in Farnham at the start of the war and when my father retired from the UN they were strapped for cash – she went there reluctantly and made the worst of it. I have recently come across some of their wartime letters, and it is clear that they loved each other. But I think she was a deeply frustrated woman who should have had a career of her own. As it was, she lived to a considerable extent through mine. My father once told me that it would not have occurred to him to send me to university; it was my mother I had to thank for that. I should also mention that my mother had a lot of ill health in her life. Apart from the TB, there was scarlet fever in Palestine and later a hysterectomy, tachycardia, hip replacements and ultimately strokes.

The title of this book is borrowed from the headline of a newspaper article written when I became the first woman regularly to take the Foreign Office daily press conference. *Juliet Plays Britannia*: the metaphor seemed to describe my long career in the Diplomatic Service, much of it spent overseas. There were very few women diplomats when I started and as I slowly advanced up the ladder I had regular bouts of imposter syndrome. Apart from trying to be on top of my brief I coped with lapses of confidence by reminding myself that I had a role to play as a member of an Embassy or Foreign Office Department and ultimately as an Ambassador. It is often easier to play a role than to be oneself. There is a touch of theatre in much diplomacy anyway. Playing also suggests fun, and I had a lot of that along the way.

So now I have set the scene it is time to dive in. But first a word on place names: many spellings have changed and were often transliterations anyhow (eg Beyrouth/Beirut). I have used current versions in the narrative but in quoting my letters I have left whatever spelling I used at the time.

Apart from my granddaughter Elizabeth I want to thank the two kind readers who read the first sprawling draft – my stepson John Campbell, whose perceptive comments often made me think a bit harder, and Harry Mace, whom I met through Girton while he was researching the Diplomatic Service and whose own book I eagerly await. My grandchildren Josh and Naomi made later helpful comments. My grateful thanks go to Brian Eastgate for his help with so many things. Then there were Mary Sandys, whom I cannot thank enough for her patience in helping me put the book into its final shape, and Maureen MacGlashan, a Foreign Office friend, who turned out to be a demon indexer. The Holywell Press were a pleasure to work with. My final thanks go to Harry Bucknall for his enthusiasm in helping me publicize this book.

Chapter 1

A PILLAR-TO-POST CHILDHOOD (1935 – 1953)

I was born in a nursing home in Blackheath called Stonefield which was run by two doctors with lovely names: Dr Pink and Dr White. My father was at that time (1935) a Captain in the Royal Army Service Corps which had its headquarters in Aldershot, and my parents were living in a house called Combe Orchard on the outskirts of nearby Farnham. From photos it looks quite substantial with a big garden.

I was christened in the Town Church in Guernsey. There was a good deal of discussion beforehand as to what to call me. Asked for suggestions my brother Francis, then six, proposed Blossom, while Philip, then four and a half, preferred Mountain. The final decision was apparently only taken in the car on the way to the church and I ended up with three given names – Juliet (inspiration possibly Shakespearean), Jeanne (after the first known Guernsey girl to marry a Collings when the family arrived in the Channel Islands with the exiled Charles II) and d'Auvergne (a name given to all our branch of the family). My mother was a great one for nicknames and in practice I got called Kitten, Poodle and Jenny Wren – as well as Hag by my elder brothers. Jenny dwindled over the years to Jen, which has stayed with me all my life. It was only when I started on a career that I put away childish names and became Juliet. For a long time I had a semi-split personality depending on whether I was addressed as Juliet or Jen. The main difference is that Juliet took herself a bit more seriously.

In 1937 my father was posted to Palestine, which was then governed by the British under a League of Nations Mandate following the Anglo-French carve-up of the Middle East. My mother, brothers and I followed him shortly afterwards. My first memories come in snatches – picnicking among the wildflowers in the olive groves that surrounded Jerusalem, leaving my precious stuffed rabbit Yellow in yet another of the Holy Places, or standing with my father at the door to my mother's room when she was recovering from scarlet fever. Palestine was a troubled place, with Jews and Arabs at each other's throats and both sides blaming the British. There was an Arab rebellion and increasingly violent Jewish resistance. I dimly remember overhearing stories of atrocities and it was instilled in me that I should never play in the olive groves outside our house. When war broke out in Europe in 1939 we were on holiday in the Troodos mountains in Cyprus. My chief memory of the outbreak of war is of Francis telling me that now all my dresses would have to be black.

War disrupted many childhoods. For me it meant endless moves with many changes of home and later school. This chapter represents a quick dash through disjointed times. Shortly after the outbreak of war we moved to Cairo, then a major military hub, where my father was Commander RASC Cairo, with the acting rank of Lt Colonel. The job came with an official residence in Abassia Barracks called Hilmi House, a fine house with a spreading garden where I loved to play. There was also a pet goose called Wooz who enjoyed nibbling my mother's nail polish. Egypt was still very much under British influence and the centre of social life for the large British community was the Gezira Club. No Egyptians there that I recall except for servants in their long *suffragi* gowns.

Our happy life there didn't last for long. The war in Europe had spilled over into the Middle East. Egypt was of particular importance because of the Suez Canal through which much of the oil passed on which our armed forces depended. Moreover, it was the shortest route to India, then still the jewel in Britain's imperial crown. When, in the summer of 1940, the British position in Egypt was threatened by Italian forces in neighbouring Libya, General O'Connor was sent to drive back the Italians, and my father was appointed as Deputy Director of Supplies and Transport on O'Connor's staff – I have told his story in *One Small Island and Two World Wars*, which contains his own Great War memoir.

This little army was remarkably successful, chasing the Italians all the way to Benghazi before the troops (and my father) were diverted to the disastrous Greek campaign. O'Connor himself believed that if he had been allowed to continue his advance he could have secured North Africa for the allies before the Germans landed there with their talismanic leader Erwin Rommel. It was also before the United States had joined the war so Britain was fighting on its own. Historians argue about whether O'Connor was right, given the long supply lines that were involved. As it was, the desert war dragged on until 1943 as the rival armies chased each other to and fro with huge casualties on both sides.

For the family my father's posting to the desert meant a return to Jerusalem. We flew back, a great adventure in itself. We then lived for a while in the German Hospice, which was run by the Sisters of St Charles Borromeo. I am told the lovely old stone buildings are still a hostel of some sort. It must have been during this period that I went to school for the first time, to the British Community School of Jerusalem. The nuns had a property out of the city which I remember as a simple nursery garden. There were a couple of rabbits there (live ones this time) which I loved to play with. They were called Wavell and O'Connor after the two generals then commanding British forces in the Middle East. We made occasional weekend excursions to an Arab village called Ain Karem, then in the countryside but now part of Jerusalem, where we stayed with an eccentric English lady called Miss Carey. She was there to await the Second Coming, and her particular belief was that He would arrive on the Friday evening train, so every week she laid an extra place for tea just in case.

When Rommel's armies threatened Cairo in early 1942 the British Government decided to evacuate all the women and children for which it was responsible from the whole of the Middle East. My mother opted to go to South Africa. I don't remember how we got back to Egypt but I do remember the train that took us and a mass of other women and children from Port Said to Suez. We were bombed and had to leave the train in a hurry. It must have been an isolated bomber because nobody was hurt and we had a peaceful if makeshift night in some hangar-like buildings near the railway. At Suez we boarded the steamer which was to take us to Durban. The ship before us, the *Georgic*, had been sunk in Suez harbour with much loss of life. One of those who died was the nine-year-old daughter of the Hogben family with whom we had celebrated Christmas at the German Hospice. The *Durban Castle* belonged to the Union Castle line and like so many other passenger ships she had been commandeered during the war. I celebrated my sixth birthday on board. My mother was a tower of strength during these eventful years, rising to all challenges and revelling in the responsibility. She was a tartar for discipline, and at times I was a little scared of her. But it was discipline with a purpose. She told me later that she had trained Francis to take responsibility for Philip and me should she get drowned. She was, however, always there, with essential papers in her handbag which she kept on a lead attached to her wrist. Another ever-present item of equipment was the Blue Potkin, a handled enamel jug which was used to heat soup, bathe wounds and for other unspeakable emergencies.

On arrival in Durban we were housed along with a gaggle of other families in a slightly rundown beachside hotel called the Harcourt Hotel. Two long low buildings opened motel-style onto a central space. Opposite the bedroom block was the dining room which had a juke box. More excitingly, there was a disused rack railway through the few hundred yards of scrub down to the beach. It was fun for us children to explore, running wild in gangs and inventing our own currency with the used bottle tops that lay all around, but I imagine my mother couldn't wait to get away.

It must have been from Durban that we joined an excursion to visit the Hluhluwe Game Reserve in Zululand. We went in our ancient Austin which my mother had somehow managed to bring from Palestine. It was a long drive and my mother nearly didn't take me, thinking I was too young – I must still have been about six. I am eternally grateful that she relented because it was an unforgettable experience. We stayed in a village of native rondavels, simple round houses with conical thatched roofs. It was thrilling to get up before dawn and to ride in the jeeps which took us to see the wild animals – rhinos galore, along with giraffes and elephants. One morning we visited a lake covered with flamingos which all took off at once as the sun rose leaving a scattering of pink feathers on the surface of the water. Along the river there were hippos and quantities of fearsome crocodiles slithering around the banks.

My mother and her great friend Eileen Middleton soon arranged to move to Cape Town, where we took rooms in a hotel in the suburb of Claremont. It was a pleasant place and I became great friends with Sally Middleton who was much my age. Then Eileen and my mother jointly rented a small house called Oak Arch. This was when a white mouse called Popsy joined the family. Originally named Popeye, she was bought to be a companion to a black and white mouse called Samuel Whiskers, but her name was changed when the house was overrun by batches of babies. I knitted little bags for them which Popsy obligingly used as bedding. We divided the mice as best we could into a male and a female cage but still they kept multiplying. We gave mice to all our friends who would take them, and one family came back complaining that their car had become infested.

From Oak Arch we moved to Tolini, a big house in Kenilworth belonging to the Moorsom family, which was to be our home for the rest of our time in South Africa. It was a handsome house with spreading balconies and a big garden. The front drive was lined with huge oak trees, one of which contained a tree house. The back garden had an orchard of loquat trees which produced delicious fruit and were the ideal size for climbing and settling into with a book. Ann Moorsom was South African and had three children. Diana, known as Doodles, was a dreamy 18-year-old who hung out with her friends and played endless pop songs like *Don't Fence Me In*. Then there was the handsome edgy Christopher who was a little older than my brothers and, like them, a boarder at Bishop's. The youngest child was Ruth, invariably called Beetle, a feisty tomboy of about Philip's age. Ruth later became a great beauty and the toast of Cambridge where she was known as Sasha. The father of this trio was in England, an artist and a figure of mystery. The other important person living at Tolini was Jane, the Cape Coloured cook, who guarded her kitchen against all intruders, and would chase out the dog Gippy brandishing a carving knife.

I was sent to Herschel, one of South Africa's leading girls' schools. It had a smart uniform, a cobalt blue dress with an ecru trim round the neck and a badge on the front: a capital H with an arrow through it. My mother was a deft needlewoman and used to make all my clothes. I can still hear her laugh when she realized that she had sewn the badge on my dress upside down so the arrow through the H pointed to Hell rather than Heaven. This was my first serious experience of education, and the only subject I remember well is history. We learned of the great Portuguese explorers, Bartholomew Diaz and Vasco da Gama, who first sailed round the Cape looking for a route to India. Their men chewed the leather strapping from the masts in the hopes of warding off scurvy, which was in fact caused by a diet lacking in vitamin C. Funny what sticks in one's mind.

Cape Province is a beautiful area, with the backdrop of Table Mountain and a string of beaches leading out to Simonstown. I learned to swim at Muizenberg and we all had lightweight surfboards on which one threw oneself as the chosen breaker came in. We visited the splendid gabled Cape Dutch houses – I particularly remember Groot Constantia and Tokay – which still represent my ideal of domestic architecture. Ann Moorsom, a woman of many interests and herself a good watercolourist, used to take us sketching, my first taste of what would become a lifelong pleasure. South Africa was a land of plenty and the war seemed far away. But I remember groups of dreadfully scarred servicemen coming to tea at Tolini. They were from St Dunstan's, a charity now known as Blind Veterans UK, and it was obvious even to me that they desperately missed their children back home. Our only lack was white bread and I think this was enforced abstinence rather than real shortage and meant by the Smuts government as an act of solidarity with Britain. Anyway, Jane made white bread at home. She had a special sieve for removing the husks from brown flour, a long mesh contraption with a paddle to push the flour through and a handle that had to be turned. I was allowed to help with this chore and the bread was delicious.

The war in North Africa came to an end with Montgomery's great triumph at El Alamein in October 1942. By this time my father was in Persia, helping organize the aid sent to the Russians during the siege of Stalingrad. He managed to join us for a couple of brief spells of leave during our time in South Africa. With servicemen so widely dispersed across the globe it was often possible to hitch a ride on a plane going in the right direction. In late 1943, with the focus of the war shifting back to Europe, he was posted back to England and my mother started looking for ways to get us back there too. In March 1944 we embarked on the *Empress of Scotland*. Launched in 1929 and the pride of the Canadian Pacific fleet, she was originally called the *Empress of Japan*, but for obvious reasons her name was changed when she was requisitioned as a troopship. We had a small cabin for the four of us, and shared communal washing facilities with many other people: cramped conditions, but we were much more comfortable than the troops who slept in lines of hammocks strung up between the decks. We had to pick our way between the hammocks to get to the dining room which was rather grand with white-coated stewards waiting at table. The servicemen were very kind to us children, again perhaps thinking wistfully of their own back home.

Being fast the *Empress* sailed alone, rather than as part of a convoy, and she zigzagged her way around the Atlantic to throw off U-boats. This was still the height of the Battle of the Atlantic with German submarines seeking to destroy the Allied shipping which brought military equipment and other supplies from America to Europe. We had many lifeboat drills which entailed going to the correct muster station with one's life belt and other essentials when the siren went off. At all times one had to wear a metal identity disk on a chain round one's neck. I still have mine. It is tiny, half the size of my dog's name disc, and reads: JULIET D of Brig W d'A COLLINGS BG"A". It is unsettling in retrospect to think that my father's name and my blood group were all that was meant to identify me had I been washed up alone. One night the alarm was for real and I remember the tense feeling as we climbed to action stations on the top deck. It was an unidentified aircraft and fortunately gave no trouble. I don't remember ever being afraid. Children accept life as it is and my mother was always there.

We arrived in Liverpool to a heroes' welcome. As we hung over the rail a military band on the jetty played "Daisy, Daisy, give me your answer, do." Then we went by train to London, where we were met by my mother's great friend Irene Sewell, who took us back to her home near Dorking. The house belonged to Irene's father, an elderly invalid looked after by a live-in nurse known as Sister. It was called Moorfield and must have been quite a place before the war with its outhouses and gardens. My brothers found a penny-farthing bicycle in one of the garages. The only other person living in the house was the Old Lady who had been Irene's nanny and brought her up when her mother died. She was one of the small handful of people I ever met who still wore high-necked, long-skirted Edwardian dresses, a hangover from an earlier age. Her domain was the basement and she gave me supper in the servants' hall every evening. It usually included a coffee cup full of soup, which I detested and she was determined to make me like. There were also two gardeners' cottages in the grounds. In both cases the men were away fighting so only the women and children were there, but the gardens remained in apple pie order.

Dorking was the right side of London as far as air raids were concerned but near enough to see the searchlights stabbing the sky at night as well as the occasional aerial dogfight. There was the wreckage of a plane on the common and one day there was a marvellous fire there with each holly bush catching alight with a loud crack. To us children the war was rather exciting but after South Africa England was very grey with blackout and rationing. A black painted ring round the bath reminded one not to take more than the permitted four inches of hot water.

Moorfield was a temporary solution to the problem of where we should live. Combe Orchard had been sold at some point during the war so we had no home. We saw very little of my father during this period. He was busy helping train soldiers for the invasion of Europe until just before D-Day when he joined Montgomery's staff as Director of Supplies and Transport for Operation Overlord. From June 1944 until March 1946 he was away in Europe. The boys were sent as boarders to Wellington College while my mother and I went from pillar to post. I find it difficult to remember where we went and in what order. To make matters worse, my mother was not well; she eventually had a hysterectomy which was a big operation back then. I had a spell with a family called Charrington who were related to Irene Sewell. They had a big house at Ingatestone, near Chelmsford. It was the only time in my life that I lived in farming country and despite wartime shortages it was in many ways the country as it must have been pre-war. The eldest Charrington daughter, June, was a land girl – one of an army of volunteers helping to feed Britain while the men were away at the war – and one morning I got up at dawn to accompany her on her milk round. A big horse pulled the open cart on which were piled huge churns of milk from which she ladled out milk as we stopped at various houses. I was there for the harvest and saw the cut corn piled into stooks to dry and then heaped on to a beautiful Monet-style haystack into which it was fun to climb. There was a daughter called Dawn and another paying guest called Christine, both of about my age, and someone came to the house to teach us.

For a number of months our family was based at the Frensham Ponds Hotel outside Farnham in Surrey. The hotel had a small resident community while neighbours came in for meals or to drink in the public bar. This bar was forbidden territory for me during opening hours and was apt to get noisy on Saturday nights. There was a dachshund called Max, a great character who would hang around waiting to be given a glass of beer. The country round Frensham was very quiet at that time with no cars on the road because of petrol rationing. The Great Pond had been drained to prevent its use by German bombers for orientation. When we arrived it had a thick growth of hazel and other shrubs and I used to follow Richard Webster, son of the hotel owners, when he went there to shoot rabbits which later appeared on the menu. The Little Pond was particularly beautiful with its bullrushes and resident heron. At Christmas we gathered holly there to decorate the public rooms. The winter of 1945/46 was particularly cold with deep lying snow and we had a toboggan. I got terrible chilblains which were treated by sitting for an hour with my feet in a basin of hot wax. I made a friend called Deirdre Thompson who lived in the neighbouring village of Churt and we would walk through the fields to visit each other.

It was about this time my mother disappeared from my life to go to hospital. An elderly lady called Miss Mulligan was engaged as my governess. She is one of the few people in my life I remember being deliberately nasty to. She was ugly and I loathed her. But she had been recommended by my favourite aunt who had loved her. Looking back at my ten-year-old self, I realize that I owe Miss Mulligan an apology; I would probably have resented anyone who was not my mother. Anyhow the Thompsons' house in Churt was a welcome refuge and I spent as much time there as I could. There was a big party at the hotel to celebrate VE Day. With the war in Europe over, the Great Pond filled up again quite quickly but it became infested with water hyacinth and soldiers came with amphibious vehicles called ducks, or more properly DUKWS, to clear it. The Websters later acquired a couple of sailing dinghies which we greatly enjoyed using before the more lucrative clientele returned.

A little later my mother and I spent some months in London staying at Durrants Hotel in George Street. As at the Frensham Ponds Hotel there were a number of elderly residents who had found a home there during the war. We shared a room overlooking the Wallace Collection. When in bed with a bad dose of flu I whiled away the time by looking through the window at their collection of armour; I was amused when I visited the museum a few years ago to discover the armour still in the same place. Durrants is still there too but has become distinctly up-market. For those few months I went to Queen's College, Harley Street, a school my mother had been to and to which I was to return later on.

Guernsey was liberated from German occupation on 9 May 1945, the day after VE Day, and we soon received pressing invitations to visit from my father's brother Bernard and sister Maidie, who had been in the island throughout the war. We went for the summer holidays, staying with Aunt Maidie at Beaumont, a house with a splendid view over the rocks off Cobo. Food was still scarce, even by English wartime standards, and my aunt (never a great chef at the best of times) was cooking in a hay-box – vegetable stews that were warmed on the stove before being left to cook in the heat-retaining hay overnight. They were very nasty and tasted bitter. My mother, unwell, had her breakfast in bed and I still remember the row when she asked one of the boys to dispose of her hay-box porridge down the lavatory and he forgot to pull the plug.

There were still many German prisoners in the island being employed on various projects. In Sark my father's cousin the Dame made those who surrendered to her build a new harbour. One of their recently abandoned fortifications, the Napoleonic Fort Hommet, was just down the hill from Beaumont and it became a fascinating playground to us children. There was an acrid stench in the waterlogged interior which was strewn with damp discarded bits of uniform, but for my brothers there was wonderful booty such as abandoned helmets and spent ammunition which they took back to Wellington and sold to other boys. The first words of German I learnt were ACHTUNG MINEN (Danger – mines) but we ignored the warning. Francis, who was good at carpentry, built what he called a sand yacht which he hoped would use the wind to run on the hard sands at Vazon, where cars had raced pre-war. I was to be the driver as the lightest of the three of us. It was a flimsy construction and I was really quite scared, but I needn't have worried, because there was never enough wind to pick up speed. Food apart, that summer in Guernsey was fun. We spent a number of holidays in Guernsey later on, usually staying with Uncle Bernard at La Verdure. My father bought us a small fishing boat which we called *La Mouette*. She was the size of a dinghy and was kept on the hard by the Castle breakwater in St Peter Port harbour. Francis was of course the Captain, Philip the mate, while I was known as the bow-worm. Francis became a very good sailor and took care to learn about the dangers caused by Guernsey's giant tides. He would sit at the top window at La Verdure by the hour watching to see which rock appeared above water at what stage of the tide and marking it on his chart. I learned how to keep two leading marks in line so as to steer a safe course and to duck when the boom swung over.

I remained in Guernsey when the boys went back to school. My mother was in hospital again and I stayed with one aunt after another. At first I was at La Verdure with Bernard and his young wife Dorothy, known as Jum, who was fun. He was a doctor, she had been the dispenser of medicines at his small practice and they had married shortly before the war. She escaped before the Germans arrived but he did not. The story goes that he planned to take his aged father and aunt to England in his yacht, but when he got them on board the motor wouldn't start, so they all got stuck on the island for the duration. My grandfather and my great-aunt Gertie both died in Guernsey during the war. Anyhow, to return to Jum, she was an attractive woman, quite a lot younger than my uncle, and she had a good time in wartime London with the help of a Polish count. Relations were therefore rather tense at La Verdure. There must have been many such sad stories at the end of the war with all its separations. Jum went back to England and I moved on to another aunt.

I went to the Ladies' College in St Peter Port for about a year. I was teased a bit for my English accent and my overcoat, which, like many other of my clothes, was a cast-off from my brothers. Most of the girls had been in the island through the war and when a medal was issued to children to mark the end of the Occupation I was given one too. There were of course many reminders of the war so soon afterwards. Under a floorboard in the basement at La Verdure there was still the radio on which Bernard and Maidie had secretly listened to the BBC. One day I went with my elderly cousin May to inspect piles of furniture which had been requisitioned by the Germans and were now stored in a tunnel by the bathing pools awaiting identification by rightful owners. Bonamy House, which belonged to May's family, had been used as the telephone exchange and a lot of furniture had disappeared. May suspected some people of laying claims to nice-looking items that were not theirs. There was a memorable party at a friend's house to dig up their family silver which had been buried in the front garden but nobody could remember quite where. Eventually the prodding fork was rewarded by a clunk and a large wooden box was retrieved complete with treasure.

But Farnham was the main focus of our lives in the immediate post-war years. We lived in four different houses there, and I went to two different schools. The more memorable was run by an eccentric elderly lady called Mrs Fillery who had great difficulty keeping order. She put culprits in the corner and slapped palms with a metal ruler. Once when really exasperated she banged my head against that of another particularly irritating little girl. A happier memory is of the tall maypole which was raised in the school garden. Long coloured ribbons hung down from the decorated top and when the music started each child grabbed its appointed ribbon and began to circle the pole, weaving in and out between the children coming in the opposite direction. Gradually a decorative mesh formed on the pole and the ribbons got shorter and shorter, until we all turned round and reversed the procedure. It was all very pastoral. I developed my first crush on a boy called Duncan and behaved badly when I was made to dance with another boy instead. The school occupied a house in Castle Street, a beautiful broad street running up the hill to the 12th-century Farnham Castle, then the residence of the Bishop of Guildford. Behind many of the Georgian facades lay a rabbit warren of hidden Tudor buildings. The school was next to a shop which roasted its own coffee, filling the neighbourhood with the most delicious smells.

We spent a very cold winter in a large and beautiful house in West Street with a garden running down to the river behind. The gardener had used most of the coal ration to heat the house while it was empty before we arrived. My mother, who was learning to cook, had to contend with an old Esse coal-fired range, as well as our limited rations and three ravenous children. She coped remarkably well with the aid of a book called *Basic Cookery*. We ate a lot of mackerel which were off the ration. But my favourite of our Farnham abodes was 61 Castle Street, another fine Georgian house where we lived for rather longer, with my father catching the daily train to London and the War Office. We were certainly there in September 1948, because I remember listening to the radio with my parents in bed and hearing of the assassination in Jerusalem of Count Bernadotte, the UN mediator.

We got a dog called Zig. She was a basenji, a rare barkless breed originally from the Sudan, with a wrinkled forehead, corkscrew tail and a tripping gait like a deer. We took her to Crufts but alas she was declared undershot because of faulty teeth and won no prizes. The idea was to breed from her and sell the puppies, but she escaped from my father in Castle Park and had a mesalliance with a mongrel the day before the rendezvous with her approved partner. The result was five pups. After a long battle with the Kennel Club it was pronounced a mixed litter – two were declared authentic basenjis while the other three were vetoed.

This was the year my father retired from the Army and started looking for another job. He joined the UN as part of UNRWA (the United Nations Relief and Works Agency for Palestine Refugees) which was set up in the immediate aftermath of the creation of the state of Israel. This meant that the family base moved briefly to Geneva and then to Beirut – more of that in the next chapter. The dogs had to be given away while the immediate result for me was going to boarding school. After looking at one or two – I particularly remember Upper Chine where the girls wore glamorous scarlet capes – my parents settled on the Beehive which was run by a Guernseywoman called Miss Adele de Putron. My mother was worried about my toughness at this stage and thought I would do better in a school which was not too big. Originally founded "for the sisters of Eton boys," it started life in Windsor, but when I arrived the school had recently returned from Wales where it had been evacuated during the war and it was now established at Broadoak Manor, outside Bexhill. It only had about 50 girls in the main school though there was also a junior school just down the road. Truth to tell, the school was barely big enough to be viable academically and at that period with so many men still away in the forces good teachers were in short supply. We had no science lessons and maths was taught by someone different every couple of terms. The Beehive had no tradition of sending girls to university and, though this was never stated, I think the aim was simply to produce decent young women to be good wives and mothers. Having reconnected with a number of them in later life, I can say that in this the Beehive succeeded admirably.

Sports were very important. We played hockey and netball in winter and cricket and tennis in summer, all in the school's spacious grounds.

Every Saturday there were matches against neighbouring schools and the girls who played in the first teams were the queens of our little society. The only time I ever represented the school was for a 13-and-under cricket match and my score was one not out. I was very lucky in making friends early on with Sophia Mortimer, known to all as Soap or Soapy, who became a pillar of the school as well as a life-long friend. She had been at the junior school but was jumped up a class about the time I arrived so we were both in need of a companion. Shortly after we met her father became the Bishop of Exeter and her parents were endlessly hospitable to me during holidays when I couldn't go home to Beirut. The other outstanding feature of the Beehive was the importance of the Chapel to which we went twice every day and three times on Sunday, the girls wearing veils over their hair, strips of material about 18 inches by 24, with strings attached to the top corners. To put them on one hung the veil over one's face, tied the strings behind one's head and flipped the fabric back over. The choir had white veils while the other girls wore yellow ones which when new had a strong smell of curry powder. Anyhow it was a great inducement to get into the choir which I soon did; my voice was true if pathetically small. Miss de Putron reigned supreme over the Chapel (and indeed over the whole school). I can still hear her beating out the time with her spectacle case on the lectern during choir practice; whenever we went wrong the beat became a sharp rat-a-tat accompanied by an exasperated "No, no, no…" On Rogation Sunday we used to process, singing hymns, through the grounds on our way to bless the crops. My brother Philip, who was then doing his National Service nearby and came to take me out that day, was so taken aback by the sight that he hid until we had passed. The whisper came down the line – "There's a man in the bushes!"

Miss de P's younger sister Miss Peggy had been roped in to do the cooking and it must have been a nightmare. Neither of the sisters was young and the old-fashioned kitchen and limited rations would have been a challenge to the most experienced cook. There was a rota of girls to do the washing up and we never got the mugs entirely clean so the mid-morning milk ration always smelled a little rancid. The diet was healthy if plain and the Matron (known to the girls as Bathbun) believed in regular purging. My mother was very cross when she heard that after she had taken me out for lunch at half term I was dosed with syrup of figs.

French was admirably taught by a disciplinarian called Mademoiselle Rolin (we called her Melle) who drilled us in grammar. I still know my past subjunctive, which causes quite a stir when used today. The girls had to speak French all day until 5 o'clock and there was an honour system requiring us to declare each week how many words of English we had used. We developed a fluent Beehive slang of fractured French; for instance "handsome", a word important to teenage girls, became "main-des". I owe to Melle as well as to Beirut the strong grounding in French that served me so well in my diplomatic career, but I sometimes wonder if my ineradicable English accent also has its roots at the Beehive. I was not unhappy at the school but I felt that my life was on hold, and I couldn't wait to get out to Beirut. For two years running I was able to go there in June, not returning until after Christmas. No wonder I was always a semi-outsider at the Beehive. The pressure of schoolwork was greatly eased by the decision of the then Labour government to introduce a new exam, the O level, to be taken at the age of 16 and not before. When I sat this exam in the summer of 1951 I did unexpectedly well and my mother decided it was time I went to a more demanding school.

The following autumn I was enrolled for a second time at Queen's College, Harley Street, to do a course called Modern Studies. It was a class of about thirty girls, from a variety of backgrounds, and some of them were very clever. We had a number of outsiders coming in to teach us subjects such as economics. Meanwhile I lived in a hostel off the Finchley Road. It was run by a couple called Mather who took in half a dozen girls as semi-chaperoned paying guests. I shared a room, with a shilling-in-the slot gas fire. The most memorable of my roommates was a Thai girl called Noi Osuthanakraw, whom I became very fond of. Years later when I was posted to Thailand I saw her again, so she will reappear in this story. In the evenings we all ate together round a big table and Mrs Mather would ask about our day. Her husband was a member of the MCC (Marylebone Cricket Club) and at weekends some of us would go to Lords to watch Test Matches. It was exciting to see England's fast bowler Freddie Truman firing rockets down the pitch at the Australians, but my favourite was the elegant batsman Tom Graveney. We used to go to the cinema once a week and would occasionally join the early morning queues for cheap theatre tickets. It was a time of great musicals such as *Oklahoma* and *Annie Get Your Gun* and it was a thrill to see them from high up in the gods, as the vertiginous top balcony was called.

It was my first experience of living on an allowance. I had £5 a week to cover lunches, bus fares, and other incidentals. Queen's had a canteen in its gloomy basement, but it was much more fun to eat sausage, egg and chips for half a crown in the Marylebone Lane. Another regular expense was getting ladders mended in my prized silk stockings. One could buy an ingenious gadget with a hook and laboriously pick up the runs oneself stitch by stitch but the girls who did it professionally were like lightning. One could see them sitting in shop windows stabbing away. I began to buy a few clothes for myself, my first chance to begin to develop a taste of my own as distinct from my mother's. And I began to get to know London, an adventure in itself.

I was already beginning to set my sights at Oxbridge and decided to have a first shot at the entrance exams at the end of 1952 instead of waiting until the following one as most girls my age were doing. I was called for interviews at Lady Margaret Hall in Oxford and at Girton in Cambridge but that is as far as I got. However, I felt sufficiently encouraged to plan another shot the following year. Meanwhile I went back to Beirut for six happy months, the idea being that I would be set weekly essays by a young don in Oxford and return to a crammer there for the exams in the autumn. This was an establishment run by a clever but rather eccentric elderly lady called Miss Keays-Young, who liked to spell my surname with an aristocratic "y" – Collyngs. For teaching she drew on the pool of young academics always available in Oxford who needed to boost their income. The girls I met doing the exams there became my core circle of friends at LMH.

When I hear people today worrying about their children changing school I think back to my own disrupted childhood and wonder if it did me any harm. I certainly missed the continuity of friendships and became for a while better at mixing with my parents' age group than my own. Educationally there were gaps, but the additional experience compensated and I was not the only child whose life had been upset by the war. I always felt privileged and a bit special for living abroad and having travelled so much. The most important point was that I never doubted my mother was there for me – even when she was not there physically.

Chapter 2

THE HEYDAY OF BEIRUT (1949 – 1956)

In the summer of 1949 the family moved to Beirut which was to be home for the next eight years. While I went to different schools in England and then on to Oxford, Lebanon provided the stable background to my teenage years and I spent considerable stretches of time there. It was very different from England and I sometimes felt as if I were living two parallel lives. I loved Beirut and it certainly deserves a chapter to itself even though the time scale inevitably overlaps the chapters that come before and after.

The adventure began with the trip out from Geneva with my parents on a Dakota loaned to the UN by the United States Air Force. The two pilots, Captains Jack Mansfield and Pete Washbourne, glamorous figures who might have come from a wartime film, invited us into the cockpit of the unpressurised plane as it wound its way between the Alpine peaks. The main hull had metal seats down each side and the journey took three days; we spent a first night in Rome and a second in Athens before finally arriving in Damascus on 14 August, in the middle of a military coup. It was the end of the brief period in power of Husni al-Zaim who was executed along with his Prime Minister. My introduction to Middle Eastern politics. From Damascus we were driven across the Lebanon mountains, a beautiful three-hour drive to Beirut and the Mediterranean.

We went to Beirut because my father had been recruited by the UN as one of the advance team dealing with a major new refugee problem. 1948 had seen the tensions between Arabs and Jews break into open warfare as Britain prepared to give up its mandate in Palestine. Jumping the gun by 24 hours David Ben-Gurion declared the creation of the State of Israel on 14 May. Some quarter of a million Arabs fled or were driven from their homes. The initial UN response was coordinated from Geneva but refugees were scattered around the countries of the Middle East and after a brief spell it was decided that the new organization should be based in Beirut. My father's job was to organize the provision of food and other essential supplies. Given his years of service in the Middle East and his background in logistics he was very well qualified for it.

Beirut, the capital of Lebanon, is an ancient port city founded by the Phoenicians at the foot of a range of mountains. Lebanon was itself part of the Ottoman Empire until the First World War, when it was taken over by the French. In the Second World War it was briefly in the news when the Allies helped de Gaulle to claim it for the Free French from the *Pétainistes*. The Lebanese unilaterally declared independence in 1941 but it was not until 1946 that French troops finally withdrew. The population belonged to a patchwork of different faiths and this was reflected in the new constitution which laid down that the President must be a Maronite Christian, the Prime Minister a Sunni Muslim, the President of Parliament a Shiite, and so on through every constituency. This careful balance came under increasing strain over the years as the Muslim population grew faster than the Christian.

When we arrived French cultural influence in Lebanon was still strong. This was particularly true of Beirut itself where the elite, whether Christian or Muslim, spoke French most of the time and the ladies dressed in the latest Paris fashions. It was a city on the make, with great contrasts of wealth and poverty, of old Arab buildings with five-arched balconies alongside modern blocks, and slums where people lived in dwellings made out of petrol tins. On the southern fringes were two tented camps of refugees from Palestine. The life of the British community, of which there must have been a thousand or so, was centred on the St George's Club and the adjoining British Church which had a prime site on the seafront. There was an active British Council and much dancing of Scottish reels. And for teenage girls in particular there was the attraction of the Middle East Centre for Arabic Studies, the school in the mountains where the Foreign Office taught young men Arabic.

But I am getting ahead of myself. I was barely 13 when we first arrived in Lebanon. After a few days at the Hotel Normandie in the centre of Beirut, we moved up to Broumana, a resort in the mountains which form the country's backbone. The Hotel Printania where we stayed was an old-fashioned French *pension* surrounded by stone pines and the sound of crickets. It had a big terrace with long views down to the sea and the twinkling lights of the city far below. We were sitting there over a meal when a group of obvious foreigners came into view: a thin man in shorts and sandals accompanied by two girls about my own age. Joy of joys – they were English, had rented a house nearby for the summer, and invited us back for a cut-throat game of Racing Demon. So began a great friendship between the two families. The Goslings had a flat in the Asseili building on Avenue Clemenceau near the American University. Fortunately the flat below theirs was free and my parents decided to rent it. But not before my mother had done a bit of househunting. It was a good way to get to know the city so she set out by taxi armed with addresses. There was one house she rather liked. The owners were out but the polite servants showed her whatever she wanted to see, including the kitchen where she proclaimed that the drains were smelly. It was only afterwards that she discovered that she had mispronounced the address and that the house she had visited was the home of the Prime Minister!

The Asseili building was surrounded by balconies and had a fine view of the American Ambassador's Residence opposite, a traditional house with a five-arched balcony. In the other direction there were glimpses of a small mosque and beyond it the sea. We three girls were in and out of each other's flats all day long playing endless games of canasta. I can still hear the muezzins calling at dawn as well as the sound of Win Gosling's high heels clack-clacking on the marble floors overhead. The Asseilis themselves lived on the top floor with their two boys. At the weekends there were joint excursions to picnic by splashing rivers at Jisr el Qadi or in the Damour valley.

The Goslings hired a house in the mountains overlooking Beirut each summer. There the hot sunny days and cool evenings were wonderfully refreshing after steamy Beirut. It was a simple life with mosquito nets and paraffin lights at night. My parents went for a different solution, renting the ground floor of a very superior beach house at the Plage Saint-Michel. The house was on a rocky point and the sea often swirled round it. There must have been a spring close by because ducks congregated in a pool beside the terrace.

When I was 14 my parents decided to take me out of my English boarding school for the autumn term and to enrol me in the Collège Protestant de Jeunes Filles Françaises de Beyrouth. After testing my French the *directrice*, Madame Weygman, put me in the second top class with girls two or three years older than me. Her argument was that the curriculum for that year would be a good introduction to French culture. She was right. There was Racine and Molière and the wonderful poet Ronsard, though to my disappointment the history was English, the inevitable Tudors and Stuarts.

It was a good school and had an interesting variety of pupils, Christian, Muslim and even Jewish, who switched languages between French, Arabic and English in a single sentence. I was of course tongue-tied to start with and had a moment of shame when taken to a Latin class at a neighbouring boys' school. For some reason the teacher picked on me to answer some question and, not able to say a word, I began to cry. But on the whole things went well.

The following year (1951) my parents decided that I should again come to Beirut for the summer holidays and stay over Christmas, with another term at the Collège Protestant. The UN only paid for one trip a year and fares were very expensive. This time Madame Weygman decided that I could not go into the top class which was preparing for the Baccalauréat, and that there was no point in repeating what I had done before. So I went down a class instead of up. It was a bit odd adjusting to a new lot of friends while my former classmates were now the elite. But there was a nice Canadian girl in my class, and I could meet the Gosling girls for a *pain au chocolat* during break. These were served through a hole in the playground wall and were absolutely delicious – two small chocolate bars in a hot crusty roll.

Our flat was a few minutes' walk from the American University of Beirut, AUB for short, a respected university founded by American missionaries in the nineteenth century. When I had finally secured my place at Oxford for 1954 I hurried back to Beirut and signed up for some courses, taking pleasure in its spacious grounds with their old established trees. Students came from varied backgrounds and from all over the Middle East. I remember having to fill in a questionnaire in which I was asked if I wore a veil in my native village. The course that really made an impression was on Arab nationalism, given by a young Iraqi called Tewfiq Hussein. My fellow students were a mixed bunch, including some with fiery views. One day the question arose of how to get rid of dictators, and one of them asserted that the only solution was assassination. "But, but, but…" I spluttered trying to articulate the basic arguments for a peaceful way out. I didn't make any impression and doubt if I would do much better now. The incident brought home to me that not everyone shared the assumptions of my English upbringing.

Around this time my mother decided to visit friends in New York. She stayed away all summer. The flat in the Immeuble Asseili was sub-let and my father and I moved full time to the beach house. (When we paid our respects to the French family upstairs, our hostess looked archly at my hand for a wedding ring. My father was highly amused.) Our cook Shukrullah came to look after us and prepare meals. All went very well until I fell ill with jaundice. Shukrullah, who was a loyal friend as well as an excellent cook, proposed arak as the best treatment. When I recovered we had some wonderful parties there. Christine and Pauline Gosling, both younger than me, were still at school but I made great friends with Gilly Gough and some of the other secretaries working in the Embassy, as well as among the young men doing their Arabic at MECAS. Beirut really was a wonderful place to grow up. One could visit Crusader castles, or dance under the stars at restaurants in the foothills. One could ski at the Cedars in winter and water-ski at the St George's Hotel in summer. Some people claimed to have done both in one day.

I also had chances to see other parts of the Middle East. Damascus was three hours' drive away. Once I drove with my parents to Hamma with its creaking Roman water mills and then on to Aleppo where we stayed in the famous Baron's Hotel. We had an introduction to a family who lived in a fascinating house in the old city – I believe it was once the Venetian Consulate – and as we sat on the roof with our drinks we looked down through the domed skylights into the medieval souk while cherry jam bubbled in a huge cauldron, cooking in the sun. The trip took us on to Sahyoun, one of the most spectacular castles, with the rock cut away to leave a single pillar which once supported the drawbridge entry. Another time we went to Jerusalem, staying on the Arab side in the American Colony where one could still see the bullet marks from the recent fighting. From there we went on to Gaza where my father had business and I saw the refugee camps. It was Thanksgiving and a Quaker couple doing their year of service abroad invited us to share their meal. I have had a soft spot for the Quakers ever since. A trip to Cairo was pure holiday. We stayed at Shepheard's Hotel, still in its pre-fire glory, and visited the Pyramids and Tutenkhamun's sarcophagus. The souk – al Muski, which we just called "the Muski" – was out of the Arabian nights, but equally memorable were the chocolate cigarettes at Groppi's café.

These years were the heyday of the Baalbec Festival. I first heard Brahms' Double Concerto in the Roman Temple of Jupiter, looking at its six iconic standing pillars while the sun set behind a backdrop of mountains to the west. One year, when I must have been on holiday from Oxford, I was recruited as an extra for the visiting Regent's Park Theatre which was putting on a couple of Shakespeare plays. My chief memory of *Hamlet* was the heavy task of carrying off the dead who littered the steps of the temple at the end of the play. We all stayed in the Palmyra Hotel right beside the ruins. I made good friends with a boy called Nuhad es-Said, the son of prosperous Palestinians, who was another extra. When the theatricals were over we partied with the cast in Beirut, and I well remember Nuhad's mother Salwa asking me never to leave him alone with them. As a girl I was considered safe from the undesirable attentions of some of the cast!

That was also the year that we rented a house in the village of Ainab, where the long-established American families of the AUB had their summer retreats. There was a gathering each evening under the pine trees that fringed the tennis court. Our Arab neighbour meanwhile pounded meat by the hour, while listening to Nasser's endless speeches full blast on Radio Cairo. My brother Francis came for a visit, the only time I remember him in Beirut. Six years older than me, he had been five years in the Army but was by then doing a degree at Queen's University in Toronto. Philip came to Beirut a couple of times in the early years while he was at Oxford and then during his national service in the Canal Zone in Egypt. But for most of the time that we lived in Lebanon I was effectively an only child.

At the end of the summer of 1955 or 1956 my parents and I decided to drive to England from Beirut, a journey of nearly 3,000 miles which took us about three weeks. Although friends had made the journey and had given us advice it was still a great adventure, through country untravelled by tourists. Heading north through Syria, we spent a night in the ancient city of Antioch (now in south-eastern Turkey and called Antakya), and stopped long enough to see some fine Roman mosaic floors. From there we followed the Turkish coast to Antalya before heading north to Ankara and then on to Istanbul. This zigzag itinerary was largely dictated by the state of the roads through the interior. Antalya was memorable for a very personal reason. It was an American military base and while we were having dinner at our hotel a very polite young man in uniform came up and asked my father if he might invite me to dance. I was of course delighted, but when he announced that his name was Romeo I certainly did not let on that I was Juliet. My double identity came in useful as I firmly announced myself as Jen. He was the only Romeo, by name as opposed to nature, that I ever met.

Istanbul was memorable in very different ways. As we were nearing the city on a long straight road, I saw something ahead that looked like a pile of cardboard. I still do not know whether my father saw it or what he thought it was but he drove straight into a pile of stones which took out the sump. As we sat beside the road wondering what to do, a lorry stopped and offered help. The driver and his mate spoke only Turkish but they were the nicest of men who announced themselves as *iki doktor* – two doctors. They took me and my mother into Istanbul after stopping in the nearest town to arrange for a garage to collect my father and the car. My first magical sight of the city was from the cab of their lorry as we crossed the bridge over the Bosphorus which links Asia with Europe.

Istanbul, we soon discovered, had a couple of days earlier been the scene of ferocious and organised anti-Greek riots. There was widespread destruction of houses and shops as well as damage to many Greek schools, churches, etc. People must have died too, though this was not publicly confirmed. The ground floor of the little hotel we were booked into had been wrecked, but they gave us a room anyway and – despite the bed bugs that kept my mother and myself awake half the first night – we stayed there for a week until the car was repaired. I was impressed by the resilience of the family who owned the hotel. It was astonishing how quickly they set about repairing things day by day. By the time we left their downstairs café seemed back to normal. It was an unforgettable chance to see the sights of Istanbul. We had an introduction to the endlessly hospitable Air Attaché who included us in a day excursion on the Sea of Marmara, and we spent another day on the Bosphorus looking at the fine mansions on either side. I marvelled at the Blue Mosque and the view of the whole city from the terrace of a smart hotel, but the image that remains clearest in my mind is of a shop in the market which contained nothing but a great heap of shredded fabric. It had been owned by Greeks.

The rest of the journey was much less eventful. Our route lay through Greece and Yugoslavia (in Split my school Russian came in handy for the only time in my life), then on into Austria with a night in Salzburg. It was tantalizing not to be able to see more of the places we passed through but we were hurrying on because of the time lost in Istanbul. Once across the Channel we headed straight for Oxford where I was due back for the beginning of the autumn term.

Chapter 3

A HAPPY DILEMMA
Oxford (1954–1957)

I must now go back a year or two in time. I went up to Lady Margaret Hall in the autumn of 1954 with great excitement, but warily at first because I did not know anybody. By good fortune I was allocated a corner room overlooking the gardens and the river and I loved it immediately. Even better, several of the girls whom I had seen taking the exams the previous autumn had rooms in the same corridor. We went down to dinner together that night in the College Hall as we were so often to do over the next three years.

LMH was still very much a woman's college with strict rules about male visitors (only allowed between 12 and 7pm) and about staying out late (sign out to come back after 10.30; permission needed for 11.15–midnight; never given after that). This made for a close community and we were in and out of each other's rooms, drinking endless cups of cocoa and toasting crumpets over the coal fires. We had no central heating and the coal ration was only enough for a couple of fires a week, so the temptation to congregate in the warmest room was great. Astonishingly the College let me furnish my room with family furniture that had not gone to Beirut, and this made it a particular draw. There was even a radiogram, a piece of furniture the size of a modern fridge, with not only a radio but a gramophone which took ten 78rpm records at a time. My father had bought it as part of his post-war bonus. There was also a pile of jazz records inherited from my brother Philip who had gone down from Oxford a year before I went up. Fats Waller and Hoagy Carmichael were favourites. I welcomed the decision for colleges to go mixed when it came in the following decades and would have probably tried for a place at Christ Church or Magdalen myself, but the all-girls college had its advantages as a safe place where one could let one's hair down.

I read PPE (Philosophy, Politics, and Economics) which was a minority subject for girls. That was partly why I chose it; from the start I wanted a subject which would help me towards a career and I slightly disdained as soft choices the subjects then typically read by women, such as English or European languages. There were half a dozen of us reading PPE at LMH, and I was soon paired up for tutorials with Felicity Hall, who is still a close friend. She was the daughter of two Oxford academics, both of whom became Heads of Colleges. For the first two terms we were working for a set of exams called Prelims, the main purpose of which was to sort out those who were not up to standard. There was a limited choice of subjects and I found myself doing symbolic logic and maths as well as basic economics. I got through but it must have been a near thing in maths because the calculus was unfathomably far from anything taught at the Beehive and two terms did not bridge the gap. After Prelims it was time to decide on the papers to take in Finals two years later. There had to be two in each of the three PPE subjects and two more that one could choose from a long list. My special subjects were both in Economics – one was called Currency and Credit, and the other The Economics of Underdeveloped Countries. Both turned out to be relevant to later stages of my career.

My mother was keen to present me at Court. In earlier times it had been part of a ritual for girls of a certain class to “come out” at about 18 and to “do the season” as debutantes, going to many balls and often ending up engaged. This was one of the last such ceremonies and it already seemed out of keeping with the times for the monarch to hold several receptions a year for girls with social pretensions. I came up from Oxford for the afternoon, joining my parents who took me to Buckingham Palace. There must have been some 60 girls there but Cleodie Macdonald, a friend at LMH, was the only one I knew. We were marshalled into a long line which crept up a corridor before emerging into a huge room in front of two thrones on which sat the Queen and Prince Philip. Our parents were all seated in the body of the hall. As one’s name was read out one had to do a deep curtsey in front of each throne, hoping desperately not to wobble. I got the impression that the Prince was sizing up the talent, probably to avoid boredom. Curtsies complete, we were ushered off to another room where tea was served and in due course we were rejoined by our parents. When decades later I went to Buckingham Palace to receive my CMG the ceremony seemed much the same despite the different clientele.

The absence of exams in my second year made for a carefree time despite a regular pattern of two essays each week. Face-to-face tutorials involved reading out one’s essay to a tutor appointed by LMH and defending what one had written. The tutor then produced a very long reading list relevant to the essay subject for the following week. Like most girls I worked quite conscientiously, but I left the writing until the last minute and had twice-weekly essay crises, often into the small hours. We went to recommended University lecture series, often in the medieval Halls of other Colleges, but these were not compulsory, so we dropped those we found uninteresting. Gowns were worn for tutorials and for lectures as well as dinner in Hall. Scholars (those who had come top in the entrance exams) had long black gowns, but mere commoners such as myself had unflattering short ones known as bum freezers, which could be used to help to create a draft to get a fire going with sometimes disastrous results. Once as I hurried late to a lecture in Christ Church I was stopped by a group of Americans who wanted to take my photo; I could almost hear them saying, "These ruins must be inhabited"! For exams clothing had to be sub fusc, ie black and white, and girls' stockings had to be thick enough so "no flesh could be seen".

Coming from Beirut with a patchy education behind me set me slightly apart from most other students. Travel was still a rarity for most British people; for many years after the war there was a limit of £50 – or at one time £25 – on the currency one could take abroad. Though there were a handful of foreign students I felt a bit exotic and secretly proud of it. As time went on I enjoyed the social life of Oxford more and more. There were four all-women Colleges to a couple of dozen for men so the ratio was very much in the girls' favour. We got to know young men through lectures and often through the friends of friends. There were parties in other Colleges and we gave tea parties in our rooms at LMH in return. Inevitably there was some pairing off, but in those pre-pill days most girls played very safe. (There were one or two who left for other than academic reasons but remarkably few.) I was never in a one-to-one relationship, but accepted whatever invitations came my way. I made very good friends of both sexes. There was, however, a slight edge of disappointment to my university life. I had looked forward to Oxford as a place where I would be surrounded by brilliant minds. What I found was a lot of people very like me and I could never get the more sophisticated world of Beirut out of my mind.

Looking back, I think my generation of students who had grown up among the shortages of grey post-war Britain were trying to recreate the university experience of the 30s. This was reflected in a fondness for slang reminiscent of PG Wodehouse. Words were altered to end in "er" – St Giles became the Giler, football matches were Cuppers, and the Prince of Wales (not that there was one just then) was the Pragger Wagger. Students seemed totally uninterested in current politics, until the shock of Suez and the brutal Russian suppression of the stirrings of democracy in Hungary.

My mother started keeping my letters in my second year but in what follows I have started with my third year when the prospect of having to find a job after Oxford was beginning to sink in. There is more than enough material to paint the day-to-day life and concerns of a 20-year-old girl at Oxford in the early 1950s. I thought of myself as quite serious-minded but the earlier letters are mostly about parties, boys and clothes. I also included reports to my father on the state of my finances. At that time most students had their fees and maintenance paid by their local authority but living overseas meant that I was not eligible for this support. My father paid all my expenses and I was very conscious of being a drain on the family exchequer.

With my final year looming, I returned to Oxford in September 1956 in time to do some work before the term began. We were expected to move out of our rooms in College during the vacations, and along with some of my friends I had booked myself into "digs" in Keble Road. It was run by Miss Pollicott, a fine example of that now largely defunct breed, the Oxford landlady. My room was comfortable, if a bit dark, and we were given a very good breakfast. Apart from some friends from LMH the only other lodger was a German boy called Gerrit, who was hoping to go to Keble, and bowed to us each morning at breakfast. Miss Pollicott herself was a real tartar. Having to eat out was rather nice for a change, and one could eat well remarkably cheaply in Oxford. There was a café in the market where one could get an excellent helping of roast beef and veg, followed by a sweet for 2/6 – cheaper and better than I used to eat in London.

There were more of my friends back in Oxford than I expected including two South Africans called Robin Plumbridge and John Cooke. I went with them to a party given by some Australian to celebrate his Ph.D. We were given a lift home in a ramshackle car and John was just laughing about bits falling off when there was a series of thuds and jerks, and the car ground to a halt, sitting down on one side behind. Silence, then someone said, "Look! the wheel's come off; it's over there on the pavement!" We were lucky to have been in an empty street and going pretty slowly, and I was luckier still that it actually happened in Keble Road. Another evening Plum came round to show us his slides of the Continent, which were really beautiful. Since all the walls were covered with appalling wallpaper, we took a sheet off my bed to show them against, and Miss Pollicott appeared, having found my bed in a ball, and obviously expecting an orgy of some sort. Fortunately she soon calmed down, but she was in quite a fluster.

A later addition to our breakfast table was a very pleasant Dutchman who was doing a PhD combining Arabic with a study of the Economic Problems of the Middle East. He took me to a graduate class on Stability in the Middle East, which was followed by a very interesting discussion. Two members of the Mahdi family were there. This name struck a chord with me because as every schoolgirl then knew "the Mahdi" had been responsible for the siege of Khartoum and the death of the Victorian hero General Gordon. During the discussion I was aware of a man opposite staring at me. I thought he looked familiar, and about five minutes later it came to me that he was Tewfiq Hussein, whose lectures on Middle East history I went to at the AUB a couple of years previously. I was very pleased to see him, for I liked him, and admired him for tackling a tricky class. As we walked home the Dutchman told me who everyone was. I would never myself have contemplated going to a graduate class even if I had known of its existence so I was grateful to him for suggesting it. He was in Oxford as a British Council scholar and was fascinated by the Middle East, an obvious bond. He seemed more mature than my other friends and had a sense of humour so was good company.

Term started and I moved back to LMH, but not before my new Dutch friend invited me to the theatre. It was when someone I knew came up in the interval that I suddenly realized I hadn't an idea how to introduce the Dutchman. Miss P had firmly introduced us by surnames of course. It really didn't sound too good to be out with someone whose name one did not know! Fortunately I got away without introductions and hastily made up for my mistake. He was called Deodaat Breebaart – Daat for short.

At this point, to my great regret, there is a gap of one month in the letters. It covers the two great political events of my student years – the Soviet suppression of the uprising in Hungary and the Suez crisis. I would dearly love to have my contemporary account of living through this brief period. In retrospect it marked the political awakening of my generation of students.

The Hungarian uprising began on 23 October 1956 with popular demonstrations demanding independence and free elections. The pro-Soviet government was quickly overthrown and a new one formed under Imrc Nagy promising reforms. For a moment it looked as if the Russian government might acquiesce, but instead they invaded with brutal force, reaching Budapest on 4 November. The heroic courage shown in the face of Russian tanks was heady stuff. But already international attention had been diverted to the Middle East.

On 29 October Israel invaded Egypt with support from Britain and France who a few days later sent troops into Egypt, ostensibly to keep the two sides apart. The fact that there had been prior collusion soon became public knowledge. In the face of widespread condemnation at home and abroad, especially from the Americans, Prime Minister Eden did an about-face and on 6 November announced a cease-fire. By Christmas all British and French forces had been withdrawn. In January Eden resigned, a shattered man in health and reputation.

There is no way that these two brief paragraphs can do justice to the momentous impact these events had on the world as well as on the lives of Oxford students. When the Russians threatened to send troops to Egypt to support the Egyptians it briefly seemed possible that there might be a wider war. My mother wrote urging me to go to Canada if the worst happened. While opinion in Britain was united in support of the Hungarian uprising, it was bitterly divided over the rights and wrongs of the Suez intervention. It was a subject that divided families and friends much as Brexit has done more recently. To some Nasser was a petty Hitler who had to be cut down. But I was in no doubts: to side with Israel against the Arabs was contrary to all the instincts I had accumulated in Lebanon; moreover, to invade Egypt was morally wrong especially when the degree of connivance became clear. I was intensely relieved when the Anglo-French operation was called off but the humiliating retreat could only underline the damage to British influence. Most of my Oxford friends felt similarly. We were further outraged that attention had been diverted from events in Hungary. It was not easy to condemn the Russians for invading one country while we were helping to invade another. Nowadays one is apt to put past crises in different boxes but at the time these two were almost inseparable. We listened to the radio obsessively (no TV of course) and sat up arguing into the small hours.

Daat helped drive a lorry-load of clothes and other help to a big Red Cross centre near Vienna, for the Hungarian refugees who were pouring across the border. I had dinner with him when he got back and heard about it in detail. He said the International Red Cross had moved in with the precision of a regiment. There were not many refugees in Vienna itself; many had been housed in the vast empty German barracks left over from the war that dotted the countryside. Daat and another boy from Oxford called David Brierly set themselves up in a village near the frontier area, in a marshy area round a lake, where most of the refugees came over. They found that the most useful thing they could do was to talk to refugees, find out if they had any contacts in Western Europe or the States and if so to write to them, telling them their friends and relations were safe and could be found via the Red Cross in Vienna. This they did till their money ran out and then hitch-hiked back to Oxford.

***

I was relieved to find I was interested in economics again after the summer in Beirut where whatever I tried to read seemed a bit boring. Finals loomed, and were all the more nerve-racking because of the absence of university exams in year two. The question of what to do after Oxford was also coming into focus. One of the songs of the moment came from a lightweight musical by Julian Slade about a group of graduating university students; it was called *Salad Days*. The refrain ran, "If I start looking behind me, and begin retracing my track, I'll remind you to remind me we said we wouldn't look back." We were already beginning to feel nostalgic for what we would leave behind.

LMH, 27 November 1956

To my infinite relief my economics are doing better again now: the turning point was an essay on Devaluation I wrote last week, which earned high praise, and restored my morale. It's a great help also having got onto the subject of International Trade which I find infinitely more interesting than subjects like the Rate of Interest. Anyhow it's as well things are looking up, cos a series of bad essays was beginning to get me down. And I am sure it was largely psychological, for my philosophy essays, which don't interest me specially and I didn't do much work for, have been consistently goodish... One of my next essays is on whether it is possible to prove or disprove the existence of God, and the other on the theoretical analysis of the Dollar Problem. What a week!

We are still industriously knitting squares for the Hungarians. Felicity is sewing them together in red cross-stitch, and the effect is really rather gay. It will indeed be a lucky Hungarian. However, the blanket has got to the stage where however much more we knit it remains the same size!

The following term a Hungarian student arrived at LMH – a refugee. The JCR gave some money towards her support while the SCR gave their guestroom. It was all arranged very quickly because the girl had studied English in Hungary, so was easy to fit in. I thought she looked rather glamorous, and not a bit "refugee."

***

Apart from exploring bursaries at universities in the US which were surprisingly widely available to British students at that time, I decided to do the exams for entry to the Fast Stream of the Diplomatic Service. Life overseas seemed much more attractive than working in grey post-war Britain. I didn't really expect to get very far in what was known to be a highly selective competition, but the Diplomatic Service had been open to women for nearly a decade and there was nothing to be lost in trying. I sat the first round of written exams in a room in the Old Schools. There were about 50 people of whom only two were girls. I wrote a detailed account to my parents:

5, Keble Road, 9 January 1957

The three-hour essay I chose was on a quote from Aristotle: "The best political community is formed by citizens of the middle class." I thought it was a good non-specialized subject in which I could bury a little economic theory, and what I know about the Middle East. I think it was a fair example of the sort of essay I write, but not in itself very good. I don't think I have ever written an essay of that length to time before. That was followed by a general paper with a fair scope of questions, out of which one had to answer 3 in 1½ hours. Not too grilling except for the pressure of time. Finally, this diabolical I.Q. test, of which my private opinion was that anybody who excelled in it must surely be mentally deranged! There were queer series of letters and numbers of which one had to fill in blanks, many of which seemed to be completely random; then there was a collection of 30 passages, which had odd words switched which one had to straighten out, and finally a dozen little problems of the type: 6 men were sitting in a railway carriage, the one on the left was a builder, what was the name of his next door neighbour? I finished the hour's paper feeling absolutely exhausted – but was relieved to hear a number of people say that they had only done about 40%. I think I may have done a bit more than that. After such a tense day, I decided to go with Margaret Tyson to the flicks to relax, and was lucky in that a particularly good light musical was on: "High Society" featuring Grace Kelly, Bing, Frank Sinatra, and best of all Satchmo (for the uneducated, that means Louis Armstrong!) – story weak, but well worth seeing. [I still regularly re-watch it today.]

Back the next day to the exam room, which I felt I was getting to know pretty well by this time. They were a couple of lovely days too, as always seems to be my luck when I am doing exams. We started off with an English paper: a v. long and difficult précis, which left me scant time for the other question on literary criticism. In the afternoon another general paper, far worse than the other in that... there was a whole sheet of statistics on Farmers' Income and Capital to interpret – I couldn't find any wretched trends at all! The last paper was yet another IQ test, but that does not count towards one's marks at this stage; as somebody else said that's to be a mill-stone round one's neck later on, if one gets that far! I'm told that one qualifies with half marks, which doesn't sound too bad, except that one's scope is cut down a lot by the shortage of time not letting one finish or amplify anything. Still, who knows? I gather we will be told if we have passed this stage sometime next month.

***

After Christmas with relatives in Guernsey I returned to Oxford to work, staying again at 5 Keble Road. I was surprised to get the impression that Miss P. rather disapproved of me – my previous landladies had always thought me "such a nice young lady". It seemed to date from the famous evening when she came in to find the room in darkness and the bed in chaos while we were showing Plum's colour slides. I don't think she ever got over her suspicions that something very improper had been going on. Anyhow, if there was a crime, it was always attributed to me. I didn't mind, because I got so much entertainment out of the idea of my totally new role of scarlet woman.

A belated Christmas present arrived from my brother Philip who was now in Canada. It was a wooden dish shaped like a maple leaf and it was pretty but I was at a loss to know what to use it for. I happened to ask for suggestions while Plum and John were there and was startled to be met with prolonged peals of laughter. It wasn't till afterwards that I realized that they thought it was a fig leaf!

***

February brought some good news. I had passed the first stage of the Civil Service Exams. A rather impersonal letter starting *Dear Sir or Madam* said, “The marks you have obtained in the January written examination qualify you for admission to the language oral test and the series of tests and interviews.” I was so pleased with myself that I told my parents I was “literally dancing.” I had been cultivating a fairly low opinion of myself for fear of disappointment and was glad to be proved wrong

My ego also received a boost from an anonymous Valentine - *A nice long one with a quaint picture. As you can guess, I’m trying to deduce who it could be from in true Sherlock Holmes style. It was posted in Oxford, addressed in black capitals: only clues are that it is from someone who knows my name is Juliet (most people in Oxford call me Jen, but surely most know my real name so it may be double bluff!) and that since it arrived on Feb 1st, it was presumably from someone who didn’t know when St. Valentine’s Day is! Not very conclusive...* I never did find out.

My LMH friends and I took to going to Christ Church Cathedral on Sunday mornings where there was usually a glass of sherry available in some friend’s rooms after the Service. Once Cleodie and I went out for an afternoon’s beagling with the Christ Church pack. There was a bus which left from the College gate just after lunch, so we ran down through the Parks to catch it. The meet was at a rather nice small manor house quite near Oxford; petrol rationing meant they could not go far afield. We alternatively strolled and tore round for a couple of hours. I am sure at one point we were nearer a hare than any of the beagles were all afternoon! It was great fun and terrific exercise and a welcome break from a hard week’s work.

I was lucky in my final year to have two very interesting tutors in economics. Paul Streeten was at Balliol and had a dramatic back story of which I was totally ignorant – political activism in his native Austria and internment as an enemy alien in Britain before joining the Commandos and being landed behind enemy lines in Italy. He went on to a distinguished career in Development Economics. To me he was the challenging and rather unsettling man with a sardonic wit to whom I had to read a weekly essay.

The other was Michael Posner who later made his name in public administration but was then a young Research Officer at the Institute of Statistics. He was not much older than me and I found him a very stimulating teacher. One week he set me to do a collection (ie a mock timed exam paper) on monetary theory. He said it didn’t matter at all how well I did, it was just for practice, but nonetheless I felt I had to do some revision. When I next saw him we had a serious discussion on the feminine attitude towards work, and to exams in particular. It started because I asked him how I’d done in my collection. The answer was that I wouldn't get a first on that, but that he was expecting me to do quite well in the paper. What I needed, he said, was confidence. I said meekly that you always felt such a fool being dogmatic in case you were wrong. There followed a diatribe on that being the attitude of all women undergraduates, and that they were therefore far too likely to have the "correct" views, without any kick to their opinions. He thought I knew enough, which was reassuring, and that the thing to do was to forget what I had learned rather than revise it. I had probably developed hybrid opinions of my own on most points which were much fresher than my best essay of two terms ago rehashed. On each paper one should answer one question about which one knew nothing – choosing one about which other people were likely to know little as well.

I thought it very sensible advice but to take it required courage. I don't remember anyone else ever talking to me like this. Girls were schooled to study hard. I found it difficult to shake off doubts about how much I knew despite recognizing that in my most conscientious periods my work seemed to deteriorate and lack originality. But what he said bucked me up. *"My moral of the moment is down with conscience! I am not going to develop the "3rd year frame of mind", which it is so easy to get into. I'm going to go out when I want to, and I'm going to have a good time to the bitter end!"*

This conversation had resonance decades later when I was at Cambridge and looking at the same problem through the other end of the telescope. More men than women were getting first class degrees especially in the Arts subjects such as History, and the suspicion was that in looking for originality examiners were giving more weight to what they saw as "flair" than to evidence of knowledge. Many women suffered from a lack of confidence which was almost baked into their upbringing while public schoolboys in particular knew how to wing it to cover up ignorance. Was this line-shooting skewing things? I hope that highlighting the problem encouraged those marking exams to think twice and also that as the intake as a whole becomes more diverse and more women reach the academic heights their successors are more confident of their own opinions.

Another conversation that echoes down the years was with my German friend Hasso Buchrucker, who dropped in for tea one afternoon. Felicity Hall appeared after a while too, and the three of us really settled down to it and told each other things we had probably been longing to get off our chests for months. Felicity and I cast ourselves as true feminists, saying we found intelligence of the utmost importance and would never dream of marrying anyone about whose intelligence we had any shadow of doubt. Hasso said darkly we'd change our ideas and find out that maturity of outlook was what mattered – or that I'd have to anyhow (presumably because Felicity was engaged already). We parted very amicably, saying firmly that everyone else's views were adolescent. I never changed my view, though of course Hasso was right too. The man I eventually married was clever enough to pass my youthful criteria.

***

1956 saw the negotiations leading up to the Treaty of Rome and my essays included one on the European Common Market. The subject already interested me though I had no premonition of its importance to my later career. Another essay which I enjoyed less was a rather technical one about a special model of a trade cycle. It was, I complained, all curves whose movements caused the economy to shoot up and down like a shuttlecock, and despite my struggles I found it almost impossible to connect these convulsions to anything in the real world at all. "Rather like Hamlet, without the Prince!" was Paul Streeten's comment, which I thought rather hard. This was before the days of computers, I was no mathematician and I instinctively disliked models of the economy that left out the human factor. Another of my interests was development, a field which was then preoccupied by the problems of "take-off". I attended a class run by Professor Herbert Frankel who argued against the prevailing purely economic view, stressing the crucial role of law and stable institutions. He was an outgoing man who kindly invited us all to tea. It was the sort of don-undergraduate contact of which I didn't think there was enough.

***

On 14 February I had my French exam for the Foreign Office. I prepared by going to see Cocteau's *La Belle et la Bête* and reading *Bonjour Tristesse* in French. For the exam itself I had to go to Queens College where I found about a dozen people. A pleasant man read us a dictation which wasn't too hard apart from a sentence in the middle, which should have read, "*les folliculaires entonnent à notre égard des dithyrambes*" – or at any rate something much more like that than the queer jumble I made of it. "*Folliculaires*" I later learned are the gutter press, while a dithyramb is a Greek form of poetry. Hardly fair! I went back in the afternoon for a personal interview which went quite well.

I was also exploring scholorships to the States. I must have given my mother the impression they were there for the asking because I begged her not to go around telling everyone I was getting one. I only had two applications in at that stage – to Radcliffe and Stanford – though I also later applied to Cornell and MIT. It took a great deal of time to find out addresses and write innumerable letters to universities which were tiresomely slow in answering. Then one had to get referees, and fill in the forms which took about three hours apiece. On the advice of an American friend I marked up all my expenses by $500 because he assured me that they were longing to hand out the cash but would mark down what one asked for on principle. But I had no real idea of my chances. It worried me sometimes to think what I should do if scholarships and the FO both came to nothing.

During that last Easter vacation I based myself in Oxford trying to sort out the knowledge which I hoped I had accumulated over the last two and a half years. With a group of other girls from LMH I sub-rented some digs at 11 Bevington Road while the young men who usually lived there were away. We had to get formal permission from the College authorities. The digs were on two floors at the top of a house, and self-contained: one pleasant living room, three bedrooms (a bit sparsely furnished but quite adequate), kitchen and bathroom. Cleodie was going to be there almost all the time, like me, and a series of other people occupied the third room. The total rent was six guineas a week, which made two guineas each.

I got there by taxi one evening accompanied by one of the others and by dozens of packages of various size and inconvenience, not to mention my triple mirror which I refused to be parted from. On the doorstep we unpacked it all, paid off the taxi, rang the doorbell – and then realized to our absolute horror that the house was locked and empty! We had been told that we could fetch the key any time after lunch and were so taken aback that we alternated between being dumbly silent and giggling weakly. Finally I rang the next house's bell, and was lucky in that a very nice woman came to the door. She kindly let us leave our luggage in her hall, go off for some supper – we were ravenous – and come back to try our luck later. But at 10 there was still nobody in the house. In desperation, we went back to the woman next door, and were just borrowing her phone to find ourselves a room in some hotel, when, by immense good fortune, she heard the woman who lived in our basement calling her cat, and so we were let in after all. But once in, another nasty shock:

The place looked positively lived in, beds unmade, washing up, etc. On closer examination, however, their clothes had gone (or most of them) and letters for us were propped up on the mantelpiece so we decided it was just that they had left in a hurry and were v. untidy. Once we settled down to it the chaos was pretty superficial, and by soon after midnight we had remade beds and installed ourselves. But I did have a moment's panic: what if they had gone to a party, came back late somewhat tight, saying like the 3 bears, "who's that sleeping in my bed?"

Meanwhile I was sent the list of marks for the written exams I had sat for the Foreign Office – everybody's marks, pass and fail alike. Mine were remarkable for their relentless mediocrity – the worst was 50% for the essay; the best 62% for the IQ test(!). Total marks for five papers were out of 500; they interviewed everyone with marks over 260, and about three dozen in the 240–260 bracket. My marks were 275; ie a comfortable non-brilliant margin. There were about 180 people over the 260 mark and about fifteen over 300. It was a fascinating document. I spent some time looking up friends and acquaintances, and seeing how people varied between the very sustained average of my own marks, and people who got 80 in one paper and 30 in the next. One person got 92% in the IQ paper and I profoundly hoped not to come up against him in the next round.

When I was summoned to London for the next stage of interviews, which were spread over three days, my first worry was where to stay in London. My preferred base would have been with my godfather Sir Alec Bishop who was then working in the Commonwealth Relations Office but he was in Canberra for a conference, the flat shut, and his wife Molly away staying with friends. I didn't like the thought of a hotel alone, so decided to write to Luke and Meriel Asquith. Luke, a grandson of the former Prime Minister, was a banker and his much younger wife Meriel was a ballet dancer. I had met him in Beirut and they had given me kind invitations at Christmas. Back in Oxford I gave my parents a blow-by-blow account.

11 Bevington Road, 23 March 1956

I duly turned up at no 9/10 Saville Row on Wednesday morning at 9:15, and somewhat tentatively made the acquaintance of the other 13 victims. We were divided into groups of 7 (which was only effective for some of the exercises) and each given a number to pin on fore and aft. I was number 13 and wondered what would happen if I applied to be

12A! We started off filling in a number of forms, and then were addressed by the chairman. There were six people supervising us who seemed to be of some importance – a chairman, observer, and psychologist for each 7 – and sundry other people who came and went.

The tests were of three kinds. First there were those that were written. Some were exercises – simple and though under pressure didn't really strain one much – ie filling sheets of words that mean such and such and rhyme with so-and-so, or giving references for where patterns went wrong. (I think that was experimental). At another time we were given a dossier on an imaginary trust, called Warden Hall: supposed to be an old house of the Hatfield type, with a famous collection of pictures left as a trust, with lots of strings. The information was all pretty higgledy-piggledy and one had to sort it out, and write a report on what one advised should be done with the estate. We had to draft a letter at another time, to someone who offered to bequeath a series of dreadful Victorian watercolours to the Trust, but who wasn't to be offended at any cost! Then another exercise was to write in 15 minutes two appreciations of oneself: one from the attitude of a fairly biting critic, the other from an admiring friend. (Strangely, my two seemed to say almost exactly the same things!)

The next sort of test were the ones the groups of 7 mattered for: discussions, and a morning of mock committee work. The Committees, to my surprise, I really rather enjoyed. Each of the seven in turn had to chair the committee in the discussion of one particular aspect of the Warden Hall Trust. Mine was the selection of a principal (by this time we were assuming that the Trust was being made into a vacation residence for overseas university students) – what his duties should be, the necessary qualifications, and pay etc. I got a bit shouted down over that, but I don't think it mattered, and on the whole I think I did that better than most.

Finally, there were individual interviews. The first that I had to have was with the "Observer" of the group. As a personality he was the least impressive of the three who interviewed me but the interview itself, though fairly tough, wasn't too dreadful. Most of it was devoted to discussing some propositions we had put forward that we were willing to defend in one of the early forms. There was no guide to what sort of proposition was expected, and I found it v. difficult to know what sort of thing to put forward. Finally I put one on the importance of recognizing the role of inferiority complex in Arab nationalism (v. rash, and difficult to defend, but I believe it), another on financing development schemes, as the Indian 5 year plan, and another on a point of Central Banking…

The next interview was with the Group chairman and lasted about three quarters of an hour. He was rather an imposing man, very much the civil servant, a bit awesome, but meaning well. I found the interview hell. He started off by asking the usual sort of questions: why did I want to go into the FO, was my interest in foreign affairs genuine, if so why was I ashamed of my ignorance. Mother, it was dreadful, I got myself into a position of feeling I was being grilled, and I more or less broke down: I mean chin up all the time, but I had to get out a handkerchief. I felt all kinds of a fool, cos though they were tough questions, and asked in a fairly uncompromising way, I knew the old chap wasn't really trying to get at me. I just don't know what came over me. I was really rather relieved that the psychologist whom I had to be interviewed by the next day, asked me about it. He said that the chairman had been absolutely baffled, for I seemed perfectly self-possessed otherwise and the poor man felt he must have been a brute, and unfit to interview girls. I said straight away that this really wasn't so, that I had been horrified at myself, and that I really couldn't explain it apart from saying that I was pretty tired straight after the term when I started these exams, and that they themselves were quite an ordeal. Anything but a reason as I said. He couldn't have been nicer to me, and suggested very tentatively that perhaps it was something to do with setting myself very high standards, and getting really upset when I didn't feel myself to be living up to them. (For what had got me upset in particular was a question why, when I had been perfectly at ease and constructive in the committee exercise, I had been more or less speechless in the earlier discussion: meant to be as much a compliment on the one, as a reproach on the other I know). It doesn't seem an adequate explanation but there may be something in it for all that. All I could do was say how sorry I was, that I couldn't really explain it, and had been horrified at myself. I was really pleased to have had it out a bit, especially with such a nice man because I really feel it must have given a fairly false impression of me, and I'm sure he realized that – in fact he said so. I can only think that I must be much more strung up than I realized. From the point of view of my chances for the FO, I just don't know how much it will count against me: looking back on it, I think I did most of the rest quite competently, if not brilliantly. Anyhow I put my faith in the nice psychologist to defend me as not being an unbalanced female, liable to tears in any stress. None-the-less it is something I would rather not have behind me.

Socially I enjoyed the few days in London very much indeed. I was the centre of attention in a most gratifying way, with competition to give me lunch and supper each day. About half a dozen of my rivals were really very nice indeed, particularly a boy from Cambridge called Richard Kershaw, who was most good-looking into the bargain. Later he briefly joined the Commonwealth Office, before becoming a journalist and anchorman for ITN. He and Andrew Crawshaw who was also from Cambridge took me to *Anastasia* when we had finished our first day, and then gave me dinner, and I had lunch again with them the last day. All told, it improved morale immensely to be in such demand, and I felt really great when on the last day we had to grade each other as we thought suitable for the FO and as we would choose for a holiday companion – confidentially, thank goodness. Richard said that it would be too easy to choose a companion if one were in my group, and an appreciative grunt went round the room! I hoped to see that pair again somewhere even though I realized things wouldn't be quite the same when I was no longer the only attractive girl to 12 men.

The next evening I went with Luke Asquith and his niece Annabel to the ballet – we saw *Sylvia*, which I enjoyed, with a lovely girl in the lead called Anya Linden (who later became Lady Sainsbury of Preston Candover). Meriel herself danced Persephone in the third act, which wasn't too bad as a part, but had the most dreadful costume of white tulle which she told me later was her despair. Afterwards we went behind the stage to her dressing room which she shared with another dancer: it was chaotic, and there wasn't really enough room so we felt somewhat in the way, but it was very interesting to see their makeup gadgets etc. Then we went back to one of Luke's gigantic dinners.

Friday was our last day. I was lucky in not having to be there till 10:30 in the morning but paid for it by having to dash back after lunch for the psychologist's interview. After that was over, it being a lovely afternoon, I walked meanderingly up Regent Street with Andrew Crawshaw who had also had an afternoon interview, stopping to have a cup of chocolate at Fullers, and wander round a fairytale toyshop – Hamleys. It is still there.

I was thankful on Friday evening to realize it was all behind me. I spent the next 24 hours just sitting around (11 of them in bed), and resolved on a bit of a rest cure before starting working seriously for my final exams.

***

In early April a letter from the Civil Service Commission arrived summoning me to an interview with the final board on Tuesday, 9 April. I was delighted and a bit surprised after my tearful performance. Resolving not to let my hopes go up, I told myself that to fall at the very last hurdle would be quite honourable anyway. The summoning letter was very formal, even to the paragraph reading: “Women candidates are requested to remove their hats before entering the Board Room.” I wondered if they objected to hats as camouflage or as unbefitting the dignity of the Civil Service. Determined to arrive properly rested this time I invited myself to spend the previous weekend with my mother’s great friend Irene Sewell in her lovely Old Vicarage at Fovant, near Salisbury. I decided that I needed long nights, outdoor days, and very little work, except to read the *Economist* from cover to cover.

I had to be at the main Civil Service Commission building in Burlington Gardens at 4pm and came up from Salisbury earlier in the day, having lunch in the train. As I walked down Bond Street I was getting a bit scared – I had never coped with a Board before – but I resolutely window-shopped just as usual. The building itself was very imposing and I seemed to have to give my name to dozens of porters before being finally settled down to wait in a room with a vast desk and some forms to fill in. A few minutes later the candidate who had been in before me came out. I knew him from the last lot of interviews, and he talked to me for a while telling me what to expect. He described an enormous circular table, with a hole in it, and interviewers sitting all round the edge: I had awful visions of being in the hole myself! Fortunately it wasn’t as bad as that. I was isolated on one half of the circle with the interviewers round the distant other half.

There were 7 of them: the chairman, a rather good-looking man in the 40s, started questioning me fairly generally about my interests, varied education, etc. He sat in the middle, and when he had finished each of the people on his right questioned me in turn. I should guess from the questions that they represented FO, C.R.O., and Home Civil Service in that order: questions mostly of the type of what did I think British policy in the ME should be, what was my opinion of US foreign policy, how would I define the bonds of the C’wealth… Mostly pretty tough questions to answer in a sentence or two, even if one did have any bright ideas, but fortunately

> *by dint of having been asked them before I had my pattern of answer a bit readier. For all that I don't think I had anything particularly bright to say, and one always feels a bit silly with 7 people all of whom obviously know much more about what you're talking about than you do, hanging on your lips. Finally the only woman of the seven, who was on the other side, started to question me. This time it was all about what I thought of the position of women in the FO, if I thought keeping a job there compatible with getting married, how much that would count against it as a career from my point of view, and finally how much I liked the idea of pioneering at jobs that women hadn't done much before, and if I would like to be the first woman at a post (which I thought I rather would).*

All this took little more than half an hour, after which I caught the train down to Oxford and retired thankfully early to bed.

The following week I went to stay with the Mortimers who had offered me unfailing hospitality ever since I first knew Sophia (also known as Soap or Soapy) at the Beehive. Her father was at this stage Bishop of Exeter and they were living in the Palace, a huge house beside the Cathedral. My stay was punctuated with dozens of church services of all degrees of "height" – from blessing oil and choirboys to processing through the streets of Exeter singing Salvation Army hymns behind the band and the Bishop. Good Friday afternoon we spent picking wild daffodils: it was lovely and there were masses, but Soapy insisted on taking us to a spot where we had to brave bog, stream, mountain and masses of stinging nettles before we got them. There was a point-to-point on Easter Monday and, though enjoyment was somewhat damped by a sudden downpour, it was fun. And one day we went to see *The Hunchback of Notre Dame*, which was rather good, if gruesome at times. Soapy's younger brother Edward (who had just gone to Eton) announced afterwards that 'tummy dancing' was all very well for African wenches but that Gina Lollobrigida (who, as Esmeralda, had quite a lot of it to do) was made for higher things! Edward went on to have a long and distinguished career, becoming a Fellow of All Souls and right-hand man to UN Secretary General Kofi Annan.

We laughed a lot, particularly when for some reason we examined statistics on illegitimate children. The variety of occupations given for putative fathers ended with an egg-packer, which somehow reduced everybody present to prolonged giggles. I was loaded with goodies on Easter Day, along with everybody else. Fortunately from prior experience I had got sufficient provisions myself too. Mrs Mortimer gave me exactly the same as Soapy – a magnificent chocolate egg and a pretty little leather purse, mine being pink. They were so kind, the Mortimers: I saw them as Christians in the very best way, with their faith leavened by a strong sense of humour.

While I was with them I received a surprise communication, and wrote immediately to my parents.

The Palace, Exeter, 17 April 1957

I've just got a telegram from Stanford University (California) offering me a fellowship for next year to the tune of $2,400! They asked me to cable my reply and I have accepted saying that I am writing. It's a princely offer... and no strings, as far as I know. I didn't dare to hope for more than $2000 at best anywhere, and last week was envying Cleodie being granted $1700 at a University rather inferior to Stanford... If I don't get into the FO, it is certainly what I would most like to do next year.

I was relieved to have something definite to look forward to. Stanford was my first choice among the universities I had applied to; it had a particularly good reputation in economics with at least two Professors whose work I had actually read. Socially, it was said to be a paradise – blue skies and long sunny beaches. It was the biggest grant I had heard of – except for Richard Kershaw's at Yale – but I would need to apply for a Fulbright Travel Grant to cover the substantial cost of getting to California. I felt incredibly flattered to think there were people willing to pay $2400 (in hard currency too!) for the pleasure of my company for a year, I reassured my father that I wanted to do an MA and would go for a year only. Both my brothers had emigrated to North America and he was afraid of losing me too.

The rest of the vacation passed peacefully in Oxford. I was to be a bridesmaid at Prue Pedder's wedding. Prue was one of my closest LMH friends and I should have mentioned her earlier. One day I went to London to try on my dress at Fenwicks. It was a copy of one of Prue's own dresses, long and in white corded silk. I thought it very pretty and sent my parents a sketch. I loved the fact that it would be a naval wedding and hoped for crossed swords. Another day I went to a reel party with Andrew Muir, a friend studying law at Magdalen, and then had coffee in his digs afterwards – only to find that it was after the time women were allowed in, and I had to be smuggled out. The landlord was taking out a vast St. Bernard dog at the crucial moment, and Andrew was so cloak and dagger about the whole thing that I was convulsed with laughter. I was living back in College by then and to my fury ended up earning a 1/6 fine for being out after 11:15 without permission. Nobody seemed to mind in the least when this happened, but if repeated it became a strain on the exchequer.

I was seeing less of Daat who had rather belatedly confessed to having a fiancée in Holland. I was cross and disappointed in him but there was no heartache on my part – or, as I confessed to my parents, "only a little occasionally." Part of the trouble was that all my friends seemed to be falling in love. With Prue and Felicity both planning their weddings I, subconsciously really, wanted to fall in love too to see what I was missing. And there were few people among my Oxford acquaintance I could even think of falling in love with. But with so many other excitements in my life the grief such as it was did not last long.

A letter came from Stanford formally offering me the Fellowship, and I wrote back to accept. There was also a letter from the Foreign Office, saying I was in the Not Wanted category. I was a bit disappointed but felt I had had a pretty good run for my money and consoled myself with thoughts of California. Then there was a most unexpected development. I received a letter from the Principal of LMH, who sat on some of the Selection Boards, saying that she had an encouraging message for me and suggesting that I should not make any further plans before seeing her.

When I went to see her she told me that, though I did not pass the interviews, the Board were very interested in me, and it was most probable that I would be offered a job in the Foreign Office on a temporary basis, having to pass the exam again the next year, but in the meantime serving in a department just as if I already had done so. This offer couldn't be made till they had seen all the other applicants, but she didn't seem to consider at all seriously the possibility that they would think better of it. The point was that they wanted to accept me but were upset by my display of nerves which didn't seem to tally with the rest of my behaviour (thank goodness I wasn't too nervous at the Final Board) nor with my record, so they were willing to give me a trial. Whether I was confirmed after a year would of course depend as much on what the Department said about me as on my actual exam performance. She strongly advised me to take up the offer if it was made.

The drawback would be forgoing Stanford, and I would feel a bit bad about letting them down though they doubtless had a waiting list. If I had got into the FO by the front door I might have been able to persuade them to give me a year, but I couldn't expect to if they were making a back door for me specially, so to speak. I explained my dilemma to the Principal, and said that I would like to know if it was a definite offer as soon as possible.

All this put me in an agony of indecision. It seemed to be an opening to the career of my first choice, and it was a chance unlikely to come again because there was a very strict age limit to entry to the Diplomatic Service. If I were in the States it would be difficult to try the exam again the following year and I would be too old after that. I thought the fellowship to Stanford would be more fun for the coming year, and that I would learn much from it, but I didn't know what I could do afterwards. Apart from the very vague idea of a job in the United Nations, there was nothing which compared in my longer-term preferences to a job in the FO

I longed for my parents' advice. When I received a letter saying that I was definitely going to be offered a job as Temporary Assistant Principal in the FO I sent them a telegram. This really set the cat among the pigeons since it arrived in Beirut before my letter explaining the background. In the end it was for me to do what I wanted but the problem was to decide what I wanted most. I expected my father to advise the FO, and my mother Stanford. The Principal repeated that she thought I should jump at the offer if my career interests lay in that direction and the more I thought it over the more I thought she was right. Moreover I felt I really had achieved something, and that it would be a shame not to make something worthwhile of it. I wanted to show that I could, as a woman, do what was often thought of as a man's job, as well as a man, and be thoroughly feminine into the bargain. The idea of making a go of the Foreign Office appealed to my feminist streak.

International calls were then a rarity and I had never spoken to my parents in Beirut during my time at Oxford. But this was an emergency, so I determined to book a call which involved a connection via Paris.

3 May 1957

I am now feeling thoroughly frustrated after my abortive attempt at ringing you up. I was dancing attendance on the phone this end for an hour, too. But anyhow they've counted all that as only a minute and are giving me two more tomorrow morning, which will be ample (or just enough at any rate!) to tell you the bare facts – or those you haven't got. I could hear you perfectly for the first couple of minutes, though you obviously couldn't hear a word I said… Perhaps it was stupid to try phoning, but one hears so many tales of its being just like the next room – and it was nice to hear your voices – even if they did just go on saying "hello"!

We had better luck early the following morning. I had been so cross at the fiasco of the first telephone call that I had a long discussion with the operator who was most helpful and got Paris to promise me a two-minute call some other time: in fact we got nearer five. I was so afraid my parents would be out that I asked for a stand-by call to warn them in advance. But I sat by the phone for a good hour and began to wonder if I would ever get through. The phone was eventually answered by Marie, our Armenian maid, and her voice really took me home: it was so very distinctively Beirut. It was wonderful to talk to my parents, however briefly.

The following Wednesday afternoon I had an appointment at the Foreign Office. I was deposited at the door by my godfather Alec Bishop, who was then working in the Commonwealth Relations Office, and we discussed everything comfortingly over lunch first. He agreed that it was a very worthwhile chance to take, and it would be a most interesting experience to have worked in the FO for a year anyhow. He surprised me by taking rather more seriously than I did a question I had been asked at the Final Board as to whether, with so many interests abroad, I felt myself to be representative and in touch with British attitudes. Better forget Stanford for now, he said, and not show too much anxiety to get out of the country at all costs.

Mr. Adams of the Personnel Department, on whom I called, turned out to be an affable young man, pleasant enough but un-pin-down-able, who was obviously there just to brief me and put the proposition to me. He particularly did not want to be pinned down on the chances of success next year and was very patently trying to avoid giving the impression that this was the acknowledged back door into the FO. He told me that my pay would be £605 pa; I would be eligible for usual amounts of leave and sickness care, and pension rights would start from the beginning if I was taken on. (I could scarce forbear a cheer!) More interesting to me was that I would be assigned straight away to one of the desks as a Third Secretary and would be more or less expected to find my own way. The normal batch of entrants were sent on courses for a few months, but I would not get them yet anyhow. I never got them later either.

When the final marks came through for the Civil Service exams I read them with fascination. They were out of 300 in each case and marked separately for the Home Departments and for the FO with a divergence sometimes as big as 50 marks. The pass mark was 240, in both cases. Twelve passed for the FO, no less than four from our group of 14, including both Richard and Andrew. The marks jumped in tens – below the pass mark there were 230s, a large bunch of 220s, another of 210s, and me in a cluster of 200s. (I only got 175 for the Home Civil Service.) So once again I wondered, and this time I came to a tentative conclusion. No woman was listed as going into the Diplomatic Service, and this must have worried them because it didn't look right and because it might have been more of an ordeal for us. (It probably was.) Anyhow, of the women candidates for the FO I was number 3. The first, a brilliant girl at Somerville called Anne Guthrie, got flying colours for the Home Civil Service (270) and was going into the Treasury. The next had 210 and I don't know what happened to her. It was all very odd, but I was by now determined to have a go.

Meanwhile Schools loomed. Under the Oxford system everything depended on one's performance in those few days of Finals and I was not the only one who was nervy. In LMH everyone seemed to be on the verge of tears at any harsh word. One man I knew simply took the train to the country on the day of his first exam. It was a tough ordeal but though there are good arguments for some element of continuous assessment I continue to think that the real test of an education, at least at university level, must be what one can draw on when put to the test. I was myself lucky in that exams made adrenalin flow. Once back in the Old Schools where I had so recently done the FO exams I got an extra boost of energy. I doubt if I remembered much of Michael Posner's advice but for the record my degree was a good Second Class which was what was required by the Diplomatic Service.

One final thrill was an invitation to a May Ball in Cambridge from Richard Kershaw, the young man who had chatted me up during the Civil Service exams. The Ball was at Clare College on 17 June, a few days after the end of Schools. Richard was a charmer and excellent company. Strictly speaking I should not have gone away from Oxford while it was still Full Term, but after three law-abiding years I threw discretion to the winds and had a wonderful time.

***

Since, thanks to my mother having kept my letters, I have described the Civil Service selection procedure in such detail, it perhaps deserves a comment from the older me. The system was said to be based on ancient Chinese practice, which is apparently why British Civil Servants are called mandarins. Later on I found myself sitting on a number of final boards as a representative of the FCO. By that stage in the procedure the weaker candidates would have been weeded out and those we saw were either firmly recommended for acceptance or borderline. Almost all would have done fine. The chief difficulty was to assess how 21- or 22-year-olds were going to develop. What sort of person would they be at 40 or 50? Would they be self-sufficient and adaptable enough for a life involving many new starts away from family and friends? It was, I found, much easier to form a clear idea of personality when candidates were a bit older. I have sympathy with my predecessors' caution about taking a girl who wept.

I still find it difficult to explain my own emotional collapse during the interviews. Nothing similar ever happened to me in a working situation though I did once find myself weeping in a training exercise where I performed badly and thought the odds had been stacked against me. Perhaps the psychologist was right in suggesting that I was a perfectionist who expected too much of herself. I remember feeling that the Chairman's questions – Was my interest in foreign affairs genuine? Why was I ashamed of my ignorance? – were some sort of attack on my integrity which it was painful to answer. I was also partly weeping from sheer frustration. But the question that caused me to crack up – Why so quiet in the discussion when I was chatty in the mock committee? – seems simpler now: the committee was discussing an imaginary scenario so it was like playing a game, while the earlier discussion exercise required me to express personal views among people I didn't know. Role playing – or later in my career talking to a brief – always came to me quite easily but it took me years to have much confidence in my own opinions. All things considered I think the Civil Service Commission handled the situation pretty well, and all credit to the mysterious personal connections which led to my being offered the chance to prove myself.

Chapter 4

AMONG THE PINSTRIPES
Foreign Office Western Department, London (1957–1961)

One sunny day in September 1957 my parents drove me up Downing Street and through the Foreign Office archway into the main courtyard to start my first day's work. My father recalled it in a letter he wrote me nearly 20 years later. *You have come a long way since that day when I walked with you to the FO for the first time and left you on the steps there dressed in a natty black coat and skirt. I well remember your last words before you walked inside: you said you had never felt more out of place in your life! You should remember that as a quote for the time you come to write your memoirs.*

My parents had returned to London after Suez put paid to my father's ideas of doing business in the Middle East and I was living with them in a rooftop flat in Queen's Gate Gardens. I certainly did feel very small as I went up the Foreign Office steps and through the great main doors into that splendid, daunting palace of a building. I had to give my name at the desk but there were no other security procedures. Then I was escorted up a big staircase to the Western Department which was mainly housed in a set of imposing rooms on the first floor looking directly over 10 Downing Street. I was to report to Martin Anderson, one of the two assistant heads of the Department, who received me very kindly and handed me a large pile of files; I should read them, he said, and come back later to discuss what to do with them. I also had to sign the Official Secrets Act. Then he took me to a small cubicle of a room with a very high ceiling overlooking the main courtyard. In one corner was an ornate pillar. We were in part of the Locarno Room (now restored to its former glory) which had been divided up with temporary partitions to provide more office space.

I was to share this little overflow office with Don McCarthy, a talkative Irishman in his mid-thirties who turned out to be a fount of useful information. Don was dealing with claims against Germany left over from the war, a pretty soul-destroying job, and had plenty of time to chat. I was officially the desk officer for France, Switzerland, the Benelux, and all their territories not in Africa. This was in reality a training post and closely supervised. I took over from another young woman, Catherine Pestell, who had joined the Diplomatic Service a couple of years earlier and had just gone on her first posting abroad to The Hague. The other desk officers were all men, and a rather glamorous bunch too. It was still the days when young men about town wore a black jacket and pinstriped trousers, with a rolled umbrella and bowler added for going out. The Head of Department and the Assistants – the next layer down – had their own secretaries but the rest of us depended on the typing skills of a small pool called the Departmental Ladies. Many of the secretaries were older than me and I had to get over the awkwardness of giving them dictation. The Department was also supported by its own Registry which did the filing and it was important to be on good terms with one's corresponding registry clerk.

All this Martin explained to me, as we undid the pink tape which bound the files and went through them one by one. Each file dealt with a different subject and the individual papers were attached inside with India tags. I don't remember what they were about but I do remember the bewildering array of different sorts of paper that were to be used for different purposes – draft letters (blue), draft telegrams (also blue), minutes (white, or blue crested if they were to be submitted up beyond the Department), little slips on which one could add temporary notes to be headed "eph" (short for ephemeral). Letters to embassies abroad were usually to be addressed to "Dear Chancery" and signed "Yours ever, Western Department" – but formal dispatches were to begin "Sir, I am instructed by Her Majesty's Secretary of State to inform you..." and to finish with a truncated flourish "I have the honour to be, Sir, etc." There was a variety of coloured boxes locked with special keys for use if papers were sent from one Department to another. They were carried by the Messengers, a splendid group of elderly ex-servicemen who wore a uniform with navy frock coats. As one walked along the echoing corridors one would hear the distinctive whoosh and crash of the pneumatic tube system in which papers could also be sent to Number 10.

When I arrived in the Foreign Office in 1957 women were still scarce in what was known as the Fast Stream or Administrative Branch though entry had been open to them since 1948. Many of those first recruited had already left, usually on marriage. Ernie Bevin, Foreign Secretary in the post-war Labour Government, is reputed to have complained that the Foreign Office had been turned into a marriage bureau! I can only remember a handful of women – secretaries apart – amongst the many officials with whom I had dealings. This had its advantages. People from the Permanent Under-Secretary down soon knew who I was and were nice to me. There were very few old buffers who didn't think women should be there at all. But we were not yet on equal terms: there was a quota on numbers, pay was not yet equal though it was getting there, and most importantly a woman who got married had to resign. A more practical disadvantage was a distinct lack of facilities for "Ladies." I got plenty of exercise walking the long corridors in search of them.

The leisurely day typically started at 10 o'clock after the telegrams had been deciphered and distributed to Departments. There were telegrams about the latest events from all over the world which made fascinating reading. So did the dispatches that had been printed for Whitehall distribution. Every Ambassador was expected to write a First Impressions dispatch on arriving at a post as well as a Farewell dispatch on leaving and these were usually circulated, along with others of special interest. Inevitably there was a good deal of competition about getting one's dispatches printed and the standard of writing was very high. These privileged sources of information were among the things I missed most after I left the Diplomatic Service decades later.

My companions in Western Department were a very agreeable bunch and I was just beginning to get the hang of things when I came down with the worst dose of flu I remember. I was in bed for a fortnight after which on the doctor's recommendation my mother took me down to Fovant for a few days to stay with Irene Sewell, whose comfortable Old Rectory was a haven for all the family. I didn't get back to the FO for about three weeks all told and was rather taken aback to learn that there had been speculation as to whether I would ever come back at all.

After that I really settled in, and stayed in Western Department for about four years. It was a fascinating period and gave me a wonderful grounding in the politics of Western Europe. The department had a tradition of gathering for tea, and visiting Ambassadors and other bigwigs tended to drop in too. The talk was often of the gathering tensions with the Russians over Berlin which was still under quadripartite rule. There was also much discussion of the new European Economic Community between the Six (France, Germany, Italy and the Benelux), which was established when the Treaty of Rome came into force on 1 January 1958. This had happened contrary to most British hopes and expectations, and attention quickly turned to organising an alternative free trade area with the Nordic countries. (This eventually became EFTA which created an extra web of commitments which Britain would have to untangle when the Macmillan government decided to join the EEC.)

Meanwhile in France, which was part of my bailiwick, the Fourth Republic was in its death throes as the government struggled with rebellion in Algeria. Waiting in his retreat at Colombey-les-Deux-Eglises was the towering figure of Charles de Gaulle. Our Ambassador in Paris, Sir Gladwyn Jebb, went down to Colombey to call on the General, and recorded the conversation in three telegrams which received a wide distribution throughout Whitehall. When they arrived on my desk in neat dockets I simply initialled them which had the effect of sending them straight back to the Registry to be archived. The next day Sir Gladwyn came steaming into my office to ask what on earth I had done with his telegrams! I discovered the hard way that formal action was supposed to be initiated on the entered copy: the telegrams should have been submitted to the Secretary of State with considered comments from the Head of Department and any other grandees who might have an interest. But I had some minor triumphs too, such as when the Prime Minister was suddenly presented with a million begonia tubers from Belgium. Told to find a diplomatic use for them, I had the bright idea of giving them to London's parks, thereby earning some gratifying praise. The Chief Parks Keeper later called on me at the FO to give me a bag of tubers to grow on our windowsill at home.

After de Gaulle returned to power in 1958 the British Government was very keen to get alongside him. He was invited to pay a State Visit to Britain in April 1960. As desk officer I was involved in the minutiae of planning the event which involved close contact with the FO Protocol Department and the Palace. I will never forget dealing with the sidekick of the Lord Mayor of London, whose title was the City Remembrancer. There have been many times in my life when I have longed for a remembrancer of my own. There were endless letters to be drafted asking permission for this and that, guest lists to be drawn up and speeches to be drafted, including those for the Queen. Needless to say my drafts were usually rewritten by my superiors. Programmes for such visits are literally coordinated to the minute. The payoff for a lot of hard and detailed work was a series of invitations to the public events of the Visit, including lunch at the Chelsea Barracks and an evening at Covent Garden. At the reception in the French Embassy the General received the guests individually. He was very tall and seemed an almost regal figure standing there, and when my name was announced I had consciously to suppress the urge to curtsey. I treasured his words: "Enchanté, Mademoiselle"!

All told I had a good and most interesting time in Western Department, and I got to know a number of people who were important to me later on. I served under three Heads of Department – the admirable Pat Hancock, who went off to be Ambassador in Reykjavik, was followed by Eddie Tomkins, who was to be my Ambassador in The Hague, and then there was Bernard Ledwidge, who was number 2 in the Embassy in Paris during my brief spell with the NATO delegation. Of the next layer up, the Assistant Under-Secretaries, Sir Anthony Rumbold was to be my Ambassador in Bangkok, while Sir Evelyn Shuckburgh who became something of a special patron was, as Head of the UK Delegation to NATO, responsible for my joining his staff there in 1965. Even more importantly, I made a number of lifelong friends. Twenty years later I married one of them!

By now I knew that I would like to make a career in the Diplomatic Service – at least until I married, if I did, when I would of course resign. I had another unsuccessful shot at the Foreign Office exams and rather expected to be asked to leave. But that never happened so I stayed. Martin Anderson, my immediate superior, once asked why I didn't transfer to the Friends (MI6) which recruited separately and would probably have welcomed me but I was very clear that the element of double life involved was not for me. Then, one day in late 1961, Personnel Department proposed that I should go to Brussels. The idea was to join the Secretariat for the negotiations for Britain's entry to the EEC, with the possibility of transferring to the EEC institutions if the negotiations were successful.

Chapter 5

A FRONT SEAT IN THE THEATRE OF EUROPE
Brussels (1961 – 1963)

I had been interested in developments in Europe even before joining the FO so I didn't hesitate even though it meant leaving London at three days' notice. It was November 1961. The negotiations for British entry had opened formally in Paris a month earlier but they were about to start up again in Brussels. It had been decided that they should be serviced by a special group drawn from the Secretariat General to the EEC Council of Ministers, reinforced by British officials. I was being offered the chance to be one of initially two British members of this team which was responsible for such things as recording proceedings, producing papers for discussion and generally oiling the wheels of the negotiations. I would still be employed by the Foreign Office and would be part of the UK delegation for administrative purposes. I packed a suitcase and negotiated an extra paid fare back home to London to sort out my things.

To my great regret no letters to my parents remain from this period of my life, though I must have written them. I do, however, have a few letters I wrote to my great friend Celia Hensman which give some day-to-day impressions of my much younger self. But in describing what was one of the most crucial episodes of my career I will have to rely mainly on memories which are still vivid, though not totally reliable. The people are still alive in my mind as is the broad arc of what happened but the details of what we were negotiating about are often hazy.

On arrival the British delegation was housed in the Metropole Hotel, a stately pile in the heart of the old town. Downstairs was very grand, complete with Palm Court orchestra at tea-time. The delegation offices were on one floor, while our bedrooms were scattered around the hotel. Mine was a dingy slice of a room overlooking an alleyway where dustbins were cleared with a great clatter at 6am each morning. I was too unsure of myself to complain, but I didn't spend much time in the room anyway. The other problem was finding where to eat. The Metropole was expensive as well as daunting and

1. My mother, Nancy Collings, aged about 80

2. My father, Wilfred d'A Collings, in old age

3. St Peter Port, Guernsey. La Verdure, the family house, is on the skyline left of the big trees.

4. With my parents and brother Francis in Jerusalem c 1939.
The car went with us to South Africa.

5. With my brothers in the olive grove near our house in Jerusalem, c 1939

6. With Sophia Mortimer and, aloft, Edward and Kate Mortimer, in Exeter, 1949

7. The front entrance of Lady Margaret Hall in the 1950s

8. With brother Philip skiing at the cedars in Lebanon, c 1950

9. Part of the 1954 intake at LMH. In second back row Margaret Tyson, Felicity Hall, Cleodie Macdonald and JC (no 29).

10. Boona, my Thai housekeeper, and her children, Bangkok, 1965

11. My house in Soi Asoke, Bangkok, 1965

12. My brother Philip and family outside 26 Sudeley Street N1 in the 1970s

13. Mrs Bennet who fought my domestic battles in London, c 1979

14. The British Embassy Bangkok as I knew it
Crown Copyright/Foreign, Commonwealth and Development Office

15. A Press Officer's view of the Aden independence talks in Geneva. Don McCarthy, in profile, sits next to Lord Shackleton, November 1976.

16. The Club du Jeudi, the diplomats' club in the Hague, on an outing to the Rhineland, 1972

17. Visiting the Dutch Parliament as President of the Club du Jeudi, 1971. JC with the Presidents of the First Chamber, (left) and the Second Chamber (right)

18. Leslie Fielding reading out the referendum results with JC and Celia Hensman, Brussels, 1975

19. Thames barge waiting for the tall ships, London, 1975

20. The Château d'Epoisses in Burgundy where the Queen was besieged by French farmers, 1979

21. The interior of Seaford House, the home of the Royal College of Defence Studies

22. RCDS visit to Korea: the conference room at Panmunjom with North Korean guards looking in, 1981

23. RCDS visit to China: JC by the Great Wall, 1981

it took a while to track down the many little restaurants tucked away in the back streets, on the *quais* or by the spectacular Grand'Place. But I soon made friends with the other young members of the delegation and after that each evening became a supper party as we explored the gastronomic delights of Brussels.

The first major event was a dinner at the Metropole for members of all the delegations. It was hosted by Edward Heath, the leader of the British delegation, and was a big affair with speeches and many tables in a huge room. It went off pretty well, and when all the guests had left the British delegation gathered round Heath who seemed visibly to relax. I made the great mistake of sympathetically asking if he was tired. This is not a question one should ask a rising politician, perhaps particularly if one is a young woman, and he was not pleased. Heath was never at ease with women anyhow and he became a bitter curmudgeon in later life but at that stage he was a rising star and he quickly gained the respect, even affection, of those who worked closely with him.

At official level the delegation was drawn from all over Whitehall. The senior official was Sir Pierson Dixon, then also British Ambassador in Paris, a very nice man whom I had got to know a bit while in Western Department. The appointment was made with a view to placating the French who from the start were seen as key to the negotiations' success. Apparently it was only the Queen who suggested that the two jobs were too much for one man. In practice he only came to Brussels a few times and the key role was played by Sir Eric Roll, one of those brilliant immigrants from Central Europe who so enriched British life. Eric Roll already had wide international experience having been involved in the setting-up of the OEEC and NATO among other things and was then with the MAFF (Ministry of Agriculture, Fisheries and Food). It was a bonus that he already knew personally many of the senior players on the EEC side. He and the other senior British officials would come to Brussels for meetings each week, returning to London for Fridays in Whitehall. They became known as the Flying Knights. Once a month all this would culminate in a Ministerial meeting in Brussels to discuss the major issues that had been thrown up. Meanwhile the lesser mortals of the delegation stayed there full time.

At the heart of the Delegation were two very able First Secretaries, John Robinson and Christopher Audland, who cultivated a wide range of contacts in the other delegations. There was also a younger group who quickly became fast friends of mine – Peter Pooley from MAFF, Rosemary

Edwards from the Board of Trade, Martin Morland and later Patrick Laver from the Foreign Office. Together we explored all that Brussels could offer and took advantage of lulls in the negotiations to go further afield for happy weekends in the Ardennes and elsewhere.

At first we continued to live in the increasingly dreary Metropole, but when it became clear that the negotiations were going to last some time we were authorised to rent flats for ourselves. This was a great release and I found a nice airy studio in a modern block on the Avenue de Tervueren. As described to Celia, "*it is rather minimal in accommodation but distinctly Hollywood in style: a large all-in-one room, with bathroom and kitchen adjoining (all beautifully equipped) and long windows out onto a balcony facing SW, with a splendid panoramic view. I had meant to get a flat with a separate bedroom and perhaps a spare room as well, but I fell for this one, and since I can have it on terms requiring the briefest of notice I decided to move in for the time being anyhow.*" I also bought my first car, a pale blue Renault Dauphine, and got the concierge to give me driving lessons. Believe it or not, there was no Belgian driving licence at that time so I just got in and drove as best I could. I did not let on to visiting friends quite how debutante my driving was.

Back to the job. The Secretariat to which I belonged was headed by a Belgian called André Dubois. The other Brit apart from myself was a man called Jimmy Newing who was a good deal older than me – a highly intelligent but socially awkward man with excellent French. Apart from us the Secretariat consisted initially of one person from each of the six EEC member states but as the negotiations went on the numbers grew. They were all seconded from the Secretariat-General to the EEC Council of Ministers which was headed by a Luxembourger called Christian Calmes who appeared for some Ministerial meetings. The British had wanted the negotiations to be between seven equal partners with a neutral Secretariat which, in the words of Eric Roll in his memoir *Crowded Hours*, would be "an independent force that could be relied on, with the Chairman, to push negotiations forward, to be constantly on the look-out for agreement, and, generally, to act as a catalyst." At first the British delegation kept Jimmy and me at arm's length in the interests of neutrality. But it quickly became clear that the Six were playing by different rules. Before each meeting with the British they would have long meetings amongst themselves to hammer out a line which would be presented by a spokesman, usually from the Commission. Once their line had been agreed, often with much pain because of their very different interests, they were extremely reluctant to alter it. There were strong echoes of all this in the Brexit talks, with Michel Barnier of the Commission speaking for the EU as a whole and British hopes of exploiting differences between other member states coming to nothing.

The highlights of our lives were the monthly Ministerial meetings and then one would see many of the heavyweight politicians of Western Europe in action. I particularly remember Paul-Henri Spaak, the Belgian foreign minister, a man who had played a major role on the post-war international scene and a heavyweight in all senses. Then there was the tall jovial figure of Joseph Luns from the Netherlands who had a habit of taking his shoes off under the table. Some wag asked him if he proposed to use them to bang the table as Khruschev had just done at the UN. For France there was the urbane Couve de Murville, who had been with de Gaulle in London during the war and whose perfect English apparently dated back to an English nanny. Ted Heath was always there for Britain, sometimes with other Ministers such as Christopher Soames (Agriculture) or Duncan Sandys (Commonwealth Secretary).

Jimmy and I sat in our rooms discussing everything under the sun while our colleagues of the Secretariat serviced the meetings of the Six. A few employees of the EEC would hang around with us too, for instance Richard Mayne who had been a trusted advisor to Jean Monnet but was now excluded from meetings of the Six on grounds of nationality. Some members of the British delegation were dab hands at light verse and as time went on a collection of clerihews featured all the major players in the negotiations. Occasionally our friends among the other delegations would give us a private steer about what was going on which we would pass on to the British side. Then suddenly someone would burst into the room asking us to summon our delegation. When the meetings with the UK began Jimmy and I slotted in at the head of the table near the Chairman, a role which changed monthly among the Six, while the British delegation were at the far end of the room and the other delegations ranged down either side. A bank of simultaneous interpreters sat behind glass panels. The spokesman for the Six would present their agreed line to which the British side would respond. This usually left Britain in the position of *demandeur*, asking for changes. (In *Crowded Hours*, Eric Roll said that in retrospect these organizational aspects of the negotiations appeared as significant as the substantive issues, or perhaps even more so.)

One of the main jobs for Jimmy and me was to negotiate and sometimes draft the detailed official record of what had been said and agreed. A bevy of translators were responsible for turning out written versions in the three working languages – French, German and English. With officials looking over their shoulders at how their hard-fought compromises would go down back home the exact wording used in each language could be very sensitive. Unlike Jimmy and myself the translators did not sit in on meetings so they missed some of the nuances. I remember a very difficult discussion with the head of the English translators who was in fact Maltese and deeply resented my changes to his text. His English was not perfect and it was as if he felt his identity was being called in question by my corrections.

All this took place in a brand new building near the Porte Louise which had been built for the Belgian Foreign Ministry. It was opposite the ornate Palais de Justice which André Dubois used to describe as "*le chef d'œuvre de la pâtisserie belge*." I had a splendid big corner office with a wonderful view over the lower town which was, however, often bathed in fog. No wonder the Metropole got so depressing. The British delegation set up offices in the Rue de la Loi.

I do not want to go through the details of the negotiations which were essentially technical. At the opening meeting in Paris, Heath had asked for full membership of the EEC, accepting in principle the common customs tariff and agricultural policy as well as the Community institutions, while setting out a long list of areas of difficulty for which Britain asked for special treatment. A series of working groups was set up to deal with these. The groups I was assigned to dealt with trade issues and they reported to the weekly meetings of the Deputies (ie the Dixon/Roll level) which Jimmy and I both attended. British trade was still based on a system of Imperial Preference which we would have to give up as we adopted the common external tariff of the EEC. A remarkable feature of the negotiations was the extent to which, agriculture apart, they dealt with the interests of the Commonwealth and Colonies rather than domestic issues. (This was a major contrast with the successful negotiations leading up to British entry in 1974 by which time much of the Commonwealth had diversified their trade so as to be less dependent on the UK.) There were long lists of goods to be considered, ranging from kangaroo tail soup from Australia through willow for cricket bats from India and Pakistan to such staples as zinc and aluminium. I remember Sir Herbert Andrew, a blunt Northerner from the Board of Trade, making an impassioned plea on behalf of tinned Canadian salmon which he would have us believe was an essential part of a Yorkshireman's tea. For some items we asked for zero quotas (imports of agreed quantities duty-free), for others tariff quotas (imports paying reduced duty) for varying lengths of time. For our African and Caribbean territories we asked for parity of treatment with French colonies, which usually meant Associated Overseas Territory status. (The clerihew about the Colonial Office representative read: "Sir Bill Gorell Barnes/Spins the colonies yarns/About how AOT-dom/Is better than freedom"). For New Zealand, which was almost totally dependent on the British market, we hoped to negotiate free entry of its lamb.

A large international press corps in Brussels followed every turn in the negotiations. There were also influential representatives of the many countries whose interests were involved, such as members of the Commonwealth and EFTA. In their every public statement British spokesmen had to be conscious that they were speaking to many different audiences at the same time, not only in Britain and the EEC but also in the wider world.

It is important to remember that in 1961 the EEC was still in its own transitional phase, with many of its new policies not yet fully formed, particularly in the agricultural field. While we British were negotiating our would-be entry in one building, representatives of the Six were negotiating between themselves in a different part of Brussels to agree the Community's basic Regulations. There was a contagious feeling of excitement and idealism about the European project (most of the officials concerned on the EEC side had been at the Val Duchesse negotiations leading up to the signature of the Treaty of Rome) but issues that mattered greatly to the individual states were still being fought for and haggled over. We were essentially trying to get on to a train that was moving quite fast.

Broadly speaking, by the summer of 1962 settlement of the trade issues was in sight with the help of some all-night sittings. At this point there was a major crisis. The Six agreed on a system of financing the Community that was profoundly unhelpful from the British point of view. Member States were to pool their customs receipts as well as levies on agricultural imports. Britain imported far more from the outside world than did the existing Six and thus would pay the lion's share of the common kitty. We had hoped to have a say in shaping the decision but were presented with a *fait accompli*. There was a very tense Ministerial meeting of the Seven. I remember a particularly fraught buffet supper in the rue Quatre Bras. As I was looking for a place to sit I was hailed by the Dutch Foreign Minister Joseph Luns and made to sit with him, the French Foreign Minister Couve de Murville and Sir Duncan Sandys, then Commonwealth Secretary. I had the distinct impression that my presence was being used to prevent heavy discussion of awkward subjects. Luns asked my opinion as to the so-called special relationship between Britain and the US which the French were suggesting was an impediment to British entry. I said that I was not sure that it really existed other than in the minds of some Englishmen but it is a question on which my mind has changed from time to time since.

As I wrote to Celia, *"Here the future doesn't seem to extend visibly very far ahead. Nobody is daring to fix summer holidays, and it is generally assumed that we will work through August, harder and harder until people start collapsing. I have firmly made up my mind that I will be the first to collapse in that case!"* We did get our summer break and when the conference regathered in September the focus shifted to agriculture and the Regulations the Six had recently agreed covering individual sectors. By this time I had got very familiar with the Secretariat drafting style and I was sometimes asked to draft a paper in French. Agreement on the technical issues seemed to be in sight.

But it had always been clear that the fate of the negotiations depended on developments elsewhere and ultimately on the decision of the President of France, General de Gaulle, who was known to be unenthusiastic if not downright hostile to the idea of British entry. The other Five were broadly in favour to a greater or lesser extent, with the Dutch being unconditional supporters, but de Gaulle saw Britain as a rival to the dominant French position in the EEC and more widely. Set upon restoring France's position as a world power, he was hostile to American influence and saw Britain with its close links to the US as a Trojan horse. De Gaulle was a splendid orator of the Delphic kind and the British delegation would crawl over the texts of his every pronouncement looking for hints of his intentions. We also devoured the telegrams from British Embassies in Paris and elsewhere which reported what other people thought he might mean by his every comment. The delegation had quite early on agreed that Jimmy and I could read the telegrams provided we went to their offices to do so.

That autumn of 1962 two major developments overshadowed our negotiations, one within France and one in the wider defence field. In France a referendum proposing the direct election of the President was approved by a large majority at the end of October. This greatly strengthened de Gaulle's position domestically. A meeting between Macmillan and de Gaulle at Rambouillet on 15/16 December went badly. A few days after this Macmillan had a meeting with President Kennedy in Nassau which led to an agreement for the provision of American Polaris missiles as the delivery vehicle for British nuclear warheads. This reinforced de Gaulle's conviction that Britain was in effect an American satellite with its nuclear deterrent dependent on the United States. The delegations regathered in Brussels after the Christmas break in a cloud of foreboding. De Gaulle was due to give one of his periodic press conferences on 14 January. I watched this for the first time recently – there was no television available in 1963 – and it made a remarkable impression even after nearly 60 years. The tall figure of de Gaulle dominated the packed room. He was treated with the utmost respect by the assembled journalists, who were invited to put their questions before the President began to speak which he did without a break for about 30 minutes. He dealt first with a range of domestic issues before eventually coming to the question of British entry to the EEC. Many of the things he said seem almost prophetic today. Pointing to the very different wartime experience of Britain and the continental countries, and to Britain's extensive links with the Commonwealth and the USA, he wondered aloud whether *nos amis britanniques* were really ready to commit themselves. It was clear he thought not.

It was devastating, but still we foot soldiers in Brussels hoped against fading hope that the negotiations might continue. In a letter to Celia on 18 January I wrote:

> *This week has been very exciting here with the battle on with the French who were trying to break off the negotiations. That they have not so far succeeded is a considerable triumph for Heath, and for the five other EEC Delegations who have shewn a quite new toughness and ability to stick together in the face of de Gaulle's attempt to cow them. But so far there is only a truce and the battle will be on again on Monday week. If the French refuse to budge despite all pressure, the negotiations can only break off (and me presumably return to London). The hope is of course that the toughness of the reactions to de Gaulle may persuade him to think again, especially if he doesn't get the backing of Adenauer (the other chief question mark).*

Two weeks later when ministers met again in that long room in the rue Quatre Bras, Couve de Murville made it absolutely clear that the negotiations were at an end. It must have been a difficult meeting for him and as he sat chatting and laughing with others of the French delegation he looked distinctly embarrassed. The representatives of the other Five gathered round the British delegation shaking their hands in solidarity, almost as if they were congratulating them. It was all very emotional. Wandering round the building afterwards I ran into one of my Luxembourg friends, Guy de Muyser, and we had a drink together almost in tears.

Afterwards Heath called a meeting of the British delegation and this time Jimmy and I attended as full members, sitting at the back of the crowded room. Heath started by analysing the negotiations in which success had seemed so close. He speculated whether we might have succeeded if they had been conducted more quickly with the crunch coming before the summer. When it became clear de Gaulle would veto our entry, the next objective had been to rally the Five so as to make clear where blame lay, and this at least had been achieved. Heath did not believe that Britain would be able to join the EEC while de Gaulle was alive. (This turned out to be correct.) He had hoped that membership would invigorate our economy as had happened with the original Six. But now Britain must tackle its problems alone. He then set out a brief manifesto for the modernization of Britain. Heath's talk is etched in my mind. It was remarkably forward-looking from a man who had just had such a huge set-back to his hopes.

But there was nothing to do but pack our bags and return to London. The delegation had a sort of afterlife in helping write a history of the negotiations which was put together by Sir Con O'Neill and then suppressed for political reasons about which I am not clear. I sent my copy by confidential bag to the Embassy in Bangkok when I was posted there a few months later and to my great regret I left it in the Embassy strong room on departure and never saw it again.

I was sent back to Western Department for a few months. I then happened to notice that I was eligible for an "over-age exam" for the Diplomatic Service which had recently been introduced as an alternative to the post-university entry. I decided to try my luck again and this time I sailed through. I was told later that my immediate boss, the splendid John Killick, had gone into the Personnel Department and thumped the table, telling them to make sure I got their full backing. I remain immensely grateful to him. As promised from the start, my membership of the Service was backdated to 1957, and it is now as if those years of uncertainty never were. Indeed, looking back I realize that, had I succeeded in getting myself established earlier on, I would by 1961 have been sent on a regular posting. I would never have had my front row seat at one of the formative experiences of British post-war history. Failure though it turned out to be, the attempt to join the EEC in the early 60s accelerated Britain's transition from fading empire to modern European state.

Chapter 6

A LAND OF GOLDEN BUDDHAS
Bangkok (1964)

My first regular posting was to the Embassy in Bangkok, where for the second time I was to replace Catherine Pestell. As etiquette demanded, I wrote my letters to the Ambassador, who had the wonderful name of Sir Dermot MacDermot, and to the Head of Chancery. I was sent a copy of the Post Report which included all sorts of useful tips about local conditions and what I needed to bring. There followed an orgy of essential shopping; supervised by my mother, I acquired sheets with my name embroidered in the corner, a set of cutlery, cotton clothing and beach wear, and much else besides.

The "approved route" to Bangkok was by sea taking about five weeks, but I decided to go by air stopping off on the way in Beirut and Delhi, where I had introductions from my godfather Alec Bishop who had just finished a posting as Deputy High Commissioner in Calcutta. The main disadvantage was that I could only bring very limited luggage with me and had to wait many weeks for my heavy baggage to follow.

My job in the Embassy was to be the SEATO desk officer. SEATO, the South-East Asia Treaty Organization, was one of the string of alliances set up under American inspiration to contain Communist influence as the Cold War settled in. The substantial headquarters was in Bangkok and the Ambassador there doubled as the Foreign Secretary's representative on the Council. There were eight members – Thailand, the Philippines and Pakistan in the area, as well as Australia, New Zealand, France, the US and the UK. Though originally intended as a collective defence organization, by the time I arrived in 1961 its members' aims had diverged: Pakistan was cultivating China as an ally in its feud with India while France under de Gaulle was taking its distance from the United States. The two countries effectively paralyzed SEATO in the defence field. In my job on what was called the Permanent Working Group we would spend fruitless hours arguing whether or not a press release concerning some military exercise between the more active members should refer to a threat from the North-East, which could only mean China and North Vietnam. But the job had some positive content too. SEATO was active in the social and economic field, particularly in Thailand which remained a staunchly loyal member. There was, for instance, a SEATO research project looking into the life cycle of the river fluke, a pest which took a heavy toll on the health of populations living along the Mekong and other waterways. There was a project to settle the hill tribes who wandered across the northern Thai border and were seen as vulnerable to Chinese influence. And perhaps most successful of all was the SEATO School of Engineering which survived its parent organization to become the Asian Institute of Technology.

In the mid-1960s the Vietnam war dominated the wider political landscape though SEATO played no direct role in it. Britain was never a combatant in Vietnam but the British government had a special status in the area as Co-Chairman (with the Soviet Union) of the Geneva Conference which had attempted to bring peace in the wake of France's withdrawal from Indo-China. Much had changed since 1953 when the Geneva Agreements setting up these arrangements were signed, but when fighting erupted in Laos between two princes who were on different sides of the ideological divide the Agreements were invoked in an effort at peace-making. This was the background to my secondment to the Embassy in Vientiane of which more in the next chapter.

In late 1964 the US began bombing the Ho Chi Minh trails through Laos and Cambodia which were used by the North Vietnamese to infiltrate the South. Some 80% of the bombing took place from airfields in North-East Thailand, though the Thai Government did not admit to this publicly. The refusal to talk about such a large elephant in the room meant that Thai politics had an unreal atmosphere. Thailand itself was a dictatorship run by the army but it was also a kingdom. The young King Bhumibol had come to the throne in mysterious circumstances following the violent death of his elder brother – another subject one did not discuss in polite Thai society. But the King and his beautiful wife Queen Sirikit held a very special place in what was still a hierarchical country. Degrees of closeness to the throne were reflected in the titles of the many princes and princesses who would bow before the statues of earlier kings. There was a special court language so that when the King walked along a road he did it with a different verb from an ordinary mortal. And I found that I myself was expected to use different words for "I" and "you" when addressing the servants from the words they used to address me.

On arrival in Thailand I moved in with Catherine. For the only time in my life I had an overlap with my predecessor and we shared a house for about a month until she left for the UK. This was fun and gave me the chance to get to know her friends at her many farewell parties. I remember with particular pleasure our breakfasts together on the roof in the cool of the morning under a spreading flame tree. I didn't altogether take to Catherine's house which, though modern and convenient, to my mind lacked charm. I had, however, no doubts about taking on Catherine's household which consisted of a cook-housekeeper called Boona, her "husband" Boon, three children – Yid, a girl of about 12 who I later heard was adopted, Boona's daughter Bee, who was about eight, and a chunky little boy called Num, not to mention a dog and a goose. I never regretted this decision and the family became the mainstay of my life in Thailand.

One of my first concerns was to find out about the Diplomatic Bag. Though this was primarily for confidential material I was allowed to use it for letters, which in those pre-phone days were my only sure means of communication with my parents. They could equally send letters or small packages to me care of the Outward Bag Room at the Foreign Office. My mother was due to go into hospital to have a hip operation which was a much more serious operation then than it is now. Apart from worry I felt guilty for not being close at hand when needed. It turned out that the bag to and from London went once a week escorted by the Queen's Messenger Service. This was mostly staffed by retired officers, one of whom, Major James Nairne, turned up at a number of my postings and became something of a friend. Allowing for UK posts the gap between writing a letter and getting a reply was about three weeks.

Here is the letter I sent my parents describing my arrival in Bangkok.

Bangkok, 28 February 1964

I arrived here yesterday afternoon, brought from Delhi by Qantas who looked after us well, and it is now time for me to give you a "first impressions report" (This is what Ambassadors are expected to write shortly after taking up a new post, though few would dare to rush in after 24 hours!).

Catherine was at the airport to meet me accompanied by a sweet-looking and silent Thai woman with a bunch of flowers, who turned out to be Boona, the feminine half of Catherine's staff whom I expect to inherit. It was a pleasant welcome... I was glad to find that no hectic social round had been arranged for me in advance, so last night we could talk peacefully of life in Bangkok and the job. This morning I went into the office with Catherine to meet the people in the Embassy. They all seemed very pleasant as far as one could tell on first acquaintance, including the Ambassador who was very much as I had been led to expect: tall and thin, shy-looking and with a kind face. I didn't intend to consider myself at work this week and so after my round of introductions, I went out to explore the town. Bangkok is a sprawling place with no obvious centre, and the residential area in which this house is (Bangkapi) is away from the river. At the end of the lane (or "soy"), there is a broad road leading into town, and also to the Embassy which, as I had been told, is in a pleasant compound with lawns and shady trees. On my inaugural trip I was advised to take a taxi to a place called "the thieves' market" in the Chinatown district. It was a good choice, because I drove through a lot of the town on the way, and when I got there I found a series of narrow lanes lined with booths (a suk, in fact) with all sorts of interesting alley-ways leading off. I found a particularly insalubrious bit of river where fishing-boats were drawn up and people inspecting crabs and cooking unspeakable bits of innards. I went past several temples (though I decided against going in until I had someone to tell me what not to do) and what was obviously a monastery, with a number of very young monks sitting about in orange robes. (The robes really are the colour of those pictures, even if they are called "yellow.") I also found a Chinese theatre playing to an enthusiastic herd of school-children – it looked rather like a Punch and Judy show on a bigger scale – the main characters were a little boy and a splendid villain with a painted face and a padded tummy requiring much hitching: the others spent most of their time hitting him and he squeaked and groaned to the delight of the audience. After all this, I thought I had had enough and took a taxi back home for lunch. The afternoon I have spent quietly unpacking and reading, and now sitting down to write to you...

My first day at work went without mishap despite the immediate problem of mastering the mass of new names and faces, not just in the Embassy but also at the large SEATO Secretariat. Catherine couldn't have been kinder in showing me the ropes and generally easing the pain of new arrival. We went together to a meeting of the Council Representatives (i.e. Ambassador's level) where slightly to my alarm I found myself being formally "introduced" by the Chair. (I only had to bow and smirk in reply!) It wasn't a very lively meeting, but I began to feel better able to cope with whatever the job might hold.

Soon after my arrival I was invited to dinner at the Residence. It was a largely Embassy affair because there was a lot of coming and going among the staff just then, and the MacDermots were doing their stuff. They were a low key but friendly couple who did not stand on ceremony despite the fact that he was, I have since discovered from Wikipedia, Prince of Coolavin and a descendant of the Kings of Moylurg. The dinner was not a scintillating affair. In fact, I was the main scintillation myself because I wore a new evening dress with a sequined top, which I was rather conscious was lower-cut than the Bangkok norm. The other main attraction was an enormous punkah that waved to and fro over the dinner table.

Before leaving London I had had visiting cards printed. It was the custom to distribute these to embassies and others on first arrival but fortunately the Embassy drivers took care of this formality. I almost immediately had my first taste of Court mourning which was declared by Buckingham Palace when the King of Greece died, because he was related to the Royal Family. For me that meant wearing black, white, or at a pinch mauve for a few days. I also had to go with the Counsellor to sign the Book of Condolence at the Greek Embassy.

I had my first lesson in Thai which was a great excitement. My teacher was an old lady called Khun Sanghat who had taught generations of Embassy people (including language students) and had the reputation of being something of a slave-driver. She wore a sarong and I was fascinated to discover that she had grown up in the Thai Court. I explained, with some shame, my limited objectives – to be able to get around, make myself understood and read simple texts – and arranged to have two lessons a week. The five tones felt very queer in my self-conscious mouth, but apparently I had made a good start in being able to tell the difference at all. For lesson two I was supposed to be able to count up to 100 and to know the days of the week.

My other immediate preoccupation was deciding where to live. After some house-hunting I found a house to rent which I liked much better than Catherine's. It was fortunately within my rent allowance and the Admin Officer approved.

Bangkok, 10 May 1964

For me the week has been dominated by the Great Move. All things considered and largely thanks to Boona it went very smoothly. The Embassy provided a lorry for the afternoon and onto this were piled all my possessions and an incredible collection of odds and ends in inadequate containers which belonged to the Boons. The picture was completed by an extremely worried pet goose who sought comfort from every bystander in turn. (He belongs to the little girl and I don't see much of him as a rule.)

And now we are all installed in our new quarters. After being here three days I am very pleased. It is a pleasant companionable house. The landlord tells me regularly that it is ridiculous that one person should live here alone and he is of course right. It is certainly bigger than I need (not much bigger than Catherine's house but more spacious and of course with a much bigger garden), but on the other hand it is cheaper than many horrid little boxes I saw, and the spaces feel airy rather than empty… I wish you could see it and hope somehow that you will in time.

About this time Sir Edmund Hillary of Everest fame visited Bangkok in his capacity as the founding President of New Zealand's Voluntary Service Abroad Foundation. I met him a couple of times casually, once at a cocktail party and once at a beach party, as well as at a more formal dinner given for him by Paul Edmonds who was the Acting Chargé d'Affaires at the New Zealand Embassy. I thought Hillary very nice and unassuming; rather endearingly in one who had braved such ordeals, he was thoroughly alarmed by Thai food and by Thai driving.

Another beach party was an all-day affair thrown by Konthi, the Secretary General of SEATO, at a brand-new bungalow down on the Gulf of Siam. I was asked to go down with Lady MacDermot whom I found very easy and pleasant during our long tête-à-tête (a 2½-hour drive each way). It was a treat to swim, which was difficult to do in Bangkok unless one belonged to the right clubs. But most of the time we were there was taken up with an enormous Chinese meal – there were 10 meat or fish dishes followed by a sweet and fruit. I wilted before we got half-way through and a good many others did too. It was really rather a pity to have spent so much time over lunch because afterwards we had to go almost straight back to Bangkok.

There seldom seemed to be an evening without some sort of engagement, even if only a cocktail party – not my favourite form of entertainment, especially in a limited circle which had too many of them. I would have loved to have one or two of my old friends in Bangkok but found quite a few congenial people and decided to give supper parties to cultivate them. There was an inevitable touch of loneliness but I found that my Thai lessons were a good stimulus and filled a time of day when I might have felt at a loose end. My new house was a place where I found it pleasant to be alone. To my relief Boona was delighted with it too.

Bangkok, 18 May 1964

She was the person who brought first news of it which was a minor triumph, and the garden is of course splendid for the children – I am out so much that I haven't been strict about them playing wherever they wish. The trimmings of furniture remain to do of course – picture frames, lampshades, extra cushions – but even so the place looks nice. Did I tell you about the trains? After deep thought I had asked the landlord if I could have the covers in the living room in a particular shade of purple muted with black (good with coral etc, I thought): I turned up one day to find that some were like that (and look very nice) but he had run out of material and used his own judgment for the others: express trains roaring across each panel. (Khun Achava is Chief Engineer of the Thai Railways!) I am afraid I couldn't stifle my shock entirely but I have decided to have spare covers made (coral this time) which won't cost very much in local cotton.

I went one weekend on an excursion to the North-West with my new friends from the New Zealand Embassy to see the King open a new dam – the biggest in SE Asia, and really very impressive. The country up there was far more attractive than Bangkok's central plain. The hills, though not very high, were definitely mountains by inclination, and the vegetation much more interesting. I particularly liked the flame trees which were at their very best. The nearest town to the dam site was Tak, where we spent the night in a hotel reminiscent of some we stayed in during our famous Beirut to London drive, particularly as to the plumbing. The beds were board hard – no sheets provided but bolsters, often called Dutch wives and useful to put your feet on to create cooling drafts. I was sufficiently tired to sleep exceedingly well despite all. The ceremony at the dam itself was interesting, though unfortunately I was too far back to get a good view of what was going on. A row of Buddhist monks sat across one end of the room looking like a frieze in their formal cross-legged position and with a fan in each hand. There was a lot of chanting and the King on arrival presented each with a tray of objects which those nearer the front told me ranged from roses to sweets and tobacco. There were then a couple of speeches by the King and the Prime Minister (which I suspected would have been even duller if one could have understood them). Then an array of balloons bearing the veil to be removed from the inscription were loosed off, only to sink with farcical determination into the river bed below the dam. None of the papers reported this incident and I hoped it wasn't a very bad Buddhist omen.

Back in Bangkok I had a dinner party, partly as a small-scale house-warming, and partly to provide accounts for the inspector, who was due to come in a week or so. In going over the costs with me Boona was most insistent that I should mark them up. She obviously didn't think the Embassy should be allowed to believe that other servants could get things as cheaply as she could. The trouble about entertaining was that I kept on thinking of little additions to the house that would make things so much nicer – a carpet here, cushions on the dining room chairs, a screen across the pantry door, etc. I could have spent far too much with very little trouble at all.

It was good to get away from Bangkok and I did again as soon as I could in the company of Jean Cameron, a junior New Zealand diplomat.

Pattaya, 24 May 1964

I have been celebrating my birthday weekend in an exceedingly pleasant and indeed ideal way in one of the Embassy's two bungalows by the sea. We get a turn for one or other bungalow about once every three months, and I decided this would be a particularly nice weekend to have my first experiment. I chose better than I knew because tomorrow, Tuesday, is a Buddhist holiday (the anniversary conveniently of Buddha's birth, enlightenment, and death), so I begged Monday off to "faire le pont" as they used to say in Brussels.

From various hints which I can't remember very clearly, I had got the impression that the bungalows were very primitive and without a great deal of charm. We were very pleasantly surprised. We are housed in a little round house (rather like a rondavel) within a few yards of the sea. It is divided into a very adequate bedroom for two (screened and no leaks) and shower, and a balcony with comfortable sitting accommodation and a rudimentary kitchen alcove. Our days here have reminded me strongly at times of our summer at the beach in Beirut – the bikini-spotting and the speculation about the neighbours, even the fishing boats which light their lanterns at night... There are speedboats which come round plying for hire, and Jean and I have been wasting our substance on water-skiing. I reckon it is eight years since I last tried in Beirut, and I was afraid the knack would have gone entirely – fortunately not, though I certainly have taken quite a number of pearlers. I even tried one ski...

I have in fact broken the rules by bringing Jean with me. The landlady apparently wrote it into the lease that no guests should be entertained at the bungalow who were resident in Bangkok but not part of the Embassy staff. I can't think how the Embassy ever agreed to anything so unreasonable – she apparently thinks that people might be invited as guests who would otherwise have bungalows of their own. Anyhow I complained that it was particularly hard on single people like me if one didn't happen to have bosom pals in the Embassy and was advised to go ahead and break the rule with the minimum fuss. I hope there is no difficulty about it, because it would obviously not be much fun to come alone...

Just as I was beginning to settle in I was whisked off to Laos.

Chapter 7

A FORGOTTEN WAR
Vientiane (1964)

I should at this point say a little more about the situation in Laos, a remote country which was briefly on the front line of the contest between the Communist and Western worlds. The Kingdom had been part of French Indochina and when the French left three princes jostled for power: the right-wing Boum Oum; Souphanouvong, leader of the Pathet Lao, who was supported by North Vietnam; and the so-called neutralist Souvanna Phouma who was supported by the Western powers. Because of its geographical position Laos had become an offshoot of the escalating war in Vietnam. At the time I arrived on the scene Souvanna Phouma led a Tripartite government based in Vientiane and international concern focused on the outbreak of fighting around an area in Northern Laos called the Plain of Jars. In deciding to invoke its special role as co-Chairman of the Geneva Conferences to convene local talks in Vientiane, whether or not the other co-Chairman (the USSR) joined in, Britain must have been acting as a stalking horse for the Americans. The US had no role in the Geneva arrangements, though they were already heavily involved in shoring up South Vietnam.

Vientiane, 28 May 1964

On Tuesday morning I was sitting on the balcony of the little cottage by the sea at Pattaya – where I finished off my last letter to you – and 24 hours later I found myself descending from an aeroplane on the Vientiane airstrip. As you will imagine what happened in between was rather rushed, and I still feel that I am in the process of catching up again. The story briefly is that the Chargé d'Affaires here (a chap called John Denson), faced with the prospect of convening talks locally between the 14 signatories of the Geneva Agreements, appealed for extra staff; the FO told Bangkok to send someone; and Bangkok sent me. The Ambassador (i.e. MacDermot) said that he thought me most suitable since my SEATO job had already given me something to do with the Laos problem; in fact I think that since SEATO has been fairly slack I was the most easily spared. In any case, I am delighted. I don't know how long I am to be here but I suspect that a fortnight is a fairly conservative guess. In the meantime, I live in solitary splendour at the Residence because the Ambassador is away and the Embassy decided to put me here rather than in a hotel. I find the arrangement very much to my taste!

After the panic to get me here in no time at all (in fact the Bangkok Embassy sent a car to fetch me back from Pattaya though I missed it and did not get the news until I got home), things seem to have calmed down. This is because the talks, which at one time looked like starting yesterday, are now more probably to start on Monday. (Nobody expects the bloc countries to agree to go which is rather sad because I would have loved to see somebody say "niet.") The breathing space is most welcome to give me a little time to read up the basic documents and get my bearings. I think I have had a very lucky break because John Denson, the Chargé… is obviously a person who likes a Watson to his Dr Johnson (or do I mean Sherlock Holmes!?) and looks like adopting me for this purpose. It is anyhow his intention that I should give all my time to the talks when they start, and this is obviously the most interesting thing to be in on. I can't help feeling that the resident members of the Embassy must feel a bit peeved, but I find to my surprise that I am senior to the other people on the political side. This is what comes of a small post.

Vientiane at first sight looked like a small-scale and much more primitive Bangkok. There were the same wats and monks, the same trees and climate, and the same rather unattractive ribbon development. The facts that it was French-speaking and that traffic kept to the right on the appalling roads were the main differences. Westerners who lived there seemed to suffer from a sort of claustrophobia, partly from the lack of amenities such as cinemas or restaurants, and partly from the absence of outlet – the security situation was bad and it was forbidden to go far from the capital. The significance of the sudden crisis seemed to be mainly political: defeats suffered by the neutralist forces had upset the balance of power on which the tripartite government rested and nobody knew what would happen next. There was, however, no sign that the Communists wished to cross the 1961 ceasefire line which had taken on an almost mystical significance as a test of intentions. The fighting all seemed very remote from Vientiane which was quite calm.

The consultations soon took on a rather strange life of their own: a diplomatic half-world which had something of the fascination of chess. The Times immediately debunked them as useless, but I thought they might make some small contribution to the higher-level talks which everyone expected to follow. It was anyway a chance for countries like Thailand and South Vietnam to state their views as very near neighbours of Laos, and the whole exercise had some value as a demonstration of support for the Neutralist P.M. Souvanna Phouma, who needed whatever help he could get. Personally I thoroughly enjoyed my first set of negotiations in a more than bow-worm capacity. It helped that John Denson, the Chargé, was only 38 so that it was not so very absurd to see myself cast as first lieutenant.

But the date of my return to Bangkok kept retreating and I soon began to realize that it would be a mistake to stay too long. Though people were perhaps more friendly than in Bangkok life in Vientiane was very restricted. I continued to live in state at the Residence where I rattled around. The talks were in the Residence too and the total lack of public transport meant that I saw hardly anything of the town. Fortunately I didn't have much spare time, what with long hours and kind invitations, because in my hasty exit from Bangkok I hadn't brought much to occupy myself with – no sewing, no Thai books. When Paul Edmonds turned up for a couple of days – the New Zealand Embassy covered Laos from Bangkok – it felt almost like a breath of wind from home.

My introduction to Vientiane society, a dinner given by someone in the American Embassy, turned out to be Chinese, with 13 courses because there were 13 guests, and we were at table for over three hours. I think most of the guests – at any rate the Western ones – found it a bit of an ordeal. One usually drank beer through these evenings, and since some of the dishes were rather hot, one got through a large quantity which added to the general sense of bloating. I was interested by the Lao guests – three couples of varying degrees of sophistication. All the women wore the typical Lao skirt, a length of material draped sarong-wise from the waist, with a heavy band of embroidery (metal thread in the posher instances) around the bottom. The skirts came half-way down the calf and were worn with a remarkably European style of blouse. Some of them were very pretty, and I resolved to go prospecting in the market when I got the opportunity.

I was glad of an evening at home to sleep off the after-effects of the Chinese meal. The airconditioned bedrooms in the Residence were very welcome though the Vientiane climate was a degree cooler than Bangkok.

The Residence was a pleasant Western-style house and looked over a peaceful garden surrounded with trees. I enjoyed drinks on the terrace, and was often driven there for meals while the conferenciers were in possession of "my" dining table. When I came down to dinner on my first evening I was horrified to find my place set at the top of a long table laid with blotters and notepads, rows of water jugs down the middle, and place cards saying "India", "United Kingdom", etc.

After a couple of weeks of near stalemate a group was set up to draft a communiqué. This became largely my responsibility in keeping with the fact that the UK was chairing the talks as a whole. My colleagues were very amenable and I enjoyed the challenge of trying to steer the group's activities in the most useful direction. But my probable departure date seemed to recede whenever I got near it.

Vientiane, 18 June 1964

As you see I am still here…I am tempted by the idea of taking a couple of days to go to Luang Prabang (where the King lives) before I go back to Bangkok. I am told that it is a very attractive town, unlike Vientiane, and it seems a pity not to see the sights of Laos while I am here. It is incidentally well clear of the fighting. I have been away from Bangkok so long that I don't think they will miss me for an extra couple of days, and I have worked hard enough here to feel I have justified it.

The pace of the work has actually suddenly slackened in the last day or two – this is because we have done as much as we can on the spot until people get another round of instructions from their Capitals. I have on the whole enjoyed the "negotiations" very much, largely (says she smugly) because I think I have done my bit rather well. John Denson as Chargé has of course a lot of other things on his plate so I have tried to make it my job always to have an idea of how the next lap might go. I think I mentioned in my last letter that we had got a drafting group of which I was de facto chairman: I have got quite a kick out of this and I think we have been as effective as we could. Of course it is all child's play compared to [the negotiations with the EEC in] *Brussels, but having watched skilled negotiators at work for so long it is rather fun having the chance to play the game a bit oneself. In this case our difficult partners have been the Indians, who having agreed to participate at the 11th hour, have ever since been having self-doubts that they may have compromised their neutrality.*

> *But yesterday, as I find so often happens to me after a period of special effort, I suddenly felt excruciatingly bored. It is in fact partly justifiable because there is nothing to do in this great house except read (which I have done voraciously, for me), and given the complete absence of public transport it is quite difficult to get out. Thursday is technically an Embassy half-day, though this is the first time since I have been here that one would notice it. (Last Sunday was in fact the first Sunday I didn't visit the Office too.) This afternoon I celebrated by commandeering an Embassy car and going shopping. I bought myself a miscellaneous selection of paperbacks, and also a watch… Afterwards I went to have my hair done (not particularly well) and I am glad to report that the result of this minor spending spree was that my black dog had vanished. (Do you remember catching my black dog in a shoebag and drowning it once when I was in a particularly sour mood?)*

I told myself that I shouldn't grouse, because people were very nice in looking after me. A particularly good outing was the annual Rotary Club Dinner, of all unexpected things. The meal was Chinese – though not thank God so overpowering as the last one – and interspersed with much drinking of toasts and references to the "*chers rotariens de Vientiane*." Most of the Laotian notables seemed to be there either as Rotarians or as guests. In particular, I was introduced to Souvanna Phouma, the so-called "Neutralist" Prime Minister, who not surprisingly looked rather preoccupied, and to General Kouprasith, who was the nominal head of a right-wing coup a couple of months earlier, a coup which seemed to have merged with the scenery to a remarkable extent. Kouprasith was rather an engaging little man, surprisingly young, and there was something pathetic in seeing him cast in the role of the sinister right-wing threat to Laotian stability.

The next day I had a rather unexpected lunch party myself. I wanted to ask the Beales, a young couple who had been nice to me, and I found to my horror that I had invited their three small children too. I immediately had visions of food stamped into the Ambassador's carpet and the gold-crested plates in smithereens. But with the connivance of the steward – a usually taciturn Vietnamese who brightened the moment I mentioned the children – it all went off very well. We ate on the terrace, which I thought was a minor brainwave. The children enjoyed the garden and were out of harm's way. In the afternoon the Beales took me to Nong Khai, the nearest

Thai town which had until recently been viewed as the local Mecca. To get there required a drive of about an hour on Laotian territory (along the worst roads I had yet met) followed by a ride in a small boat across the Mekong, an impressive broad river. The far bank was Thailand and one dutifully handed in one's passport before setting out to explore the town. In fact there was very little to see – a few poorish silver shops and some not very exciting fabrics. I bought an attractive brightly coloured strip of material which was meant to be a skirt border and was delighted to discover that Lao skirts were called "sins"! The reason for Nong Khai's attraction was the Lao currency crisis which kept many foreign goods out of the shops. Things had improved with a massive devaluation and there were now about 1500 kips to the pound. One was still given single kips from time to time but people used them as bookmarks. I sent one to my parents.

I was fiddling with the radio one night in a vain attempt to find a friendly station when I came across a cool BBC voice which announced it was Radio Beijing and then launched into a diatribe about Americans bombing Khang Khay (the Pathet Lao headquarters) and surrounding villages. The wave of hate and the bland distortions were somehow all the more shocking when contrasted with the voice. In fact, the US planes were grounded on the day in question as we happened to know for an unconnected reason. Somebody did the bombing though, because John Denson visited Khang Khay and saw the results – Laos presumably, and one could hardly blame them in this state of civil war. The worst of it was that I didn't feel the Western-orientated side could ever win, nor even achieve the draw which they had really been trying for, because their opponents were Asians. This, I told my parents, was the dilemma the US were trying to get round in Vietnam: whether to continue an endless fight or to cut their losses. What little countries like Laos, or rather their sparse vocal elements, wanted had not got much to do with the matter.

Vientiane, 25 June 1964

I think this really will be my last letter from Vientiane – this stay, anyhow. It looks as if our communiqué (always assuming it is eventually agreed) will be published at the beginning of next week, and with that our consultations will come to a resounding close. If it gets published in the British press I hope you will remember what struggles have gone into each hackneyed phrase.

I have had one or two pleasant outings this week. The Densons invited me to a dinner which they gave for the P.M. – in the Residence, so that was not really an outing. Quite a turn-out of Lao notables were there. Souvanna himself I didn't find very impressive, though he has the reputation of being the only Lao politician who has any idea of the international repercussions of what goes on in this little country. He is very Frenchified, speaking with the thick accent they all have, and has an absent French wife. He was rather fond of holding forth in order to hear his own voice, I thought, but I suppose if you are a feudal Prince you get used to people listening whatever you say. Certainly his relationship with the other ministers present struck me as one between the school master and the boys. I sat next to the Minister of Finance, an elegant young man who only really perked up when we talked about water-skiing. He, just to ring the changes, has an absent Danish wife. Another Lao personality who was there, and someone I had very much wanted to meet, was the Neutralist General Amkha. He has the reputation of being one of the most independent-minded, not least because he survived 3 years' solitary imprisonment underground by the right wing without any noticeable after-effects. He turned out to be a tall shy young man in an ill-fitting dinner jacket with a remarkably sweet smile. He had a new wife whose French was an example of a will not always providing a way. The only other Lao wife I talked to had no French at all and just smiled showing betel-nut stained teeth. Apart from Embassy supporters the only non-Lao guests were the IMF representative and his wife...

Another party which turned out to be rather a good one was given by the Indian Ambassador (who is of course a participant in the negotiations). He and his wife are both from Nepal and are rather a colourful pair. He sculpts as well as being a crack polo player and keen racer (little outlet in Vientiane, poor man). I don't quite know what she does, but she does it with great vigour and always takes a pep pill whenever she begins to find a party dull. The party was for the departing Australian Ambassador (to whom I seem to have said many goodbyes though I never knew him before) and "le tout Vientiane" was there.

The consultations nearly ended with a bang rather than a whimper. At the 11th hour, John Denson (who for all his virtues was a very moody man) lost his temper with the Indians who had all along been the difficult factor. We didn't realize that much harm had been done until the next day when as it happened John had gone away from Vientiane for the day. In his absence I was summoned by the American Ambassador to discuss how to soothe

the Indians down – a slightly over-whelming honour, but Leonard Unger was a very nice man and my morale was helped by having something to say. Anyhow everything was eventually smoothed over, and the documents signed amidst sweetness and light on Monday afternoon. Unger went on to have a significant role dealing with Vietnam in the State Department. When I said goodbye to him, he congratulated me which I appreciated.

With the consultations over my job was quickly done. There was a final rush of reporting and then suddenly I seemed to be spare. This was splendid because it meant I got away for my trip to Luang Prabang which I described in a letter written back in my Bangkok home.

Bangkok, 5 July 1964

I had a series of misadventures in my attempts to get there – it is very much in the wilds and plane services rather unpredictable... It was a crack of dawn departure. The first stop, about which nobody had warned me, was at a place called Sayaburi where I very nearly left the plane by mistake thinking we had got to LP: there was nothing to tell one. Fortunately, however, the herd instinct stopped me from straying too far and eventually I found a Filipino who spoke English and told me what had happened. We had quite a wait at Sayaburi because of cloud, which was quite interesting because a number of the local tribespeople (whom one never sees in Vientiane) came out to look at the aeroplane. Their clothes reminded me surprisingly of some of the Palestinian costumes (Bedouin really) – black mostly, with coloured embroidery and heavy silver jewellery. I think from discussion later they must have been from two tribes – Meo and Yao.

Morale was pretty low on arrival at LP because it was pouring with rain and the crew and all passengers decided to stay put rather than getting soaked. I was just contemplating rather dismally the prospect of a very wet day sightseeing in a town where I could speak to no one (and which I wasn't sure how I would get to anyhow) when a Land Rover with a large red cross turned up, driven by a British doctor who is employed by the Colombo Plan [a British aid programme] *who had been warned that I was coming and met the plane on spec. He and a young Voluntary Service Overseas chap who was helping him were very kind to me and made all the difference to my stay. Luang Prabang has a great deal of charm. It is situated at the junction of two rivers and the high ridge between the two is surmounted by a gilded conical wat (temple). The town, which is the capital of a province and also where the King lives, is full of wats, some very beautiful. There was one which I was particularly taken with which was covered with mirrored mosaic: One wall had a series of pictured mosaics illustrating the local myths and holy stories which reminded me in its vivid characteristics of the mosaics at Antioch (or was it Tarsus) which we saw on our famous drive* [to England from Beirut].

After supper I was taken on a tour of the night spots including an opium den. It was in a palm thatched shack of a house, and the room inside about 12 foot square. When one's eyes got accustomed to the light one saw that there were benches all round and groups of people lying around three lamps. The atmosphere was very calm and almost dignified – there was obviously a ritual in preparing the pipes which someone else seemed to do for the smoker. There was hardly any talking, and we foreign intruders were stared at with a passive but in no way resentful curiosity. The staring effect is heightened by the fact that people don't seem to blink when they have been smoking. There was a woman there who must have smoked about 8 pipes in quick succession while we were there, and towards the end a man started to massage her by treading up and down her back as if he was making wine.

Few people remember the Lao crisis today and I doubt if anyone recalls the talks in Vientiane which so preoccupied me and which led nowhere. The main Geneva Conference was never recalled and Laos, like Cambodia later, was gradually sucked into the war in Vietnam, with much bombing of the Ho Chi Minh trails in both countries. But the domino effect which so preoccupied Western policy makers at the time stopped more or less there. Thailand held firm against communism and with it most of the rest of South East Asia. Indeed, with the fall of Sukarno in 1965 Indonesia rejoined the Western camp.

Chapter 8

"FROM YOUR CORRESPONDENT IN THE EXOTIC EAST" Bangkok (1964–1966)

I went back to Bangkok with mixed feelings. I remember thinking that as a single woman with diplomatic standing I was socially neither fish, nor fowl, nor good red herring: I did not belong in the wives' circle, nor in that of the Embassy secretaries who shared a Mess in a pleasant old house, and I felt clumsy beside the petite Thai beauties who crossed my path. I missed close male company too. My colleagues were friendly, but over-friendliness could be misinterpreted by their wives. Though I was not prepared to admit it to parents, or even perhaps to myself, I was lonely and yearned for my old friends in Europe. I was quite sad to leave Vientiane, partly because I had quickly made friends there. Squalid little town though it was, my stay there had been most interesting and I had enjoyed it as one tends to when one has a job to do. But it was very nice indeed to be back in my house, which I found as lovely as ever, and to be surrounded by the ministering Boons.

The Densons were taking a few days' well-earned leave in Bangkok and, in a slightly rash moment, I asked if they would like to stay with me which they accepted with disconcerting alacrity. I immediately began to recall that the guest rooms were very partially equipped, and that in a month almost anything might have happened to the household. It was not a house in which to put up formal guests because there was only one bathroom where one washed by scooping water over oneself, and the two main bedrooms inter-connected giving precious little privacy. But Boona took all in her stride, and after borrowing a couple of mattresses everything seemed pretty well under control.

We had quite an excitement one night. The door of the small room John Denson was in had a Yale lock – because, the landlord told me, when he lived in the house they used to keep a Buddha there. Later I learned that his father's ashes were kept there too. Anyhow, the door slammed and we found that both keys were inside. There followed an anguished spell while John circled the house like a prowling lion trying to work out how to get into the room, which overhung the garden on stilts about 10 feet high. Eventually, as it was getting dark, Boon came in and proceeded to get out an incredibly rickety ladder which was far too short, to which he nailed a most inadequate piece of wood up which he shinned until, waving perilously high above us, he managed to get into the window. I must say I was thoroughly alarmed, not least, as I held the ladder, by the thought of the scimitar kitchen knife he might come tumbling down on us with. The knife was to cut the netting so the window could be unbolted, and he held it between his teeth. But the silent Boon showed unexpected determination and the only answer to my desperate "*mai dai*" (not possible) was a monosyllabic "*dai*" (possible). He was right, thank goodness.

It was about this time that Birabongse Kasemsri returned to Bangkok. I had known the handsome Bira slightly at Oxford. He was a British-educated minor prince (Mom Rajawong) who had been at school with my friend Prue Pedder's brother and, like me, had spent holidays with her hospitable family. After Oxford he had gone to the States to study at the Fletcher School at Tufts University. He was now coming back to Thailand after 12 years away, together with a Cheltenham-educated young wife called Rampi. She was a Mom Luang, one level higher in the Court hierarchy, and very beautiful. By an odd coincidence Bira was going to work in the SEATO department of the MFA where he would be my Thai opposite number.

The other person I really wanted to see was Noi Osuthanakraw, my Thai roommate when we were both day girls at Queen's College in London. We had been very good friends but meeting on her turf rather than mine and after a long gap was bound to be different. I had already concluded that, unlike Bira, her family was not one of those that mixed in Embassy circles. From time to time I mentioned her name to people who might know her and finally struck lucky when the wife of a Thai colleague in SEATO told me that she had been a class-mate of Noi's. The next thing I knew Noi rang me up. We had lunch together and, though she now had a husband and two children, it seemed relatively easy to take up where we had left off 10 years before. I got the impression, however, that her husband would not be brought into things very much. He was in the police and "not very interested in work." Noi herself sounded a bit nervous of formal entertaining. I was really most pleased to see her again, and she seemed very pleased to see me.

At my request my mother sent me a copy of *The Devil's Discus*, a book investigating the death of King Bhumibol's elder brother, the former King. It was banned in Thailand and feeling about it was high locally, not only because the Agatha Christie-type discussion of which of the Thai Royal family might be a murderer was felt to be *lèse-majesté*, but also because it set out to whitewash the Leftist Prime Minister (Pridi) who was exiled shortly afterwards and sought refuge in Red China. I found it most interesting, if a bit irritating in its condescension about the cuteness of the Thais. Many people were asking who put this relatively unknown novelist up to writing the book and particularly who paid the costs involved in his fairly extensive research (eg, he visited Bangkok, Switzerland, China). It was in fact very much the thing to have in my bookshelf with the dust cover reversed to hide the name.

***

I had been longing to visit Angkor with its many thousand-year-old temples. It lay across the frontier in Cambodia and the long hot drive of about 450 kilometres was a deterrent. Moreover, the border was closed to ordinary traffic though not to diplomats. Relations between Thailand and Cambodia were strained because a dispute about ownership of a small temple on the frontier had grown into a major row, ending up at the International Court of Justice. I leapt at the chance when I was invited to join a group excursion.

Bangkok, 27 July 1964

Setting out from Siem Riep at 9:30 this morning we reached Bangkok about 6pm this evening – this was much better than the journey up when, flogged on by the enthusiasts of the party, we were on the road by 4:15 am but thanks to long sessions on the frontier and other incidents including a car which managed to get lost we didn't arrive very much earlier. The roads were not too bad on the whole despite stretches of potholes on the Cambodian side and laterite (a red sandy substance which is apt to skid) in Thailand. We were three cars in all, the others belonging to a family in the Embassy called O'Keeffe and a family in one of the banks… The party was made up by a nice woman who has the daunting job of teaching midwifery in one of the Thai hospitals… The other cars were much bigger and more powerful than mine but all told I think our team put in a pretty good performance on the rough roads. Around Angkor my Dauphine came off best…

> *I lose courage at the thought of trying to describe Angkor itself – so many people must have done it much better than I could. I think the main impression I had was of sheer size – these were towns (or rather the temples and outer walls mainly, for the dwellings were of wood and have not survived) of a million people. The temples – and there are so many that we saw only a few – cover areas up to more than 100 metres square, with tier rising upon tier to end in the strange cone-shaped towers which seem to be the most characteristic single feature of Khmer architecture. And when one realizes that in many cases each tier is carved for its whole length with human figures, animals, trees, etc., the labour force that must have been involved is incredible. Most of the sculpture is in bas-relief, which probably explains why so much of it remains* sur place. *One is very conscious – as with Petra – that these monuments are made to be seen from the outside: inside the towering masses one finds only the occasional small dark room, now stinking of bats and frequently with a modern Buddha inside showing signs of recent attentions. One of the many confusing things is that some of the Khmer Kings were Hindu and some were Buddhist – but today both sorts of temple seem to have indiscriminate mystical attraction to the locals. I suppose it would be impossible to live in the shadow of them and be unaffected.*
>
> *The grandeur is undeniable, especially of the temples with the jungle growing amongst them. And the carved murals are fascinating, giving endlessly varied pictures of the people about their work, or the Hindu myths. I want now to read about the place, sort out my memories of what I most enjoyed in the hopes of paying another visit in a few months' time. I know now that the journey is quite a feasible one, though for preference one needs a little longer there than we had. I calculated that the cost of the trip there and back (i.e. excluding board and lodging when there) was about £2.10 – i.e. about 25/- a head – and we could easily have had a third in the car.*

Following my weekend at Angkor I began reading up on the history and culture of Indo-China. My visit there had made me realize my ignorance and just how different it all was from the terms of reference in Europe and the Middle East. I was much impressed by a book called *Indochine*, in the Albin Michel series *Arts du Monde*, by an archaeologist called Bernard Philippe Groslier, who was the curator of Angkor through the 1960s. He was born in Cambodia, his grandfather had been a civil servant in the French administration there and his father, George Groslier, founded what became the National Museum in Phnom Penh. George died under interrogation by the Japanese in 1945. Bernard himself joined the French Resistance and returned to Cambodia with General Leclerc's army in 1945, earning a Croix de Guerre. He then supervised the restoration of the Khmer temples. What a family story. For all its many faults, French colonialism made a great cultural contribution.

Bangkok, 3 August 1964

The Bangkok World *has for the last few days been full of rumours of a coup. Police and army have been confined to their barracks since last Friday. I can't make out what it is all about, but it is related to the return of Gen Prapart (alternatively spelled Praphas but still pronounced the same way), the rather mysterious Deputy P.M. who has been away in the States having an eye operation. I think it is a security precaution against any over-enthusiastic supporters of his. Anyhow everybody seems very relaxed about the whole affair. I find that I am still remarkably in the dark about Thai politics – in a place this size one doesn't meet the characters concerned as in eg Vientiane and the Embassy is so big that one is not involved in its activities outside one's own sphere. Though the papers print a certain amount, they are fairly limited in what they can say. (Gen Prapart himself cracks the whip.) And the very fact that it is a dictatorship run by the military makes it all seem more remote...*

The next letter describes local reactions to incidents between American and North Vietnamese ships in the Gulf of Tonkin which led to a major escalation in American involvement in the Vietnam War. There was a good deal of confusion as to what had actually happened – American retaliation seems to have been based partly on faulty intelligence and the second incident mentioned below probably never took place. Casualties were low, but as a result of the confrontation Congress granted President Johnson special powers which were used as the legal justification for deploying US forces on the ground. My information must have come mainly from briefings by the Americans at SEATO.

Bangkok, 9 August 1964

We have had quite an interesting week in many ways, overshadowed of course by the news of the incidents in the Gulf of Tonkin and the

Americans' retaliatory action. I expect you will have seen in the papers that SEATO had a special meeting. This was the first that we had heard of the second incident or of the bombing of N. Vietnamese bases and I must say it was quite a shock. There is still no authoritative version of what the N. Vietnamese were trying to achieve by their attacks and how far the Chinese were privy to them. I am inclined to suspect that they were not and that the NVN were trying to drag them more thoroughly into their war in much the same way as the SVN seem to be trying to do with the Americans. But everybody is just guessing. Anyhow so far, touch wood, it looks as if the Chinese response has been as moderate as it could be in the circumstances...

I was tired after Angkor and one morning I didn't wake up until an agitated Boona thumped on my door at 9 am, an hour after I ought to have been at my desk. But things were fairly idle in the Embassy so it didn't matter much. I started my Thai lessons again and went around the house crooning little up and down notes as I practiced my five tones. Thai is a fiendishly difficult language with its tones and complicated script so I knew I would never become very proficient but I was determined to reach a level where I could communicate with the people I met in my daily life. This paid off later on. I was very proud of myself when I made a trip one weekend with two non-Thai speaking friends to Chantanaburi in the south-east where foreigners were obviously still a rarity. We stayed in the simplest of hotels where the locals watched fascinated as we cleaned our teeth at the single basin at the back and I negotiated some delicious street food for supper.

I have already mentioned the midwife, Dorothy Spengler, whom I got to know during the excursion to Angkor. I liked and admired her very much. When I paid a visit to the hospital where she lived and worked my admiration was fully confirmed. It was an interesting afternoon, not least because we had to cross the river by one of the local ferries which was very colourful – the terminal each side seemed to be part of a market and to get to the boats we picked our way across an assorted collection of flowers and foodstuffs. Our fellow passengers were pretty assorted too, including a number of the orange-robed monks who were one of the most picturesque features of Bangkok. Dorothy had two rooms in the hospital facing each other across a busy corridor. The bedroom was tolerable and an air-conditioning unit gave it a sort of privacy, but the living room was a nightmare – a noisy slit of a room, which one could only cut off from the corridor by shutting out any hope of a cooling breeze. The Thais were not respecters of privacy and her fellow-nurses barged in on her at all moments. I offered her my spare room as a bolt-hole. The familiar feeling returned to me of slight shame that my own job was by comparison so very plush in relation to what I really did.

Naval visits had been a feature of life in Beirut so I thought I knew what to expect but the visit to Bangkok was on a quite different scale: *...5 ships. One of the officers I met commented that he didn't remember seeing so many RN ships together for years! There was the usual round of parties – a luncheon on board, a vast reception, and a slightly stiff drinks party at the Residence. I had a couple of chaps to lunch on Sunday (with Jean Cameron to help) and then took them off to buy quantities of Thai silk afterwards – so worrying when one thinks the colours they have chosen are frightful... But I couldn't help wishing we had the navy here permanently as a contribution to our social resources.*

I finally induced Noi to come to supper one night, and that went some way towards breaking down barriers. We made a joint excursion to the weekend market accompanied by her small son Mon (pronounced with an upward lilt), where I bought a few plants including a gorgeous purple lotus for the klong (which I now discovered was not a klong at all but a *sa*, ie, pond, not water channel). I was then invited to a family event: Noi's mother had a new house, and it was customary to have the priests in and then have a party. I felt that it was quite a thing to have been asked.

Bangkok, 17 August 1964

Noi's mother's house-warming party took place on Wednesday, which was a national holiday to celebrate Queen Sirikit's birthday; the festivities took most of the day. I was bidden to turn up at 10:30 am for the first session. When I arrived I found that the priests were already there. The main downstairs room had been converted into a chapel with all the furniture removed apart from a series of lacquered tables which had been arranged to form a stepped altar with two Buddhas sitting on it – a large one behind and a little one in front. From the Buddhas a piece of string went all round the room, and I gather all round the house too, so as to carry the blessings to all parts of it. Seated in a long row with their backs to the wall were nine orange-robed monks – nine seemed to be a special number. The monks sat cross-legged with their robes most ingeniously folded to conceal every part of their feet. Each was on a tiny square carpet and each had a leaf shaped fan which he held in front of his mouth as he chanted. In the meantime the family, and in due course me, sat around on the floor with soft drinks, frequently chatting, and swarms of children ran in and out. Soon after 11 am the chanting stopped and the monks sat expectantly until they were bidden to go and eat a vast Chinese lunch – they can't eat anything after midday so their interest is understandable. When they had done we all reassembled around the shrine for some more chanting, and then Noi's mother presented each of the monks with gifts – mostly very practical things like toothpaste, cigarettes, and a towel, but with each set of presents went a bunch of lotus blossoms which they stowed away in the bags they always carry slung on their arms. The priests did not of course say thank you: it is the giver who does this. The final stage was that the chief monk collected from the altar a bowl of water and a green branch with which he sprinkled water first over Noi's mother, who prostrated herself, then over the rest of the congregation including a rather surprised Julie, and finally in and out of all the rooms in the house. The monks then piled into a mini-bus and left us to finish off the remains of the lunch, by now cold but still good.

So far only family and close friends were there – though even so there seemed to be swarms, and I was thoroughly confused. When we regathered for the evening there were lots more people, but still no other foreigners. We then had a big Chinese dinner after which the guest of honour, an uncle who had once been a Minister, made a speech which of course I did not understand, and then people took photographs. The whole thing broke up pretty early, much to my relief, for though I greatly enjoyed it it was a bit of a strain. It will be much easier when my Thai is a bit more serviceable. At the moment, though everybody seemed to speak more or less English, to talk to me meant breaking off the train of their general conversation. Anyway it was a most interesting day and I am very pleased that Noi invited me.

Bangkok, 23 August 1964

Last week I was entertaining the British Navy – this week it has been the American. (Incidentally I understand the Italian Navy is due in about 10 days' time!) We have been having a SEATO Intelligence Conference for which delegates have been coming from far and wide... At the end of the first day I was efficiently picked up by one of the American contingent, a Naval Commander from Honolulu, who provided most pleasant company

> *for the next few days. Tall, remarkably good-looking as well as interesting to talk to, he was altogether too good to be true. In fact he would be nice to have in Bangkok instead of 6,000 miles away... The name is Danny...*

I asked Boona to make a stew for us to take down to the beach. Alas, I didn't realize that it was not in the car when I set off to fetch Jean and Danny (who came down for the day before setting off for Saigon and Honolulu). It must have been nearly an hour later when complete with my flock I was steaming out of Bangkok on the main Pattaya road and to my astonishment we were hailed by Boona from the pavement. It was miles from home but she had found the stew and was determined we should have it. Frankly, it was a miracle we saw her on a fast-moving road, but she had chosen the spot because, assuming I had been into town first, I was almost bound to go past.

One morning my household was shaken by a blaring family row. I never discovered what it was all about but Boona sat in the back premises with the assumed look of a thunder-cloud dealing out blows from time to time with a ruler. The little girls were the culprits and furious they were too. Bee, who was the more spirited one, stood there stamping her foot and roaring like a small vixen. When I asked Boona what it was all about she just laughed and said they were very naughty and she must slap them. It was the first real row since I had arrived as normally the family were very peaceful. I got quite a lot of amusement from the incident.

My mother wanted to know about house-keeping matters. I explained that I ran a cook book which I inspected whenever Boona wanted some more money. I got through about 200 baht (c. £3) a week including the odd casual guest but excluding big parties. This covered my food, but not the servants' – though I didn't enquire closely about left-overs. Nor did I pay bills for the cats but since they looked well I didn't interfere. I ate a lot of fruit and there were a great many I had never seen before. I didn't order meals as a rule but let Boona think up what to give me. We discussed party menus and sometimes I tried to explain new ideas, not always very successfully. One day I gave what I thought was a graphic description of a stuffed egg, and was slightly shaken when they turned up at table as whole eggs complete with shell but for a small hole at one end through which the contents had been removed and put back. They tasted excellent but looked a bit bizarre.

A lot of foreigners in Bangkok went to Pattaya almost every weekend. I hesitated on the grounds that it tended to become a rut, and one that had very little to do with Thailand. But having overcome my scruples, I decided to try a place in the main Pattaya village called the Varuna Club which I enjoyed and thenceforth used as a bolt hole from time to time. The Club was very simply run. There were two enormous dormitories for men and women as well as a few small rooms for families. Apart from that there was a terrace on the beach where one could buy soft drinks, and another big room behind where one could eat – primitive cooking facilities were provided but no food. The place had at that stage been going three or four years and had become the centre for the sailing enthusiasts. I went out with people from the Embassy who had a racing dinghy and dutifully pulled on ropes when ordered. It was fun and very invigorating after Bangkok's lethargy. Water skiing was also available and I proudly reported when I had mastered the stylish art of using one ski.

My official life was enlivened by a splendid row in SEATO. The key character was Konthi, the Secretary General, a Thai with an inflated sense of his own importance. He was very piqued that the PWG (my working group) had treated some of his proposals with less respect than he thought their due, and when Ambassadors next met he launched off into a furious harangue: the PWG were exceeding their authority, the Ambassadors should assert themselves, and his – Konthi's – proposals should be considered at a higher level. Needless to say, everyone got thoroughly aroused, though I am glad to say that Sir Dermot was one of the Ambassadors who came staunchly to the defence of the PWG. It was only a couple of days' later, however, that the full effects made themselves known. A usually down-trodden member of the Secretariat staff went to the Secretary-General saying he viewed the outburst as a personal attack on the Deputy Secretary General (a New Zealander who presided at meetings of the PWG) and that he, the down-trodden member, felt himself unable to accompany the Secretary General on a tour of Australia and New Zealand as planned. I didn't know the PWG could be made to sound so glamorous as in Konthi's denunciation.

SEATO celebrated its tenth anniversary in early September. The Organization made the mistake of having too many "dos" on the same day – the audience got a bit bored and one got the impression that all the speakers were making the same speech. I can in fact vouch for the fact that the one Sir Dermot made was different because I wrote it, but it sounded much like the rest except for a joke which fell rather flat at the end! The various ceremonies for dedicating buildings and laying foundation stones were reminiscent of Noi's house-warming – chanting priests, strings to keep the bad spirits out and presentations – and some unlikely auspicious objects were buried in the foundations. I amused myself by drafting a dispatch to the FO describing the odd ceremonies attached to the anniversary. It was quaint to think what strange allies were invoked on SEATO's behalf. It is also ironic to remember that these new buildings were being put up for an organization that had only a few more years to live.

Meanwhile my expat life continued with its usual concerns. There was an enormous cocktail party for the Italian Navy at the Sports Club. Some of the Embassy girls complained that they had been pinched unmercifully, and I was beginning to think I must be slipping when I escaped unmarked. Anyhow I got taken out to dinner by a very punctilious and very young officer called Franco: I felt very maternal and hoped it didn't show. He was a nice lad, but conversation was rather heavy going since we only had half a language in common (his English). I preferred punctiliousness to pinches any day.

Bangkok, 14 September 1964

> *My kittens are all flourishing. In desperation I sent a circular note round the Embassy asking anyone who wanted cats to get in touch. Among a few helpful replies, I got a note from one wag who said his bull terriers would like them for hors-d'oeuvres! I also heard rather to my astonishment that a copy had been sent to the New Zealand Ambassador. My little note, which was meant to be mildly humorous was certainly only meant for Embassy consumption, but I now have uncomfortable visions of its circulating the diplomatic corps.*

My life was beginning to settle into a slightly boring routine. The long days at the Embassy were punctuated by regular meetings at the SEATO Headquarters. The hot and sweaty drive across town in my Renault Dauphine QQ (named for its temporary number plate) took about an hour each way, much of it in standing traffic. Evenings were often spent in entertaining or being entertained mostly among the expat community. There were all too many national day receptions. The occasional visits from people I knew in other posts in South East Asia were particularly welcome and often an excuse for more ambitious sightseeing. My pleasant house with the wonderful Boona and family in attendance provided me with a comfortable if solitary base and I realized how lucky I was. I tried to reach out to other people on their own, particularly the volunteers with VSO many of whom were teenagers. It was only later on that VSO came to the conclusion that they should concentrate on older volunteers with some expertise to offer.

Despite the special briefings SEATO was a bystander in the main political events of the time in South-East Asia – the growing war in Vietnam, the confrontation between Indonesia and Malaysia. My job was repetitive with monthly meetings at the level of Ambassadors and weekly ones at working group level. In reporting to the department in London I always told them what instructions I would assume for the next meeting if I heard nothing to the contrary and I seldom heard back. I had a small budget from which I could recommend grants to a handful of SEATO-run projects to which British experts were attached. This was separate from the main British aid programme which was looked after in the Embassy by Laurence O'Keeffe. Unfortunately, nobody explained to me that the Government budgetary system did not allow unspent money to be carried forward from one year to the next so I wasted some of my grant in the first year and one expert in particular was very cross with me.

In the back of my mind there was always a worry about my mother who had more than her share of health problems during her life. At this stage it was the aforementioned hip replacement, and the development of tachycardia, which causes the heart to race uncontrollably. My long letters were meant to divert as well as to show my parents how often I thought of them, but they also became a sort of diary. I described the world in which I found myself, took stock of my doings and marked the time until I would resume my normal life, self-consciously signing myself "*Your correspondent in the exotic East.*"

I took every opportunity I could to get out of steamy Bangkok. For weekends I often went to Pattaya, to one of the bungalows when I could, otherwise to the Varuna Club. Sometimes we went along the beach to the local café, which was open to the stars and where *"all the hip cats were dancing the latest wiggles. The twist seems to be* vieux jeu *now which is a pity because I have only just mastered it. Nowadays to be with it one has to surf and shake, both of which activities require a few extra double joints in the lower part of the spine."* I was amused to see the French Ambassador sitting in one corner reading a book through it all.

The rains came and I woke up one day to find the house surrounded by water, reminding me of the beach hut in Beirut. When I got downstairs I had to paddle to the breakfast table since the water had crept into one corner of the dining room which proved to be a little lower than the rest.

Boon rigged up a landing stage beside the car complete with a perilous catwalk to keep the feet dry.

Every house in Bangkok had its chinchuks, a sort of anaemic lizard varying in size from an inch to nearer six, and fortunately quite harmless – unlike another lizard also called after its cry – *tokay* – which had a nasty bite. I am glad to say I had no tokays inside, but there were plenty of chinchuks and I found a morbid satisfaction in watching them. They were too bloodless to be attractive, but they moved in nice curves and had strange hypnotic battles in which I could not decide whether love or hate was the motive force. They were reputed to eat the mosquitos, but that was a losing task. Another periodic plague was frogs, who would take over the garden. Fortunately I was spared snakes of which Thailand has some particularly nasty specimens. There is a theory that having a goose keeps them at bay, and being very scared of snakes I profoundly hoped this was true.

***

In October we had a long weekend holiday to celebrate Chulalongkorn Day (Chula was the boy Anna Leonowens brought up, as enacted in *The King and I*) and I decided to make the most of it with John Cambridge who was visiting Bangkok from Jakarta. John, an old friend from the Western Department, was working in the Embassy in Jakarta and regularly visited Bangkok bearing diplomatic bags for onward transmission to London with the Queen's Messengers. I had some qualms about how our weekend à deux would be viewed in Bangkok society but decided "*not to let any Victorian ideas about chaperones stand in the way of seeing places when pleasant company offers.*"

Train from Chiengmai to Bangkok, 25 October 1964

The weekend didn't go altogether according to plan but I, for one, enjoyed it very much. To start at the beginning, John turned up from Djakarta on Thursday morning and we caught the train for Chiengmai leaving at about 5 pm. The sleepers are surprisingly good: on the way up I was in one of the first class cubicles – shared with a Thai lady – but on the way down I was too late to book one, for reasons to be explained later, and had a couchette which was considerably cheaper and just as nice. The seats are divided by a centre aisle and at night each pair facing each other are ingeniously converted into an upper and lower bunk, each secluded from the rest of the carriage by a green curtain. I am sitting in this compartment, now back in its daylight form, as I write.

We were met on arrival by Donald Gibson [the Consul in Chiang Mai whom I knew slightly while in the Western Department], *who was very kind in looking after us. He took us to the Prince Hotel where we were to stay. It had only been open a few months and was obviously by Chiengmai standards very plush. This remained our base and we teamed up there with an English family called Martin to hire cars for seeing the sights.*

Chiengmai turned out to be a very attractive town and despite its many mirror-mosaiced wats, more homely than I had expected. It is set on a wide fertile plain, already quite high and with higher mountains visible all round. One mountain in particular dominates the town and it is on this ("Doi Suthep") that the most beautiful and famous wat is situated. The day we drove up, the summit was close to the cloud level and – imagine my surprise – it was bitterly cold. (People said it was probably about 70° and that it was the contrast we felt.) Even a climb up 300 steps between balustrades of undulating nagas (snakes to you) did little to warm me up. However, the Wat really was attractive and worth all the sufferings: it was in the shape of a hollow square with shrines in the middle of each side and rising from the courtyard in the centre a golden spire. The habit of hanging bells all round which ring in the breeze adds to the charm of the place, as do the yellow-robed monks.

Chiengmai is famous as the handwork centre of Thailand, so we had quite a lot of shopping to do. I was quite restrained on the whole. I bought my first length of Thai silk – monk's orange; I hope it isn't blasphemous – and some pretty black and gold enamel owls who hold cigarettes. Apart from that only nick-nacks, including painted umbrellas for Boona's two girls from a village which seemed to make nothing else.

The misadventure concerned our return trip. We had got tickets to return by air on Sunday afternoon, but when we went to the office to confirm, the airline told us there were no seats. Fury and consternation. It didn't matter so much from my point of view, but John was very worried about his return flight to Djakarta and decided that the Sunday night train didn't give him enough time. So after much discussion he decided to take the bus – quite an experience in these parts where they pack the passengers in with the luggage and the produce. I opted more tamely for the train…

My last day in Chiengmai, after John had left on his bus, Donald Gibson organized a picnic into the mountains. We went with a pleasant

British Council couple and our day was made by seeing some elephant at work hauling timber. Donald had also arranged a dinner party for us earlier as well as our accommodation etc so I really felt he did us proud.

On return home I was dismayed to find a new lot of kittens – three this time and all black – born the day before in the charcoal hoard. They were so well camouflaged that it was only when the charcoal started miaowing that anyone realized what had happened. I already had some prospective owners, so I was not as worried as I had been. Boona had also persuaded a friend to take one of the big cats and I gave a kitten to Noi who seemed very pleased. She came to collect it with her two small sons who were amusing little toughs. They spoke no English and I was heartened to find that I at least understood a little of what they said. So when my father warned of the dangers of becoming a cat slave I protested that I was still a free woman.

About then we had one of Thailand's most publicised annual events. The King went in a procession of gilded barges to present new robes to the monks at Wat Arun, the Temple of the Dawn. I sent my parents a postcard of the Royal Barge, with a prow like a swan. Another of the barges was like a *naga* (a seven-headed snake), and there were shoals of "monkey class" and "demon class" attendants. It was really a very colourful procession, particularly as the oarsman were all in period costume. Helped by the current, they came swinging down river at a cracking pace with oars dipping in rhythm to ceremonial chanting. It was something of an anti-climax to see long strings of barges being towed back upstream afterwards.

I amused myself one night by getting Boona's views on politics. It couldn't be a very sophisticated conversation given the language problem: Boona suffered from the usual Thai trouble with "r"s and one had to guess from the context whether she was talking of Malaya or malaria. But I was interested that she had such strong views. She was very angry with Sarit (the ex-dictator whose sins were now being systematically exposed) – "too many ladies." He apparently at one time raised a subscription to get back the temple on the Cambodian border which the International Court had awarded to Cambodia – and pocketed the proceeds. Boona gave two baht (a few pennies) and it obviously still rankled. The present lot of Ministers seemed to be judged OK but without much enthusiasm.

***

In November the cooler weather arrived at last. The temperature dropped a good five degrees and Boona kept on saying she was cold, but for me it was a great relief to be able to drive into town without soaking my dress with sweat and at night I revelled in pulling up a blanket for an hour or two. There had been a good deal of thunder and lightning, but the rains seemed to be almost over. I hoped the water in my lily-pond would now stay within its banks and the lawn would come into its own for my croquet set.

It must have been about this time that Group Captain Paul Mallorie took over as the UK Military Advisor's Representative in Bangkok, which was great good luck for me. In practical terms he was my opposite number on the military side of SEATO but though older and senior to me he never pulled rank. He and his wife Ursula had a house on one of the main klongs and threw a party there to celebrate Loy Krathong. This is one of Thailand's most attractive festivals. It takes place at a full moon and each person launches on the water a krathong, which is a little boat or floating raft made of lotus blossom and banana leaves and bearing a lighted candle. The krathong floats downstream representing a wish or the expiation of your sins, and if it doesn't sink until it is out of sight all is well. I enjoyed describing this event to my parents.

Bangkok, 22 November 1964

The Loy Krathong party was great fun… I bought my Krathong in the afternoon: after careful choice I opted for one in the shape of a lotus, whose petals were alternate pink and white with silver tips. The whole was made of paper and sat on a cardboard base. In it were placed a candle and a joss stick and it was necessary to add one's own coin. Some of the other guests at the party had brought Krathongs made of banana leaves plaited to form petals and scattered with fresh flowers. The most ambitious Krathong I saw was made by one of the servants in the house. It had the shape of a boat, the hull being made of banana stalks, the deck trimmed with zigzags of plaited banana leaves and flowers, and the superstructure an imposing array of candles, joss sticks and masts carrying miniature umbrellas. The Mallories' house is on a big klong and it was there that after supper we all entrusted our little vessels to the water. I was rather surprised to find that mine did float – but the candle wouldn't stay alight so I am afraid it didn't bear away my sins. In any case it fell victim to a lot of little pirates who were waiting indecently close downstream to collect whatever they could from the party. I have little doubt that it was sold to someone else the next day!

My cat disposal prospects received an unexpected set-back when I heard a piteous yowling in the hedge and found two very small black cats. Thinking they were the latest of the home stock I picked them up, only to be told by Boona that they were strangers. Apparently a trishaw driver had left them in the garden saying this was obviously a good house for cats! The usual thing to do with unwanted cats in Thailand was to leave them at the temple – I was horrified at the thought that people might take to leaving them at my house instead. I gave Boona firm instructions to resist any further donations, but couldn't very well turn out the two tiny strays. We put them tentatively with the other two kittens, and surprisingly the mother accepted them all without a word.

December brought a garden party when all the Diplomatic Corps was invited to the Palace to celebrate the King's birthday.

Bangkok, 17 December 1964

The setting was delightful, in a large square garden flanked by parts of the Palace which were mostly built in wat-style with pretty rooves with tilted edges. Most of the square was lawn and dotted on it here and there were little Thai-style summer houses in some of which musicians were playing on weird instruments. In the early stages we were ranged along one side of the square (Ambassadors in front with staff ranged behind in strictly descending order of seniority) in front of the Royal guest quarters which were housed in a most attractive modern building of traditional design. Eventually the King and Queen descended from some upper region and did a slow procession round the square shaking hands with Ambassadors en route and with govt officials on the other side of the square. According to the papers there were 10,000 people there which I can't quite credit. Finally the King and Queen went into the middle of the lawn and we were able to break ranks and go in search of a by this time badly needed drink. The Royals stayed with the party a long time and by the time they left most of the females were suffering agonies from trying to stand so that their high heels did not sink into the grass! But despite these discomforts I enjoyed the afternoon very much.

Another social event was the Oxford and Cambridge dinner which Bira took me to. It was a bit stuffy in some ways; too many speeches and disappointing food. But I was glad to meet Bira's friends. The occasion was livened up by a sleazy looking individual who kept on interrupting the speakers. I afterwards heard he was a dipso and nobody threw him out because he was a Prince and related to some of the speakers.

Just before Christmas I got permission to pay a familiarization visit to Singapore in an attempt to understand the complex military set-up there. This concerned me because the C-in-C Far East (Admiral Sir Varyl Begg) was UK Military Adviser to SEATO and the UK contribution to SEATO plans would come from forces under his command. I had only met him a couple of times previously and was most impressed to find that not only was I to call on him, but I was also asked to lunch. Most Ambassadors certainly wouldn't pay so much attention to a casual visitor of my level. The lunch party didn't come off, alas, for the unexpected reason that Singapore was largely flooded that day having received 8½ inches of rain in 24 hours.

I was struck by the Britishness of Singapore at that time; the street signs, the tempo of traffic, and even the balance of population felt very different from Thailand. This, however, didn't come as a surprise. What did was the fact that one looked out across the water and saw Indonesia sitting on the near horizon, so close that the Confrontation problem had an almost physical urgency. Confrontation was the name given to Indonesia's armed response to the creation of the Federation of Malaysia. The communist-leaning President Sukarno was trying to cause the new Federation to unravel by infiltrating the Malay states of Sabah and Sarawak and playing on their ethnic and religious diversity. These two states and Brunei are on the island of Borneo, the rest of which forms the Indonesian province of Kalimantan, and this is where most of the fighting took place. It fell to Britain as the former colonial power to provide most of the defensive effort, especially in the early days, and British air and sea forces were involved as well as the land forces fighting in the jungle. It was a hot war in all but name and only brought to a close in 1966 after the fall of Sukarno. The various aspects of this question seemed to absorb nine-tenths of the energies of most of the people I met. Once again SEATO was a bystander so it was not surprising that it engaged so little of people's attention among the military in Singapore. I managed to fit in a little Christmas shopping between meetings and went back to Bangkok hoping I had learned enough to justify calling the trip official.

Bangkok, 28 December 28 1964

So Christmas has now come and gone and I have that familiar feeling of surprise that it went with so little fuss. This is partly anti-climax, I suppose, but also in the circumstance relief that a season so apt to provoke homesickness is safely past. Fortunately for me I don't suffer acutely from homesickness, but even so Christmas does bring it rather near. This time I found going to church the worst nostalgic moment – inappropriately enough since we are scarcely a churchgoing family. But the rest of the day was so full that one had no time to think. A Christmas Eve party went on until the early hours so that I was only just up in time for Church. After that drinks at the Counsellor's for all the Embassy, and an enormous lunch party at the O'Keeffes' which I left still going strong at 5:30 pm in order to have a quick zizz before the supper party I was bidden to. Even so, I am afraid I failed signally to do justice to the second load of turkey and plum pudding in the day.

I thought of you all at Fovant. I suppose you all went to sing carols at the Church next door. I hope you will have got my offerings. I saved up the likely looking envelopes which arrived during the few days before Christmas so as to have something to open on the day and found myself with a Penguin book on Indo-China and a year's supply of bead thread. Thank you for both which will be very useful, and also for the nice collection of letters. Today's bag was a disappointment, but I expect that the UK mails have been upset over Christmas.

I celebrated New Year with a party that didn't end until the small hours weren't so small any longer. There was a dance at the Sports Club, where I was inveigled into going into the Beauty Contest – with no success, I may add. The winners were all twenty-year-olds, so I consoled myself by deciding that the Thai taste was for the very young. It was quite a good party even if a terrible band called the Filipino Shadows put a damper on some of the later stages. My friends and I eventually forsook them and ended the evening in a nightclub eating onion soup. The worst of the occasion was that I had to parade at 9 am the following morning to go to sign books at the Palace and the MFA as the local custom demanded.

I had an accident one day when driving QQ to the airport to meet some guests but I of course played it down in writing home:

Bangkok, 4 January 1965

I regret to say I had a prang in my car the other day. Don't worry, I wasn't scratched and nobody else was hurt either. A car overtook a lorry wide coming towards me; I swerved, and skidded, and went off the road and down the bank to the left hitting an up-sticking pipe on the way. Somebody gave me a lift to the airport where I knew that Charles Booth (the new Head of Chancery) was seeing off some other visitors, and he got an Embassy driver to collect poor dear QQ.

What I didn't tell my parents was that I had turned the car over completely and was extremely lucky to be unhurt bar some spectacular bruises. I still recall the way the world went into slow motion as I realized what was happening. The car ended the right way up and I immediately got out and hitched a ride to the airport, arriving before the plane I was hurrying to meet. This strange behaviour must have been the result of shock. It was only when I saw Charles that I burst into tears. I felt so helpless by myself with the crowd which sprang up from nowhere jabbering at me in Thai.

The Red Cross Fair was a big event for the diplomatic community with Embassies competing to show off their wares. I was roped in to help at the British stall which was very badly organized; all the helpers arrived at once instead of taking turns and the crowd were let in before the stall was open. We were selling cigarettes below the market price (which I considered wrong anyway) and as a result a rabble crowded in on us waving fistfuls of notes and we sold the cigarettes as fast as we could hand them out. It was quite frightening for a moment. When the cigarettes were done we turned to laying out the whimsy china which was our other stock in trade. The stall developed a quite different character as upper-class Thai ladies pondered which free-hand flowers and which arty pot they liked best. All told we apparently cleared about £1,200. I was thankful to have the excuse of a dinner party to prevent my staying to the bitter end.

***

I received nice compliments on my draft of the annual review on SEATO's activities which the Ambassador was obliged to send. It may well have been the last dispatch that Sir Dermot ever signed because he was about to leave the Service on retirement. All the Embassy staff paraded at the airport to see him off. Then we waited a few weeks for the new Ambassador to arrive.

The appointment of Sir Anthony Rumbold had been announced during the autumn. He had been the Assistant Undersecretary for the Western Department when I first joined the Office. I expected a very different sort of Ambassador from Sir Dermot, one who would keep a much closer eye on what the Embassy was up to, and that, I thought, would be no bad thing. About this time a boy called Robin Martin arrived in Bangkok as one of the new batch of VSO volunteers. He had an introduction from his aunt, one of my mother's many friends who had provided me with an alternative home during my childhood. I invited him to lunch with another lad called Eric. They were pleasant boys, easy to talk to, and still very much teenagers. They clearly found their all-Thai environment a bit trying at times so I encouraged them to drop in when in Bangkok. Robin only worked 20 miles away so he became a quite frequent visitor and I grew very fond of him. It was through Robin that I found some unexpected Guernsey connections in Bangkok. He took me to a gathering organised by a man called Anhuphon Kritachorn (but also known as Peter) who turned out to be an old boy of Elizabeth College, Guernsey's public school. On hearing that my father was an Old Elizabethan too, he immediately asked what his school number was! Peter had been there in the 30s and every detail appeared to be engraved on his memory in gold. A picture of his Elizabeth College XI was under the glass on his desk. The meeting led on to further connections:

Bangkok, February 1965

I was introduced yesterday by my Thai-Elizabeth-College-Old-Boy-Crony to an Englishman called Kenneth Lawson, who used to be Legal Adviser here when Britain still had judicial rights over foreigners in Thailand. He was here during the eventful pre-war years and was shut up by the Japanese. I questioned him particularly about an old boy known locally as Judge Sparrow who was here at the same period and wrote some colourful and probably very misleading books about life in Thailand. Lots of splendid gossip emerged. The two were obviously at daggers drawn. Kenneth Lawson (now in his 60s at a guess) was the nephew of a Colonel Lawson who was Chief of Police in Thailand during the first world war and who retired to a house overlooking Saints' Bay in Guernsey...

***

Bullets were flying again in Vientiane and in Bangkok we anxiously waited for news. I was having lunch with someone from the American Embassy when a message came through from the U.S. Embassy in Vientiane saying that shells were falling in their compound and that Donald Hopson (the UK Ambassador in whose Residence I had so recently been living) was stranded with them, unable to go the odd half-mile back to his own office. It all seemed so unlike the calm which was the rule during my stay. The Laos had seemed such a tranquil people. Word came through to the Embassy later in the day that Hopson was back and he seemed quite unruffled.

Soon after his arrival Sir Anthony Rumbold went to present his credentials at the Palace. I was very disappointed not to be one of the party. Apparently the Ambassador wanted to take me but when it was suggested to the protocol people at the Palace they were horrified and said they had never had a woman at such an occasion.

Meanwhile I took what opportunities I could to get closer to the culture at less rarefied levels.

Bangkok, 1 February 1965

I have just come back from Hua Hin, where I spent a very interesting weekend. Anhuporn (alias Peter)'s old parents have a farm down there, his sister a cotton factory, and an aunt several properties including a wooden house near the seashore which is where Robin and I stayed. Anhuporn himself unexpectedly disappeared at bed-time to sleep somewhere else! It was an attractive house with wide balconies and capacious mosquito-nets, the latter being very necessary because I have never seen so many mosquitoes. Hua Hin has a lovely beach with a long stretch of gleaming white sand and we spent Sunday morning swimming and lazing there. Then at lunch-time the parents turned up, a charming couple. The father, Mom Chao (which means grandson of a King) Sittiporn, is an old Harrovian who last set foot in England in 1901. A courteous old boy speaking perfect English, with a cap of neat white hair above his brown face. He said he thought he had been at prep school with our new Ambassador's father, which of course tickled H.E. when I told him about it. His wife, who at 75 seemed a mere chicken, was also word-perfect in English though she hadn't been to England since she was 12 – but she explained that she had an English governess for a year after that when her father was Thai Ambassador to the Czarist regime in Moscow! Another titbit I discovered was that it was from their house in Hua Hin that the then King was summoned back to Bangkok in 1932 by the revolutionary clique who made him sign away his absolute powers.

Prince Sittiporn then fell out of favour with the new regime and I gather that he was virtually rusticated there for many years. I longed to know more but didn't know the right questions – apart from being diffident about asking them.

Bangkok, 1 March 1965

I went to dinner at Bira's house last week. They have had an English guest staying with them, Mrs. Dunlop. She must have provided a pied-à-terre for Bira when he was at school in England; I can't make out if it was a P-G relationship or not, but Mrs. D. certainly seems to have oodles of boodle now... The oddest thing of all was that Bira and Rampi referred to her as "Mother". I gossiped with her in the corner the other night and she passed me some very interesting titbits of insight into Thai family life – even the life of such a Westernized couple as Bira and Rampi. I knew that they lived in a house in the same compound as Bira's parents. What I didn't realize was that the relationship was still thoroughly satellite. They and several other sons and daughters live in outhouses of the main parental home, and all the catering is done jointly and controlled by the matriarch. There are apparently frequent family conferences where all personal questions are decided. The careers of the children for instance are a matter of family policy, and where one child, like Bira, goes into government service which has great prestige and pays virtually nothing, others will be sent into paying jobs. Family finances will then be used in such a way that they all live in an appropriate manner. The other thing that interested me was that each of Bira's three children has a personal servant who at night sleeps on the floor across the door of the child's room. The servants were waiting at dinner the night I was there, and they followed a custom which one still often sees in Thailand of keeping the head lower than that of the people they are serving. So, coming in with the coffee tray for instance, when they get close to the guests they crouch or kneel and shuffle forward in a way that looks very dangerous but in fact doesn't spill a drop. Like so many Thai customs it is very gracious...

I made a great, and not really voluntary, step forward in my language studies when I was forced to do the cook book in Thai. This was because Boona's friend who used to write it up for her went away. Boona's own written English was non-existent though she could speak a bit. Her powers of addition were a bit dodgy too as I discovered when finding an error of 25/- in my favour. When I queried this she asked with a puzzled look if I could explain what 9 plus 0 came to. After that I did the sums and we struggled jointly through the accounts with the help of a good dictionary. When Boona's daughter Bee developed chicken-pox I discovered that my name was being invoked to make her drink her medicine, a dubious compliment. Num, the little boy, had grown a lot and was by now very mobile. Waving me off to the office became such a tradition that he began to wave whenever he caught sight of me.

The whole Embassy buzzed with activity as the result of the new man at the top, but also because of a stream of VIP visitors. Royal visits always create a special stir and in March Prince Philip (the Duke of Edinburgh) came briefly en route to somewhere else before paying a proper visit on his return journey. A special SEATO study group of "economic experts" had been set up to consider economic relations between the member states. London did not think much of the idea and decided not to send any experts. In their absence Laurence O'Keeffe and I had to do our best to fill in. I knew absolutely nil about the subject. Since UK policy on the question was negative this didn't much matter but I still felt rather a fraud. Laurence was better informed since his normal work was in the field of economic assistance and anyway he had a splendid gift of being able to hold forth at length on virtually any subject, which was just what was required on such an occasion. For me personally there was also the job of preparing the new HE for his first SEATO meeting and I completed all the briefs with a sense of triumph despite an unusually busy few days.

Another Second Secretary arrived at the Embassy for a short spell. She was called Sheila Milsom and was what was known as an information floater, which meant she had the unenviable task of filling in a few months here and a few months there all over S.E. Asia with no fixed base. She had been in the Embassy a month before I knew of her existence which was a rather poor comment on our staff management, I thought. We went together for a long weekend at Pattaya. It was a full load for QQ because as well as Sheila I took Boona and her two girls. Bee and Yid had new scarlet two-piece swimsuits for the occasion and were very thrilled. It always amused me that the two girls were dressed in a completely Western style while Boona herself never shed her sarong, even for a swim. It was a good weekend in many ways. We wasted our substance on water skiing and there were enough favourable comments to make me glow with vainglory. Sheila tried skiing for the first time with considerable success and the girls rode in the boat, so everybody was happy. Boona spent her time fishing and caught a weird selection of fish and crabs, some of which to my slight dismay accompanied us back to Bangkok

Pattaya was agog that weekend because a sailing race was arranged in which both the King and the Duke of Edinburgh were to sail. We got an unexpectedly good view, first when they arrived by car and then when Prince Philip came to the Varuna Club to pick up his dinghy. The latter was the neatest little manoeuvre. A motor-boat appeared out of the blue and it was several seconds before anybody realized that the chap who leapt out and into the nearest dinghy was the Prince – and by that time he was already sailing out to sea. Unfortunately, they didn't have a very good day for their outing. It was overcast without much wind.

The following day Prince Philip was taken to the River Kwai to see the cemeteries and the railway. In the evening there was a monster cocktail party at the Embassy, hosted jointly by the Commonwealth Ambassadors. There was a rehearsal when a group of us who had been designated as "route officers" were allotted the positions from which we would desperately try to catch the Royal eye to present selected guests.

9.30 pm (post-Duke), 8 March 1965

And an exhausting performance it was too. By the time the Prince got to my presentees he was going at a rate of knots, and it was only with great difficulty and the help of the Ambassador that I got him back again. There was then a bit of confusion as to which wife went with which husband, and after meeting my little group of military he rounded on me and asked if I was military too! All told it was rather a nervous strain but the great thing was they all got presented. The worst of a system of warning people in advance was that they would have held it against me for life if they had failed to shake the royal paw.

The Prince himself made a very good impression, full of energy after a long day visiting the war cemeteries. His manner though is a bit too challenging, I think. He has a question for everybody but he almost throws it at them in a way which is apt to put people who are already a bit nervous on to the defensive. Speaking personally of course!

Anyway, it is all over satisfactorily now. It was nearly cancelled at the 11th hour because Court mourning has been ordered for the Queen of Sweden. It really would have been dreadful to turn all those hundreds of

people away. The Duke himself decided that the party should go on. I put on a black dress instead of the new flowery one I was planning to stun everyone with and was very hot into the bargain.

A visiting friend introduced me to a minor princess called Pimsai who had been at LMH but rather before my time. She took us to a Thai-style restaurant which I hadn't before visited, and very good it was too. Shoes were left at the door and it was a case of sitting on the ground, propped up as well as one could manage on *wat* cushions. I noticed that Pimsai was as uncomfortable as we were after a bit. The meal was prettily served in Thai celadon green dishes. Pimsai explained that Thai meals were supposed to have a certain balance. Apart from rice the basic ingredient is a curry. The other side dishes are one sharp (a vinegary bean salad), one sweet (crisp noodles cooked in sugar), one salt (crab, which wasn't very), and one bland (soup with queer floating oddments). The idea is that you start with a mouthful of curry and if it is too hot, you move on to a soothing mouthful of something else, and so on. Most of the dishes we ate were very good, especially the curry.

In April a Heads of Mission Conference was held in Bangkok, gathering Ambassadors from all over the Far East. I can't say I contributed very much although I was given the honorific title of Secretary. Sir Anthony Rumbold was such a do-it-yourself Ambassador that there wasn't much left for lesser mortals to do. But I was able to attend the whole way through and was in fact the only member of the Embassy apart from the Ambassador who did. It was very interesting: not perhaps very productive but then it was planned more as an exchange of views than as a decision-taking meeting. The chief amusement as far as I was concerned was to find that of the two politicians present – Lord Head, a former Tory Minister who was then High Commissioner in Kuala Lumpur, and Lord Walston, Under-Secretary for Foreign Affairs in the then Labour Government – the latter seemed to hold the more right-wing views! There were several familiar faces among the conferees. James Adams, of MECAS long ago, who was there as Lord Walston's private secretary, had a back seat beside me. Leslie Fielding, representing Phnom Penh, and very much the youngest of the front line, held his own admirably (and was mercifully prevented from talking too much). Myles Ponsonby, a very nice man whom I remembered from Beirut, came from Hanoi, which must have been the toughest of all the posts represented – hardly any Western colleagues, and who knew when the bombs would start falling. He seemed in quite good heart but was obviously longing for the day when his year-long appointment would be over.

***

There follows a gap in the letters of a couple of months covering my trip back to England for the SEATO Council Meeting in London and the leave that followed. The meeting itself took place in Lancaster House, a spectacular Georgian palace used by the Foreign Office for grand events, and was chaired by the new Foreign Secretary, Michael Stewart. There was a special session in the Banqueting House in Whitehall to impress the visiting dignitaries. With its magnificent paintings and sad history – Charles I was executed there – it certainly impressed me. My most memorable success was to table in one of the preparatory meetings a proposal for the SEATO School of Engineering to be launched as an entity in its own right. This was agreed by the assembled ministers with the result that the School survived the demise of SEATO a few years later and continues to flourish today as the Asian Institute of Technology. When I claimed credit with the Dean of the School on my return to Bangkok it became clear that he had primed a number of people to make sure the idea got on the agenda. But I am still glad that I was the one that put it there.

When I got back to Bangkok the routine of ex-pat life in a tropical city quickly re-established itself with the usual round of visitors and dinner parties, excursions to the beach, and worries about the heat and my hair. All this I recorded in detail in my weekly letters home together with my worries about my mother's health and questions about family and friends. I was conscious that most of things I did I had done and reported on before, but even in this blasé mood I singled out one party because it was given on the river. An enterprising chap from the Australian Embassy had borrowed a boat for the occasion from the Thai Ministry of Agriculture: a splendid boat with lots of brass railings and the aggressive respectability of the *African Queen*. (I found that most steamboats in Thailand reminded me of the *African Queen*; they perhaps dated from the same period.) We all packed on board from a jetty beside the Oriental Hotel and I felt very superior to all those poor plutocrats who gaped enviously. The boat took us further up-river than I had ever been before; and I was surprised how long it took to get clear of the town. I should have liked to do the trip in daylight when we would have seen far more but since the Thais don't believe in curtains we got a good view into all the little houses.

On the political front the easing of Singapore out of the Malaysian Federation came as a bombshell. I thought it a very ill-considered step provoked largely by jealousy of Lee Kwan Yew. This latter point was true but my doubts were misplaced: Malaysia remains a successful federal state, while Singapore became the star performer of South East Asia. At a more gossipy level the *Bangkok World* was full of the latest Miss Universe, who was a Thai beauty called Apasra.

Bangkok, 16 August 1966

She has been received by the Queen, had a Reception given for her by the Minister of Foreign Affairs, and has been on TV non-stop for the five days of her visit to Bangkok. A rumour is going around diplomatic circles here that the whole show was staged by the State Department so as to give the victory to a "good" South-East Asian country. Unfortunately I did not see Apasra myself so I can't comment. A nice touch came from Boona who told me that she was in a quandary because Thai TV were showing Apasra on one channel and a school play in which Robin Martin had to perform a Thai dance on the other at the same time. It was the neighbour's TV and not unexpectedly they chose Apasra.

We celebrated Remembrance Day in true outpost-of-the-Empire style. The chaplain conducted a short service at the war memorial in the Embassy grounds and Commonwealth Ambassadors and various other representatives laid wreaths while the British community looked on. A few wreaths of orchids lying amongst the artificial poppies made an appropriately exotic touch. The British Embassy compound in Bangkok was spectacularly large and beautiful with echoes of the Raj. Entering the main gates one was confronted by a tall flagstaff and an imposing statue of Queen Victoria, often adorned with flowers left by women hoping to become pregnant. There were four fine buildings, including the residences of the Ambassador and the Counsellor, each with balconies all round and big windows to catch any breeze; in the case of the Chancery these had been closed in to provide office space. My own office, though of grand proportions (being about 18 feet square), was a glorified corridor. The pre-air-conditioning colonial style meant that all the rooms opened out of each other for maximum coolth which had its disadvantage as regards privacy. Further back were spreading lawns, a small lake and the living quarters of the Gurkhas who guarded the Embassy. This was prime land in a rapidly expanding part of the city.

Perhaps it is surprising that it was not until 2018 that the British government decided to sell it – for a cool £420 million. I can't help being a bit sad.

One of my tasks was to take my turn as Embassy duty officer. This meant in practice sitting by one's phone (or somebody else's if the Embassy was informed in advance) waiting for messages which scarcely ever came. It was rather a bore, but if one ratted that would be bound to be the night of a crisis. One had to do five nights in a row but it only came round about once every three months with a duty weekend just about as often. For fear of worrying my mother I didn't mention that the duty officer was expected to make a night inspection of the Embassy compound to check that the Gurkhas were doing their duty. One also had to check inside the Chancery building. I found it very unnerving to be interrupted by a quiet voice right beside me in the darkness while I struggled with the combination lock on the main door. The idea of my catching the Gurkhas out was absurd and I was a bit frightened, but to have asked to be excused this duty was of course unthinkable, an admission of female weakness.

Robin Martin and his friends went on their way when their year was up. The next lot of VSOs were girls, one of them blind.

Bangkok, 6 September 1965

All four of them came to lunch last Wednesday. I hesitated about asking them en bloc but it seemed the best thing to do since two were off up-country almost immediately. The girls seem a little older than the boys doing the same thing – though I always noticed that Robin who was the only public schoolboy out of the last bunch in many ways seemed the most youthful of all. Actually most of these girls had done a year or two's training since school and one, the blind girl, has just finished Oxford. They were an interesting variety, from one very stolid girl who said hardly a word and who is off to Chiang Mai (the best job of all I should think), to a very debby lass who is to stay in Bangkok where she will certainly fall on her feet. One of the others is going to Korat ... a typically unprepossessing and restricted Thai provincial town by all accounts. She was a bit disgruntled, poor girl, and I couldn't but sympathise, especially when she told me that her predecessor hadn't even had a bed to herself but had shared with one of the Thai women teachers. I encouraged her to stand out for one to herself, and offered her the use of one here for emergencies. The fourth girl was the blind one, Helen Starns, and in many ways the most interesting of all. I hadn't quite taken in the completeness of her blindness – or rather her helplessness – when I met her first. It was rather a shock to realize that she couldn't know what was on her plate until she tasted it and that she had to be helped like a child. Poor girl, she is not a placid type either, and will I am afraid find the shame very great at first. She is working at a school in one of the busiest parts of Bangkok and I don't see how she will ever be able to go out on her own. I am not sure that the Thais are very understanding about physical weakness, although they are not unkind.

Later that month I visited Phnom Penh at the invitation of my old friend Leslie Fielding. He had been sent there as head of a much-reduced Embassy after carefully staged anti-British riots during which the British Council was burnt down but nobody was hurt. I had met some of the previous staff when they were evacuated to Bangkok with their families. I arrived in Phnom Penh to be met by the current Embassy staff en masse – all three of them. Leslie was an actor manqué and I got a good deal of amusement out of his acting the Chargé d'Affaires. He was certainly very good at it, however, and got through an incredible amount of work.

Bangkok, 27 September 1965

I found I was expected to work too and was given mounds of paper to read and was taken to call at the Ministry of Foreign Affairs. The Cambodians to whom I was introduced seemed friendly enough, but the British are officially in semi-Coventry. You will probably remember that our Embassy in PP was attacked by rioters last year – I was shown the point on the stairs where the mob were held back while the remaining staff huddled in the only corridor out of reach of flying stones. Then Cambodian-American relations deteriorated to the point where the US Embassy went last May. At some stage Sihanouk announced that Cambodians should not go to the houses of the Anglo-Saxons – or else. This ban in fact now applies only to the British since the Australians are considered to be good boys.

This all makes the place sound rather sinister, but it certainly didn't look that way last week. Phnom Penh is quite a small town, and most of it built since the French left. The general atmosphere however is distinctly French-flavoured, and the French certainly have a far more attractive influence on city building than the Americans as seen in Bangkok. P.P. has broad tree-lined avenues with the occasional road-side café and a startling number of nude statues at the junctions (obviously a special taste of Prince Sihanouk). Like so many towns it does not make as much use as it might of the river; a pity, because the Mekong is pretty impressive, especially at the point known as Quatre-Bras where it joins up with a couple of lesser rivers. We ate out a few times, very well, another happy French legacy.

For the weekend Leslie drove me down to Sihanoukville, an embryo town which is being developed as a port (to prevent dependence on traffic up the Mekong which can be blocked by the S. Vietnamese) and as a holiday resort. The beaches were beautiful, white sand and clear water fringed with handsome trees. The town was weird, a ghost of what may (or may not) be to come. Once again there are miles of broad boulevards, but this time no people and hardly any houses. I was taken to see a luxury hotel on an impressive perch above the sea which was finished 18 months ago and is still uninhabited except by packing cases. Apparently, there was an engineering mistake and everyone is now waiting for it to slide into the sea. The whole place bears signs of the Prince's sudden enthusiasms which cause funds to be switched from one grandiose project to another, so that much is never completed or becomes something quite different from the original plan. Everything in the country depends on Sihanouk. While I was in PP he was away – in China trying for aid.

***

In October I spent three days in Singapore. The purpose of the visit was quite a short meeting chaired by the C-in-C to go through his briefs for the following week's SEATO meeting which he was due to attend in Bangkok. There was a new C-in-C since my last visit, Air Chief Marshal Sir John Grandy, who went on to be Chief of Air Staff and Governor of Gibraltar. I found him impressive – though less smoothly charming than his predecessor Varyl Begg. Compared with diplomats the top service commanders I met struck me as being far more direct, even compared with Rumbold who was pretty outspoken. I supposed it came from having much more power.

Singapore itself seemed exactly the same as my last visit despite the separation from Malaysia. Still just as friendly. Still just as swamped with British. It was not a situation that I felt could go on indefinitely. The people I met were not very confident about relations between Singapore and Malaysia in the long term. But the immediate issue was Confrontation and it was particularly interesting to be there during major disturbances in Jakarta. These turned out to be the coup which overthrew Sukarno and changed the situation unrecognizably but nobody knew what would happen so Singapore was full of speculation. SEATO was far from the front of people's minds.

I got back to find that Boona had gone to hospital. I couldn't discover from the others what was wrong but Boon assured me that she was "only a little ill". After a day or so I summoned up courage and went to visit her with Boon. She was in the women's hospital where they took in poor patients for free. The conditions were not at all bad, considering. Boona was in a bed in the wing of a huge ward; trimmings were admittedly pretty sparse, but the bed was clean and the room cool. She looked pretty grey, and I only stayed a minute or two because I felt that my presence was a strain. Anyway, to my surprise when I got home the next day I was greeted by Boona herself looking very much better. I asked someone from the Embassy to ring up the hospital to find out what was wrong and they told me that it was a miscarriage.

***

One of the SEATO-financed projects in Thailand was designed to settle the nomadic hill tribesmen who had traditionally wandered across the Northern borders from China, Laos and Burma. The idea was that if they became farmers they would be less of a security threat. The Thai Government hoped to persuade them to grow crops such as coffee and tea rather than opium. An excursion was arranged for diplomats to see for themselves what was happening. It was a most enjoyable few days.

As far as I was concerned the party started at 5 am on a Thursday morning, which was the lowest ebb of the whole trip. An Embassy car took Charles Booth, the Head of Chancery, and me to the airport where a plane chartered by SEATO took us up to Chiang Mai. The centrepiece of the trip was the opening of the new Hill Tribes Research Centre on the grounds of Chiang Mai University; the University had only been going two years but was a favoured project as far as money was concerned and had a very beautiful site beneath the mountain overlooking Chiang Mai.

Chiengmai-Bangkok train, 25 October 1965

The opening ceremony followed lines which are becoming familiar to me: rows of chanting priests, long detailed speeches in Thai, painstaking photographers who bow to the VIPs after each shot. The special feature in this case was that a group of Hill Tribesmen attended in costume. Bill Geddes, the Australian anthropologist who has been watching over the birth of the Centre, told us afterwards that they had quite taken him by surprise and were in any case the dead-beats who had not got the initiative to move away from the Government Settlement. Certainly it was noticeable that the same faces reappeared at different stages of our trip. After a splendid curry lunch we all piled into Land Rovers and set off for Doi Chiang Dao, one of the govt sponsored Hill Tribe settlements in the mountains. Mountains they certainly were and we were taken up a hair-raising road with precipitous drops to the settlement where we were to spend the night. It was a lovely spot with spectacular views – from the window of the room which I shared with Mrs. Booth I counted seven successive rows of mountain peaks away to the North. For dinner we had a mountainous curry and afterwards some of the stage army of hill tribesman performed tribal dances. But the real fascination of the evening was the television. While the European visitors watched the dancing, the other tribespeople stood transfixed by a T.V. set which had been put in the open air. By this stage we were terribly sleepy what with the early start and the cool mountain air (I was very glad of a vest and my thickest cardigan) and we retired to bed about 8:30. The beds were as hard as boards, which is just what they were, but none-the-less I slept splendidly, disturbed only by a colossal crash when Carl Walstrom fell through his bed next door – happily unhurt. [Carl was my – rather senior – opposite number in the American Embassy, a solidly built man who came down with a good crash.]

The next morning another early start, and we were taken sightseeing. First to a tobacco plantation belonging to a jovial character called Khun Prasit. He was quite a pioneer in his way having set up the plantation 18 years ago when all his machinery had to be taken up in small pieces. He employed hill tribespeople from all the surrounding villages to work on the plantation and seemed to get on with them rather well. Next we were taken to one of the villages belonging to the Lahu tribe – rather a tidied up one I am afraid, with fences and house numbers, but still interesting – houses on stilts of wood and leaves, with threshing, poultry keeping and all sorts of other things going on underneath. This village was apparently particularly untypical as a result of its being Christian – this particular branch of the tribe had come over from Burma about 60 years ago complete with missionary. The most picturesque of the tribespeople I saw were Meo like some I saw in Laos last year but unfortunately we did not see any of their villages (except from a distance. They are usually rather inaccessible).

All the anthropologists – and there are dozens wandering round the hills, of all sorts of nationalities – are a bit scathing about the Thai Govt's Hill Tribes programme. On the basis of what we saw I think they are probably right. The centre where we stayed was a splendid holiday camp but it wasn't at all clear what it did; generally the official attitude is either patronizing/condescending or straight uninterested. It is only recently that the Thais have started bothering about their minorities and this is because they suddenly see them as a potential subversive threat. So now they want to do something, they really don't know enough about the tribes to do much good. This is where the new Research Centre is supposed to come in. One hopes it will develop into something more than just another administrative centre.

We (the Booths and I) returned to the Consulate after parting from the SEATO party most of whom were bound straight back to Bangkok. There were two guests for lunch at the Consulate: a Swedish anthropologist in town from the Far North, and his protégé, a Yao headman, who had apparently never eaten with a knife and fork before. They were a fascinating couple: the Swede tall and very elegant with pale blue eyes which looked slightly mad, and the Yao, who was very self-possessed and remarkably evolué, *speaking several languages but not unfortunately English or any other known tongue. My Thai was up to making polite contact but not up to asking the questions one longed to know the answers to. Apparently the Yao are the most cultured of the Hill Tribes being very close to Chinese, and this chap certainly bore the verdict out.*

Donald Gibson, the Consul, was once again a splendid host and took us on the most varied sight-seeing tours. On Saturday we went up the mountain behind Chiang Mai and visited a lovely temple there, and then the King's Summer Palace, a beautifully sited house decorated for the most part in an elegant combination of traditional and Scandinavian-influenced modern which was presumably the taste of Queen Sirikit. We then went along another barely Jeepable mountain track to a point where a panoramic view included a Meo village in the valley below – I was game to climb down but was quite relieved when the others voted for lunch instead.

We came away, the Booths as well as myself, wishing we had the luck to be Consul in Chiang Mai. It was a delightful town, so much more peaceful than Bangkok, and the surrounding countryside was full of endless possibilities. The Consulate itself, where we stayed, was a miniature version of the Bangkok Embassy on the banks of the river. It was built about 1916 by an old boy who still lived in Chiang Mai where he had been drawing a pension from the FO for close on 40 years! We were lucky enough to meet him one afternoon, and he was still remarkably on the ball. His name was W.A.R. Wood and his book *Consul in Paradise*, which was published in the 60s, describes the days when as a very young member of the Consulate he was responsible for administering summary justice to the many British nationals then working in the area who were mostly from India.

***

There is a long gap in the correspondence at this point, covering my mother's much-anticipated visit to Bangkok in late 1965. My parents were rather hard up at this period and air fares were expensive so I offered to part-fund my mother's ticket though this was rejected. I had a slight sense of grievance that the Foreign Office seemed to get single staff on the cheap. A married officer with children doing the same job as me would have been entitled to a bigger house with local allowances to match, air fares to bring children out for holidays and boarding school fees paid by the state. As time went on children could come more often and wives were allowed an extra trip back to the UK. All this seemed good, but I did feel that single officers should be given an extra fare too, either to go home themselves or for a family visit. But anyway, now the great thing was that she was coming. We did everything we had planned and more. Friends were very good about looking after her while I was at work.

Perhaps the highlight of her stay was a splendid week we spent in Hong Kong with Ursula Mallorie making up the party. We stayed at the glamorous Mandarin Hotel in the heart of Kowloon. Paul Mallorie had a brother in Hong Kong who looked after us well. One day he took us on a tour of the New Territories, stopping at a viewpoint to look into the forbidden world of Red China. He worked in the Housing Department and talked to us about Hong Kong's relationship with China on which it was dependent for water. He also took us to a development being built to house refugees from the mainland. The huge blocks of flats brought home to me the scale of the refugee problem, which was to grow so spectacularly over the following decades.

I loved crossing to Hong Kong Island on the Star Ferry as the many junks zigzagged around the harbour, and took it several times for the joy of the scene. The inevitable shopping spree included visits to a tailor who in 24 hours made up elegant suits in heavy Indian silk for my mother and myself. My other major purchase was an intricate gilded carving, originally the door of a small shrine, showing a lively cast of characters, one wielding a sword. It is now on the wall in my house in Oxford.

It was a great pleasure for me to have my mother's company. But in retrospect perhaps she stayed a bit too long. Though we were great friends she had a tendency to take control of my household which occasioned one of our rare rows. It was my practice to let Boona's little girls hand round the eats at drinks parties in the garden. My mother disapproved and one day when they were doing this she sent them away with a scolding. I expect they were showing off but I was furious at the challenge to my authority.

By the time the letters resume in May 1966 the end of my posting was in sight. Because of its climate Bangkok was considered a "hardship post" and the average posting lasted two years. (It also counted for extra when it came to calculating one's pension.) I had made a point of looking in on the Personnel Department when in London to discuss what they had in mind for me next but got no clues. The nomination of my successor, David Burns, unsettled me a bit. He wrote saying he wanted to take over my house. Despite its many flaws and discomforts it was the first place I had really made myself a home and I knew I would miss it. I was inclined to regret that I was going without the zest of excitement of knowing what to look forward to. But I realized it was time to leave Bangkok. I felt myself getting slower at things, a sure sign of lost energy or enthusiasm. Ironically, in other ways my life in Bangkok had been looking up because I had made some real friends. The arrival of Daphne Blackman as the Ambassador's Secretary provided me with a compatible woman friend, while Paul and Ursula Mallorie welcomed me into the life of a family. As I got to know Bira and Rampi Kasemsri better, I also had more of a window into Thai society.

I took the plunge and booked the Rama Hotel Penthouse for a super farewell party. I wanted to go out with a bang, rather than a whimper – and practically, it would be a great help in the last hectic few days to know that the catering was in capable hands and that I need not worry. But even after negotiation with the management I was slightly shocked at the bill.

Then suddenly in mid-June disaster struck. I was brought to bed of an unknown fever. The original diagnosis was flu, but my temperature was high and didn't respond to antibiotics. When a blood test confirmed it was dengue fever the doctor ordered me into the Bangkok Nursing Home. I was very frustrated. This could scarcely have come at a worse time with my farewell party scheduled for the next Monday and departure for the annual SEATO Council Meeting in Canberra the following Wednesday. Dengue is mosquito-carried and I might have picked it up anywhere in Bangkok or up-country. The expected pattern was eight days' fever followed by a week to recuperate. I felt sick and achy but not very seriously ill after the first couple of days. Dr Ettinger (the Hungarian who was looking after me) said that it had been regarded as a much more serious disease in the past, and I have been told that is once again true now. For the moment I was comfortably installed in a room with air conditioning. The nurses were pleasant; the food medium (not that I was interested) and there was a pleasantly informal atmosphere, so after the fever wore off things were not too bad. But morale dipped as I continued to lie there, and the prospect of going to Canberra faded. The inadequate cause of the delay in my release was a rash which had become slightly haemorrhagic:

Bangkok, 20 June 1966

My legs in fact look a bit like the face of someone who drinks too much. It doesn't show unless one looks pretty closely but the doctor is afraid of complications and says I must stay put until it is gone.

I could scarcely have had a better publicized illness if I had tried, since I had no sooner sent out invitations to almost everyone I knew in Bangkok than kind Daphne sent out the cancellations. So I had lots of visitors and lots of flowers – which certainly helped to console me. Louis-Jacques Rollet-Andriane, the senior Frenchman in the SEATO Secretariat, a colourful character whose wife was a minor film star, did his best for my morale by bringing round a bottle of champagne complete with ice-bucket.

The end of the month brought my release and two bits of good news. I heard that my next assignment – a short one – was to Paris to work in the UK Delegation to NATO who were struggling with the French after de Gaulle's announcement that France would leave the organization. And a real stroke of luck was the offer of what sounded like a super flat in Paris. It belonged to Guy de Changy, the Counsellor in the Belgian Embassy in Bangkok, who said it had been unoccupied since he himself left Paris about six months earlier; he didn't mind how much or little rent the FO would pay because he didn't like it lying empty, but he wouldn't let it to anyone unknown who might break up his antiques. To add to my pleasure, I would be going to Paris on promotion to First Secretary. I rearranged my farewell party.

Bangkok, 5 July 1966

It's a piano daughter that you have today, because "The Party" went with such a go that the last bodies, including the hostess, were only swept out with the crumbs at 2 am. The Hotel did me proud in the way of food and service, the Penthouse was just as nice as I had hoped and my black and white dress on its first outing had a number of compliments. All told I think it was a great success. I have a pretty hearty programme of entertainment ahead for my last week; and I am rather glad to have got my own responsibility over before the last minute. Needless to say I have only made small inroads on the great pack-up as yet.

I am back at work this week, though in a half-hearted way. I feel completely myself again which is a blessing. The Canberra party are back now… and say it was a very dull meeting though they obviously had a pleasant time. Despite my regrets at having missed it, there are compensations at having started the final spurt of packing and entertainment thoroughly rested and having had a chance to think about what clothes I want etc. Anita is making me a last batch of things in Thai silk.

People were very kind before I left. The farewell parties were good ones and fun, making me realize that an unrepeatable episode of my life was coming to an end. The highlight was a completely unexpected lunch party given by General Kriangsak of the Supreme Command HQ for 20 including several Thai generals and at one of the best restaurants in town. My dealings with him had been in connection with fitting out a mobile clinic for use in North-East Thailand, which the British Government provided under its SEATO aid programme as a contribution to the Thai counter-insurgency programme. Not content with this splendid do I was presented with yards of beautiful green Thai silk. I must admit I was very touched and pleased especially as I had always had a very soft spot for General Kriangsak, who was lively and decisive as well as good-looking. He later briefly became Prime Minister.

But I was really very glad when D-day came and put an end to my round of gaiety. A number of friends came to see me off at the airport – despite the fact it was at 7 am in the morning – and so did a slightly tearful Boona with the children. One of my worst moments was when Boona insisted on helping in my last packing vigil sniffing dismally.

I was lucky that Daphne's annual leave coincided with my departure from Bangkok and we decided to visit Nepal together on our way back home. This entailed a night in Calcutta to pick up the plane to Kathmandu.

Kathmandu-Delhi plane, 19 July 1966

I have been following the path blazed by Mother earlier in the year. Calcutta was as grim as she painted it. We had been booked into a dingy hotel there at the sight of which spirits sank, but fortunately the beds turned out to be comfortable and the supper surprisingly good so we ignored the dirt and retired to bed very early to prepare for a 4 am start next day. Calcutta at that hour was like a morgue – hundreds of thousands of bodies stretched out on the pavement, often sleeping on nothing but a bag; and ghastly gaunt cows wandering about.

Our stay in Nepal by contrast has been a marvellous success. The weather was unbelievably kind – crisp clear days of hot sun with only occasional showers, and though the mountains were shrouded in cloud as we had been warned, they lifted as we left this morning to give us glimpses of the snowy peaks. The people we met were kinder still and after doing our own sight-seeing the first day, the rest of the time we were taken around and often fed by unknown benefactors. We had an introduction to the Ambassador – which he hadn't in fact received! – and he introduced us to the most helpful people. One other good move was to go over to the Royal Hotel for lunch; we immediately got summoned into the bar, given lunch, dinner, taken sight-seeing for the afternoon etc – and then we never looked back. The Royal itself was the most bizarre place – the front wing of a baroque palace with the Rana owner still living in the back. Now terribly run down because Boris, the owner, has switched his interest to a pig farm – proof to be seen in the pigs trampling down the flower garden in front of the hotel. Boris himself apparently used to be a well-known ballet dancer – took the lead in "The Miracle" in London. His wife is a Scandinavian who… hates Kathmandu after 14 years there, poor dear. There is no doubt we were much more comfortable in the Annapurna!

I found the Kathmandu valley a fascinating place, its life incredibly untouched by the outside world. The complete lack of self-consciousness about traditional clothes and customs was very refreshing. We went to see both the other towns in the valley and various other temples, including a very beautiful one beside the sacred river where there were three little fires burning which we were told were people who had died that morning. The river with people walking down the steps to wash themselves in the water made an unforgettable picture.

Daphne and I then had a wonderful week in Kashmir, staying in a pleasant hotel where the charming elderly "houseboy" would watch out for us each evening so the bath was ready when we got to our room. Srinagar was still a dream holiday destination, uncrowded, with picturesque streets and splendid handicrafts. We took boats across Dal Lake to visit the well-kept Mughal gardens with their ornamental channels of sparkling water and spent a long day in a mountain resort where we rode horses amid scenery reminiscent of Scotland. Somehow memories of the Raj seemed much closer in Kashmir than elsewhere in India. When I took my husband to visit Kashmir some 30 years later we stayed on a houseboat on the lake and were visited every morning by a small boat almost invisible beneath its load of flowers. But the Mughal gardens with their beautiful terracing had gone to rack and ruin.

Chapter 9

THE JOB THAT WASN'T THERE
Paris (1966)

France had been a founder member of NATO but in March 1966 President de Gaulle startled the Western world by declaring his intention to withdraw from the military (though not the political) side of the Alliance. All American forces were to leave France by 1 April the following year and SHAPE (Supreme Headquarters Allied Powers Europe) a bit later. There was much argument among politicians and diplomats about how to respond to this challenge. In particular Sir Evelyn Shuckburgh, who was now the British Permanent Representative to NATO, initially wanted to take on de Gaulle in public hoping to force him to reverse his decision, while Sir Patrick Reilly, Ambassador to France, thought this was pointless since the General would never change his mind. Frustrated that the Embassy's press section was supposed to speak for both missions, Shuckburgh asked the Foreign Office to provide him with an extra member of staff to deal with the press. This was the background to my posting to the UK delegation to NATO, but by the time I arrived in Paris it was clear that NATO would have to move and Shuckburgh was about to leave on posting to Rome anyway.

Paris, 3 September 1966

Well, here I am, having survived the first week of that frenzy in slow motion which always seems to go with a new job. I am as you see installed in a Hotel with the unlikely name of Martha – a small bed and breakfast house tucked down a side street between NATO and the Arc de Triomphe – unpretentious but comfortable.

I was met on arrival at the airport by the Delegation admin officer who took me to my hotel and then to the delegation. There I met the people I am to work with – those that weren't still away – including Willie Marsden and Richard Thomas, the two young FO members of the del who have been showing me around. – both quite a lot junior to me which is an odd feeling. Evelyn Shuckburgh reappeared the following day – sporting a new beard, which I didn't take to much.

It was anything but clear what my job was to be or indeed whether an extra person was really needed. The decision to have a press officer in the delegation itself took the heat out of the argument between the two Ambassadors for a time. But the dispute was still there and centred around what I was to do. The Embassy didn't want me to talk to the press directly – they wanted to keep that side in their own hands; but if I didn't there was very little I could do except read the papers. Evelyn Shuckburgh did in fact introduce me to the British press when he gave them a background briefing about British defence cuts in Germany. This was a very easy way to meet people and some began to ring up with difficult questions. But even at that stage I expected that I would in practice become just an ordinary member of the delegation with a bit more to do with the press than the others. I was doubtful if the delegation needed an extra member anyway but it was very pleasant to be in Paris and I was determined to make the most of my stay, however short.

I eventually found my way into Guy de Changy's flat and decided to take it despite the inconvenience of being in the Marais which was a bit far from NATO. It was rather a splendid flat in its very elaborate way – Richard Thomas and his wife Catherine commented that it was just like a stage set for the interior of a French château – with damasked walls, heavy drapes, and consciously period furniture. At first view there appeared to be a chain of gracious reception rooms – but nowhere to sleep. In practice, however, various sofas turned out to be beds in disguise. I decided to take over what the inventory described as the "Salon bleu" for my bedroom – the spare beds were in the "Salon jaune." There was a bath that stood on four moulded feet and the water gushed into it through swans' open beaks; as I later discovered, it also gushed onto the floor.

113 rue de Turenne, Paris 3^{e}, 12 September 1966

I have a sense of triumph in writing the address, because it seems unbelievable that I should be established so soon. There is a long way to go before everything functions properly and all my things are settled in, but none-the-less, it is splendid to be here and with a nucleus of my own things scattered around me I am just beginning to feel at home. The Spanish concierge's sister-in-law is prepared to come and do for me

> *which is a great weight off my mind. Kind people have rallied round to lend me the minimum of china and cutlery, and now I wait impatiently for the rest of my belongings from Bangkok.*
>
> *The great move was on Saturday, and I was in great luck that Tony Curnow (whom Mother will remember from Bangkok) was in Paris and had nothing better to do than help me. I am sure this created lots of wrong impressions chez les voisins, but it's a good thing to create interest at the outset and in any case the advantages of having a strong arm to help heave things and willing eyes to look for meters were overwhelming...*
>
> *To return to the move, I am at the moment confined to part of the flat at night because not all my advisers have managed to discover why the lights in the bathroom, w.c., and "the den" don't work. I hope this will be fixed tomorrow. There has also been trouble with a water leak, but the poor concierge who has suffered more than me (being underneath) has summoned a plumber who also should come tomorrow. Finally the Embassy have promised to deliver a fridge, so tomorrow really is a red-letter day. Not to mention that I am having lunch with – and at the expense of – the Daily Express!*

My journalistic contacts began quite well. I had a good many phone calls each day from people who wanted to find out what was going on – the French cut-down on NATO budgetary contributions was one point of interest, the move of SHAPE to Belgium another, and threatened British cuts in Germany a third. But one wit in the Delegation who was a professional pessimist made a point of coming to me each morning with some bit of misreporting to show, saying, "It doesn't matter what you tell them, if you've talked to the press at all you'll be held to blame." This Job's Comforter was called John Sabatini. I was intrigued by the name because my mother had often spoken of Rafael Sabatini, a popular author during the first half of the 20th century. She had told me she was the model for one of the characters in his swashbuckling novel *Captain Blood*, which was published in 1922 when my mother was about 21.

I started quite well as far as the night-life of Paris was concerned too. Tony Curnow took me to a jazz cellar one night and I was delighted to find that the French still played New Orleans style and I didn't have to struggle with the Shake and the Surf and the other dances that used to defeat me in Bangkok. Then another night after dinner with some people from the delegation I was taken on to a discotheque by a newly-met American from their Embassy.

Meanwhile, I settled myself into the flat and began to explore the interesting neighbourhood. But alas, there were problems.

Paris, 19 September 1966

A plumber took away the bath taps to mend a leak a week ago and won't bring them back; and potentially more seriously the bathroom and study are largely blacked out because of a suspected dangerous short circuit in part of the electric wiring – but an electrician did discover for me that the points were still live so I have plugged in lamps to keep the forces of darkness at bay. The loo is still a problem having no points, but fortunately one has a good deal of experience of what is required. Otherwise the house is getting much more human. My concierge and her Spanish sister-in-law are a blessing. It is they who have tackled plumbers and electricians on my behalf while I was at NATO... I am going to have an attempt at a bath. The concierge obviously has decided it is high time because she appeared with a length of rubber tubing and showed me how to transfer water from the basin and back again. Most welcome!

PS. John Sabatini is no relation of Rafael, alas – perhaps just as well, because he might have been taken aback if it was his father who used to write those poems to Mother's eyebrows!

The effort of unpacking and settling in my belongings from Bangkok absorbed a great deal of spare time. At long last somebody came to mend the hot water system and the flat began to feel more homelike. I still needed a carpet for beside my bed – bare toes and antique parquet were a bad combination – and decided it had better be white to go with the colour scheme which included blue watered silk walls and curtains, green velvet furniture and mottled pink mock marble trimmings. I slept on a green velvet sofa underneath a picture of the Mystic Marriage of St. Catherine!

The British Embassy had a night-club in the Cellars. It was started by Willie Marsden in the Delegation and opened once a month. I volunteered to help at the first night of the new season and was given charge of the *vestiaire* from 12.00–1:30 am. A new friend in the US delegation came with me to investigate. It was remarkably un-amateurish with a good band and a West Indian cabaret. The décor by the trendy department store Au

Printemps featured nude window-dressing figures with grasping hands detached – effective in a slightly surrealist way.

I was also invited to dinner by the Shuckburghs. Lady Shuckburgh was charming and looked absurdly young to be a grandmother three times over. All the ladies were in long dresses and I was glad I hadn't worn a short one. I found myself sitting between Guy Millard (the number 2 in the delegation) and Sir Patrick Reilly, the Ambassador in Paris (whom I had known distantly during my years in the FO). Both turned out to be easy to talk to. The main snag in the evening was getting there. Taxis were not prolific in the Marais and I did not feel like searching the streets in my long dress so I tried to phone for one. Eventually this worked but only after 20 minutes on the phone thinking desperately of nails unpainted and jewellery unsorted as panic built up that no taxi would come anyhow. I longed for my car to arrive from Bangkok. As a diplomat I was able to buy a car duty free while I was posted overseas but selling it locally at a profit was frowned on so I took it with me. It seems extraordinary that the Foreign Office were ready to ship my car from Bangkok to Paris as part of my effects – of course they did not know I had turned it over!

Paris, 12 October 1966

Today, at last, I have my bath taps back. I had my first normal bath for weeks yesterday, but only to find this morning the leak as bad as ever and the concierge who lives underneath near tears. Apparently the nit-wit plumber's boy had put something in wrong. Today they are supposed to have fixed it. It really will be nice to have a functioning bathroom. For the last few weeks I have had baths decanted from the basin taps…

Another struggle has been to get a needle for my record player. None of the ordinary places stock this Japanese make (National) and surprisingly it doesn't seem to be a crib of anybody else's machine. As a last resort I have telephoned the Japanese Embassy and will see tomorrow whether their lead is helpful.

The letters stop abruptly at this point and by Christmas it had become abundantly clear that I didn't have a proper job in the delegation. By the time I arrived in Paris any ideas of getting de Gaulle to change his mind had given way to making the best of a bad situation. In retrospect the thought that Juliet C could have made much difference seems ludicrous. I attended several meetings considering where NATO should physically go.

The Belgians were determined to have the Secretary-General and all the political side in Brussels, with SHAPE (Supreme Headquarters Allied Powers in Europe) and all the military side in Mons. They made a generous offer of premises and facilities that was quickly accepted.

Sir Evelyn Shuckburgh was replaced by a very different character, Sir Bernard Burroughs, who was said to be the inspiration for the character of Mountolive, the British diplomat in Lawrence Durrell's *Alexandria Quartet*. He was an engaging and strangely silent man of obvious intelligence and quiet presence. I didn't see much of him except for going to his inaugural Christmas party which was a cheese and wine do in his residence, a big flat off the Champs Elysées. My chief memory of it was that the Burroughs, who I think were teetotal, had grossly underestimated the appetite of the hungry delegation! But in Paris there was no shortage of nice little restaurants for us to go to and stoke up at afterwards.

All told I much enjoyed my first introduction to Paris and my brief spell working in the NATO delegation was interesting if a bit frustrating. I made lifelong friends in Richard and Catharine Thomas with whom I explored France at weekends. I also enjoyed my first taste of dealing with the press. But by Christmas I was back home and looking forward to a new job in the Foreign Office.

Chapter 10

SPEAKING FOR BRITAIN
Foreign Office News Department, London (1967 – 1970)

Back in London I needed somewhere to live. I moved in with Alison Crawshaw whose brother Andrew had been one of my companions in the long-ago interviews for the Diplomatic Service. She had a small flat in Radnor Mews near Paddington. It was a friendly place if rather a comedown after the glories of Guy de Changy's flat in Paris. I had a tiny bedroom where black dirt from the steam trains settled on the window sills and the whole flat shook with the Underground passing underneath. It was an easy commute to the Foreign Office and I caught the bus each morning from a stop opposite Kensington Gardens where I found an unexpected pleasure in watching the elegant Guards officers exercise their horses.

But it was only a temporary solution and I soon decided that this was the moment to start looking for something to buy. My wandering childhood had left me with a longing for a place of my own; I never wanted to be in the position of my parents on their return to England in 1944 when we moved from pillar to post without a permanent home. Eventually I narrowed the focus of my house-hunting to Islington, then a rundown area full of early 19th-century houses in need of restoration and therefore going cheap. Visiting the many houses that were for sale was a social education. I had not known such poverty existed in England and often felt intrusive. The small terrace house I eventually settled on had been divided into four dwellings with a single shared privy in the garden. But it was pretty and I knew as soon as I walked through the front door and saw the sun shining in that 26 Sudeley Street was the one for me. It was on offer for £5,000 and I held my breath waiting for the survey which would tell me if it was basically sound.

Sudeley Street is one of the streets near the Angel which opens directly off the Regent's Canal. The terraces on either side of the street appear at first glance to be of two storeys but the houses are more spacious than they look with a basement as well as a single room on the fourth floor and a garden at the back. There was a corner shop and a friendly pub, both of which became regular haunts. It was in the pub that I met a builder who was restoring a house round the corner in Vincent Terrace. I was finding it difficult as a single woman to get a mortgage and he advised me where to get one. Including the costs of conversion to a comfortable dwelling I needed to find about £12,000. Thus began a fruitful relationship and a busy nine months or so, while we agreed plans and his team of builders – Arsenal supporters to a man – got to work transforming my little house. The first problem was to open out the dark dank basement. The whole house above had to be propped up while reinforced steel joists were inserted and internal walls removed. I remember standing there and wondering if everything would come tumbling down on my head. But gradually my dream house took shape. We retained as many period features as possible and my one extravagance was to commission a carpenter to make a round-topped sash window of the design special to the street. The week it was installed someone else a few houses down replaced an old sash with a metal casement like the one I had despised. The builders were highly amused.

Islington was then a very mixed community in the early stages of gentrification. When I moved in about a third of the houses in the street had been done up. I later learned that the aunt of Arthur who ran the pub had lived in no 26 and had died there falling down the stairs. But neither she nor any other of the other earlier residents ever gave me any trouble. Islington bloomed over the years with Camden Passage becoming a trendy antiques market full of bargains and good restaurants. The house remained my base until after I was married and I loved it.

Meanwhile I was working in the Foreign Office News Department. The Department's role was to brief journalists in London on current foreign policy and to answer their queries. Its head when I joined was Donald Maitland, a small dynamo of a man with a gift as a mimic. He had been the Director of MECAS, the Foreign Office Arabic school in the mountains above Beirut, so I knew him already. The Head of the News Department was one of the Foreign Secretary's closest advisers, travelling with him and attending his meetings with world leaders. This access to first-hand information cascaded down to the rest of us. We were expected to be well informed on all the main issues of the day. There was an interconnected phone system and whenever it flashed whoever was free was expected to pick up. But each spokesman concentrated on one particular area of responsibility. For me, to my pleasure, this was the Middle East. I also understudied a colleague on Europe.

The day followed a well-established pattern. On arriving in the Office one's first task was to read the newspapers and the telegrams that had come in overnight from posts around the world and to identify the questions likely to be of interest to the press. Then one needed to get in touch with the Department with responsibility for the policy area concerned and agree a line to take. This could be "on the record", "unattributable" (which meant that the information could be used without mentioning the source) or sometimes "for background only." I soon got to know which of my diplomatic colleagues had the knowledge and confidence to help – sometimes it was a desk officer but often I had to beard the head of department who would inevitably be busy. At 11 o'clock the News Department met to exchange the information we had gathered. If Donald was not satisfied with any proposed line he would pick up the phone and speak to a senior official. Our meetings were fascinating and sometimes hilarious. I will never forget Donald's re-enactment of a meeting between Foreign Secretary George Brown and the Secretary-General of the UN, the Burmese U Thant, complete with gestures and accents.

Then followed the daily press conference at which ministerial engagements and other routine on-the-record announcements were made. This was mainly attended by the news agencies but it was open to any journalist who wished to attend so could occasionally throw up awkward questions. The senior members of the Department took it in turn to be spokesman for a month at a time. When my turn came round it caused rather a stir, with articles in the daily papers reporting that it was the first time that a woman had presided. (One article commented that out of 1,100 British diplomats only 26 were women.) The title for this book is taken from my favourite headline – *Juliet plays Britannia*. But I was not quite the first, after all – Joan Burbidge wrote to the Yorkshire Post to say that she had taken the press conference in 1950. It turned out that I was, however, the first regular spokesman. Later that first day the correspondent from the Central Office of Information brought me the transcript he was proposing to send out to posts abroad. It started "A Foreign Office spokeswoman said today…" Instinctively feeling that it was the role that mattered, not the gender of the speaker, I insisted that he change it to "spokesman." I don't know if I would do the same today. Usage has changed and with it my understanding of the unconscious impact of masculine words. My priority at the time was to be seen as a paid-up member of what was still essentially a male environment rather than to mark a feminist milestone.

The real work of the Department took place during the afternoon when self-selecting groups of correspondents came into the Office for confidential briefing. There were the 3 O'Clock Group, also known as the Trusties (Christopher Serpell of the BBC, Sandy Rendell of the *Times*, Mohsin Ali of Reuters and some others), the Circus (including John Dickie of the *Mail* and Willy Wolff of the *Mirror*), the foreign correspondents (mostly from US and European papers) and several others. We briefers were allocated which group to talk to each day and this was when all the information gathered during the morning became important.

The system depended on mutual trust. One's reputation as a briefer depended on being accurate and as informative as possible. I remember one correspondent whom I didn't know very well saying that if what I had told him turned out to be wrong he would never speak to me again. In turn we briefers depended on journalists respecting the basis on which information was given. If a statement was attributed publicly to the Foreign Office which should have been off the record it could cause international embarrassment as well as trouble for the briefer. I often found myself reading out confidential telegrams from posts abroad as background. This kind of relationship (which was mirrored in the lobby system at No 10) has more recently been called into question as an establishment stitch-up and I don't believe that anything like the system I knew in the 1960s could exist any longer. It belongs to an age of greater mutual trust. The advantage was a very well-informed set of foreign correspondents with some of whom one could share much raw information as it came in.

I memorably got it wrong one weekend when I was the duty officer on a Sunday. It was the height of the Vietnam war and the Foreign Secretary Michael Stewart had sent a tough message to the Americans criticizing their latest actions. My colleague who had been on duty the day before had left me a bunch of telegrams about this with a note on top summarizing events which I took to be the authorised line to take. I briefed the journalists who came to see me that afternoon accordingly and it made headlines the following morning – but by that time I had happily gone off on holiday so I missed the excitement that followed. I later discovered that what I said had been denied by the Deputy Head of Department as untrue. However, I had the last laugh because when the Foreign Secretary next had a meeting with the press he was asked about the incident by John Dickie of the *Daily Mail*.

I am glad to say Michael Stewart confirmed my version. In the event this played quite well for him politically because Harold Wilson's government, which had refused to get involved in Vietnam, did not want to be seen as the poodle of the US.

The Middle East was an exciting brief in the late 60s. The creation of Israel had left a host of unsolved problems and Israel was digging in on land claimed by the Palestinians. United in opposition, the Arab world was led by President Nasser of Egypt, who grew ever more bellicose. There were almost daily incidents, with the two sides giving conflicting accounts of what had happened. In News Department briefings the statement "We condemn all breaches of the cease-fire" became a reflex. On the night of 22 May 1967 I was on duty at home when John Dickie phoned me to say that a news agency was reporting that Nasser had closed the Gulf of Aqaba to shipping going to the Israeli port of Eilat. Did I think this would mean war? I said I thought it probably did, and hastily phoned the Resident Clerk at the Foreign Office. When the news was confirmed from Tel Aviv some four hours later the Foreign Office swung into action with a meeting in the Foreign Secretary's office. This episode was picked up in the press in a cartoon entitled "Anatomy of a Crisis." Fame comes in many forms!

War did indeed follow a fortnight later and it radically changed the map of the Middle East. Israel took Sinai from Egypt, the Golan Heights from Syria, and most importantly the West Bank from King Hussein of Jordan, not to mention the small island of Tiran which was claimed by Saudi Arabia. There followed a period of intense activity at the UN leading up to the passage of Resolution 242 which was based on the proposition that Israel should withdraw from the territories it had recently occupied in exchange for assured peace. This was largely the achievement of George Brown, then Foreign Secretary, and it remained the key document in Arab-Israeli relations for decades.

George Brown was ultimately a tragic figure. From humble roots he had risen to become the leader of the Trade Union wing of the Labour Party and a key figure in Wilson's government of the late 60s. His problem was drink, and during his time as Foreign Secretary increasingly scandalous stories began to circulate. My favourite, true or false, recounted what was supposed to have taken place at an official reception in South America. George Brown asked a tall red-robed figure to dance: the apocryphal answer was, "I cannot dance with you for three reasons – you are drunk, the tune they are playing is the Peruvian National anthem, and I am the Cardinal Archbishop of

Lima!" The situation couldn't last. One evening in the spring of 1968 the Foreign Secretary gate-crashed a News Department party. We were saying farewell to someone and a number of journalists were there. Brown began holding forth about the harlots of the press and started a slanging match with Michael King of the *Mirror*. Tempers rose and the language got very blue; a comic detail which sticks in my memory was one of my more self-effacing colleagues stuttering, "Sir, sir, there are ladies present..." A similar row happened in public the following week and that was the final disaster. George Brown had to resign.

The staid Michael Stewart returned as his successor. Apart from the press conference mentioned above, my chief memory of him is from a meeting in the Foreign Secretary's office in the House of Commons that I was sent over to cover from the News Department angle. Getting there was an adventure in itself, involving a special pass and making my way up the winding back staircase that led to the surprisingly tatty ministerial offices. As so often, I cannot remember what the meeting was about but I do remember the awkward moment when the Foreign Secretary turned to me as the only woman present and asked me to type up a text. I had to say that I couldn't take shorthand or type. I am not sure which of us was the more embarrassed.

The Labour government was determined that Britain should wind down its commitments east of Suez. One of the hotspots was Aden which had been under British rule for 128 years. British troops engaged in a desperate fighting retreat while the two rival resistance movements, the Front for the Liberation of Occupied South Yemen (FLOSY) and a shadowy group known as the National Liberation Front (NLF), were at daggers drawn. Britain eventually decided to hold secret talks in Beirut with representatives of the NLF. If this became public, my friends in Arabian Department told me, the NLF representatives would almost certainly be murdered. It is the only time I remember steeling myself to tell a deliberate lie to a journalist. Of necessity I learned how to dodge questions and to be economical with the truth but a failure to deny could be taken as confirmation. My personal rule was never to lie unless lives were at stake.

The secret contacts in Beirut led to more formal talks in Geneva in November 1967. The British side was led by Lord Shackleton, son of the explorer, then a Foreign Office Minister, and a very nice man. I was appointed as spokesman to the delegation, with my own secretary and a special suite in the Hotel Beau Rivage in which to brief the press. It was here that I introduced the main members of the delegation to the British correspondents for an informal briefing on the eve of the negotiations. When the talks opened the next day with the usual session for photographers, I leaned forward to ask Don McCarthy, now Head of Arabian Department, who was who so I could tell the journalists. Don replied that the British team had never seen even a photograph of any of them before. Both sides in the negotiations were keen to avoid leaks and my job turned out to be keeping the press happy while telling them virtually nothing. When Lord Shackleton wrote to thank me afterwards, he added, "I am afraid it was probably a rather disappointing exercise for the Press; nonetheless I think we kept their goodwill." I can't resist quoting a titbit that appeared in one paper: when the reporter who was covering the negotiations rang me at the hotel my secretary replied, "Miss Collings' suite". "Yes," he quoted himself as replying. "She is, isn't she?" He must really have been short of stories.

Responsibility for the Middle East brought me into contact with Arab and Jewish correspondents. I used to dread being phoned by the *Jewish Chronicle* who were deeply critical of British policy and not above twisting anything I said. But Gaby Strassman of the Tel Aviv-based *Maariv* became quite a friend. On the Arab side there was Ali Zaghloul, son of one of the leaders of Egypt's early independence movement. Zag, as he was known, and his English wife Joy invited me to dinner several times in their flat off Gloucester Road. He was intrigued to learn that my father had served in Egypt during WWII so I got them together over dinner at my house in Sudeley Street. All went very well until my mother noticed that the biscuits I was serving with cheese were Jewish matzohs and tried to carry it off with an ill-timed joke. Zag went purple with anger. My father and I recovered the situation as best we could but I doubt if Zag forgot the incident any more than I did.

One of the journalists with whom I was on closest terms was Richard Johns, the Middle East specialist of the *Financial Times*. We used to have lunch together from time to time to discuss whatever might be going on. When the time came for me to leave News Department he invited me to a nice restaurant in Whitehall. After we had discussed all the usual subjects, he suddenly asked me if anything was going on in Oman. Now it happened that I had just been reading a secret Foreign Office telegram which gave the most vivid account of British officers of the Oman Defence Force kidnapping the aged Sultan in his palace and escorting him into exile. This was most definitely not public knowledge. I gulped mentally but I think I simply asked Richard if he was expecting any developments there. Anyhow

I succeeded in diverting him, though later, when the story came out, he said that he should have smelled a rat because I looked rather peculiar.

***

The time had come to move on and I got just the posting I wanted. I was to go to The Hague as Head of Chancery with special responsibility for EEC affairs. As I phased out of News Department there was a hectic round of briefings as well as a spending spree. My main purchase was a white sports car, an MGB GT, one of my two favourite cars ever. I felt very dashing and my friends in the News Department teased me that I had bought it to wear as much as to drive.

Chapter 11

CLOGS, CARNIVAL AND THE CLUB DU JEUDI
The Hague (1970–1974)

This time I had no problem about where to live. Dick Faber, the Ambassador's number 2, wanted to move and it was proposed that I should take over his flat opposite the vast building that contains the International Court of Justice. It was modern, airy and comfortable and a short drive away from the Embassy. Indeed its only disadvantage was that it was overlooked by the Bulgarian Embassy which was generally supposed to be a nest of spies in the pay of the KGB. Most Dutch people do not draw their curtains at night, but I drew mine just in case.

The Embassy itself occupied a handsome house on the Lange Voorhout, a broad street of 17th-century terraces which is one of the most prestigious in the city as well as one of the most beautiful. It had a double band of trees down the middle which in spring was carpeted with crocuses. As Head of Chancery, my office was one of three elegant first-floor rooms looking out on this peaceful view. The Chancery was the political section of an Embassy and was in this case run by the Counsellor, Dick Faber. As Head of Chancery my job, despite the title, was to ensure that the Embassy ran smoothly and the staff were happy. There were about 30 UK-based staff as well as a sizeable locally-engaged contingent who worked in the less sensitive sections – commercial, information, consular and administrative. I dealt with all personnel matters such as postings and confidential reporting on staff and, though the Administration Section dealt with most day-to-day problems, sensitive issues such as housing, parking and security often came to me to be adjudicated. I was also formally responsible for checking and signing the accounts which I found a daunting task. Though briefed about scams to look out for I was all too aware that a clever accountant could pull the wool over my eyes with the greatest of ease. Fortunately my staff never put me to the test.

A Head of Chancery really needs a wife to help keep in touch with Embassy morale and any personal problems that may be brewing. Not having a wife of my own I made a point of adopting somebody else's. In The Hague this was Jasmine Blakeway who played the role to perfection, being very sociable but also reliably discreet.

When I arrived in The Hague the Ambassador was Eddie Tomkins, who had been Head of Western Department during part of my time there. I had always got on well with him and liked his wife Jill too. They were very hospitable and I loved going to the Residence, a historic house made all the more beautiful by Jill Tomkins's lovely collection of paintings. (She was a Benson of Kleinwort Benson fame.) It turned out later, however, to be quite literally a death trap. In 1979 the then Ambassador Richard Sykes was ambushed and killed by IRA terrorists as he got into his car in the courtyard entrance. I knew Richard Sykes, a thoroughly nice man with an outstanding war record. I also knew Alyson Bailes who was in the car with him and survived. Richard was not the first British Ambassador to be killed by the IRA. Christopher Ewart-Biggs was assassinated in Ireland in 1976. As a British diplomat in the 70s one could not be unaware of the terrorist threat. We all knew how to look out for doubtful packages and how to check the underside of our cars for bombs. Our offices had extra-long net curtains with weights at the bottom which were supposed to balloon out and contain flying glass in case of an explosion. But the deaths of people I knew brought it all much closer to home.

To my great pleasure, as well as the key job of Head of Chancery I was given responsibility for dealing with EEC affairs. De Gaulle had left office, Edward Heath was Prime Minister and the UK was again trying to negotiate its way into the European Communities. I was delighted to be in on the new chapter of a story that was so devastatingly interrupted by the French veto in 1963. I followed in great detail the telegrams reporting what was going on and went to be briefed by the UK Delegation in Brussels where the formal negotiations were taking place. The Dutch were again the strongest supporters of British membership and I saw my job as being an outlying cog in the machine, feeding in useful information about Dutch intentions.

The world had moved on since 1963: Commonwealth countries had mostly diversified their trade patterns to be less dependent on the UK and the EEC had put in place many core policies to which it expected the UK to adapt. But if much of the substance of the negotiations was surprisingly different, many of the personalities involved were the same. The heads of the two key departments dealing with the subject in the Dutch Foreign Ministry turned out to be old friends from Brussels days. Agricultural questions now loomed large with the Dutch being key players: Sicco Mansholt, the influential European Commissioner for Agriculture, was a Dutchman. I boned up on agricultural matters and developed contacts with the Ministry. I also made a good and useful friend in the Finance Ministry. All told, I found the Dutch officials unfailingly helpful.

Holland was a good place to be British in the 1970s. The fund of goodwill left over from the war spilled over into personal relations. Virtually all the Dutch I met spoke English fluently, though sometimes they came up with funny literal translations. It was quite common for a workman needing to see the rear of a house to ask to see one's backside. One certainly didn't need to speak Dutch to make friends but I decided to learn the language anyhow. I took lessons with a clever and inquisitive lady called Mary Makowski who was married to an Eastern European and, I was warned, was probably a spy. She was an excellent teacher and I have never forgotten the first phrase she taught me – "twee handjes op een buik" – meaning hand in glove, but literally two hands on one stomach! I eventually passed the Foreign Office Intermediate exam in Dutch, earning a small extra allowance. I got to the point where I could read a novel, if painfully slowly, and could get the gist of newspaper articles and public speeches. But the main value as far as I was concerned was that I could spend an evening with Dutch friends without forcing them all to speak English.

I also made friends through the Club du Jeudi, which was open to all diplomats below Ambassador rank serving in the Hague. After a while I was made President of the Club which became an important feature in my life. The Committee was an interesting bunch of young diplomats such as Charlie Salmon, who followed Dutch internal affairs in the American Embassy, and Tony Vincent, a Canadian who later played a notable part in an Embassy siege in South America. Our main activity was to invite eminent Dutchmen to speak at our monthly lunch in some hotel. With the help of the Dutch authorities we also organised outings to places of interest such as Parliament and the radio station at Hilversum.

There are no letters to my parents from The Hague but I did keep an occasional diary which gives a contemporary account of my work and play. Here are some extracts:

19 November 1970

I want before the memory is too dim to write a little about the conversation at dinner at the Embassy the other night [8 November 1970].

I think it was a rather impromptu affair because I was commandeered at the last moment. The other guests included Erik Blumenfeld, an attractive if over self-confident German Deputy and his rather dull wife, Sir Fitzroy MacLean (as nice as ever but sadly older than when I met him last) and Harold King, the ex-Reuters correspondent in Paris, who really made the sparks fly. From where I sat at dinner I could hear Harold King launching attacks on a variety of subjects such as miniskirts and man's search for another war. It wasn't until after dinner that the attack was aimed at me and then it was about how shockingly the Foreign Office misjudged the French. We were all prejudiced; we never knew the people who mattered; some of the things he had heard our Embassies say about de Gaulle were libellous. Inevitably it got around to the Affaire Soames. Here, he affirmed, we had done the General a dirty trick, slapped him in the face when he held out a hand in an attempt to get over years of mistrust, etc. etc. I tried a skirmishing defence but was not at all equal to the wily old bear's tactics. The red herring, the claim to special knowledge, the ad hominem argument. It was a fascinating virtuoso display. Anyhow at that point the Ambassador (Eddie Tomkins) scented a lively discussion and came over to join in, making a much better job of it than I did. He even got Harold King once or twice to admit that we might have had grounds for doubting the General's motives, given the timing and manner of what he said to Soames, not to mention the background.

At this point I should explain the Soames Affair. It originated in a private lunch that took place the year before, on 4 February 1969, between Christopher Soames, then British Ambassador in Paris, and General de Gaulle, at the Elysée Palace with no officials present. The General, still President, ruminated about Europe, suggesting that a wider, looser grouping than the existing six members of the EEC might be desirable, led by an inner core of Britain, France, Italy and Germany. He apparently suggested bilateral talks. Soames' reporting telegram put the Foreign Office in an agonising dilemma: should they tell the other five member states, who had supported Britain's wish for membership of the EEC? Or should they respect de Gaulle's confidence? They opted for the former; the story leaked, and all hell broke loose. Two months later, on 28 April 1969, de Gaulle resigned having lost an ill-judged referendum on domestic constitutional reform. Negotiations for British membership resumed under the new President Pompidou and this time ended in success.

The day after the Embassy dinner – 10 November 1970 – the world heard that de Gaulle was dead. In fact, the old man must already have been dead when we were so hotly discussing the rights and wrongs of his behaviour. The news provoked a number of odd thoughts and memories: Edward Heath telling us in Brussels that Britain would never get into the Common Market while de Gaulle was alive, the State Visit to London in 1960, meeting de Gaulle at the French Embassy when he said, "Enchanté, mademoiselle", and the marvellous ceremony of his speech in Westminster Hall. There was a piece in the *Times* Diary about Harold King's comments on the event. There it was, just the same – the perversity of the FCO, the generosity of the General. Clearly Eddie's arguments had been like water off a duck's back. But in a strange way it was comforting to know that even if we did unwittingly try to stick pins into the old man's wax image as he lay dying, the image was unscratched in Harold King's mind. I admired and was fascinated by de Gaulle despite his perversity.

Meanwhile life had its lighter moments too. I went to the opening of an exhibition of Salvador Dali's work in Rotterdam. The occasion was itself quite as surrealist as the paintings.

The Hague, 12 November 1970

The exhibition was huge, but even so there was such a crush of guests both inside and trying to get in that our eventual entry through the one swing door might, I feared, have provoked a riot among those still forced to wait outside. The question everyone was asking was "Will Dali come?" I had quite decided he would not when suddenly there was a stir and in he marched, like a wax figure complete to the moustache ends. He was looking crossly straight ahead with one arm protectively round a shrivelled old lady who was apparently his wife Gala. He stalked round with a perfunctory glance at the occasional picture, a word with the Spanish Ambassador's wife for the benefit of the photographers, and then was gone. The pictures did not mean very much to me. Those that stay with me are the double portrait of a battle-axe of a woman (one face realistic, the other dissolving into a rocky peak with trees and paths), some fine line drawings and the Crucifixion which I have known since a child... Like them or not, I will never forget the lip-shaped sofa called "Mae West" or the crowned gold heart with its window into a pulsating, rubied interior.

But it was difficult to do justice to the exhibits given the competing demands on one's attention of the other guests. I doubt if I have ever seen such a mixed assembly. The shaggy, the long-haired, the exhibitionist rubbed shoulders with the properest of Dutch high society. There was a girl whose gauze trouser suit was so completely transparent that she might have been wearing nothing but the miniest bikini... There was another girl whose tight jeans caught my attention by the enormous butterflies sewn strategically across her person fore and aft. And with all this, as in disconnected film sequences, one saw jostling the smart set, some out of place local dignitaries and a smattering of old people for whom the dream-like atmosphere must have been a nightmare. Were they all invited? One will never know.

Geoffrey Rippon, the Chancellor of the Duchy of Lancaster, was the Minister responsible for leading Britain's renewed negotiations with the EEC which had reached a critical juncture when, in April 1971, he visited The Hague for discussions with Joseph Luns, the veteran Dutch Foreign Minister. I was responsible for taking the record and I enjoyed the feeling of being briefly nearer the hub of the negotiations. I found Rippon himself arrogant and self-satisfied but I admitted to myself that he imposed his personality admirably on the political discussion. The meeting lasted about an hour and was dominated by the inability of both sides to judge what the French were really up to.

The Hague, 22 April 1971

As a result it was a confused discussion, often with several people talking at once. The Dutch are much more undisciplined about this than British officials. The only bit of light relief in the meeting arose out of this. It was clear that Luns and Hartogh [the senior Dutch official] *had different ideas about the sort of move the French really wanted from the British – an erosion of negotiating positions, as Hartogh seemed to think, or some grand unconnected gesture, perhaps in the nuclear field, as Luns has been proposing to the press. Anyhow after much sibilant whispering on their side of the table Luns started to contradict H: "As I was just saying to Mr Hartogh, my dear Ambassador..." Hartogh interrupted, "In fact that is not what the Minister said at all. He said, 'You negative fool'!" Roars of laughter all round, Hartogh slightly pink and not minding at all. Luns: "In Dutch that is almost a term of affection."*

Luns was on the point of leaving the Dutch Foreign Ministry after 19 years. He no longer seemed quite so vitally exuberant as when I had first seen him in action in Brussels: a bit whiter and inevitably a bit older looking. But Dutch politics would certainly be duller without him.

Being Head of Chancery seemed to involve me in endless administrative chores. To be woken up by the phone at 7.45 to find Duncan Sandys, a former Tory minister and Churchill's son-in-law, expecting me to provide a car in fifteen minutes to take him to the airport was one of the lesser joys of life. It was more fun to slip back into my old skin of dealing with the press. Roger Beetham from News Department, who was accompanying Geoffrey Rippon, asked if he could stay in my flat – and was naively surprised to discover a rumour circulating in the Embassy that we were having an affair! I laid on an Indonesian meal for those journalists who turned up for his briefing – some old friends such as the eternally scruffy Walter Farr, and some familiar names such as Reggie Dale. Poor Roger got in a bit of a state by saying that an Anglo-French summit had now got a "certain inevitability," a phrase that got picked up and echoed in various articles, starting a typical two-day flurry and questions on the subject at the press conference Geoffrey Rippon gave at the end of the talks.

On 22 May 1971 I had dinner with Herman Posthumus Meyjes who was now Head of the European Department in the Ministry of Foreign Affairs. He arrived at 7 o'clock saying, "Are you listening to the press conference?" But for this I would certainly have missed hearing for myself what Pompidou and Heath had to say after their anxiously watched meetings in Paris. What a contrast with that other press conference in January 1963, when de Gaulle said that Britain was not ready for Europe. It was difficult to believe one's ears. Here was a French President saying that even if some people had thought that true, he was not one of them, and that it would now be unreasonable to suppose that an agreement couldn't be reached next month. And here was Edward Heath, less eloquent in success than in disaster, calmly talking of British entry as something within reach. I was afraid of being too euphoric – these moments of political elation can be so insecurely based. But there really are historic moments and this was one of them. I was glad to have shared it with Herman, not only because he had been my most consistently helpful contact since I had been in the Hague, but also because he too had been in Brussels last time when things ended so differently.

***

The Club du Jeudi organised a visit to Maastricht, an attractive town in the south of the Netherlands which later gave its name to one of the EU's most important Treaties. I think it must have been at the suggestion of Mr da Costa, a nice old man in the Dutch Information Service who took great pains to ensure that our group of fairly junior diplomats saw the best of his country. I sometimes even wondered if he had anything much else to do.

1 March 1972

It seemed a very bright idea at first to organize a Club du Jeudi excursion to one of the Carnival towns. But when I actually came to get on the bus with my assorted collection of companions, I was in two minds about the whole thing. I needn't have worried. I had a ball.

We had a handsome Prince in exotic clothes who must have kissed thousands of girls during his brief reign without showing any signs of strain. We had lots of processions, with floats often devoted to local political themes. There were Carnival officials in funny hats and people giving each other back-handed salutes. But most of all I think the fun lay in the crowds who surged from bar to bar, singing, and wearing odd vestiges of costume, and drinking enormous quantities of beer. It was lucky for me that our self-appointed guide from the VVD [Dutch information service] *turned out to be so nice, and that he decided I was a good thing, because Carnival is obviously more fun à deux. As it was I enjoyed myself no end, wearing the very smart scarlet felt top hat which I bought myself for Fl 6 and a pair of fetching false eye-lashes which I was given by somebody else in the party. I am not sure I want to repeat the wild "hossing" (when the crowd pushed and shoved in time to music rather than danced) – but by next year I will probably feel up to it again. The rest was great fun: singing, dancing, briefly meeting other people who came and went with the crowds, and finally riding with my new friend Guy in a battered car which was towed in the procession to publicize some old car rally. I wonder if I will ever see him again or like him so much if I do? I daresay Carnival friends don't look so good to either side by the light of the working day. But it was nice to meet someone sympathique in such an unexpected way, and I must admit I did not expect the dejected young man with a nice smile whom we met at the beginning of the evening to have such a spark.*

This confidential memo would not really be complete without recalling the advice given by a friend to lock my hotel room door at night. I did, but was still a bit surprised when shortly after my very late return on Saturday night I heard someone try it. "Go away! I am trying to sleep." Persistent knocking and a voice asking to be let in. Me, a nut, opening the door and faced with a totally unknown figure asking "Do you want a boy in your bed?" Door hastily shut with prudish comment. But to be honest I must admit that that incident too made me feel a success!

Another Club du Jeudi excursion was to the Rhineland, to taste the local wine. A long weekend organized with splendid – and very acceptable – Germanic thoroughness by the German Embassy allowed the oddly assorted group to do its own national thing, and the resulting mixture would have been a joy to Lawrence Durrell. The small group from the British Embassy – Pat Nicoll, her fiancé Peter, and myself – were kept in The Hague by the need to attend our Ambassador Eddie Tomkins's farewell party. By the time we caught up with the party at Schloss Böckelheim, they were already well into their second wine-tasting.

29 October 1972

The tasting room was a large room with windows looking down over the river below. A large table nearly filled it and round it sat my colleagues listening intently to the explanations (which very few of them understood) of the Director of the winery. They had already reached No.8 on the wine list and we arrived very appropriately as the Director announced that that was where the quality began. Minions went round pouring a little into each person's glass: then followed a thoughtful sip, a rolling around the mouth, a few knowing comments and then – horrors – the rest of the sample was tipped unceremoniously into an enormous communal vase, to make room for the next exotic vintage. Eiswein followed by Auslese, followed by Spätlese, and I was thoroughly befuddled when it was borne in on me that I had to present my first clogs – an absurd recurring gesture of thanks (as recommended by the German Embassy) which reduced me to near giggles each time I caught Pat's eye.

We drank our way happily through Friday and Saturday – scattering clogs as we went – but the highlight of the trip was the party on Saturday night, all of us transported to a small village winery where we were entertained in the tasting parlour and fed with two whole roasted sucking pigs. There were a scattering of local notables, including the "Lord Mayor" (an amiable man who didn't speak much English). The ex-German Agricultural Attaché in Paris kept on saying that he had never seen diplomats like us before. The party was going well when Mary Panabaker, the wife of the Canadian Military Attaché and the heart and soul of the party, stood up, necklaces jangling, and demanded to know "who would dance the polka" with her. A subdued hush was followed by a click of heels and Pazout, our Czech colleague, rose to the occasion. The dancing grew fast and furious. The ex-Agricultural Attaché took to the floor, protesting that he had been crippled for 20 years but was now as right as rain. And then Mr de la Loza, the Mexican Counsellor, came into his own. One by one, he swept the girls (including me) onto the floor and, one by one, they fell away exhausted. He twirled, he whirled, he poured with sweat, but never hesitated, although most of his partners were twice his size. At the end of the day, he alone held the floor.

But Mr de la Loza was not the only person to find himself that night. The Thai Third Secretary mustn't be forgotten. I had just noticed Chalermporn's method of drinking the night before – he regarded it as a challenge and whenever anyone drank his health, he took a deep breath, said "Scholl," and drained the glass. I had seen him do this when offered a sip by two totally unknown young Germans – who looked a bit surprised but fortunately accepted the situation in the spirit in which it was meant. On Saturday night the festive spirit got into the inscrutable Chalermporn and he was scholling all over the place. It was on the way home in the bus that he took the initiative. Mary Panabaker was determined not to let the party die. She found a microphone and announced to the now somewhat somnolent company that we would all sing our national songs. The British contingent held their breaths, modesty reinforced by reluctance. But we needn't have worried. Up leapt Chalermporn; taking over the mike from Mrs. P he settled down with it cupped in his hands and proceeded to croon in nasal noises for the next half hour. He would have gone on till we got home too, but Mrs. P. wouldn't let him. Happily, by then, enough others were brave enough to try their voices, and the English contingent just made it home before the finger pointed inescapably at us.

***

On 1 January 1973 Britain finally became a member of the European Communities. The Embassy in The Hague shouldn't have had any role in this, but just as I was setting out for a late lunch, I had a phone call to say that a small plane bearing the two new British Commissioners, Christopher Soames and George Thomson, plus a mountain of luggage was coming into Rotterdam Airport. Could the Embassy please rescue them?

After a frustrating hour of attempts to telephone (best unrecorded), I made contact with the party and sent a couple of cars out to meet them. Then the Ambassador got back from lunch and decided to go to the airport too, sweeping me up with him. We arrived to find the party – Thomson, Soames, David Hannay and one other – tucking into a hearty lunch. (I was getting rather hungry by then.) After some discussion they decided to catch the train to Brussels.

4 January 1973

As we began packing the Embassy cars the full glory of the luggage became visible. There were about 15 suitcases and a dozen despatch boxes (labelled variously "Secretary of State for Commonwealth Relations" and other inappropriate titles), not to mention various parcels tied with coloured ribbon.

We got to The Hague station in time for brandy for the Commissioners ("more brandy" would be more accurate) and piled the luggage in the best place to dash for the train when it came in. Dutch trains only wait 2 minutes and are no respecters of persons. It came. Somehow the people and motley collection of luggage were all piled in and my last glimpse of Christopher Soames was looking like a disconsolate stranded sealion surrounded by a desert of suitcases. George Thomson had earlier described the expression as "if this is Europe, I don't like it"!

The highlight of my social career in the Netherlands was probably when we entertained Prince Claus – Prince Consort of the Netherlands – as our Guest of Honour at the Club du Jeudi. Prince Claus was a German aristocrat and former diplomat whose marriage to Crown Princess Beatrix in 1966 was controversial in Holland, a country where war-time memories were still strong. This had largely died down by the time of our luncheon in 1973 and when Beatrix became Queen in 1980 he became very popular. He struck me as rather a cold fish – good looking in a way, but rather drawn and a bit older than I had expected.

I waited to greet him at the front door of our usual haunt, the Belair Hotel, and was relieved not to be more nervous. He launched immediately into a steam of conversation which may have been intended to put me at my ease but was in fact faintly unnerving. I led him down to our usual gathering place by the bar and introduced him to the rest of the Committee and various others. We had the luncheon in a big L-shaped room on the ground floor, having overflowed the accommodation we were originally allotted. Our table was at the apex of the triangle, with a mike and rostrum beside it from which one had a good vantage point over the assembled crowd – about 150 people all told, a Club record. The lunch itself passed quite easily if not very memorably. The Prince seemed to talk quite easily to the Indonesian on his right, as well as to the rather smooth Belgian we had put opposite him, and rather to my surprise he seemed to get on well with Sue Tanguy, the off-beat wife of the American number 2. Also close was our obligatory East European, this time Kuznetzov, a Russian who didn't seem to me to be trying very hard. I thought at the time he was perhaps a bit out of his depth but perhaps Princes were not quite his line.

I can't say the Prince's speech was very inspiring. He admitted to me afterwards that he had given little thought to what he would say. He was obviously really interested in Africa and had strong views on development questions but he let himself get led into some rather oversimplified clichés about recipient countries knowing best what aid they required to fit their cultural pattern and about the pollution of development being better than the pollution of poverty. It was not a sustained argument and he gave a rather cheap reply to a question from a Filipino girl as to what influence he had on the areas of concentration chosen for Netherlands aid. He said that if she were working on the political side of the Embassy she would know how little influence Royalty had on policy questions. Now this was scarcely the point, as he was Chairman of what was called the National Committee on Development Strategy. When I asked him about this he explained that his Committee's work was restricted to harnessing public opinion, and had not even advisory functions as regards policy. The general view was that he could have found a more courteous reply to the question but it was basically a social occasion, and people had flocked to see him rather than to listen to any message he might have. At that level it was very successful. It was nice to bask in praise of how I chaired proceedings, and I did feel smugly that without saying anything very original I managed to hit the right note between ease and formality. So when someone said I was "just perfect" I could purr very comfortably!

***

About half-way through my posting, Edward Tomkins was replaced as Ambassador by John Barnes. They were very different personalities. Whereas Eddie was relaxed and genial, John had strong ideas of how everyone should behave. He was kind to me personally but as Head of Chancery I often felt caught in the middle when he got at other members of the staff. It really was extraordinary how one person's personality could alter the atmosphere. We used to be a relaxed and friendly group, but I thought fairly efficient. Now the Embassy was a tense place, with a pervading feeling of pressure, and I did not think its output was any greater than before. It was a subject I brooded about at length in my diary.

The Hague, 6 March 1973

What then is my verdict on whether he is a good Ambassador?... I do not think it can be right to direct such a large proportion of an Embassy's efforts inwards – so many of his requirements make a quite unnecessary amount of work which has no bearing at all on what I regard as the real purpose of our being here at all, the representation of British interests in the Netherlands. One cannot help regarding much of it as a sop to personal egotism... But I must admit I also wonder whether his didactic manner is very successful with the Dutch. He is a bit too given to telling people what they ought to think. And I have been surprised by his reluctance to get to grips with such important political questions here as Dutch views on the future of the EEC – the role of Parliament, economic and monetary union etc. Of course these are questions I myself find fascinating which may make me inflate their importance. But I really do believe that since British entry into the EEC, the question of what sort of Europe we want is one of the main questions we as a country face. It is a question we face together with Holland, and it is a question on which the Dutch have definite and in no way nationalistic views to contribute. One has the possibility here to add one's own small effort to the major constructive policy of the Government – the building of Europe.

Nearly 50 years later I still find John Barnes a puzzle. I am more than ever convinced that the best Ambassadors work with their staff, building a team and motivating them to work together to achieve the Embassy's aims. John Barnes's lack of interest in the European story still seems extraordinary to me. He came to The Hague from Tel Aviv where he became very pro-Israel. It felt as if he couldn't leave all that behind.

The next diary extract was written over a year later by which time I was back in London, but it obviously belongs here rather than with the next stage in my career.

London, 14 August 1974

I left Holland at the end of January after 3 and a half years. If I was an Ambassador and had to write a valedictory despatch what would it have said? I would certainly have said with the best of them that I found the country a very rewarding one and like to feel I left many friends behind. It was the openness and friendliness which I met from so many people which set Holland apart among my postings so far. It is a country quite without frivolity and to get on one has to be very straightforward oneself. Subtlety is a waste of time, and if one tried to be too clever or smart, the most likely result would be to make people ill at ease. At that level I feel quite pleased with myself really. Of course it was an enormous bonus to be English, and to be a girl was also an advantage.

All told I left the Netherlands with many regrets…but they weren't unmixed. Though I came to some sort of terms with life with John Barnes in the last few months, it was only at the cost of lowering my standards – of neglecting what I felt ought to have been done, to try to conform (inadequately) to what he wanted. Not a happy time. I felt that my work vis-à-vis the Dutch was getting squeezed out, that I was an inadequate buffer between an unreasonable Ambassador and an unhappy Embassy, and that I made very heavy work of the admin which seemed to be John's main interest. Really an enigma of a man, with all his talents and intelligence. I kept on saying that I didn't dislike him, and that is basically true, but I am really thankful to be free of him.

Chapter 12

THE EYE OF THE STORM
Foreign Office European Integration Department, London (1974–1977)

When I heard that my next posting would be back in the Foreign and Commonwealth Office dealing with the EEC (European Economic Community) I was thrilled. I saw it as the chance to be at the centre of things as Britain settled into its rightful place as a member of the Communities. But we were all in for a rude shock. I arrived in London at the start of 1974 in time to witness the death throes of the Heath government. A cap on incomes designed to curb rampant inflation had led to industrial action, notably in the coal industry. Hoping to conserve stocks the government had issued an Order limiting commercial consumption of energy to three days a week. The miners came out on strike as did some other categories of workers. London was grey and miserable. I found candle ends on my desk and rubbish was piled high in the streets. Heath called an election in February on the theme of "who governs Britain." It was a close-run thing: the Conservatives got more votes but Labour got most seats in the House of Commons and Harold Wilson formed a minority government.

The change of party turned my new job upside down. Instead of basking in the success of getting Britain into the EEC at last, we were now working for a government committed to "immediately seek a fundamental renegotiation of the terms of entry." To many of those who had been involved in the entry negotiations this was a matter of national and personal shame. Britain was reneging on a major international commitment while the ink on the Treaty was scarcely dry. If there were few resignations in the Foreign Office this was because word quietly began to spread that Wilson and Callaghan, the new Foreign Secretary, would negotiate to stay in the EEC. But many sections of the Labour Party had different ideas, as did several leading members of the Cabinet who were bent on getting out. The issue split families and friends in the same way that the Brexit referendum has done.

There were at that point two FCO departments dealing with Europe with the unedifying names of European Integration Department (Internal) and (External), covering respectively the EEC's internal affairs and its relations with the rest of the world. My job as one of two assistant heads of EID(I) involved responsibility for issues concerning the functioning of Community institutions, law and finances. (Fortunately there was a very clever chap whom I only notionally supervised covering the Community's financial arrangements; I never fully understood them!) It turned out to be a remit with very fuzzy edges. My immediate boss was a clever, hard-working, low-key man called John Fretwell. As I took up my job someone in Personnel Department told me that he was marked out for great things in the Foreign Office but needed all the help he could get in EID(I). So did I. We were in the eye of the political storm and there was a continual barrage of Parliamentary Questions, debates and other meetings for which the department had to provide material for ministers. For each PQ one had to anticipate the follow-up questions that might be asked and provide suitable replies. There were so many complicated new subjects to master that for some time I found the job overwhelming, both intellectually and in terms of pressure of work.

The Assistants in the two EIDs took it in turn to commission and collate the briefs for Meetings of the EEC Council of Ministers which took place about once a month, as well as for bilateral meetings of all kinds. I often had to produce the first draft of the Steering Brief, attempting to put a shape on the meeting as a whole, spelling out British priorities and the likely positions of other key Member States. There were often about 20 subject briefs to be drummed up including some on subjects for which I was responsible. Chasing up laggards from other departments could be a nail-biting experience as the deadline for submission to Ministers and senior officials approached. One of the compliments I most treasured from that time came from one of the secretaries who was helping put the collections together (all still done by hand; it was long before the days of computers). "You don't fuss," she said, "as so many of the men do!"

In an ordinary Diplomatic Service career one does not have much to do with Parliament because the FCO seldom initiates legislation. But membership of the EEC blurred the distinction between domestic and diplomatic issues and between European and national law. How was the UK Parliament to deal with the tide of legislation being negotiated in Brussels? It was of course a problem for other Member States too, and I went with one of the Parliamentary Clerks and a senior official of the Lord Chancellor's Office to Bonn, Copenhagen and Dublin to investigate how they were dealing with it. It was eventually decided to set up Scrutiny Committees in both Houses of Parliament to examine draft EEC legislation and single out proposals of sufficient importance to be debated by the full House. I thought a joint committee would have been better but this foundered on jealousy between the Commons and the Lords. A procedure was later established to ensure that proposals went to Parliament with a brief explanatory memo. Implicit in a lot of this work were two major constitutional issues – sovereignty and the balance of power between Parliament and the executive.

Another major subject that landed on my desk was the result of a proposal for devolution of certain powers to Scotland and Wales: how could the UK government ensure it implemented EEC legislation in fields where power might be devolved? I couldn't begin to see the answer to this question but was bailed out by the chief Legal Advisor, a splendid man called Ian Sinclair, who was a Scot. He provided me with wonderfully clear minutes on the subject which I simply had to submit to Ministers. The quirk of Foreign Office procedure was that the policy department had to own the subject while the Legal Advisors advised.

There was little time for a private life (other than in August when the EEC went on holiday) and I became totally absorbed by the politics of it all, and particularly the personalities. As time went on I gradually got on top of a range of arcane subjects and began to submit papers over my own signature rather than through the Head of Department. The occasional diary that I kept over these years gives a flavour of the work with all its excitements and pressures, as well as the state of my morale. Many of my judgements of the Ministers of the day must surely reflect how they were seen more generally in the Office. The exception was the glamorous David Owen whom I saw quite a lot of. He was apt to throw his weight around and had many critics but, as will become clear, I enjoyed my dealings with him.

London, 15 August 1974

I was delighted to get a job in the European Integration Department because I felt that if I am to stay in the Foreign Service a future in Europe is what appeals most. It is moreover a subject about which I feel quite strongly. I am sure that the personal experience of being in Brussels in 61–63 has a lot to do with this. But I have found it all very hard work and am not at all sure that I am making a very good job of it. Intellectually it has been very demanding – and I hope that however hard the autumn turns out to be, the greater knowledge I have accumulated will help me to avoid being quite so overwhelmed as I have at times felt in the last few months. But that apart, I have also been worried that the job has brought me up short against a debilitating trait in my temperament: indecision. I suppose this in turn has its roots in lack of confidence. I might have made a better stab at the job if I had gone to it glowing with good reports from News Department instead of after a rather demoralizing spell with John Barnes.

All of which has made me think quite seriously about where my future lies. The upper reaches of the Foreign Service don't really look all that promising as a way of life. In London if one is in a good job the pressures which I already find a strain are likely to increase. And yet I don't think I would be satisfied by anything but an inner stream job. And though there are certainly prestigious jobs abroad where the going would be less hard, the idea of increasingly lonely eminence does not appeal either. All told it is difficult to know what to do. The obvious and convenient way out would be to get married. But I have never found that an easy answer, and I do not really see much prospect of anyone presenting themselves whom I actually wanted to marry...

So for the immediate future I can see no alternative but to slog on, and to hope that after a good summer's rest and with the help of experience I will find the job easier. I must remember that John Fretwell (who gets through an appalling amount of work himself) clearly thinks it a heavy job. And if I really find it is too much for me I will have to get myself moved. But I certainly don't want to do that, which would be an admission of failure, and which would I fear inevitably dim my career prospects. When it comes down to it, if I am going to stick to the FCO I still want to shine.

Looking back I am struck by the self-doubt of the preceding passage. Perhaps the psychologist from those long-ago interviews to get into the Diplomatic Service was right: I was a perfectionist and had a tendency to despair if I didn't come up to my own expectations. To me confidence always came from feeling I was on top of my job and EID(I) was in many ways the toughest challenge of my career. As a woman in what was still essentially a man's world I was daunted as well as inspired by the very clever men I worked amongst, most of whom oozed confidence. But tenacity saw me through and I was determined not to be beaten.

***

During these years I was living at 26, Sudeley Street in Islington, the pretty little house I had bought during the 1960s. From time to time I shared it with a friend who lived in the top room. The house was looked after by the redoubtable Mrs Bennet who had worked for my parents in Guernsey. Small, rising 70, with a beady eye and a fondness for gaudy colours, she had left school at about 12 and then went into service. She was a splendid character, rich in courage and loyalty, and she took a proprietorial interest in my house, as well as in me, to the great benefit of both. She was a tiger with workmen and defended my interests far better than I could myself.

She came twice a week. She would begin by fiercely scolding me about some of my sins of omission, of which there were many, only relenting when I was properly penitent. She had a wonderful gift for malapropisms. One day she was lecturing me about the kitchen floor, a subject dear to her heart; she wanted to clean it with "a pint of distergent and a pint of pneumonia to a gallon of water." Another time she had been "bitten by a midget." I particularly enjoyed her description of my father's struggles with the inventory when letting the flats at La Verdure: "the General and the infantry." One had of course to receive these remarks without comment or the flicker of a smile, and it was just as well that usually there was no other witness.

***

Labour came to power in February 1974 as a minority government in a split Parliament with a manifesto promising to leave the EEC. Both parties were split on Europe but at this point the Tory leadership was firmly pro, as was most of Whitehall. Trying to strengthen his hand, Harold Wilson called another election in October the same year and this time got a majority of just three; his manifesto promised to renegotiate the terms of British membership and to put the results to the people in a referendum. It is clear in retrospect that Wilson intended Britain to remain in the EEC but he had huge problems with the antis in his own party including the Cabinet Ministers Tony Benn and Peter Shore. Some of the officials in departments with anti-EEC Ministers colluded against them in a way that completely cut across the traditional doctrine of ministerial responsibility. The febrile political atmosphere fascinated me.

By the spring of 1975 the negotiations were done. Wilson had defined his negotiating aims in pretty slippery terms and the only substantial change conceded by the EEC was to establish a complicated financial mechanism that put a ceiling on how much Britain might have to pay into the Community coffers. It was a tense day when the Cabinet met to decide whether the outcome justified recommending yes in the promised referendum. There had been a frenzy of briefing beforehand. I had drafted the brief on the results of renegotiation as a whole; even at the time it struck me as peculiar that someone at my level should attempt to tell the Foreign Secretary and Prime Minister what to say on a subject on which they had clearly made up their minds. It was difficult to arrange the arguments in so wide a sphere – the history, the alternatives and their dangers, the realities of life in the Community. However, my draft got through, embroidered but gratifyingly unscathed. My other effort, the sovereignty brief, was scarcely altered at all. I was still a bit surprised to find myself an accepted expert in such a very legalistic field.

For officials there was nothing to do while the politicians argued it out. Wilson was expected to win but I listened to the evening news nervously. I felt very invested in the outcome and for want of anything more useful to do I took to my diary. About this time I began to write it up more frequently. I have drawn heavily on the entries in the rest of this chapter to give a picture of the day-to-day pressures involved in being in the eye of the political storm, if only in a support role.

London, 17 March 1975

One has the feeling of a play in which people are playing preordained parts. There can be few if any of the people involved who have not by now made up their minds on the merits of membership. But still the drama has to be played out until the final pro and anti division lines are drawn.

It has been very interesting to watch Callaghan's development over the last year. (Watch is scarcely the right word because at my level one never meets him; but his trenchant and highly political personality pervades our work nonetheless.) In retrospect I think he had probably come to the conclusion before he came to the Foreign Office that Britain could not afford to leave the Community. But he certainly did his best to dispel any such idea in the early days. The one occasion I saw him in action was when Ambassadors in the EEC countries were called back for a conference just about a year ago, when Labour had been in office a bare couple of weeks. He was determined to get the message over that he was unconvinced, and a very uncompromising message it was too. It clearly shook the Ambassadors. His first speech in the Council was in the same tone, though it contained some obviously vital pointers to how he proposed to play the hand: negotiate if possible within the Treaties; in the meantime participate in Community business as long as the outcome of renegotiation was not prejudged...

The months leading up to the first referendum on British membership of the European Community were extremely busy. Though a Referendum Unit was set up in the FCO this did not lighten the stream of work coming to me which I often took home at night in a locked official briefcase. This was accepted practice for documents graded up to Confidential but strictly not for Secret and above. I often ended up writing Ministerial speeches on my bedroom floor with a glass of wine to help the flow of words.

The referendum was held on 5 June 1975, and 67.2% voted to stay in the European Community on the renegotiated terms.

26 June 1975 – and a long time later!

My political diary has been lagging a bit recently. I meant to write in the moment of triumph but was too busy celebrating. It is pleasant to be associated with a policy which succeeds beyond expectation. Looking back I suppose that the Cabinet decision was the true turning point, but there were moments afterwards when the outcome was far from clear. First when the majority of junior ministers declared themselves against. Then one had the 3-day debate in the Commons with its vote of over 2 to 1 in favour, quickly followed by the Labour Party Conference voting by a similar majority the other way.

The public campaign was at the same time engrossing and a bit of a bore. The arguments became so familiar that one could see the reply before it left the racquet. Those on the anti side over-simplified often to the point of distortion or untruth. The arguments on the pro side had greater respect for accuracy, often qualified to the extent that impact was lost. It is very difficult to judge the public impact of the campaign. One feared that those not involved must be numbed by the sheer weight of words flung at them by either side. In personal terms, I suspect Benn will be the politician who gained most by it all – his name crowned a scare headline every other day.

> *But I also think it is true that the ultimate splendid result owed as much to those who opposed the market as to those who campaigned for it.*
>
> *And it really was a splendid result. Even after the first fine careless rapture is over, that remains the case. An over 2 to 1 vote in favour, on a higher poll than most people predicted, and spread so evenly across the country that all areas (with the trivial exceptions of the Shetlands and the Western Isles) were clearly proved to be in favour. It really was a great day for Europe, and a good day for Britain too.*

Celia Hensman and I went to Brussels to celebrate, a slightly crazy thing to do for a rather special weekend. It was blazing hot and Leslie Fielding with whom we were staying gave a champagne garden party at which he insisted on reading the results in all the languages of the Community. He stood on the steps dressed in a kilt with Celia and me standing below like a pair of Angkor guardian animals. I was quite pleased with myself for taking so unpromising a role in such good part. But then it was a very good weekend.

I can't avoid comparisons with the Brexit referendum of 2016. It may be vainglorious but I think my generation made a much better job of putting forward positive arguments about the benefits of membership. It helped enormously, particularly in that age of greater deference, that the great majority of press and business leaders were in favour of membership. The sovereignty issue was glossed over in 1975, but the public was not then much interested in this question, the British government had a veto with which it could block any changes and the Community was not in a dynamic phase anyhow. One could argue that the EEC was a success story which Britain should be part of. I regret that I have lost my tee-shirt with EUROPE OR BUST printed across the front.

By 2016 the situation was much more complicated. The move from European Economic Community to European Union was far more than just a change of name. Margaret Thatcher of all unlikely people had agreed to majority voting in many practical fields (and thus to the loss of our veto) and the increasing number of members with their different special interests had created a host of new problems. To the horror of many in Britain a further pooling of sovereignty seemed the only answer if the Union was not to become totally bogged down. It was all too easy to present the EU as a failing organization and to exploit worries about immigration.

As I write this in 2023 more and more people are realising that leaving the EU was a disastrous mistake which has added greatly to Britain's other problems. But the subject is still painfully divisive. This is not the place to refight the referendum campaign, but for me these issues feel acutely personal, and when I was asked in late 2019 to write an article about Brexit for a newsletter in Burgundy where I have my second home I let rip.

***

Life wasn't all work. I had reconnected with Daat, my Dutch friend from Oxford, during my time in the Hague. He came to stay in London during leave from the American University of Cairo where he now worked. The weekend happened to be the climax of the Festival of Sail in the Thames. This was an occasion loaded with nostalgia because once the new barrier was built across the river the following year it would never again be possible for big ships to come upstream to Tower Bridge. We went to watch the tall ships lying by the Tower, their rigging picked out against the sunset-reddened sky. There must have been six or eight of them upstream of the bridge, the *Danmark* the most beautiful of all. We watched the bridge open for a late arrival, relatively small in the distance but with masts reaching close to the span above the opening drawbridge and with crew lining the rigging. It was a fascinating sight and I determined to get up early on Saturday morning to watch the departure, a grand procession of boats setting off for Southend where the clipper race to Australia would start the following day. They were striving to beat the 80-odd day record of the old grain ships.

London, 5 September 1975

8.30 at Woolwich. It was an effort after a late night and Daat who had previously sounded enthusiastic obviously lost heart. Anyhow for once I knew what I wanted to do and my determination got us there just as the first of the tall ships came into sight. There were a fair number of people, even at that early hour, so I followed an enterprising few onto a jetty which offered a good vantage point. At the far end were one or two boats lying, including a fine Thames barge with tan sails furled. People were getting on and off and some of the men who seemed to be in charge greeted us cheerfully. More of the tall ships came down the river and, wanting to get a better view for my camera, I asked if we could get on board. "Make yourselves comfortable" came the reply, so we got on and sat down, fascinated by the stately ships passing in the slightly misty morning light.

It is what happened next that makes me feel a bit ashamed. I was aware of some activity of loosening ropes, and it seemed as if we were going to move along a bit for a better view. I realized I should have got off, but after all I had asked permission to get on and there was so much to see. Then the boat gathered way, motored gently upstream for a bit, and suddenly swung round to take up a place in the procession.

I didn't know what to do and as time passed began to get increasingly worried. Daat and I had taken seats up near the bows, away from the bulk of the people, but two or three of the men who seemed to be crew came and went and chatted to us a bit. It was from one of them that I discovered that we were bound for Southend. The weather got worse and a piercing breeze got up. We, ready for another hot day and expecting to be back for breakfast, had no warm clothes. Other people were drinking and it was clear that there was food down below. The old crew man who had befriended us said that we should go down and help ourselves. But how could we?

I eventually decided that confession was the only sensible course and asked one of my new friends whose boat it was. He directed me to a vast man in glasses who stood at the top of the hatch drinking with another man even vaster. They listened to my lame story with some amusement, twitting me with the prospect that the next stop would be Sydney. In fact they could scarcely have been kinder in the circumstances. The owner of the boat (who it turned out later was a Woolwich publican and had bought the barge earlier in the year to convert it for charter) urged us to go below and we were plied with food and drink. (Fortunately there was a fully equipped paying bar.)

From then on the day developed another sort of fascination, observing the assorted groups of people among whom we found ourselves. There was a group of drinking companions from the owner's pub, cockneys all. The super fat man, obesely repellent, rather like Peter Ustinov but with a black eye for extra colour, was Harvey. He was a life and soul character, genuinely friendly and putting us at ease to start with, increasingly sentimental as the day wore on and the liquor flowed. There was also John, who had been a doctor and lots of other things, but now drives a taxi, a man with a sensitive face, anxious to tell Daat of his time in Egypt at the end of the war, and to tell me of his beautiful daughter… There was also a booky and a variety of others. Another definite social group turned out to be a party of policemen and their wives, invited en bloc by the owner, from the police station opposite his pub. I picked up some useful information about the London crime rate. It was because these two groups did not know each other that we must have been assumed to belong to the party too. In fact it became clear as the day passed that they were like oil and water and did not mix. Indeed there was a certain amount of repressed hostility. "You can see them snarling at us," John said to me. "They never let themselves go."

The pub party certainly did let themselves go, and as first the whisky and then the gin gave out the drinks became very mixed. It was cold and damp in the afternoon and we were driven down from the deck. "We'll have a burial at sea," said Harry, and then began a charade which I found fascinating and rather horrid in its intensity... Harry produced from somewhere a Union Jack which he laid out on the long wooden bench running down the centre of the boat that was the top of the keel. He persuaded a portly young man to lie on it, then enshrouded him and intoned a mock jingo prayer. As the joke showed signs of petering out, "an autopsy" was the cry, and a string of unlikely objects were produced from the supine figure. It was the publican who acted as agent provocateur by producing a pair of maracaibos shaped uncannily like male sex organs. A roar greeted their appearance. "A transplant," cried Harry, and set to work with a sawing motion (I think he actually had a knife of sorts) on the unresisting body... One felt that the victim would have to protest to preserve a shred of self-respect as first they shoved the maracaibos between his legs, then turned him over unceremoniously and mock hammered a bung up his arse. The game could very easily have turned sour. I was thankful when some of the police party made a move to go on deck and I felt I could follow without giving offence to our strange new friends.

We got home somehow, tired and somehow subdued by an extraordinary day. But at this point my diary again changes gear rather abruptly and I should set the scene for what follows.

***

It was a turbulent time politically and Dennis Healey, as Chancellor of the Exchequer, was in the thick of it. Redistribution of income and wealth was a main plank of Labour policy and Healey had taken office threatening to tax the rich "until the pips squeak." However, as inflation took off he was obliged to change tack and try to control wages. Meanwhile sterling slid while the gap in the balance of payments yawned. In December 1976 the Government was obliged to seek a loan from the IMF which meant submitting the British economy to IMF supervision. Healey was one of the biggest beasts in the political jungle of that time and also one of the most controversial. At a dinner party given by Frank Melville of *Time Life* I found myself sitting across the table from Healey and next to Bill Rodgers, then Minister of State for Defence. The other guests were almost all American journalists and Frank M had clearly staged the party to provide contacts cum briefing for his team. A very super evening it was too.

4 April 1976

Healey held forth in super-confident mood. He had just announced another package of minor economic measures (details forgotten, I regret to say) which had had a good press reception, and Healey was very ready to add his own congratulations. Bill Rodgers, from beside me, was anxious to make his mark – slightly the would-be prefect with Healey the established senior. Rodgers commented that among his constituents he noticed a willingness to make sacrifices when these were called for in the national good. They were stirred when Healey gave a strong lead but disillusioned and disorientated when the line softened. Healey admitted readily that this was so at constituency level. He said that in carrying out his economic policy he had to deal with four levels of reaction. Within the Unions there were three – workers, the shop steward level, and union management. He thought he had educated the management level and had no serious problem with the workers. It was the middle level that caused the problems. But his major achievement of education, he said, had been within the Cabinet. He obviously regarded the education of Michael Foot to support an incomes policy as his chef d'oeuvre.

Apart from the content of what he said what struck me most was the manner. Tough, amiable, the great man holding forth rather than the conversationalist. His talk was larded with bad language, which his wife afterwards (apologetically?) said was adopted as a suitable way of talking to grass roots – perhaps as part of a conscious effort to shed a donnish intellectual image? It was a touch of irony that within a couple of weeks Healey should have got himself into such trouble by suggesting that the left wing of the PLP were "going out of their tiny Chinese minds" in arguing for an easing of the incomes policy.

Among my direct responsibilities the issue of direct elections to the European Assembly, as it was then known, had been gradually coming to the boil and, much to the chagrin of officials, Cabinet time and again dodged the necessary decisions. We finally got landed with a horrific timetable: an all-day Cabinet on 26 March to discuss European matters – not only direct elections but also the Tindemans Report, which proposed far-reaching changes in the powers of the Community institutions and common policies in crucial fields such as foreign affairs and education. It caused a great stir at the time but led to virtually nothing. Then there were to be debates on direct elections in both Houses of Parliament (with the Commons in the end deciding to extend the debate to two days) and the European Council meeting at which Heads of Government had set themselves "to finalize a draft Constitution" on 1 and 2 April.

On 16 March Wilson had most unexpectedly announced that he was resigning. Callaghan, Healey and Foot were all standing to succeed him. Callaghan, still Foreign Secretary, was the favourite and clearly had other things on his mind when we submitted a draft Cabinet paper and various other negotiating points on direct elections.

4 April 1976

Positive reaction came there virtually nil. Then on 26 March we heard that he had gone into Cabinet and immediately announced that he had decided to set up a Select Committee as proposed by the anti-Marketeers. He had not of course sought anyone's advice first, and I must say my first reaction was gloom and despondency. It seemed the all too familiar recipe for postponing decision, and the fact that the idea had originated with the antis was particularly discouraging at a time when Callaghan no doubt had an eye to popularity in all parts of the Party. In retrospect I think I misjudged the situation... In this field of political canniness he is certainly a past master.

Anyhow it was a rough few days for us and I felt flat exhausted by last weekend, during which I finished up work on the complicated brief for the European Council. The weekend before I had written an opening speech for Callaghan to use in the debate – a draft into which I received a series of requests to bring in new points as the week progressed, culminating with a bit on the Select Committee on Friday 26. Imagine my dismay to be telephoned on Sunday evening (28th) to hear that 16 points in the Secretary of State's inimitable scrawl would be waiting with the

Resident Clerk at crack of dawn for incorporation into yet another revise of the wretched speech. Fortunately the adrenalin flowed quite well that morning because I got him his speech by 12.45. John Fretwell and I got summoned about 2pm to explain to him the Parliamentary procedure preceding ratification. He was in characteristic mood of jovial pugnacity. He was friendly to us, but positively bit his PS, John Weston, who wanted to check he had got in a particular point: "I am really not the idiot the press describe me as, you know."

Then to the House where the debate began soon after 3.30. I was gratified that Callaghan delivered virtually all my speech, embroidering it as he went along. It served its purpose quite well. The Select Committee idea had a general welcome and by suggesting (a) that it could not consider the principle of direct elections which was in the Treaty, and (b) that it must work at the speed required by decisions in the Community Callaghan succeeded in disarming potential criticism of delaying tactics.

The rest of the debate was of considerable interest to me – probably more than it would be to those less involved in the subject. There was an outstanding speech by Douglas Hurd, his first from the front bench, which clearly foreshadows a considerable political future. I was intrigued to hear David Steele, for the Liberals, putting the inevitable case for PR very well. He has always been something of a pin-up of mine. Jenkins opened the second day for the Government, an adequate rather than inspiring speech, though clearly setting him to be counted on the right side. Hattersley wound up. He is a hard-working politician who writes his own speeches. I have always got on quite well with him and did again on this occasion when he accepted some of my thoughts and included them in his speech…

Anyway it has been a good week for my own ambitions. April 1st saw me promoted to Counsellor. Close friends have been comfortingly nice about it, and the occasion felt a bit like a birthday with cards, presents and a party in the evening which Daddy gave for me. I find it difficult to believe that it is really me that has reached such august levels. Let me try to maintain a difficulty in taking myself too seriously. But I have certainly been glad of the bouquets that have come my way this week over my EEC brief and the speech for the debate.

It didn't take second sight to spot that Douglas Hurd was a coming man. He went on to become a very thoughtful Foreign Secretary whom I saw quite a lot of later on. I never met the colourful Dennis Healey again, to my regret, but after leaving the FCO, I did find myself on different committees chaired by Jim Callaghan and Roy Jenkins. Both were by this stage old and long retired, and in need of a bit of practical support. Old civil service habits die hard so I made a point of being on hand with the right papers. It was a small tribute to two very different men who had borne the burden of great office in their day, both of whom I admired. It is not just nostalgia that makes me think that the major politicians of that period were much more impressive than those of today.

Back to my story; when Callaghan became Prime Minister in April 1976, he made Anthony Crosland Foreign Secretary. Crosland was one of the intellectuals of the Labour Party and had written an influential book called *The Future of Socialism*, which offered a non-Marxist vision. He had had a distinguished ministerial career and his arrival was greeted in the Foreign Office with much interest. But on 19 February he died. Not a great Foreign Secretary, but he had seemed to be getting into his stride after a slow start and he was increasingly getting the respect, and perhaps real liking, of the Office.

19 February 1977

The few times I saw him, always in fairly big meetings, he played a laconic role, always pleasant, donnishly challenging rather than commanding, and throwing in the occasional dry witty aside – often difficult to hear through the ever-present cigar. In retrospect I realize that I have never heard anyone report him as being ill-tempered, nervy or domineering on any occasion. That must be rare among politicians who have such strains upon them.

Then out of the blue last Sunday it was announced he had been taken ill at Oxford over the weekend, and gradually it became clear that he was dying. Consciousness of this fact hung over our work all last week, never far absent from the mind. It was particularly brought home to me by the morbid irony of drafting a telegram which I suddenly realized would issue as signed by a man who might never again regain consciousness.

The announcement of David Owen as the new Foreign Secretary came as a bombshell. As Minister of State in the FCO dealing with Europe he was relatively junior. At 38 he was the youngest Foreign Secretary since Eden. One newspaper headline read simply “Doctor Who?” But No 10 emphasised that this was no stop-gap appointment. There were mixed views in the Office – relief, at least on the EEC side, at not having to start again at educating a new Foreign Secretary, and misgivings about his acerbity. I had already seen quite a lot of him on the subject of direct elections which he thought a bad idea but ultimately inevitable. One day one of his Private Secretaries phoned me to pass on the Minister's irritation at my department's cautious views. "He says you've got no balls!" he said. "In my case that's a compliment," I could honestly reply. But there is no denying I had a soft spot for David Owen despite all. My own view was coloured by his undeniable charm – a feminine weakness I was careful not to display too obviously to my colleagues! He was difficult at times, refusing to listen to what people had to say to him, and looking with down-turned mouth like one of the demon gods in the tug-of-war at Angkhor; at other times the infectious smile and glinting humour were irresistible.

21 February 1977

I wonder what David Owen himself is feeling tonight – as if a fairy tale had come true, I imagine, a fulfilment of fantasy. By chance I went along to his Private Office at 6.30 to deliver some papers on direct elections on which I was hoping to get a steer from the Minister. I asked Roger Westbrook, the Private Secretary, if he had any news. "None," he said, "the Minister does not know either." The announcement was on the news at 8pm. I doubt if I will get any comments on my piece on electoral systems!

I certainly wasn't the only one to be surprised. Peter Petrie, who had taken over as Head of EID(I), commented that the many rivals who lost out because of David Owen's meteoric rise would be looking for ways to cut him down to size. This would, Peter thought, be bad for the Office, particularly with a report pending from the Central Policy Review Staff on their review of Britain's international representation. Owen would have to fight hard for his position. He had no established power base in the Party nor yet much of a public reputation. But I had no doubt that the Office would close ranks behind him, swallowing any misgivings and giving him all possible support. The Office always wanted their man to perform well.

Britain had the Presidency of the EEC for the first half of 1977 which meant chairing all meetings. A Presidency Unit was set up in the Foreign Office and there was much talk about how the time in the chair could be used to further the British agenda. My own view was that the system worked best when chairmanship functions were kept quite separate from national objectives. The weeks leading up to the meetings of the EEC Heads of Government were always a pattern of rising frenzy and when in March Britain chaired the European Council for the first time things were worse than usual. There had been much dissatisfaction with the organization of the previous meeting in the Hague, and various proposals were circulated with the aim of making sure that discussions were properly prepared and led to decisions. The British paper (largely my draft!) was full of good precepts which we were then obliged to try to live up to. It was full of the sort of detail that the great tended to overlook and my greatest contribution was probably to try to put a shape on the subject matter as it gradually became clear what people would wish to talk about.

It seemed no time until the European Council next met in London at the end of June and the frenzy set in again.

11 June 1977

Yesterday was a fiendish day. I had worked late the night before to get going on the first draft of a steering brief, and the pressure began building up as soon as I got to the Office. Brenda (my PA) didn't turn up till 10.30 which was an added frustration. First chore was to get out a minute about the Council on 21 June for a meeting the SoS had called at lunch-time…Then a meeting with Donald Maitland and senior officials in the Cabinet Office…Back to launch my draft steering brief. Interruption at lunch-time as Rodric Braithwaite from UKRep came in to talk about various things on his mind, ending up in his sabotaging a submission of Peter Petrie's with a draft letter from SoS to President of the European Parliament which Rodric thought would go down badly…Just got to the canteen in time for a sandwich which I took back to my desk. Then an attempt to get down to routine work, when Peter P returned from SoS's meeting… The fall-out as far as I was concerned was two questions, both highly complex, on which replies were required by close of play: Could we include in the direct elections bill a clause such as the French Government had proposed to safeguard against extension of the EP's powers? Could we include a clause saying that the salaries of British MEPs would be fixed at Westminster rather than by the Community? Both would cause endless problems if tried.

The Treaty providing for direct elections to the European Parliament was finally signed in September 1976 and it had then to be approved by national parliaments before ratification. The whole issue was very sensitive in the House of Commons, which was jealous of a rival centre of power. Hitherto members of what was called the European Assembly were also members of their national parliaments so some MPs would be losing perks too. Pro-Europeans argued that a directly elected parliament was necessary to hold the Commission accountable and thus a step towards eliminating the democratic deficit.

I was not very satisfied with the papers I finally produced and before I was through I had a blinding headache. But I hoped I had headed Owen away from ideas that seemed to me fraught with difficulty. I believed that he was genuinely prepared to think again if a good case were put to him and prided myself on being able sometimes to find the right wavelength to get things across. Owen had the kind of mind which threw off ideas ceaselessly. It was his way of learning, I mused. He probably also believed that it was right to keep officials on their toes, and that creative tension had this effect. The result was a lot of unthought out ideas, which we all had to treat with due seriousness, putting up carefully argued comments. But I had to admit that they did also sometimes throw a new light on a problem.

15 June 1977

My two papers reappeared early this week – devoid of all my cautionary phrases about preliminary views, complex situations, etc – in the shape of minutes addressed to the Home Secretary, with copies to PM and other Ministers. Both minutes read "I think Ministers should now consider whether it is desirable to include in our direct elections bill a provision to..." and then launched into the carefully balanced Collings prose designed (by me) to bring out the disadvantages!

Then I heard a rumour that I was about to be posted to Paris as Information Counsellor. It was more than a rumour really because Peter Petrie, who had a knack of picking up personal gossip, had learned it from someone on the Board which was to consider my nomination that day. Peter later reported that the Board went quite well. But it still had to go to the Ambassador – and perhaps the PUS – before it was settled. In the meantime I was sworn to absolute secrecy. It was a job I had long thought would suit me very well. Lovely to live in Paris, of course, and my spell in News Department, which I greatly enjoyed and apparently got glowing reports for, should provide a good grounding. Peter Petrie worried me, however, by his description of

Nicko Henderson as an Ambassador to work for: a man who wanted things done his way without explaining what that was, a man who didn't like women unless they were young, pretty and flirtatious. (That twisted the knife slightly but I didn't wince!) My predecessor had apparently broken under the strain. At least, Peter said comfortingly, Personnel Department would not write anyone off on the basis of one of Nicko's reports because he had such a difficult record! All this was surprising to me as well as worrying. My slight dealings with Nicholas Henderson had given me the picture of a pleasant man of good manners and some charm if a bit distant. I had certainly heard some rumours that he was a difficult boss but I decided not to let Peter scare me off. I didn't see how I could turn down a job like that, particularly since I had previously said no to Canberra on the grounds that it was too far away and asked for something in Europe instead. I made plans to brush up my French and my wardrobe. Life suddenly seemed full of promise again – with new opportunities waiting to be explored and new people to meet.

David Owen gave a drinks party to celebrate the end of the UK Presidency. There were about 50 people in his big corner office overlooking the Park where I remembered seeing so many Foreign Secretaries. David Owen was at his most outgoing, greeting everyone, going round with a jug of Pimms and collecting the girls from his office who had gone on working. He couldn't have been more charming, and as usual I found myself succumbing absolutely. I was thrilled to be greeted personally and, when I held out my hand with a smile and thanks at the end, to get a friendly clasp of the arm and a word about my work ahead for the direct elections debate. The party was also a useful opportunity to talk to people about my new job in Paris. I got a bit more of an idea of why Nicko Henderson had the reputation of being difficult to work for – an egoist, people said, and very publicity conscious. But I was thoroughly excited and looked forward to Paris with high spirits.

First there was the Direct Elections Bill to get through Parliament. After two long days of rehearsing familiar points on either side the Bill was approved by 394 to 141 votes. It was a bigger majority than people expected – indeed it was something of a triumph. I spent much of those two days sitting in "the official box," which is on the floor of the Commons to the right behind the Speaker's chair. It is reminiscent of a church pew and equally uncomfortable.

7 July 1977

I found it a nerve-racking experience, and come back literally shaking at the knees, though a drink and something to eat are helping to restore the fibres as I write. David Owen was winding up. He sent word last week that he didn't want us to draft a speech but only to provide "factual notes" which we duly did. I was a bit concerned to hear this morning that he hadn't read the notes properly yet. But far worse was to come. He sauntered over to the box in the early stages of the debate to say that he didn't know what he was going to say and would we please take note of points made saying by whom (with constituency) and providing a note of reply.

I had decided to take the middle of the afternoon off anyway because one can only sit in that box so long. So I spent the time preparing a few extra passages on subjects raised so far in the hopes of providing the framework for a speech. This may have been a tactical mistake because I had only just got back and taken over in the box from Ivor Roberts when the SoS summoned me out to discuss what he would say. It was not an encouraging beginning: he said that he had never looked forward to a speech in the Commons less. That the whole thing in his view was a mistake and that at least the bill wouldn't pass. (I hope he meant this session but suspect he didn't.) Then he opened our pack of "factual notes" and started going through them one by one, asking who had raised the questions covered... He wouldn't touch the rather modest passage I had provided on why direct elections were a good thing... It was a fairly combative performance though he was personally quite pleasant and even once threw in a "love" when arguing down what I was trying to say. (It might just as well have been "ducky"!) Special bon mots were that we should always talk of it as the "Assembly" hereafter, that we should make sure that the salaries of members were "non-obligatory expenditure" (this would guarantee an institutional row) and that we should get the section 1(3) requirement (ie the procedure necessary for making the Community Agreement enforceable in the UK courts) into the bill when it is resubmitted in the autumn. I feebly parried, but found myself agreeing when he commented that there seemed to be an awful lot of things officials did not want him to say. I left the meeting with one or two points to check and with the dreadful feeling that he didn't really have anything to say which would add up to a coherent speech.

In fact I needn't have worried. As the time came for the SoS to speak, the House was filling up and it began to get very noisy. He started off against a barrage of background noise and there were continual interruptions. He very wisely concentrated on a few points – and thrust at the Opposition for their free vote on entry in October 1971. He used my piece on the date, a bit about the Assembly being complementary rather than competitive with Parliament and finally (I am glad to say) some quite tough stuff about the Government's determination to use its best endeavours. It barely lasted out the 20 minutes, but against such a noisy background it was quite adequate and any detailed argument would have been wasted.

So in the end it was quite satisfactory, and it was quite exciting watching MPs massing for the vote. Of the anti Ministers it was only Peter Shore, as far as I could see, who actually sat on the front bench while David Owen was speaking. His appearance was greeted by a roar, as was a fleeting glimpse of Tony Benn who put his head into the Chamber and withdrew.

When the SoS swung out of the Chamber at the end and his Private Secretaries swung into line and made off to his office I hesitated fatally as to whether I should go too and got left behind. Anyone with a natural ration of self-importance would have gone and picked up any obiter dicta – and even possibly a drink! My morale was restored next day when David Owen sent me a message of thanks, saying he was sorry to have missed me. He was apparently quite pleased with everything, except the Deputy Speaker for letting the uproar develop to such proportions while he was speaking. I certainly sympathised with him on that.

EID(I), as it was so inelegantly called, was certainly the toughest job of my diplomatic career. Work took over my life almost entirely and there were times when it got me down. I contemplated leaving the Diplomatic Service and went for job interviews in the European Commission and at NATO. I am glad that they did not work out because in the long run I got great satisfaction from belonging to a Service of clever and interesting people most of whom I liked and admired. And in retrospect I am glad to have survived such a challenging job and to have had the experience of being so close to the heart of politics. It has certainly given me more sympathy for ministers who must try to decide what best to do amid the pressure of the many different crises competing for their attention. My next job was to test me in a quite different way.

Chapter 13

GOOD DAYS AND BAD DAYS IN PARIS (1977–1980)

Paris was regarded as a plum posting in the Diplomatic Service, and I was thrilled when I learned that I was to go there as Press Counsellor and Head of the Information Section. I had greatly enjoyed my dealings with journalists and I already loved France. With my background in Beirut and the largely French-speaking Secretariat in Brussels I was not afraid of the language. So all seemed set fair. I was only slightly worried about Peter Petrie's warning that I might have problems with the Ambassador. Brushing such thoughts aside, I enrolled for intensive French classes with the Diplomatic Language School and started on the usual round of briefings. I also wanted to spend a little time immersed in French before launching on the Parisian scene. A journalist friend gave me an introduction to an elderly couple called Maingeneaux who invited me to spend a week as a paying guest in the Château d'Olbreuse in the Charentes. The village had the wonderful name of Mauzé-sur-le-Mignon and it was a place where the world seemed to have stood still. I lived in the château and joined the Maingeneaux for chat and a drink of Pineau every evening. They were charming and generous hosts and refused to take any payment when I left.

Paris, when I got there, seemed like a different world, fast moving and competitive. At my first dinner party my French neighbour explained that to be a social success in Paris "*il faut briller!*" I was a bit concerned that sparkling was not my default mode. The Embassy was full of highly intelligent people so I was on my mettle there too. It was all very stimulating. France seemed dynamic at a time when Britain's economy was in the doldrums. These were the days when Giscard d'Estaing was President of France and Raymond Barre was Prime Minister. The haughty Giscard had a tiresome habit of measuring France's prosperity against the situation in Britain to illustrate the successes of his own administration.

Memories of the second world war were fading, and in any case sensitive given France's mixed record. Anglo-French relations were dominated, as so often afterwards, by problems relating to the EEC. First and foremost was the question of Britain's contributions to the common budget, an issue which had loomed large in the entry negotiations a few years earlier. The Community's system of financing was intended to ensure that it had its own funding – or *ressources propres* – and did not depend on the day-to-day agreement of the member states. The proceeds from taxes on imported goods including agricultural levies went straight to the common kitty and, if this did not produce enough money to cover the budget, the Community could call on up to 1% of the proceeds of a value added tax. Britain's problem was that it depended far more on goods imported from outside the EEC than did the original member states, most of whose trade was with each other. The issue had been fudged during the entry negotiations with a declaration to the effect that if unacceptable situations arose, remedies would be found. The convoluted formula agreed during renegotiation had never been triggered and the British contribution to the budget remained very high.

When Margaret Thatcher became Prime Minister in 1979, she increasingly stridently demanded, "I want my money back!" The French, who were net gainers from the existing system, were equally vehement in describing British demands as "*non communautaire*." This, and the argument about Britain's import of quantities of New Zealand lamb at prices which undercut French producers, provided the background noise to much of my work in the Information Section. The French, or at least Parisians, are intensely competitive and love this sort of argument. A British diplomat could not go to a smart dinner party without being attacked on such subjects and I got pretty tired of trotting out the counter-arguments. But it was a small price to pay for the joy of living in such a beautiful city and when official life got a bit too tense I could escape to the very different rhythm of the French countryside.

There were more chances to see to my parents and telephoning was a practical possibility in a way it was not from South-East Asia. There were thus fewer letters home but let's begin with the first one, written from the Hotel Plaza Mirabeau, 10 avenue Emile Zola:

Paris 15^{e}, 18 September 1977

My week at Olbreuse was a great success. The Ms were absolutely delightful, and I feel that I had a glimpse of the real French countryside which can have changed little for centuries. It was incredibly peaceful under the golden autumn sun which shone almost the whole time I was there. I had lunch with the Ms (apart from my day à velo) and dined mostly with the Bicyclub (pronounced Beeceeclūb) and in between pottered around looking at Romanesque churches (the area has countless of them, all alive with sculpture), read the French papers, and painted a not very successful picture of the Château. All very restful and invigorating

Paris is a little daunting, but I think I have come through my first week O.K. It is a huge Embassy. The morning meeting, at which the senior members of the Embassy meet, consists of about 20 people. There is something slightly incongruous about the diplomats meeting beneath the heavily gilded ceiling, with painted nymphs in various degrees of undress looking on. It is an interesting occasion for the newcomer to see how everyone performs. I have broken silence once or twice but haven't said very much!

The main excitement of my first week was the visit of Ian Trethowan, the new head of the BBC. It slowly dawned on me that Trethowan was coming at the Ambassador's suggestion and that the Ambassador had forgotten that he had invited him. To add to the complications the BBC had got the impression (probably correctly) that the Ambassador was against some of their pet projects and had been queering their pitch with the French. All made more difficult by my ignorance of the intricacies of wavelengths and frequencies and the other technical details which are the essentials of broadcasting. Anyhow I decided the best I could hope for was to get the Ambassador to ask questions and be as open-minded as possible. The meetings went reasonably well, but I had no clue how I had scored in the Ambassador's personal rating, which seemed to be vital to one's success in the Embassy.

The Ambassador gave a dinner for Trethowan at the Residence, my first sight of this gorgeous building and its lovely gardens. It was bought for the Duke of Wellington when he became Ambassador after Waterloo and had previously belonged to Napoleon's sister Pauline Borghese. We had a sumptuous dinner and it was all very glittering. The guests included a cross-section of personalities from the press and information world and some very elegant ladies with whom, I was told, the Ambassador liked to leaven his invitation lists. The most striking was a blonde lady from the Protocol Section at the Elysée, with a beautifully boned face, and a floating silk trouser suit, backless and pretty well completely transparent above the waist in front. Definitely eye-catching. I went demurely clad in a tucked black chiffon blouse and flowered skirt.

My predecessor came back to Paris the following week to say his goodbyes and he took me to call on some key French editors. There was a farewell dinner for him at the Residence. This time I hoped to escape before 1.45 am. Paris dinners were very late, with invitations for 8.30 and guests arriving around 9pm. I wondered how my stamina would last out. Anyhow it was all rather exciting, and my spirits were high.

Meanwhile I was house-hunting. I eventually settled on a flat recommended by the Petries who had one in the same block in Passy. Peter's wife Lydwine was French and worked at the Louvre so they had homes in London and Paris. My flat belonged to Serge Boisdevaix, the French Ambassador in Bonn. It was comfortable and rather grand and once a month I had to visit the Ambassador's mother, who lived on the top floor, to hand over my rental in cash. I could drive to the office in the rue du Faubourg Saint-Honoré and park in the Embassy courtyard.

8, Rue des Eaux, Paris 16e, 22 November 1977

I am beginning to find my feet a bit in my work – a bit hesitantly; not least because I don't think other people are very clear what they expect of me. But at least I am becoming a bit clearer about what I think I can most usefully do, which is to get out and meet the French press and the various organizations concerned with promoting the UK, to try to find out what they expect of me, and by asking questions to build up as good a picture as I can of how the various papers tick and of what their angle is on the UK and on French internal politics. On the whole the people I have called on have been very friendly, though I suspect a number have been rather surprised to see me. Perhaps other information officers don't invite themselves to call out of the blue! In some ways the question of relating what my section is doing to the work of the rest of the Embassy is more difficult. It is not a very organized Embassy, and so large that it is difficult to keep up with what is going on. And the staff of my section, while individually very nice, are all a bit on the defensive having seen many of their colleagues axed over the last 2–3 years, and fearing the axe may be about to fall again.

There was yet another and even more glittering dinner party at the Residence to mark the Silver Jubilee with a buffet for about 250 guests distributed in three different rooms. Lady Henderson, who was very interested in fashion, had invited the main British fashion houses to display their wares. The dress display took place between the smoked salmon and the serious catering and did the rounds of all three rooms.

> *The mannequins were tall thin girls – several black – who walked with an arrogant, backwards leaning, hip-swinging gait. The clothes varied from the beautifully feminine to the sick. The worst were Zandra Rhodes: mock rips and tatters studded with sequins. A number of the dresses I had seen advertised in Vogue – eg. some embroidered tartans by Bill Gibbs. Zandra Rhodes herself was as odd as any of her clothes: her fringe was dyed green, and her eyebrows had been painted in asymmetrically so that one was long and one was short… It was a glittering assembly of guests too – Princess Alexandra, who seems charmingly simple and unaffected, and looked enchanting as long as she stood still… Princess Grace in a slightly matronly caftan, Princess Caroline looking virginal, accompanied by her young man…*

Working in the smartest part of Paris had its temptations. As I walked down the rue du Faubourg Saint-Honoré one morning I passed a sale at Courrèges and couldn't resist going in. The result was a navy dress, very slim but with a longish skirt flaring out into mock pleats, reduced from eleven hundred francs to four hundred. It felt wildly extravagant but was very stylish. The label itself was worth a lot: *Courrèges: couture future*! I also bought some long boots – kid and leather-lined. Long boots were so much part of autumn dressing in Paris that I was beginning to feel quite naked without them.

Another extravagance was joining the Cercle interallié, the madly expensive club next to the Embassy. It had a gorgeous swimming pool where I could drop in for a swim, as well as a pleasant poolside restaurant where one could get a light meal. The whole sports complex was in an ultra-Hollywood penthouse décor – lots of smoked glass and potted plants (fake!), deep carpets and dim lighting. The pool was full of people earnestly swimming up and down with bodies delicately bronzed by sunray lamps. There was sauna, yoga, squash and any number of ritzy etceteras. All very soothing, despite (or perhaps because of) the churchlike calm of hushed voices. The main dining room, a fine long room overlooking the gardens, was also a good place to invite journalists to lunch. I had a generous entertainment allowance and, despite the awkwardness of inviting people I did not know, this proved a good way of building relationships.

The whole Embassy was pervaded by the personality of the Ambassador, Sir Nicholas Henderson. This tall, imposing man somehow managed to look at once elegant and slightly dishevelled. A long obituary in the *Guardian* described him as the last of the great showman Ambassadors. Supremely confident, he had strong views on policy, dealing on equal terms with politicians and business moguls. When later sent to Washington he became close to the Reagans and played a major role in putting the British case to the American public during the Falklands crisis. But I do not think he was a great Ambassador in Paris. He did not seem to have such close relations with French ministers. It did not help that his spoken French was mediocre.

The Ambassador came to my office every morning at about 9.30 to be briefed on the day's news. This involved a very early start for me or my deputy to scan the French and British papers identifying the main stories and lines of comment. Nicko had favourites in the Embassy and it soon became clear that I was not one. Though never actively unpleasant he ignored or talked over me. At one point his deputy Kenneth James organised a meeting to try to sort things out. It didn't do much good and looking back I think we talked past each other. Nicko seemed to want me to act as a personal PR promoter which was not what I believed my job to be. I was never easy in his company and found myself wondering whether he could really be as self-centred as he sounded. I did organise a meeting for him and the political section of the Embassy with the editorial board of *Le Matin* and earned some brownie points. I should have done more of this sort of thing but, demoralised, I mostly pursued my own way working for positive coverage of Britain and the British point of view. There was also a strong contingent of British correspondents for whom I was the official link. Though I had perfectly good relations with other members of the Embassy I was not properly part of a team effort.

I took every opportunity to get to know France outside Paris. There is a lively French regional press and I periodically made forays into the provinces to visit the more important papers. My first trip, in January 1978, was to Lyon where the Consul-General Howard Rigney couldn't have been kinder or more hospitable. I stayed in his handsome house on the quais where he gave a lunch and a big dinner for me to meet local journalists. Another evening we were given dinner by the biggest local paper, *Le Progrès de Lyon*, and then saw it being produced for the night. I marvelled at the almost surgical printing process, relying on computers and photographic reproduction. Very different from the noisy lead printing presses I had seen in London. *Le Progrés* produced some fifty different regional variants which all had to be correctly assembled and dispatched at successive times depending on the distance to be covered. It was a very interesting visit but as hard on the feet as the quantities of Lyonnais food were on the digestion. I later paid similar visits to Rennes and Strasbourg.

In late January I spent a weekend with the Tomkins in their ski chalet at Meribel. Eddie, who was half French, had gone on from The Hague to be Ambassador in Paris but was now retired. He was a good friend and I wished he were still in the Embassy. The skiing at Meribel was marvellous though I could have wished the snow was all on the ground: it snowed solidly for three out of my four days. It was only just before I left Paris that I realized that the Duke of Kent would be there too. The Embassy was always informed of visiting Royals. He himself could not have been less stuffy, but life with a Royal at close quarters was an odd combination of formality and the opposite. The Tomkins obviously knew him well, and most of the time conversation was totally normal apart from a sprinkling of "Sirs." But I was quite taken aback when the Duke announced he was going to bed and gave Jill a goodnight kiss, whereupon she dropped a neat curtsey. I didn't manage a curtsey, but then I didn't get a kiss!

Back in Paris, I started French lessons with a view to taking the intermediate level exam in March, and then working slowly for the highest level. (This was about degree level and required serious effort but I passed it in due course, earning a useful extra allowance.) We had a visit from the Foreign Office Inspectors which involved a good deal of preparation. I was relieved that they did not stumble over any fearsome skeletons in the Information Section. They decided to cut one local post as I had myself proposed but also our only UK-based secretary. From then on I had an excellent secretary called Barbara Geary who knew Paris well having lived there for years.

We had some horrid weather that February, very cold with snow melting just enough to freeze viciously at night. I came down with a stinking cold, a spokesman without a voice. The Ambassador rang himself to ask if there was anything I needed, and though I assured him not, in the afternoon his chauffeur delivered two beautiful packages wrapped in striped paper with brilliant ribbons which turned out to contain a bottle of champagne and a box of chocolates. Such kindness from the man I viewed as an ogre quite took my breath away.

I was still a bit wobbly when we had a visit from Eric Varley, the Minister for Industry. The future of British steel was making headlines which involved me in a certain amount of press activity including organizing and briefing him for a press conference. And then later in the week I harnessed John Davies, the Tory Shadow Foreign Minister, to do a TV interview on the fisheries question: we had been getting a very bad press on that subject, and I thought it would be good to show that our case was supported by all sides in the UK. I was pleased to have got close enough to the leading TV channel TFI to get them to do it.

The Embassy received many invitations to town twinning ceremonies and I spent a day at Fontainebleau which was twinned with Richmond-on-Thames. The programme for these events seldom gave much clue to what to expect and I was always faintly nervous that I might suddenly be let in for a speech. To my relief my part in proceedings was minimal. We started by watching a procession, which was enlivened when a brass band started off at full blast under the noses of some insecurely mounted horse-guards Then lots of speeches, an enormous lunch, and a rugby match. One thing that struck me very strongly was the difference between the Mayor of Fontainebleau – who had been in office about 20 years, and was also a senator and obviously the personality of the neighbourhood – and the Mayor of Richmond, a rather dry businessman elected for one brief year. French and German mayors who stayed in office for long periods often became good friends in a way British mayors did not. Another ceremony, this time at Orléans, was connected with Jeanne d'Arc. Being an English Jeanne, I was not sure which role I would be cast in and hoped it wouldn't be too uncomfortable.

I was lucky to have some family connections in Paris. The de Mareuils were cousins by marriage through the Bishops. Their kindness and hospitality made a big difference to my sometimes over-formal life in Paris. They had a house near Paris and another in Brittany and invited me to both at various times. Another weekend I had an unexpected invitation, from a rich and (to me) unknown textile magnate to lunch at a château in Normandy. It turned out to be a charming little late 17th-century château – more like a manor really – built *entre cour et jardin*, which means that the rooms looked out front and back. The party consisted of about 20 people – some diplomats, someone from the Paris municipality, others from Protocol at the Quai d'Orsay and the Elysée. The host and hostess were a delightful couple, most hospitable and open; he proudly told me that he was rising eighty but still travelled non-stop. I was also befriended by an interesting couple called Hugo and Marianne Tobias who had a lovely house in Lisieux and often invited me there.

In September 1978 I spent a happy week on a barge on the Canal du Midi with Celia Hensman and the Mallories. The countryside was glorious and life was never dull as the old canal wound its way along the contours and slowly climbed through its myriad locks. At barge speed, each tiny village one comes to is a place of excitement and the search for a baker is a major expedition. One unforgettable evening we bought quails in the market at Carcassone and barbecued them over cuttings from the vineyards where we moored for the night. Delicious. What with shopping, working the locks and spotting the occasional kingfisher our time was very full. But I did manage to produce two Collings masterpieces (i.e. sketches) which gave me added satisfaction.

In the late spring of 1979 there was a change of Ambassador. The departure of Nicko Henderson was a relief to me. He was succeeded by Reginald Hibbert, a very different sort of man. Brisk and with a toothbrush moustache he looked like an army officer. I got on with him perfectly well. I was, however, in for a shock when I went to discuss his first annual report on me. I mentioned that the Personnel Department had offered to send me to the Canadian Defence College but I had asked to stay out my normal posting in Paris instead. It was only then that he told me that he had recommended my removal on the grounds that Nicko had given me such a bad report that it would be better to cut my losses and start again elsewhere. I never saw what Nicko wrote but if Reg Hibbert had told me of his recommendation earlier I would certainly have followed his advice. That episode cast a slight shadow over my final months in Paris which went well otherwise and were much happier ones for me. In the long run, I don't think my brush with Nicko Henderson did much damage to my career.

May 1979 also saw a change of government in the UK when the Conservatives won the general election bringing Margaret Thatcher to No 10 for the first time. When Reg Hibbert presented his credentials to President Giscard a few days later he suggested that an early meeting between the two would be a good thing, Giscard responded warmly, and on 5 June the new Prime Minister came to Paris for a remarkably amicable meeting. (Giscard became one of her pet hates later on.) I arranged an interview for her on French TV which went well too; she flirted with the interviewer who could scarcely keep a straight face. I also found myself sitting at the same table as Mrs T at an all-staff lunch at the Embassy and I watched with fascination as she mercilessly grilled Kenneth James on the finer points of French science. Inevitably there was a good deal of conversation about

Giscard and suddenly the Prime Ministerial regard fixed on me: "What do you think of Giscard…as a woman?" she asked. I can't think what I replied, but I found the question rather patronizing. Perhaps she thought I was a secretary. I drafted a telegram on coverage of the visit in the French press which (ironically in the light of later developments) welcomed "HMG's intention to play a more positive part in the Community."

Shortly afterwards there was a meeting of the European Council in Strasbourg and I joined the British delegation to deal with the French press. For some reason I was driven there in state as the sole occupant of the Ambassador's Rolls-Royce. I didn't have much to do so I hung around with a number of others in the outer delegation office picking up titbits of news. The Foreign Secretary Lord Carrington drifted in at around 11pm saying, "Will that woman never go to bed?".

About this time I had six weeks away from my desk to take part in an exchange dating from Britain's entry to the EEC. A Heath-Pompidou initiative, the idea was to encourage middle ranking civil servants to get to know more about how the other country was governed. French administrators went to London while in Paris the course was run by the Institut International de l'Administration Publique (confusingly the acronym was pronounced "Lilliapay"). This was an offshoot of ENA, the prestigious Ecole Nationale de l'Administration Publique, and mainly provided training for African countries in the French sphere of influence. For me it was an ideal chance to get to know France better and I volunteered at the first opportunity. It turned out to be great fun as well as very informative.

The first couple of weeks were spent in intensive language training. We were divided into two groups according to existing ability. I qualified for the more advanced group of about a dozen people and the teaching was really stimulating. As well as giving short presentations and producing summaries of news broadcasts, our ears were trained by listening to singers like Gilbert Bécaud and Jacques Brel. One day we went out into the Jardins de Luxembourg armed with a large recording machine called a magnetophone. There we accosted a variety of people – a retired banker, a nursemaid etc – and asked them several questions about where they came from, what they did, and what they thought of the UK. Back in the classroom we listened to the recordings, analyzing the different levels of language used by different people. It was fascinating. I also enjoyed the sessions on slang – though I have learned to be very careful how I use it.

The next four weeks were spent in learning about the French system of government. We paid visits to bodies like the Conseil d'Etat (which is housed in the Palais Royal, one of the most beautiful buildings in Paris), the Courts of Justice (on the Ile de la Cité beside the Chapelle Royale) and ENA itself. That last visit was particularly fascinating because ENA embodied the elitism that is so characteristic of France. If you passed out at the top you could become Inspecteur de Finance which guaranteed you a salary for life and was the entrée to a dazzling career in many fields in and out of government service. The next few down went to the Conseil d'Etat and after that the Quai d'Orsay and other prestigious jobs. At the time I visited there had been some recent attempts to widen the entry but I got the impression that they were a bit half-hearted. I particularly remember talking to a disillusioned young man who was older than most and had been picked out from the civil service for the privilege of attending. Macron finally abolished ENA in 2021.

For the final week we were divided into smaller groups to see something of provincial government and the many layers of French bureaucracy. I went to Périgeux and the Bordeaux area. The mayor of a village drove me round in his very small car and explained local politics; if he greeted someone he might gain a vote but running over a hen would cost him two! What a contrast with the formality of the Prefect in his handsome Napoleonic offices which reflected his status as the representative of central government. Then in Bordeaux itself we were entertained by the former Prime Minister Jacques Chaban-Delmas who combined being Mayor of the city with representing the department in the Assemblée Nationale – a prime example of the way in which the big French cities serve as a base for national politicians. But the cherry on the cake was a visit to Château Beychevelle, one of the most prized vineyards in the Bordeaux region. I went back to the Embassy refreshed but also considerably the wiser. Back in Paris I wrote an article about the course for *Le Matin*.

Around this time the Boisdevaix came back from Bonn and I had to move. I settled on a flat in an attractive old building in Avenue Carnot, just round the corner from the Arc de Triomphe. It was an interesting area of Paris though the flat had its problems, including the drains and a tendency to grow mushrooms in the WC. I began to hanker after a bolt hole in the country. By lucky chance I was able to rent an ex-winegrower's cottage in a village called Couture which is on a tributary of the Loire and about an hour's drive from many of the major châteaux. The house was tiny and rather damp with one room upstairs and one down and could sleep four with the help of camp beds. There was a labyrinth of caves set into the cliff behind containing wine-making gear as well as hundreds of bottles of wine. I was given a huge iron key to the front cave along with permission to drink as much as I wanted of the most basic wine for a small charge per bottle. The village had added interest because of its connections to a group of 16th-century poets called La Pléiade whom I had loved on being introduced to them in my schooldays in Beirut. Pierre Ronsard grew up in a small turreted house called La Possonnière which was just along the road while one could see the château of his friend du Bellay across the peaceful valley. I took great pleasure in the place and went there whenever I could. It was there that I wrote my impressions of accompanying the Queen on what was billed as a private visit to see some French châteaux.

Couture, November, 1979

The Embassy had been doing some meticulous planning over the last few weeks. It still seems incredible to me that a private pleasure visit should be so precisely organized – and a little sad too. If I were the Queen I am sure I would want to go down the passage I wasn't shown or at least to look at the other side of the château, rather than being confined to the predetermined route. But she never deviated and we kept absolutely to the timetable till the last half hour or so when pouring rain slowed down the cortège of cars – then somehow increased to nearly 20!

The first day was in Touraine and we made an early start from Paris by car to be at Tours airport well before the Queen's arrival. "We" were myself and Michael Shea, the Queen's press secretary… At Tours we met up with a press officer from the Elysée, a nice girl called Mme Richard, who was the third of the press shepherds. It was a lovely day, late summer tinged with autumn, and the countryside looking its best. The Queen's Andover touched down on the minute and suddenly she appeared from behind the wing. (The photographers were slightly upset because the plane was pulled up nose on rather than sideways as is usual!).

One thing I noticed was that the Queen always wears singing colours that stand out from everybody else's clothes. On first arrival she was wearing a teal blue coat and matching hat with a small brim.

The Royal party went straight to Chambord for lunch, but I had arranged that the P.R. trio would go straight ahead to Chenonceau, which was the first place where the press were to be admitted. Mild crisis because the place where we had arranged for the press to stand had them looking straight into the sun – it had been a thoroughly grey day when we made our reconnaissance and the curator at the château was firm that we had chosen the best spot. Michael and I went straight along to have a look but there was nothing to be done. And then I made a dreadful discovery: we had walked along the freshly raked gravel where the Queen was to come and there were two tell-tale pairs of footsteps! We did not own up!

We got a lift back to Paris in the Royal plane which was rather fun. It has two compartments – one de luxe one with 4 seats which is where the Queen sits and one with 6 more cramped ones up forward. The hoi polloi get on first and off last, so as not to pass through the Queen's section while she is sitting there. We were served a delicious almost nursery tea, stacks of sandwiches, hot scones, cream cakes – but alas after the excellent lunch we had had at Chenonceau I couldn't cope. We flew up the Loire and I had a lovely view of Amboise.

It was then a quick rush home to get changed for dinner at the Elysée. I was in two minds about whether to wear a long dress for the occasion since my principal purpose was to herd journalists in the courtyard. But fortunately I took advice because everybody at our second class dinner was also dressed to the nines. Anyhow I opted for my Monsoon Indian red which goes so well with Mother's lovely long coat, which was much admired by a variety of journalists, Embassy chauffeurs and other old friends!

President Giscard decided at the last moment to go by car to the Embassy to fetch the Queen which was apparently an unprecedented courtesy. So they swept together into the courtyard which was beautifully lit and looked terrific with serried ranks of Gardes Républicaines framing the staircase. The Queen really looked lovely, as she came up the steps in a diamanté dress which sparkled in competition with diamond necklace and earrings. And down the steps to meet her and the President came this delightful black Labrador, Samba, which she gave the President a couple of years ago.

I went into the banqueting hall with the photographers as they took their round of table photos so had a good view. There were 5 tables of 10. Rather oddly the President sat opposite the Queen – supposed to be a sign of equality! On one side of the Queen was the Aga Khan, now a slightly pudgy playboy but still with a certain glamour. There were a number of French ministers and their wives (all remarkably glamorous!) and an unusually varied collection of other guests – actors, Marc Bohan of Christian Dior, Simone Veil etc.

Then up to our own dinner in one of the small rooms in a wing of the Elysée: there were 4 of us hangers-on from the Queen's party, and half a dozen on the French side – the Commander of the Garde Républicaine, the President's doctor and a nurse, the duty Protocol officer and the Elysée architect. We had the same meal as the main party which was delicious – and looked like a set of illustrations to Escoffier. First lobster, cut into small steaks and put back on the creature so that it sat up and looked at you. With the main course (lamb!) was a spectacular dish called a Chartreuse de Légumes aux Morilles: shaped like a sand-castle with tiny vegetables encrusted on the surface like mosaic. My mouth waters even with the memory!

It was another early start the following day to catch a train which would get us to Beaune in advance of the Queen. This time the photo facility went beautifully and the press had plenty of chances to see the Queen as she walked around the courtyard of the Hospice, a beautiful old building with its coloured tiled roof. [On our reconnaissance trip we were taken on a short cut through a ward full of old people lying in rows of four-poster beds with scarlet blankets. I am glad I had a glimpse of the great hospital serving its original purpose, but it felt intrusive.]

On to the château of Sully where once again we were entertained to a lunch for hangers-on. This is a small four-square château built around a courtyard and surrounded in turn by a moat. It is still in private hands, belonging to la Duchesse de Magenta, who is a friend of Lydwine Petrie's family. The house is a bit shabby in parts and I am not sure that it didn't add to the atmosphere because suddenly everyone seemed much more relaxed. It was at this point that we heard that a demonstration of éléveurs de mouton was planned for our next stop at Epoisses!

It is a long drive from Sully to Epoisses, through lovely country and small villages. Epoisses itself is a small medieval castle, once again moated and with an exterior wall. As we came close to the main entrance, there were a number of by-standers but they seemed very good-natured and we drove in through the castle gates. (By this time Michael and I had decided to rejoin the cortège so as to see what happened). About 10 minutes later while the Queen was being shown over the house someone came up to whisper that there were piles of tyres burning in front of the castle gates. We slipped out to have a look and it was indeed true: the bonfires created an almost festive air, despite the corpse of a dead sheep lying prominently in the road. There was a smattering of placards, one reading, "Jeanne d'Arc, revenez sauver vos moutons." It was all pretty cheerful, but one had the slightly uneasy feeling that things could get out of hand, particularly when piles of smoke began rising from other points behind the castle and it became clear that there was a danger of all the cars being bottled inside. Quite a medieval picture with the Queen besieged in the castle and the rioting peasantry at the gates. Fortunately the local police handled it well, and negotiated with the demonstrators who allowed a fire engine to douse the flames. The cars got out on time, past people waving sticks, and trying to look fierce. There were not very many demonstrators all told, I don't suppose, but it was quite difficult to tell them from well-wishers come to watch the Queen.

The last stop was Vézelay which we reached at dusk, just as it was beginning to rain. The basilica was floodlit and looked very exciting. I have been there a couple of times already since I have been in France and always find it full of atmosphere. It was particularly true tonight. The Queen was taken first into the entrance porch, where she was shown the inner screen, and then the main doors opened beneath it to show the brilliantly lit nave within. It was in the porch at the end of the visit that I was presented to the Queen, as was Mme Richard. I had not realized that the Queen herself would give me her photograph and indeed had a moment of panic as I wondered how I was going to cope with curtseying, shaking hands, and taking the photo at the same time. No disaster fortunately and I managed a few brief sentences. I was very pleased. Just you wait until you see my Royal Souvenir!

That was about the end. We went to Auxerre to see the Queen safely off and away in her Andover and then drove back exhausted to Paris. Another late night, and an impending feeling of anti-climax, but also a feeling that all had really gone pretty well… As I drove down to Couture for the weekend, I found myself missing the pairs of gendarmes on every bridge that was a feature of driving with the Royal Party. Had to stop at red lights too, and pay the péage. But I think I would rather do that and know I can slip away anonymously when I like, indulging the whim of the moment.

***

In July 1980 Prince Charles (then Prince of Wales, and now King), came to visit the French Armed Forces at the invitation of President Giscard. Margaret Thatcher was not best pleased because France was not a full member of NATO but finally acquiesced. Once again I was added to the party to deal with the press. The Ambassador and I joined the royal party at Dijon where we were taken to an air force base and given an extremely noisy trip in a helicopter. The Prince was a pilot and flew the royal plane part of the way to our next stop, Toulouse. Here we hangers-on stayed in a paratroopers' mess, while Prince Charles and the Ambassador were more regally entertained. The spartan accommodation was obviously not intended for women because there were no locks on the loo doors and I had to get a friend to stand guard. But we had a sumptuous dinner and the next day we watched a spectacular display of parachutists so numerous that they seemed to fill the sky.

The final stop was Brest, for the nuclear submarines that made up the *Force de Frappe*. I only got as far as seeing them from the dock. But I did get to spend the night on *Britannia*, where Prince Charles hosted a reception. The Marines beat Retreat on the *quai*; this ceremony, traditionally used to recall troops at sunset, is a spectacular pageant of military music and precision drill. Unfortunately we were moored deep in a security zone so the public could not watch. Dinner on board afterwards was an almost family affair with the Prince at the head of the table chatting to us all. Afterwards I was taken on a tour of the ship which included a visit to the spotless engine room. We ended up in the Officers' Mess playing some absurd game. I don't remember what the official party were doing the next day but I got invited to a tête-à-tête lunch on a small French warship which was a lot of fun.

***

I stayed in the Paris Embassy for the rest of 1980 but there are no more letters. I left France in time to spend Christmas in Guernsey and joined the Royal College of Defence Studies in the new year.

Chapter 14

HOW TO BE A BRIGADIER
The Royal College of Defence Studies (1981)

The Royal College of Defence Studies, founded in the 1920s as the Imperial Defence College, is the senior defence academy in the UK. Its general purpose is to broaden perspectives and understanding of Britain and the wider world, and its website grandly proclaims, "we provide the capstone to the strategic education of those officers ... who have the potential to reach the highest ranks." A handful of diplomats was included in each intake from the start, and in 1983 there were two of us, Peter Wallace and myself. I have no letters from this period but did write an occasional diary which describes "*my marvellous luck in spending this year at the RCDS, a wonderful return to university life in hand-picked company with the very best of lecturers and a privileged entree to a wide variety of places one could never hope to get to as an ordinary mortal.*"

On the morning of 6 January 1981 I walked up to the imposing portico of Seaford House in Belgrave Square, announced myself to the waiting desk-keepers in the hall, was fitted out with my new College identity (No 62, Miss J J d'A Collings, Diplomatic Service), duly photographed and allotted a peg for my coat and a box for papers. I felt very self-conscious, not so much as the only woman (I think I am being honest) but because the place seemed full of officers greeting old friends and I clearly did not come from any of their regiments. But of course there were many others in reality much stranger to the situation than I was. There were 76 course members all told, of which 40 were British and the others a variety of countries and colours. The great majority were from the armed services of their respective countries, but about 25% were civilians (including a few policemen). There were also a number of directing staff – again mostly from the armed services – whom one got to know as well as one's fellow students. It was a small world of its own, a cross between a public school and a club.

Our studies were launched with a lecture from Sir Max Beloff who ranged easily over Cold War issues while looking like some intelligent bird with bright eyes and quiff of hair. It is difficult to pick out the high spots from the many lectures that followed; most were of different degrees of excellence. Lord Justice Scarman, an eagle of a man, argued for entrenching basic rights in law. Geoffrey Jackson, the Ambassador who was imprisoned by the Tupamaros guerrillas in Uruguay, impressed with his courage which was obviously based on a strong faith. Then there was John Dillow, the policeman who had commanded the operation to storm the Iranian Embassy after it was taken over by Iranian dissidents and they killed one of their hostages. Dillow showed us fascinating film of the operation, overlaid with the actual police commentaries.

Among other speakers I can remember 40 years later was the Chief Scientist of the day who told us about the power of digitalisation, forecasting an almost unbelievable day when a single device would replace telephone, calculator, camera and many other familiar gadgets. Sir Laurence Martin, then Professor of War Studies at King's College, London, and the Reith Lecturer of the year, talked about the strategic balance between East and West – but I must admit that what I remember best about his lecture was that he began by addressing us all as "Lady and Gentlemen." The Foreign Secretary Lord Carrington addressed us too and I joined him and the Commandant for lunch afterwards. I got more than my fair share of such perks. We took it in turns to thank the speaker.

After a while a surfeit of lectures brought on a touch of mental indigestion, particularly during the economic phase which was perhaps too reminiscent of Oxford and all I had forgotten since. It was most welcome when an increasing number of outside trips were worked into the programme. An evening with the Metropolitan Police was most revealing. I went with about six others to Brixton, only a few weeks before the violent anti-police riots there. We began with the Commander at the Brixton Police Station, who answered our questions very freely. He said that in a disadvantaged area in hard times it was inevitably the coloured people who came off worst, and therefore inevitably the coloured youths who came up against the police most – an economic as much as a social fact. I then spent a couple of hours with two officers in a car on 999 duty. It all felt rather macho and they would obviously rather have had a man to escort. We drove round and round the mile by mile-and-a-half pitch, in and out of housing estates, back streets and trouble spots. The estates were an eye-opener. Any car left in the ground floor garages under each block got gutted and ransacked, as I saw. My companions complained that blocks which won architectural awards were impossible to police properly because they could not bring their cars into the pedestrian walkways – and when they got out they were pelted with bottles by youths from the balconies above.

It was a quiet night. There was one emergency call, to one of the estates where a man was complaining that the woman in the flat next door was threatening him with a knife. It turned out to be a typical sordid neighbours' dispute, illustrative of the tensions endemic in life lived cheek by jowl. It was a white man who had given the alarm. His pokey flat on the first floor could only be reached by going past the equally small flat of his neighbour, a coloured woman with an eight-year-old girl. He told his story – that the woman would not let him in or out and had a carving knife. Then the police rang her doorbell, but for a long time she wouldn't answer, and I realized how little they could do without the right to enter. Eventually she was coaxed to the door and gave her story – that the neighbour was a Peeping Tom. She was so strung up that it seemed likely that she had invented a lot of it, but either way there was precious little the police could do except calm everyone down, which I thought they did with good sense and humour and a strong streak of paternalism, striking in such young men. I asked what would happen next. They would probably be called in again in a couple of days, they said; after a bit, things might simmer down. They were scathing of my query whether this was a case for social workers: it's all over by the time they get there and they don't help much anyhow, seemed to be the verdict.

Later there was a call from another car for help with an arrest. We were drinking coffee in the station at the time and suddenly my companions bolted, with me desperately trying to keep up and not very clear what was going on. Suddenly everything relaxed again; apparently the situation had been defused before we got there. It was difficult to sort out the messages meant for us from the mass of noise coming over the short-wave radio. We were then all taken out to a Clapham pub for sandwiches and a drink with the Commander and some of his senior officers. An agreeable end to a most interesting evening. Listening to news of the riots a few weeks later I hoped that none of my police companions were among those hurt.

There were a number of other excursions too. Quite early on there were trips to the British regions about which I felt very ignorant having lived so much of my life abroad. I went to Wales with a group of around 20 headed by an Admiral, who drummed into me that I must on no account ever keep the group waiting. (That year certainly instilled a sense of punctuality which was not part of my upbringing. My mother believed that it was a woman's right to keep a man waiting!) We saw something of hill farming, visited a nuclear power station and went down the last operational coal mine in Wales. The deep, deep shaft, the long dirty train ride underground and the machines grinding away at the rock face all made a great impression on me as did the blunt speaking miner who was assigned to escort me and my American colleague. Coal mining was still a way of life and the closure of the pits was the cause of much unemployment but I am glad that in Britain at least nobody works in such conditions today.

Another memorable trip was to Germany. We flew in an RAF plane to an air base at Bruggen where to my surprise and pleasure a smart young officer singled me out on arrival. He turned out to be Thomas Mallorie, the son of my great friends Paul and Ursula. I had known him as a boy in Bangkok; Thomas was now flying Jaguars for the RAF. But we didn't linger long before going on to visit a tank regiment. There we were each given a turn in a tank, a terribly noisy experience despite the ear baffles. I nearly disgraced myself when my escort offered me the chance to drive and I tried a slalom turn. I had asked permission before trying the manoeuvre but in the racket all the response I had got was a charming smile which I misinterpreted. The controls were whipped away from me. Apparently I could have ripped the tracks off the tank but fortunately no damage was done. We spent the night in the barracks and dined in the Sergeants' Mess, which was very splendid with full dress uniforms and lots of regimental silver. I wore a dashing long black dress I had acquired in Mexico which I thought of as my Merry Widow outfit. The occasion was a bit sticky at first because my neighbouring Sergeant Major didn't approve of women in the Mess, but he thawed as the wine flowed and we ended up standing on our chairs together bellowing out the regimental songs.

It sometimes felt as if I were living a Boys' Own dream. Having done the army in Germany we had a day in Portsmouth with the Royal Navy and a day with the RAF. This last visit gets a long entry in my diary as follows.

6 June 1981

Thursday meant an early rendezvous outside the College to pile into buses to Northolt. There a couple of clumsy Hercules aircraft awaited us – real trooping planes where the passengers sat on metal seats along the side with the luggage piled up under nets in the centre. Dark and noisy, so it was very welcome discrimination when I was invited to sit in the dial-filled cockpit. The course was divided into 6 groups each going to a different RAF station. I was bound for Finningley, the end of the line, and we shed the other groups progressively until we finally got there.

Finningley is now primarily a training base for navigators and pilots flying heavy aircraft. We were taken round a fascinating collection of training centres with highly complex simulators designed to teach people radar, communications and other aspects of their professional skills. A busy base with some 2,000 people. The highlight of the visit was the offer of flying. I had blithely volunteered to fly upside down, with very little idea of what that involved. Kitting out is an experience in itself. Our measurements had all been sent in advance and each was provided with a set of underwear (Y-fronts! - which I spurned), flying overalls, vast black boots, soft white kid gloves, and a helmet which was fitted to one's head like some instrument of medieval torture (painless thank goodness). Then there was a demonstration of how one would be strapped into the ejection seat with its two trigger handles. An elaborate system of straps and cables attached one's person to oxygen, intercom, rubber dinghy, parachute and of course finally the seat itself - with a pair of crisscrossing leg straps designed to bring down the heels in the case of a quick exit so that one's legs weren't broken on the way through the cockpit roof.

After the rehearsal, on to the real thing. Six of us had been allocated flights in Jet Provosts, the two-seater in which pilots get their first jet training. It was an odd feeling walking out to the row of waiting planes which looked almost like toys they were so trimly neat. My companion was a stringy little chap inches shorter than me who had obviously been flying for 30 years or so. He tactfully took me aside briefly to sound me out about what I really wanted to do; I confessed to my fear, not of flying but of being airsick – all too fully justified alas. But anyhow I wanted to do whatever was on offer. So finally there I was clambering up the wing and trying to put my heavy boots on the black patches which are specially strengthened. Then into the cockpit and a mechanic was busy strapping me in. Finally out came the three safety pins that made the ejection seat operational, down came the cockpit roof and we were taxiing along to the runway. Taking off was a very easy affair. The little plane seemed to soar into the air after a very few seconds, and there was a wonderful feeling of lightness and manoeuvrability as we climbed a little and picked up the preplanned course. It was gloriously sunny as we set off and the countryside sparkled, jewelled with yellow fields of rape. We saw York in the distance on the right as we headed up to the Lakes. Once we had left the villages behind we flew very low, swooping over the hills (and leaving my tummy behind for the first time). Then along Lake Windermere, and banking sharply left to find a gap in the cloud to follow the valley to Coniston Water. After the Lakes our route turned East back to the Humber where we turned South again towards Lincoln with a tantalizing glimpse of Rievaulx Abbey down beneath us.

As we neared Finningley my mentor asked if I still felt up to some aerobatics. I gritted my teeth and said yes, so after climbing to a safe height the pilot put the stick back and suddenly there was the ground with a river flowing along it above my head. There was little sensation of being upside down but the G-force pushed me down into the seat as if a heavy weight were on my shoulders. Then before I knew it we were again the right way up. A final slow roll and we were landing again. I got shakily out of the plane and, clutching my paper bag, walked self-consciously back towards the building where there was a waiting receptacle strategically placed in full view of the windows. I feel quite queazy even thinking about the whole experience and it was a good 24 hours before my system returned to its usual equilibrium. But I was delighted to discover that I was far from alone in succumbing – and had done better than some in going on undaunted for the full hour's flight, trying the controls myself and looping the loop...

The one written requirement of the year was to write a paper on a subject of one's own choice, drawing on the information gathered from lectures and visits etc. The deadline was the summer break and as it got nearer the task became more and more of a challenge. The very fact that we had so much time made my expectations of myself rise higher and higher. In the end I decided to write about the imbalance of the propaganda war between countries with and without a free press. It was not a very original subject, as the Foreign Office member of the Directing Staff pointed out, and I wasn't very satisfied with what I wrote, but it did have echoes in a number of our lectures and encouraged me to learn more about the workings of the Soviet system. To my pleasure my thesis was one of those chosen for publication in the Seaford House Papers.

The main event of the autumn was the month-long international tour. This extraordinary experience gets the next chapter to itself. The rest of the course was bound to pale in comparison and my own mind began turning towards a posting to Jakarta in the new year. But I should certainly record our visit to Berlin with its frightening wall where so many people had been shot down as they tried to escape the Communist east. We flew into Tempelhof airfield which had featured in the Berlin Airlift of 1948/49. Going through Checkpoint Charlie, the main link between East and West, was an experience in itself. As the bus crawled along we had to hold our passports up to the window for identification. On no account were they to be touched by the Russian border guards. The point behind this proceeding was that the wartime Allies still regarded the city as being de jure under quadripartite control, whereas the Russians were asserting unilateral control over their sector and trying to incorporate it into East Germany. The painfully negotiated procedural compromise was a tiny example of many years of tortuous negotiations over Berlin. Our day in the Eastern zone was mainly propaganda tourism, including visits to the huge and impressive Russian war cemetery and to a museum of WWII showing Western "atrocities." My most lasting impression of East Berlin was the contrast between the beautifully restored prestige buildings and the dinginess of everything else.

All through the year the RCDS organised an active social programme which included wives or partners. I invited Celia Hensman to join me when we went to the Derby in a huge coach, sitting on the roof to watch the races. But I began to feel the need of a male escort and invited Alec Campbell to join me from time to time. This is the point at which I should introduce Alec who will figure largely in the later chapters of this book. We became friends when we were both working in the Western Department in the 60s. I particularly remember a dinner party given by Alec and his lively American wife Fi in their Hampstead flat. It was Christmas time, the tree was decorated entirely with white paper ornaments from Scandinavia, and under it lay a baby boy in a basket. Alec left the Diplomatic Service for academia shortly afterwards but we stayed in touch through the years. In 1972 Fi died tragically leaving two children: John, then at Winchester, and his younger sister Ann. Alec was by now Professor of American History at Birmingham. Darkly handsome, intelligent and witty, he was the ideal companion. I remember a particularly beautiful RCDS outing on the Thames when the two of us ended up walking round St Paul's in the moonlight. Alec was also my partner at the Seaford House Ball which marked the end of our course.

Chapter 15

LOOKING AT FLOWERS FROM THE BACK OF A GALLOPING HORSE

Hong Kong, Japan, Korea, China (1981)

The culminating adventure of the RCDS year was the month-long world tour. Looking back this seems an incredibly lavish way of ensuring that rising senior officers obtained an international perspective and a taste of different foreign cultures, and it was a very memorable experience. We were divided into groups of a dozen or so, some going to Southern Europe, some to Latin America, some to the Middle East. I was very lucky and got my first choice, the tour of the Far East. It was the first time that the RCDS had been able to visit China which in 1981 was just beginning to open up under Deng Xiaoping and people didn't know what to expect there. The country was clearly on the brink of immense change. Hong Kong was still a proud British colony but the date when the British lease of its New Territories ran out was not far ahead. Korea remained a flashpoint in the standoff between communism and the West while its economy like that of Japan was vibrant. For me the trip had a special interest because just before we set off I heard that I was to be posted back to South East Asia in the new year. The jam-packed programme left me ready to drop into bed at the end of each day but I decided to keep a journal and faithfully wrote up our doings often on planes or trains.

It wasn't until we boarded the plane at Gatwick at 8 pm on 7 September that I fully believed the trip would take place, but there I was, one of twelve people setting out for the voyage of a lifetime, and doing it as part of an official party, being treated like visiting VIPs. They seemed an agreeable group – a French diplomat, a German and an Italian colonel, a New Zealand official and an assortment of senior British officers. The plane was a British Caledonian regular flight to Hong Kong, of which the services regularly chartered a large section. Broad-bodied and pretty cramped, it didn't allow one much sleep. Apart from anything else I was seated by the Commandant and didn't want to end up snoozing on his shoulder! First stop Dubai, where we arrived as the dawn came up scarlet over the horizon. In the grey morning light it still had the look of a desert oasis, trees hiding the worst of the concrete that must have been there. There was a surprisingly beautiful airport building constructed of arches of traditional Islamic design – wide but pointed. Then on again. It was a very long journey gliding in that no-man's land of air travel over so many different countries.

It was already evening when we arrived in Hong Kong, though not yet noon by London time. The city looked even more spectacular than I remembered it – forests of new skyscrapers, making New York seem in memory quite provincial. A stormy sky illuminated by a brilliant sunset gave the whole picture a touch of unreality.

When we got to the hotel and gathered in the opulent lounge to be allocated our rooms, "Spike" Milligan (the efficient Squadron Leader who had the task of shepherding our party) broke the news that of the 18 cases checked in London only 17 had arrived in HK. Inevitably the missing item turned out to be one of mine, the one containing all my dresses for the trip. As I settled into my luxurious suite with its red roses and fruit basket compliments of the management, I suddenly felt deathly tired and very much alone.

But it is marvellous what a good night's sleep will do. When I woke up to look out on the sparkling city, I couldn't repress that thrill of excitement at the prospect of exploring an unfamiliar place. The news from the airport was that my case was still missing, but that I was entitled to 25 US dollars to buy extra clothes. We were scheduled to lunch with the GOC Hong Kong, so I set out urgently for the nearest shopping arcade to see what I could find. The trouble was that I was about six inches taller than most Chinese women so the choice was limited but eventually I found something pretty and practical – and rather startlingly pink.

The lunch was a relaxed occasion. General Chapple's residence was halfway up the Peak on HK Island, a lovely house surrounded by terraces with spectacular views. We ate outside and I found myself on the General's right. (I wondered about the protocol problems I must be causing our prospective hosts!) A nice man, who talked interestingly about Hong Kong, China and ASEAN – the latter particularly when he heard that I was off to Jakarta in January.

I rushed back to the hotel at 6 pm, because I was told that by then it should be working hours in London and there might be news of my case. But no. I found myself talking on the phone to the General Manager of British Caledonian Far East, who really could not have done better in the circumstances. When he heard what my situation was – two weeks' official programme in Japan and Korea and virtually no outer garments – he said I should go out and buy whatever I needed. But please not to be *too* extravagant. I duly promised, and rushed back to the morning's shopping mall to try on everything that had looked remotely possible. The result was a trio of outfits not at all in my usual style but bought from a boutique which conveniently had a sale.

In the evening I was invited to dinner by Richard and Fiona Margolis, colleagues of mine in Paris, who were now with the Political Advisor's Office in the Government Secretariat. We went to a super Chinese restaurant and ate a series of delectable dishes – some with the same names as one sees on Chinese menus in London, but not remotely recognizable in taste. Richard, a fluent Chinese speaker, obligingly demonstrated the four tones of Mandarin for me, and also explained (which I had not previously realized) that Chinese syllables can only end in three ways – with a vowel, an "n", or "ng". More practically Fiona lent me a suitcase and a few supplementary clothes. It was quite late when Richard deposited me at the Star Ferry to cross back to Kowloon. I loved that ferry: the trim little steamers crossed to and fro among the junks and other shipping of Hong Kong harbour with all the stolidity of old-fashioned tugs.

I came down to breakfast with Hanno von Kielmansegg, our delightful and highly intelligent German colleague, and chatted more than I meant to, enjoying our conversation. My real purpose was to dash to a silk shop recommended by Mrs. Chapple to buy myself one really nice dress at British Caledonian's expense. I did so too and after some whirlwind trying-on returned to the hotel by taxi on the dot of our departure time to find all my colleagues waiting expectantly – or perhaps resignedly – in the lobby. The welcome news was that my case had at last been located and should catch up with me in Tokyo. A great relief really, and I did not think British Caledonian could complain because my total purchases cannot have exceeded £80.

***

If Hong Kong was one of the world's most fabulous cities, Tokyo at first sight was one of the most appalling. The vast airport, inefficiently organized with huge queues of people, was a fortified encampment manned, so I was told, by 25,000 security staff. One left through a barbed wire perimeter fence, aware of the watch towers placed at strategic intervals and the armoured vehicle parked across the access road with riot police at the ready. The airport had opened in 1978 after a long struggle with farmers and students opposed to the expropriation of agricultural land. They were now protesting against another runway. The purpose-built expressway for the 45 km journey into central Tokyo took us 2 ½ hours, most of this time spent crawling as part of a mammoth, fume-ridden traffic jam through hideous modern suburban sprawl. By the time we arrived at the Palace Hotel (another comfortable and characterless hotel which could be anywhere) we were all heartily fed up. But once again the morning brought a new perspective. My window looked out on the grounds of the Imperial Palace. There was no glimpse of the Palace itself, and apparently it could not be seen from anywhere in Tokyo. What I could see were massive grey walls of great strength and overall regularity despite the irregularity of the individual stones. These walls, some two or three miles around, enclosed a roughly square thickly-wooded area with a few glimpses of tiled roof, and were surrounded by a broad moat, lined on the opposite side with willows. They were apparently one of the few things in Tokyo that were really old. I wondered what life was like in there, where the Emperor Hirohito, an old man born to a position of divine authority, was living out his secluded life. What memories he must have had, including the humiliations that followed Japan's defeat in the Second World War.

We were collected first thing by the minibus which was our second home in Tokyo and taken to the British Embassy for initial briefing. This too looked over the Palace grounds though from a different side. It was a spectacularly beautiful compound, dating from the days when Britain was top dog among nations. There were a number of staff houses there as well as the Ambassador's residence where we dined that night: all lovely old-fashioned houses with big rooms looking out onto terraces and luxurious gardens.

It was an excellent briefing given by the Ambassador Hugh Cortazzi with a number of his staff. We had had a couple of good lectures on Japan in London, but there was still so much to learn about a way of life and thinking so different from our own. That afternoon and the next morning we visited a series of Japanese offices – Ministry of Foreign Affairs, C Itoh (a vast international trading company), the Defence Agency and the National Defence College – at each of which we were given a briefing. The pattern soon got familiar. A presentation of the official line with no surprises, no personal touch, followed by a short period for questions. We never got direct answers to any difficult questions, or even pretty simple ones. What usually happened was that the question was followed by a short discussion in Japanese between our hosts, then somebody gave the agreed reply, which frequently had only a tangential relationship to the question asked. I am amused by how some of my service colleagues reacted to this (among ourselves, I mean, for the courtesies were strictly maintained in public). Evasive, they said, hypocritical too; no wonder the Americans got so frustrated when the Japanese were clearly determined to limit their contribution to Western defence while reaping their rich economic harvest. I myself was struck by the Eastern tradition of consensus versus Western individualism. In a public meeting, especially when their seniors were present, no Japanese seemed willing to risk a personal answer outside the safe ground of general agreement. But many of those we met were much more prepared to speak frankly in private conversation.

I experienced an example of this at the briefing at the National Defence College. I asked a question about the defence of the sea lanes round SE Asia, suggesting that since the Japanese forces were constitutionally limited to a role of self-defence and the Japanese economy was crucially dependent on Middle East oil, this might be an area where the Japanese would find least political difficulty in meeting US pressure for a greater defence effort. The answer, after the usual preliminary consultation, was largely flannel and indeed I wondered whether I had expressed myself clearly enough, or whether my point had got lost in translation. But afterwards, over a buffet lunch, two of the Japanese took me aside separately to say that they did not think I had received a proper answer. The Principal of the College said that it was not the constitutional point which was the problem since much more would be possible within the limits laid down than envisaged in current defence plans. He added that Japan had simply not got the military capability to defend the Straits of Malacca and clearly saw no prospect of this changing. A junior officer later told me that talks were going on with the Americans about the division of roles for protection of sea lanes. When I recounted all this later to the Air Attaché, he said one would never get an answer to such a question which was one of highly topical debate – and that the Japanese were probably rather startled to find a girl pressing them on such sensitive matters anyhow! Women were obviously second-class citizens in Japan. I wondered how long the swinging, intelligent and highly-educated girls we saw would accept the background role of their traditional forebears.

The other conversation which I found most interesting was with my dinner neighbour at the Embassy dinner – Professor Eto of Tokyo University, an expert on international relations and particularly on China where, he told me, he was born. A sophisticated, subtle man, with complete command of English even to its humour, he was very interested to hear that we were going on to Beijing, and when I told him that we did not yet know what our programme would be he said that it would certainly be under intense discussion. He forecast that we would be given very special treatment, all the more so because there were some clouds in the US-Chinese relationship. We would be shown the most prestigious sights – and we would probably be given one special glimpse inside the Chinese bureaucracy – possibly a day with the People's Liberation Army, conceivably a meeting with Deng Xiaoping. I asked how he found academic freedom developing amongst his university contacts in China. A sharp retreat from two years previously, he said. Whatever the economic policies, bureaucratic controls were those of a Communist State.

Sunday started idly which was a great relief. At midday I was collected by Bob Immerman, the Political Counsellor of the US Embassy, who had been warned of my arrival by the State Department student on the course, David Lambertson, who rightly assumed that I would like to see a bit of Tokyo not covered by the official tour. We dived down the subway (glistening clean and smooth, a blessed contrast to the traffic jams up above) and came up again in Ueno, one of the more popular suburbs to the northeast of the city. There we set off down some alleys, ending at a wooden Japanese restaurant on a corner which he had chosen for our lunch. We seemed to be the only Europeans there. After waiting a few minutes downstairs, we were ushered up and this was the point at which shoes were removed. (As I gingerly climbed the slippery wooden stairs, I reminded myself not to wear nylon tights next time!) There can only have been about six tables all told, with two or three people at each, all sitting neatly on the flat cushions which serve as seats. I got down a trifle self-consciously, but found I could perfectly well manage a stance with feet tucked to one side which maintained a modicum of elegance. No way though that I could have managed the position of the older Japanese ladies, who sat kneeling with feet crossed underneath them scarcely showing. It was a delicious meal – tender pork fried in a batter of breadcrumbs with a range of more exotic trimmings. Bob himself turned out to be an interesting person, serious and far from the traditional American extrovert, very knowledgeable about Japan, as David had promised me. I was glad to be able to throw at him the dozens of questions about Japanese ways, however trivial or unanswerable, that were forming in my mind.

The meal did not take long – apparently the Japanese tend to eat quickly and without conversation unless it is a party. Then we went for a walk along a street full of market stalls – exotic fruit and fish, with crimson tentacles of squid adding an extra touch of colour, shoes, clothes, and countless other little shops which seemed to be doing plenty of business. From there we went into a park with a Buddhist temple surrounded by a lake of lotus. The path to the temple was lined by those stone lanterns so typical of Tokyo and by little memorials – one, which Bob translated for me, was to the spirit of all the blowfish which had perished in Tokyo. The trees beside the temple were covered with little ties of paper – unpropitious fortune slips, Bob explained, that people exorcised in this way. Inside, it was rather like a Thai temple with people coming and going, at their devotions or buying religious trinkets. It did not seem to be the custom to lay flowers before the Buddha, though there were plenty of tassels and votive offerings.

I was sorry to have to rush back to the hotel because the Defence Attaché had arranged for us all to go to see a sumo wrestling tournament. I wasn't sure I really wanted to go, but tickets were hard to get and it would obviously have been churlish to refuse. It turned out to be a spectacular occasion in which ceremonial and costume counted for at least as much as the wrestling – and took a great deal longer. We were there to watch the top division contests from 4–6 pm, and almost as soon as we arrived in our seats, all the participants made a ceremonial parade – huge men, some unbelievably fat, with hair scraped up into formal top knots (which are ceremonially cut off when they retire). At this stage each wore a gloriously worked apron, but when later they came to fight they were only wearing a coloured belt round the crucial parts wound intricately with a knot at the back, and frequently the odd elastic bandage. The arena itself was a brilliantly lit raised area under a suspended palanquin with four huge tassels hanging from the corners, each tassel a different colour to represent a different season. Within this area a circle was traced out by a ridge made of packed straw, and each bout was decided when one wrestler forced the other out of the circle, or onto the ground within it. Some bouts were over in a few seconds with a sudden shove or flick. But it was the preliminaries that were the most intriguing, as these huge men squatted glowering at each other in traditional stances, slapping their massive thighs explosively – only time and again to get up simultaneously, each retiring to his corner where he would purify himself with a wipe of a special towel and then throw salt onto the ground before settling back into another spell of glowering. Keeping an eye on all this was the umpire, a gorgeously gowned individual with a special black gauze hat and a flat lacquer fan the position of which seemed to play an important role in proceedings. It was clear that there was a strict hierarchy among the umpires whose status could be told by the colour of the tassel attached to the fan. With their brilliant or subtly coloured clothing (I particularly liked one in pink and black) and the traditional positions they took up, the umpires looked like characters out of old Japanese prints, as indeed did the wrestlers. It was extraordinary to see some of those faces in real flesh and blood.

Monday was our last day in Tokyo and it was largely spent in visiting the Fuji school of artillery, infantry, etc. The grounds were on the lower slopes of Mount Fuji, and all day I kept hoping that the mists would clear to give us a view of the mountain the Japanese refer to as Fuji-San, just as if it were a person. ("San" is the polite word to add to someone's name.) But they didn't. The most memorable moment of the visit was the huge guard of honour awaiting our arrival and repeated before our departure. Each time the Commandant (who performed his role very well given no warning) was put onto a small dais, with the rest of us lined up to attention behind, and sundry tunes which might or might not have been the national anthem were played. There was a regrettable lack of unity in our ranks about what and when to salute. The parade was conducted on the Japanese side by a fierce-looking officer who stationed himself opposite the Commandant and issued his orders in a series of startling nasal cries.

From Fuji it was a helicopter ride to the US Air Force base outside Tokyo, where we were addressed by a tall, scraggy-necked Marine general with a downbeat line in humour. It was notable that, whereas we had been struck by how little the Japanese were prepared to do in response to American pressures for a greater contribution to Allied defence, the Americans were very keen to persuade us that the Japanese view was changing fast, that things could be discussed now that had been taboo until recently. True perhaps, but I still had the feeling we were being shot a line, though I couldn't quite think why.

I was on tenterhooks to get back to Tokyo in good time because it was my only chance to have another look at some prints I had spotted during my first adventurous exploration of one of the traditional areas. A set of three in matching shades of blue, brown and coral that had to me a beauty which could only mean they were good. But how to tell when I had no means of communicating with the shop-owner, and knew nothing of Japanese prints? With the help of a fellow customer I had got the artist's name and period written on a card with the shop's address (printed in Japanese!) so I could do my research. The more I heard and thought about the prints the more I felt they couldn't be wrong, and the more I wanted them. But, as always in Tokyo, the traffic was bad and we were late back. With an hour to go before we were due to leave for the next official appointment – did I dare go? After the briefest of dithers (and time to borrow some money) I leapt into a taxi and gave the driver my card – only to be thrown into agony as he scratched his head over the address, consulted the hall porter, who disappeared inside with it to consult someone else. But at last we were off, and I was back in the busy lane looking for the right shop. I rushed in, seized the prints with scarcely time for a second glance, put down the money and ran. Luckily taxis are plentiful and there was no difficulty in getting back to the hotel. A lightning change and I was ready to go out to dinner, hoping I didn't look as rushed as I felt.

The evening turned out to be a splendid one – a typical Japanese dinner in a guesthouse overlooking a formal garden. Our hosts were the Japanese Defence Agency who certainly did us proud. By this time I was getting rather good at sitting on the floor to eat. The meal, served by six or eight pretty girls in different coloured kimonos, was something of a magical mystery tour – there was no way of telling what could come next, or how many courses there would be. At one point I thought we had got to the end with some delicious sweets – the glacé chestnuts were particularly good – but when I put the "chocolate" which I had been saving for the last into my mouth, it turned out to be squid! Then we launched off into several more courses. The end came with soup and rice – which it is not good manners to finish because that would suggest that one was still hungry. I had no difficulty in observing that courtesy.

The next day (Tuesday) we took the Bullet Train to Kyoto – less of an experience than I had expected, because it was remarkably like travelling on the Trans-Europe Express. Kyoto was the one place of cultural interest where we had some free time – thanks to the happy chance that the day happened to be the festival dedicated to respect for the aged. It was a city full of temples and shrines (the former Buddhist, the latter Shinto, with the same people going to both) and it was rather tantalizing to be rushed around. To make matters worse I managed to get lost in one shrine. Concentrating on a photo

I wanted to take I failed to notice where the others went, and suddenly there was no sign of them. I quickly felt very lost; signs in familiar script were extremely rare, and surprisingly few people spoke English. So after a vain attempt to find the others, or to recognize our bus from the hundreds of others outside, I decided the best thing was simply to wait at the temple gate and pray there was only one way out. Happily my prayer was answered, but it seemed a slow response.

The best thing we saw in Kyoto was the last, a temple with a wonderful view over the city from one of the surrounding hills. It was a huge cedarwood construction, in feeling rather like some of the Chiang Mai temples with their huge Buddhas half-hidden under the eaves. The most remarkable thing here was the giant wooden scaffolding, hundreds of years old, which supported the platform on which the main temple sat. Behind were several attractive little shrines; one was for children who died young, to which the bereaved parents donated a child-sized Buddha clad in orange, or perhaps only an article of his clothing. It was rather touching to see a young man at his devotions in front of the shrine, ringing the bell and praying, face to face with all these tiny Buddhas.

From Buddhas to Robots. The next day we were taken to see Magasaki Heavy Industry near Osaka, then Japan's leading producer of "sophisticated" robots. I must admit I felt rather like a robot myself having got to bed late the night before after a supper party given by the Consul General and a 7 am start from our hotel. But their robots were much cleverer than me – at any rate at twisting, turning and processing. The bits of machinery we saw them working at were, I believe, parts for more robots. The robots we saw were modelled on the human arm and hand, with shoulder, elbow and wrist movements very like ours. But, said Hanno, they couldn't begin to rival the complexity of the human hand. Not then anyhow! From there it was on to Sanyo electronics, to watch the assembly of television receivers by endless lines of quick-fingered girls adding successive parts to the skeletons that slid by on conveyor belts. Very impressive too in its way. There we were each presented with a solar-fuelled calculator that we were told would run forever. It was here that I let myself be goaded into a question as to the number of women in managerial positions, to which I got a short answer: none! Clearly not about to be any either.

From Tokyo we flew to Seoul. As we drove into the city from the airport with our military escort it was very noticeable that the cortège never stopped for the red lights. Also that the place was full of people in military uniform of various sorts. The contrast with Japan could not have been more striking. We were arriving in a place where the military were in charge. The point was brought home forcibly later in the evening when we learned that there was to be an air-raid alert and that the city was to be totally blacked out at 10 pm. The nightly curfew was to be extended from 10 pm to 4 am. At first we were inclined to take this a bit lightly within the hotel. I went for a drink in one of my colleagues' rooms on a different floor, and only just made it back home before the lights were cut. Once back in my own room I kept the lights out and opened the curtains so I could watch what happened from my 19th-floor picture window. By 10 pm the city was totally black apart from the headlights of some cars which were clearly inspecting the exercise. Even the aerial warning lights on the skyscrapers were out and the electronic clock. Then searchlights stabbed the sky. It was rather sinister.

The next day we had the usual round of briefings – national defence college, ministry of foreign affairs, economic planning. The Koreans were much more direct than the Japanese had been: when we asked a question somebody answered it straight away. The Koreans are also remarkably outgoing. At the dinner given for us by the KNDC, our Korean hosts had no inhibitions at all about coming up and starting a conversation, however scanty their English. They were rather a jolly people after the impassive Japanese. Racially there was a wide range of features – from broad-faced people who could be SE Asian to slit-eyed Mongolian faces that could have come out of any film about life on the steppes.

On Saturday 19 September we went to Panmunjom, which was such a fascinating experience that I will quote my diary account in full:

> *One cannot fail to be brought up with a start by the realization that the bustling city of Seoul is only 25 miles from the demarcation line between North and South Korea across which North Korean and UN forces are still glaring at each other. The road to Panmunjom is strewn with military defences and obstacles that can be used to block them in an emergency. There must be 6 or 8 arches of reinforced concrete that can be brought down by explosives at a touch. And even so the military estimate is that the North Koreans could be in Seoul in 1¼ hours. No wonder it is a jittery city.*
>
> *After stopping at an American headquarters for a briefing on the situation and the complicated structure of UN, US and Korean commands, we went on to Camp Kittihawk which is just to the south of*

the Demilitarized Zone which stretches 2 km each side of the demarcation line. There we were given special passes to go into the Joint Security Area and made to sign a form saying that we would not hold anyone responsible for any harm that might befall us there. A special bus then took us into the DMZ which seemed strangely normal despite the fortifications – there is one village allowed in the zone on either side, and the villagers from Friendship Village, as the Southern settlement is called, cultivate rice fields just as outside. We went first to the Swedish mess which belongs to the neutral nations supervisory commission. For over 25 years this small group of officers from Sweden and Switzerland on one side and Poland and Czechoslovakia on the other have held their regular weekly meetings and generally kept an eye on the sometimes shaky truce. A strange monk-like life in some ways – only the senior officer, now the charming Admiral Blom, is allowed to be accompanied by his wife – but they have got themselves very comfortably installed and the main difficulty is trying to fill the day.

After a pleasant lunch with the Swedes we were taken into the heart of the Joint Security Area. First to the shack straddling the demarcation line in which the Military Armistice Commission holds its periodic meetings: a table is placed along the line itself which is marked by the cables of two microphones: on one side sit the UN (US and ROK, plus the occasional representative of the other countries who fought alongside them in the Korean War), on the other the North Korean and Chinese. The room was empty when we were there but we were very aware of tension as North Korean guards came up to the windows outside to have a look at us and though we were allowed to walk around to the NK side of the table it was only after the UN guards had deployed their weapons. But when our U.S. escorting officer drew attention to the two flags which sit on the table (one on a three-tiered pedestal – but the other's pedestal slightly higher; one slightly larger than the other – but the other slightly wider; one with a bigger spike etc) the North Korean guards joined in the laughter.

Safely back on the southern side of the line we were taken up to the pagoda which served as an observation post for the UN forces, and could look at the imposing edifice opposite, which is apparently only about 12ft deep! Either way along the line UN and NK observation posts stared at each other. A revealing incident: There was a U.S. soldier sitting with binoculars and phone in the observation post watching for any unusual activity the other side. The Commandant made to pick the

> *binoculars up. The soldier snatched them out of his hands with a lack of ceremony which Air Chief Marshals don't often encounter.*

Later we were taken down to the Bridge of No Return, the point where prisoners had been periodically exchanged across the line which there follows the river. The last such prisoners were the crew of the *Pueblo*, the US Navy research/spy vessel which was seized by the North Koreans in 1968. The crew were held and apparently tortured for some eleven months before their return was negotiated. Wikipedia tells me that the *Pueblo* is now a museum in Pyongyang and the only ship of the US Navy in captivity. In an earlier generation, as my French colleague Philippe Legrain reminded me, the diplomats caught in North Korea when the war broke out also came across that bridge after their three years' detention, including the spy George Blake. The spot had also been the scene of gruesome events in 1976 when an attempt by UN troops to cut back a tree on the south side of the line ended in two US soldiers being hacked to death with axes by North Korean guards.

We were then taken to see one of the infiltration tunnels dug by the North Koreans under the DMZ. This, the third known one, was discovered in 1978 after test borings had been put down on the basis of information provided by a NK defector. We were taken down the interception tunnel dug by the South Koreans; a long steep way down it was too, reminding me of my coal mine adventure in North Wales. When we got down to the bottom, this impression was even stronger because the walls of the NK tunnel had been blackened. Our SK guide said that this was to support the North Korean line that the excavation must surely be an ancient Chinese coal-mine. Ironically, as we got to the point where the tunnel had been blocked off – presumably immediately under the demarcation line – there was a cage with two birds in it. Canaries? we asked. No, lovebirds, came the answer! There was a strong aroma of a PR exercise about the tunnel, as there was about many aspects of South Korea. But I had no doubts that the tunnel was basically what it was alleged to be – a tunnel bored by NK with the intention of getting behind the Southern front defences. Whether the circumstances of its discovery were as alleged was another matter.

The next day, Sunday, was a very different sort of day. We went in the morning to a "folk village" some 20 km outside Seoul, in which the government had brought together and preserved a large number of old houses from various parts of the country. Even more interestingly, a wide variety of old crafts were kept going there. I particularly enjoyed watching the hand-making of paper from mulberry pulp. It is the paper used in screens and the light shutters which cover windows. It is also used for scrolls, and there was a marvellously colourful old gentleman who painted decorative letters. I got him to do a scroll with my name, and also one for my goddaughter.

That afternoon Philippe Legrain and I were shown around some of the palaces of Seoul by the delightful daughter of a one-eyed Korean general whom we had met at dinner. (Perhaps he had two eyes really but one was covered by a patch.) It gave us a glimpse into the position of women in that society. *It was... pleasant to find a girl who obviously took pleasure in the opportunity to practice the English and French which she was studying in University. I got the impression she was rather lonely, perhaps because she was much more Westernized than most of her peers. When Philippe asked her how many women were studying at her University, she said without hesitation 7%. And it was clear from the reaction of the Korean officers to my own presence that women were kept even more in the background than in Japan. When I asked one of them what his specialty was, he burst out laughing saying that Korean women would never ask a question of that sort. To digress further, the Koreans were even more intrigued by my height – 5ft 9. One general insisted on having his photo taken standing beside me – he came just above my shoulder!*

The palaces themselves were disappointing apart from their enchanting rooves. Supported on tiers of carved eaves, the tiled surfaces swept down only to rise again with a characteristic tilt at the corners. Clay figures strutted down the roof line and sometimes wind-bells dangled underneath. I found them irresistible.

For our last day in Korea we flew by military aircraft to Pusan, the second largest city in the country. From there we travelled in a convoy, as for so much of our time in Korea: first a flashing military escort car, then the car with stars on it carrying the Commandant, and finally the rest of us in a bus which tried desperately to keep up. This time our bus was underpowered and had great difficulties. Our goal was the Hyundai shipyard, founded in the early 70s and now the largest shipyard in the world. It was a drive of some two hours, through the most beautiful country – steep hills everywhere, terraced with rice fields using every available inch of space. There were far more old houses with their entrancing tiled roofs. And more people wearing the old costumes too.

Hyundai was very impressive. We were received in the most spectacular guest suite for a very lavish lunch – an hors d'œuvre of local delicacies was followed by excellent steak and Korean wine which I would have mistaken for claret. After this we were restacked into our bus for a quick tour of the shipyards. We drove down into huge dry-docks, and saw a vast ship being extended by the simple device of cutting it in half and putting an extra bit into it. I found it all immensely impressive, but remarkably difficult to judge in the absence of expert knowledge. One obvious point was how clean and tidy it all was, and how everyone we saw seemed to be hard at work. But most striking of all were the photos on the guesthouse wall – where all this stood, 10 years earlier there was countryside with a small fishing village.

From the shipyard, on to a whistle stop tour of Hyundai car assembly plant, where they were principally producing Pony cars, the one and only all-Korean model. Very impressive to me. But my more technically qualified colleagues said that this was quite a simple line, and that we had many the same in the UK. Thank goodness. I was beginning to feel a bit depressed after the shipyard.

Back in Seoul in the evening, I persuaded two of my colleagues to go out in search of a proper Korean meal. We were advised to try a restaurant in the colourful alley just behind the hotel, and very good it turned out to be. The food was mostly highly spiced, particularly a pickled cabbage dish which seemed to be the staple of Korean meals. I greatly enjoyed a dish of sliced beef grilled at the table on a strange mound-shaped brass dish. The beef had been marinated in advance and was delicious. There was also an array of rice, sauces and side-dishes as part of the meal and some rather bony fish. All rather good, and very good value compared with the restaurants at the hotel.

To get from Seoul to Beijing we had to fly via Hong Kong. We also stopped at Taipei, where we had no special privileges and might have been in trouble had the authorities known where we were going. During the long flight while my colleagues chatted up the air hostesses I wrote my diary. It was the half-way stage of our trip and time to gather my impressions of my colleagues. I started with the Commandant, Air Chief Marshal Sir Robert Freer, a very senior officer, now about to retire.

Mid-air, 22 September 1981

A nice man, surprisingly shy, who probably is a bit lonely in his position of eminence. I was told that some of our Korean hosts assumed I was his girlfriend. Rank seems to be much more of a divider in the armed services than it is with us in the diplomatic service, where people can very easily mix in together – provided they are compatible personally. This is his last trip in the Services and the Squadron Leader, "Spike" Milligan, who is accompanying us as Admin Officer on the trip, is touchingly keen that the boss should have a good time.

Which brings me on to Spike. A cheerful, friendly person who turns out to be much more of a loner than I had expected. He has served in Hong Kong before and I suspect that when he disappears from view from time to time, it is to look up old contacts. He swears it is to write up reports of the visits we have made!

There are two other Air Force officers in the group, Bobby Robson and Tom Stonor, who joke together like a pair of schoolboys. Bobby is the exuberant one and Tom the foil – aided and abetted by Godfrey Milton-Thompson, the smooth and elegant naval doctor. They form together a nice and high-spirited core to the party – and can be counted on to hold open house in one or other bedroom late into the night. The other evening in Seoul someone had delivered a bouquet of red roses and white daisies to Godfrey's room by mistake. They were addressed to a Mr. Eto, or some such. God knows if Mr. Eto ever knew about the gift or if the donor waited discouraged for an acknowledgement. Anyhow when I joined the party for a drink, it was to be presented with roses plucked from the vase by Bobby on bended knee. The daisies came out next, a limp bunch which Tom proposed should be delivered to Mr. Eto with the original card. I ended up taking the sad remains of the bouquet back to my room – and pinned the last survivor on my tee-shirt as I left Seoul today.

Then there is Chris Croft, the other naval Captain, a quiet man who has brought his tennis racket with him and has managed to get a game at each stop so far – though only at the cost of missing out on excursions to gather local colour. David Swinburn, the Sapper Major General, is perhaps the most potentially difficult member of the group. A man of very decided opinions, he has an irritating way of giving a running commentary on everything we pass. There was a moment when I thought some of the others would rebel. But I think the crisis has passed luckily. David seems to have calmed down, and the others who were inclined to goad him – principally Bobby – have happily laid off.

That brings me to the foreign contingent, of whom there are four: a French diplomat, an Australian civil servant, and a pair of colonels from Germany and Italy. The star of the group in many ways is Hanno von

Kielmansegg, a highly talented and charming man who turns out to be widely read in the cultural background of China and Japan. Poor Hanno has back trouble and some of our rougher bus trips have had him looking bleached with pain and fatigue. To me he is really the most congenial company of the whole agreeable group, with always some interesting insight or observation to offer. He fits in well with the British hard core too – having been at Cambridge and Sandhurst no doubt helps.

The Italian, Lenny Zenotto, is also a nice and cultured man, though not in the same class of intellect. Lenny is a dedicated sightseer, and when posed in front of a local monument his normally serious face takes on a slightly wolfish grin for the camera. His English is fairly good and he has taken great trouble with it over this year, but he is obviously floored by much of the banter that is exchanged. It is bad luck for him that all the others are so fluent in English.

Then there is Philippe Legrain, former French Consul-General in Leningrad, whose wry humour is increasingly finding expression as the trip goes on. He speaks the most perfect example of Peter Sellers English I have yet to encounter which adds greatly to the effect. Philippe is also very knowledgeable about the Far East and particularly about its languages. A linguist by training, he reads a dozen languages including Chinese and has taken a great interest in the script of each country we have passed through…

That leaves the Australian member of the party, Keith Lyon. At first sight the typical Australian, Keith has the great merit of being completely unchippy. A pleasant, intelligent man with a distinctive viewpoint of his own, he fits in quite well too.

All told a very agreeable bunch. No trouble-makers and lots of entertainment value. As the only woman, I feel lucky to have such a group of companions. It is only on the rarest of occasions that I feel the odd man out!

On Wednesday 23 September, 1981, we reached Beijing at last – and, an obvious point the full significance of which had escaped me in advance, we were there as the guests of the People's Liberation Army (PLA). At the other stages of our journey we had been lavishly entertained by various hosts, but were nonetheless paying our own hotel bills, fares, etc (or our governments were). Here in China we were guests from start to finish – travel and Beijing's best hotel included. Our hosts were a series of men in ill-fitting green uniforms without badges of rank, who more often than not spoke no English.

But this is to leap ahead. After our overnight stop in Hong Kong, we caught the train for Canton and that was the first taste of the new world ahead. A comfortably spacious train festooned with antimacassars (which seemed to be very much in evidence in Communist China – the armchairs in my bedroom had them too). It was very full, and as it chugged its way slowly across the countryside, a haranguing voice was relayed in each carriage by microphone, and lots of attendants scurried up and down selling things to eat and drink. It was the "soft seat through train" to Canton, as my ticket informed me.

Crossing the border was an exciting moment. It was marked by a high barbed-wire fence which followed a small river. The train barely stopped at Lowu, the border town, except to let on a couple of uniformed officials wearing the ubiquitous red star who came down the train checking passports. The two-hour slow journey across the countryside showed us a China in which life continued as it had for centuries. The peasant agriculture – rice, or tidy market-gardens as we neared Canton – was still a matter of a man with a hoe and the occasional water buffalo. The villages looked neglected and very closed in on themselves. We crossed the occasional river, and on one there was a ferry full to the brim with people.

At Canton we were met at the station by our first representatives of the PLA, who took us across the teeming, bicycling city to the Army hotel where we were given our first Chinese banquet. It was the first taste of real Cantonese food and also of the conversational problems which arise when one has no word in common with one's neighbour. At our table of 10 there were two interpreters who helped out but otherwise it was rather sticky going. The meal itself contained some delicious dishes, particularly a barbecued fish, and some peculiar ones, notably a soup made out of snakes, and poisonous ones too. The main trouble was that my neighbour kept piling more and more onto my plate and there was no way of knowing how much more there was to come. I was almost defeated at the end by a particularly glutinous sweet rice goody which appeared to be stuffed with Christmas pudding and stuck to the hind teeth mercilessly.

From Canton it was a couple of hours flight by Chinese Airlines to Beijing, or Peking as we still called it. The plane was a Russian one – quite comfortable in first class though the *hoi polloi* were really packed in. No emergency oxygen supply, my RAF neighbour pointed out. I felt extremely sleepy after our vast meal and first saw Beijing through a haze of drowsiness. There again we were met by a couple of PLA officials, and sat round for some time in the familiar pattern of VIP suite (heavy mahogany chairs down both sides with a couple at the top for the VIPs). The Commandant was obviously struggling conversationally and sank to new lows of banality – but I was glad it wasn't me in the top chair. Then a drive into Beijing along wide streets almost deserted of cars. There were swarms of bicycles around – quite unlit – and little knots of people gathered under street lamps playing cards, or occasionally just reading.

Then to the hotel, which was obviously trying hard to be modern but had old fashioned furniture and an institutional atmosphere. The beds were quite comfortable, if hard, and by now I could not keep sleep at bay any longer. I awoke next morning tantalized to find out what I would see when I pulled my bedroom curtains. If I had got my sense of direction right it could be the Forbidden City. But when I discovered how to open the curtains (surprisingly there was an electric motor for the purpose) it was to look out on a thick white fog. Breakfast was served downstairs and the first surprise of the morning was to find a member of the PLA lurking on the landing to send me in the proper direction.

The day was largely spent in two mammoth set-piece briefings by Chinese officials, interrupted by a very civilized interlude at the Embassy, where we had lunch. The first briefing was by He Tingshi of the State Planning Commission. It took place in a large airless room lined with deep antimacassared armchairs in which we all sat looking inwards and were endlessly plied with sweet fizzy orangeade. It was a very long presentation, and as the statistics flowed, I could see a number of my colleagues having difficulty in staying awake. I wriggled in my chair and dug my nails into my palms but didn't do very well. The afternoon briefing, which like the morning one lasted two hours, was in exactly the same place, but given this time by the lively General Xu Xin (pronounced Shoo Shin) on the whole range of China's defence and foreign policies. This turned out the lesser ordeal, partly because of Xu Xin's exuberant personality, and partly because he let us ask lots of questions and actually answered them. It was an impressive performance.

The visit to the Embassy was a relief from tension. The Ambassador, Percy Craddock, welcomed us with a drink on his deliciously cool terrace. We then had a free and easy briefing session and an excellent lunch. The Embassy building was the one that was stormed during the Cultural Revolution. It dated from the 1950s, but in the garden were numerous relics brought from the Legation of Boxer Rebellion days including the big bronze bell which was rung each day while it was besieged.

We saw quite a lot of Beijing during the day from our coach – a big straggly city, and apart from some new buildings it had a very run-down air. There were still lots of old houses, secretive behind their shabby grey walls. Tantalizingly, all one could see was their roofs and the occasional glimpse through a doorway. All touches of elegance, such as the stone figures which used to stand outside the doors, had gone. We saw a number of markets which seemed to be selling a very limited range of produce – more cabbage than I had ever seen in my life. There were bicycles everywhere, and few cars. Driving was made hair-raising by the way that bicyclists hogged the centre of the road, just escaping the wheels of the honking bus. Unlike Canton, most of the men were wearing blue Mao suits. The women were in sexless trousers, but occasionally one saw a girl who had chosen a bright coloured shirt and had taken some trouble with her appearance. Once we saw a young couple holding hands.

That night a dinner was given in our honour at the Great Hall of the People. Our host was an old veteran called Wu Xinquan, who was a Deputy Chief of General Staff and had been, so I was told, one of the judges in the trials connected with the Gang of Four. We arrived in a group to find a row of uniformed PLA officers waiting in a line to shake us by the hand. Then on to a U-shaped group of armchairs: Wu Xinquan and the Commandant took their seats at the head, leaving the rest of us to find places down the side and to listen while they exchanged polite nothings through an interpreter. To drink we were offered more of that fizzy orange or tea. After half an hour or so of this we moved on to eat at three large tables. I found myself at the top table beside Xu Xin, the jovial general of the afternoon, who was I think then Assistant Chief of General Staff. Xu Xin spoke no English. The conversational range was therefore pretty limited but we chatted cheerfully about the food as he kept on loading morsels onto my plate and tried to tease me into drinking maotai, a lethal-tasting alcohol about which I had been forewarned. Much of what we had to eat was delicious. I particularly liked a crispy fried duck ("crisp and fragrant duck" was its charming name), and slices of lotus stalk. I managed quite creditably with sea slugs and shark's belly, though they were a bit slithery for my taste. The worst was the first cousin of yesterday's Christmas pudding roll – and I firmly left that after the first bite. Promptly at 9:30 Wu Xinquan rose from the table followed by the other PLA and then we were all trooping out and saying goodbye.

Next morning we left the hotel at 7:30 for the Great Wall which at the point we visited is some 50 km out of the city. It was a fascinating drive, first through Beijing itself where people were already thronging the streets though the occasional house still had its old red door shut on the outer world. Then through the sprawling suburbs, where I was surprised to see shepherds bringing flocks of sheep right into the city. Then out into the country where people were working in the fields in their hundreds, mostly with hoes and hand ploughs though we saw a few tractors too. It was another misty morning and we did not see the hills until suddenly we were in the midst of them, winding up a long valley between pretty farms and orchards of persimmon and other fruit. The Swallow Mountains, as they are called, were very dramatic, with steep peaks succeeding each other to make a spectacular skyline of receding shades of grey.

There were a number of walls at different times and we must have crossed three or four before we reached our goal, a large stretch of wall which had been restored to its former shape and size. Some six metres wide and six metres high, it marched across the landscape up the peaks and down the valleys, with every hundred metres or so a two-storeyed watch tower. We set out to climb the stretch of wall leading off to our left up to a vantage point on the hill above. It was a considerable climb sometimes on slippery sloping paving (lethal when wet) or sometimes up steep steps. I was thankful I had been advised to wear stout shoes and comfortably loose slacks. I had to force myself up the last bit, but it was worth it for the spectacular views at the top, and the atmosphere of the place. On the way up we passed a dromedary being used as a prop for photography. As we came down, Bobby Robson, our team photographer, dared me to get on it for a photo. So somewhat gingerly I did, mounting a ladder on the hidden side and then slithering into the surprisingly comfortable gap between the two tufted humps, with people shouting encouragements to me from the wall above.

The next item on our programme was a visit to the 6th Tank Division. The tanks were Chinese-built, said our commentator – exact copies of a Russian tank, whispered Tom Stonor in my ear. As we arrived a dozen or so tanks were drawn up in line with the crews standing to attention in front of them in the hot sun. I felt a qualm that we were half an hour late. There was then a demonstration of wheeling and firing which we watched from an observation room, each sitting at a place provided with binoculars, dark glasses, damp face-cloth – and of course the inevitable fizzy orange juice.

Afterwards we were able to climb into two of the tanks. Hanno, who was a tank man, was in his element talking to the tank crews and clambering down inside. He said afterwards that they were the tanks of approximately 20 years earlier in Europe.

The Tank Division entertained us to another banquet. It was less formal than the previous night's party in the Great Hall of the People, and everybody was very relaxed. There was much drinking of maotai for which I was thankful; after the heat and exertions of the morning I had quite a headache. Fortunately maotai mixes well with beer and leaves no after effects – until your knees simply give way under you, which fortunately did not happen to me. The custom was for the host to challenge the guest to a drink with the Chinese equivalent of "bottoms up". I was told that as a lady I might just sip the toast, though there was a moment when I feared I might be forced into draining my glass, but fortunately somebody must have told my neighbour to lay off. The funniest moment came, however, when the Political Commissar, who was apparently the chief host (certainly he said much more than the silent deputy tank commander), proposed my health with the unexpected comment "you hold up half the sky." Tom Stonor on my right commented *sotto voce* that he wondered if this was a reference to my beauty or my height. This remark was translated to great mirth all around.

The rest of the day was spent in more super sight-seeing. The Ming Tombs were first on the afternoon's agenda. There was an attractive approach between pairs of animals and human statues, a collection that reminded me of some of the temples of Angkor – but here there were two pairs of each species, two male elephants facing each other standing up, followed by two females very sensibly sitting down. We saw the only tomb that had been excavated, that of Wan Li. Just to be difficult the Ming emperors took a different name when they died and Wan's tomb is called Dingling. We were taken down to the rather horrid subterranean galleries where the coffins of the Emperor and his two wives were found, along with lots of treasure to speed them on their way. Some of the treasures were on view in a museum nearby but most were taken off by the Europeans of earlier days. In front of the tumulus was a high "soul" tower which seemed to float above the trees. Its roofs, like those of the palaces in Seoul, had processions of figures riding down to the corners and I finally discovered what they represented: a wicked prince who was driven out by his people and tied to the roof to die; the procession brought up behind by a dragon was there to make sure he didn't get back in again. It was a tantalizingly brief visit and I wished we had been given time to wander among the other tombs.

Another long drive took us back into Beijing. There was just time to change before going to see a performance by Chinese acrobats – a standard entertainment for visiting foreign delegations, I was told. It was a most entertaining evening and they performed prodigies of balance and precision leaps, with human chains hanging from the ceiling and fantastic piles rising from the floor. Perhaps the best of all was a contortionist who seemed to have no rigid bones in her body at all. She managed to lie down with glasses of coloured water on her forehead, feet, and hands, and then roll over without spilling a drop.

The next day we went to the Chinese National Defence College, which involved another long drive through the suburbs, this time skirting the Summer Palace. Our reception at the Academy had a markedly different flavour from our other encounters – not that the message of goodwill was any less effusive. The difference was Mao. Whereas his name had scarcely if ever been mentioned elsewhere, here it was referred to constantly. The College had been founded on his inspiration, a major part of the syllabus was devoted to Mao Tse Tung thought, and his wartime inspiration, etc. This certainly bore out the view that the rearguard action against the debunking of Mao was strongest within the Army.

After the usual speeches of welcome in the usual horseshoe of square armchairs, we were taken on a tour of the classrooms. The first one had several hundred students in it standing in descending tiers from the door at the back where we came in. As we trooped down the gangway to the front they all clapped in unison. Remembering our preliminary briefing we all clapped back. We then lined up alongside the Commandant facing them all. More speeches, during which the keen students in front kept their eyes riveted on the speaker – though I was glad to note one or two dissidents with wandering eyes further back. Then up the gangway the other side with more mutual clapping, and out. The Assistant DA who accompanied us said that that was the first time he knew of that visitors to the Academy had actually seen any students.

Apart from Mao this visit was memorable for paranoia about Russian expansionism. The briefing which ended our tour was an extreme statement of the hegemony thesis even by Chinese standards of the time, starting with the 16th century and coming on to a graphic illustrated assessment of the current Russian threat to Europe and the Far East, complete with a forest of aggressive arrows. This was followed by a brief film on the Chinese incursion into Vietnam a couple of years previously – all glorious advances with no counterfire, only Vietnamese corpses, and the verdict that China withdrew having achieved her objectives. Not a hint of the difficulties the Chinese apparently encountered during the campaign. Finally we were shown a video tape recording our own visit to the college which could only have been filmed an hour before.

I had arranged to have lunch with Stephen Jessel, the BBC correspondent who I knew in Paris and who had just arrived in Beijing. We were late back but happily Stephen and his wife were still waiting for me. It had to be a scratch lunch because time was so short and our efforts to find a table deserve to be recorded as an illustration of the frustrations that beset life in China. Stephen led the way into the downstairs restaurant where he had often eaten before but it was full, so we went to another one at the far end of the rambling hotel. Here we were stopped at the door by a flunky who said it was for delegations only. At this point I put my oar in and said I was a member of a delegation. What was my room number then? When I gave it I was told that in that case I must eat in the restaurant on the second floor – where the RCDS party had indeed been taking all its meals. So back we went. In the end it must be the PLA who paid for all three of us, though in fact Stephen was trying to invite me out for lunch.

The afternoon excursion was to visit the Imperial Palace, the Great Within where the Ming Emperors lived their extraordinary hidden lives. As courtyard followed courtyard, ever more magnificent halls unfolded, with golden yellow tiled roofs and marble balustrades. It was a place one could have spent days wandering through, but we took it at a brisk trot and I was in continual danger of getting left behind yet again as I stopped to take photos. When we had gone right through the chain of halls and reception chambers we were taken into some much more intimate rooms off to one side with courtyard gardens. It is here that the remaining treasures of the Ming were kept – we were told the Kuomintang took most of them off to Taiwan – but we saw fabulous gold reliquaries, jewellery, models in jade, coral and quartz. Wonderful things which by Western standards seemed incredibly ill-guarded.

We had to scurry through because afterwards we were due to call on the Chief of General Staff, Yang Dheje, an important figure and a Deng Xiaoping man. He had succeeded Deng in that role in 1980. Yet another reception in yet another chamber in the Great Hall of the People. More solid armchairs in which this time we students sat silent while polite speeches were exchanged between Yang and the Commandant. It was the most stultified of all the meetings yet and as the hour passed slowly I was able to note that only the leaders were provided with spittoons beside their chairs. It is also quite fun watching which of the group was having trouble fighting off sleep. Philippe got much teased because he firmly shut his eyes and put on a stuffed monkey expression that could be deep attention or pure somnolence.

Then yet another quick change for another banquet – ours this time, in return for hospitality received. It was in a restaurant where the food, from Shansi province, was quite different from what we had had so far. It was very good, I thought, but we were all beginning to feel a bit jaded. I was very glad when at 8:45 our guests all got up and left as one man.

It was rather tantalizing leaving Beijing. Though we had crammed more into three days than any normal programme, one still left with the feeling of having scarcely scratched the surface of this secretive city. And the privileged, cocooned existence of our group, shepherded at every turn, gave little chance to get the feel of the place as an ordinary person might experience it. I managed to slip the leash once for about 15 minutes and went off on my own down the shopping street alongside the hotel. It was positively refreshing to be just one of the thousands of people walking up and down. Europeans were no longer a rare sight in Beijing and I seemed of no particular interest to anyone. There were people everywhere, on the pavements and in the road leaving only a narrow path in the middle for the buses to hoot their way up and down. At one point there were a lot of people looking at a series of exhibits behind glass on a railing – a rather good photographic exhibition – and then further on, and attracting just as much attention, the daily papers in Chinese and English displayed page by page.

We flew next morning to Shanghai. If Beijing was a city turned in on itself with its hidden courtyards, in Shanghai people lived in the streets. It was a bustling, cheerful city, where people smiled at you. The houses had balconies and the ground floor rooms were open with people sitting on the pavement gambling, being shaved or doing whatever they wanted. I saw several people making baskets, and a woman making silk flowers. The hotel too presented a most welcome change from the pompous run-down monstrosity in Beijing. This was a much smaller and simpler hotel, run by the army. But it was sparkling clean and fresh. No cockroaches and standing pools of water on the bathroom floor! One could sense the rising spirits all round as the party settled in.

The afternoon involved a visit to another shipyard. Very different from the spick and span Hyundai yard in Korea. This was an old yard founded in the 1850s and far from modern. No sign of computers or robots here. The great metal sheets seemed to be cut out almost like dress material – shapes chalked on with the help of a wooden template then cut out and welded by hand. In many ways the most interesting thing was the work force – women working everywhere beside the men. A lot of people were hanging around not doing very much. We got a glimpse into some of their living quarters which were the most dreadful hovels.

In the briefing in the Deputy Manager's office I asked about orders from abroad. Yes, they were now building a ship for Hong Kong. Later we met the HK shipper's agent, a solitary Englishman amongst 30,000 Chinese workmen. He explained that the negotiations had been handled by the Chinese ship builders' office in Beijing, who had directed the order to this yard which had had no difficulty in getting the necessary materials because it was an export order. Presumably, if the foreign exchange was needed badly enough, prices were fixed at whatever level was necessary to get the order. It seemed impossible for a yard such as we saw to compete with Hyundai. The two were centuries apart.

After the shipyard a quick change for a formal banquet given by the Shanghai garrison. This time I found myself between Hanno and a jovial general who was Chief of Staff to the Garrison Commander. My conversation with the general lagged owing to the usual absence of a common language. I was apt to fall back on appreciation of the food, which had the disadvantage that our lavish hosts immediately piled more on my plate. The main common language was the toast – or *gambei*. This time the *gambeis* were flowing particularly freely and my neighbouring general took to trying to make us empty the glass on each occasion. As a female I hoped I was exempt, or at least permitted to drink in wine rather than firewater. In fact it was Hanno, a near teetotaller, who came to grief first. As he manfully downed a glass of the stuff, in his words "it went down the wrong throat" and left him spluttering. I sympathized smugly, but a few minutes later it was my turn. I was shamed (bullied?) into tipping down a glass of the red wine, couldn't stop laughing, and the inevitable happened. The remnants of the wretched stuff were in my windpipe for half an hour.

It was a considerable wrench getting myself up the next morning in a city still dark though already stirring. The train – soft class and very comfortable – left Shanghai at 6:45 and got into Hangzhou shortly after 10 am. We were met by representatives of the local Air Force garrison and taken to their base to see an air display. The planes, built in China, were apparently MiG copies and looked as lethal as any other fighters to me. After a routine low-level fly-past at speed four planes gave a firing demonstration, strafing and rocketing the strip of ground beside the runway in front of us. Live ammo too, I was assured. It was of course really some way away, but I jumped at each bang. Another enormous banquet lunch – without incident this time, but notable for the vast quantity of delicious food. I thought the courses would never stop coming. Fortunately our host at my table made it clear that he himself was going to drink the toasts in orange squash.

The afternoon was devoted to sight-seeing. Hangzhou is set beside a smooth lake with a backdrop of mountains. It reminded me of Kashmir, even to the arched bridges in the long causeways which divided parts of it. We were taken for a most enjoyable boat ride round the lake, stopping at an island with pretty pagodas, which was something of an anti-climax because of the crush of tourists photographing each other. Then on to a garden the other side. It was lovely to have a feeling of leisure after our hectic last few days, and the calm of the place added to the soothing effect. It was easy to see why this was one of the favourite honeymoon places in China – for those able to have honeymoons. The mountains in their receding lines of pearly grey, topped by the occasional pagoda, completed my pleasure.

But I was a bit shocked to see that in this most fertile part of China, men (and sometimes women) were used as beasts of burden in a way I had never seen elsewhere. Men yoked to wooden carts with immense loads of bricks, sacks or steel, strained to pull their burdens along. The three-wheel bicycle rickshaws were clearly only the rich man's form of transport.

We also visited a revered Buddhist shrine, dating from the 6th century. But today it was basically a tourist site with crowds trooping through though I did see one woman at her devotions, and a number of people burning joss sticks. I felt very sorry for the solitary Buddhist monk standing guard beside his shrine. There did not seem to be much place for such people in the China of the early 80s. The shrine itself (called the Lingyin Si or Temple of Divine Mystery) was very impressive though much of the building was relatively new. Inside there were vast and ancient Buddhas and a selection of fearsome guardian spirits who were new to me. Despite its spiritual neglect the place had an atmosphere of age-old devotions that seemed to win through. Incidentally here – as at the Imperial Palace in Beijing – it was thanks to Zhou Enlai that the treasures were kept safe from the Cultural Revolution. On his orders the temples were locked up so the Red Guards could not get in. The path down from the temple buildings was overlooked by rocky cliffs into which countless Buddhas were carved dating back to the 10th century. An intriguing place which I would have liked to have more time to savour. I particularly did not like a young woman who was having herself photographed sitting on one knee of one of the cliff Buddhas.

After a very long day which had started with a call before 5 am the train journey back to Shanghai began to drag and I was very tired. But surrounded by sleeping companions I resolved to stay awake and bring my journal up to date. The four-hour trip to Hangzhou had provided some interesting conversations with our PLA guardians, and particularly with our senior permanent companion, Dong Ledong of the Foreign Affairs Bureau, an interesting and intelligent man who had travelled abroad with the Chief of General Staff Yang Dheje. He proved unexpectedly ready to talk and remarkably freely, though occasionally it was obvious that I (or the Commandant who was sitting next to him) had pressed the button calling for propaganda. He volunteered that one could usually tell the origin of a senior officer in the PLA by his age. Those in their late 60s or 70s would come from the Yunan area, and might well have taken part in the Long March. Some 4,000 of the 30,000 survivors – such as Yang Dheje and Wu Xinquan – were still alive. The 50–60 age group usually came from the Eastern provinces and had taken part in the war against the Japanese. Younger officers might come from anywhere.

After he had talked about this for some time and about the war with the Kuomintang, I risked a question about the Chinese incursion into Vietnam. Had they not found the tactic of a People's Liberation War being used against them? He replied that the VN leaders were indeed trained in this theory, many of them being graduates of the Chinese Military Academy, but in such a short campaign the tactics – which only really took their effect over time – were not applicable. I then asked if the Chinese action had not run the risk of forcing the independent Vietnamese into the arms of the Russians – but did not get a real reply.

We had the same seating arrangement on the return journey. This time Dong volunteered to answer a question I had asked earlier in the day about how collective leadership worked in the army. He explained that each garrison (or for that matter Embassy, company or whatever, with appropriate changes in title) had a military commander and a political commissar. Both of these, with other key officers, were members of the Political Committee, and one or other was likely to be the Secretary of the Committee who was in fact the most powerful person around. Each of them was responsible for executive action in their respective spheres, within broad guidelines set by the Political Committee to whom they had to refer important decisions and report annually. Committee decisions were taken by majority vote and everyone, including the Secretary, was expected to act on the decision though they also had the right to alert senior authorities if they thought it seriously wrong. The Political Commissar was responsible for political education, promotions and discipline, while the Military Commander looked after all technical and routine operational matters, including military equipment. People normally stuck to their speciality, political or military, though switches from one stream to another did occur. In wartime situations the Military Commander would appoint a potential successor just in case someone else had to take over – it might be his deputy commander or the Political Commissar. It was odd discussing this archetypal Communist pattern of control with somebody who lived in it and made it sound just as ordinary as any other system. He admitted it was cumbersome and could be slow, but did not mention the disincentive to taking risks. When I asked whether most senior officers were members of the Party, it was with a slight laugh that he replied almost 100%.

The morning excursion the next day was to visit the East China Sea Fleet at their base a few miles up the Huangpu River. The Chinese Navy is the youngest service, having been founded in 1949. (I gathered, though nobody specifically said so, that the former navy must have decamped with the Kuomintang.) It was all the more of a surprise to find that we were received with far more traditional ceremony than elsewhere and indeed that the whole base area had unexpected touches of grace. We entered the gate into a pretty winding shrub-lined avenue decked with flags and turned a corner to find a large guard of honour, complete with brass band. The Chinese sailors' uniform also added to the impression of traditionalism – with their familiar wide collars falling square at the back and their jaunty sailors' hats with fluttering ribbons they looked very like their fellows from Western Europe, apart from the baggy Chinese trousers and of course the faces.

We were invited to inspect a whole row of ships lined up along the river bank; each was decked with flags and had rows of officers and men standing smartly to attention in the bows. An enormous amount of care and preparation had obviously gone into our visit – the paint was so new that we had the impression that all the ships we visited had been specially painted for the occasion. Ships are not my strong point, one being frankly very like another, but my colleagues were very impressed by the smartness of the place – though not by the equipment which here again seemed to be 20 to 30 years behind what was in use in the West.

We then had our first banquet of the day and here too one was conscious of the special effort at elegance – flowers on the table (for the first time since we had been in China), pretty name cards beside each place and (also for the first time) a little memento for each of us – a key ring with a medallion of the East China Fleet as its fob. It was a delicious meal too, but by this time I was beginning to flag and was devoutly thankful that the quiet Admiral who was our host went easy on the *gambeis*.

The afternoon of the day of our visit to the East China fleet was spent in a visit to a machine tools factory, the usual question and answer session followed by a drag around a series of hangars containing lathes, tractor assembly lines and various other machinery whose purpose I did not understand. The interest of the place to me (and it was a fight against an oncoming bug to maintain even that amount) was in the manager's attitude. His speech was full of statistics to show how well his factory had done: they had overfulfilled their production target and been top of the league of similar factories; they had according to latest policy been producing light industrial products in response to market forces. But when one asked how much of his production was in response to direct demand the answer was evasive. He either didn't know, or more probably was not prepared to give any precise response to a question designed to test the meaning of the political jargon. He responded similarly to questions about problems he might have with supplies. And the entry into light industry appeared to be selling some tractors to communes. The other interesting thing about his presentation was the difficulty our PLA interpreters from Beijing had in translating him. They explained afterwards that the dialect spoken in Shanghai was almost a different language: even the word for "I" was totally different.

Luckily for me we got back to the hotel early for once and I was able to retreat to my room. I had a small temperature, as I had suspected (100.5), but a couple of hours and a couple of aspirin later I felt sufficiently revived to face the evening which was the occasion of the RCDS return banquet. It was in another hotel, the Jinjiang, formerly the Cathay in the days of

Shanghai's pre-Communist glory. My memory of the banquet (the second in one day!) quickly faded into a composite memory of all those we had in China – dish after countless dish, never knowing what the next mouthful would bring; the innumerable *gambeis* in *maotai* or the sweet red wine which was also always served; the gulps of *lam-chan* – a mineral water with a taste like Epsom salts, which I greatly preferred to the fizzy orange; the stilted attempts at conversation through an interpreter if one was lucky enough to be close to one. This time I sat next to Dong Ledong, so I had an easy time. Among the many toasts and speeches Dong made one expressing his hope that we had enjoyed the visit and that the programme had enabled us to learn as much as possible of China in the time. He said that our visit was like "looking at flowers from the back of a galloping horse."

The next day was our last in China, and the first in which we had a little leisure. The morning excursion to the Shanghai Industrial Exhibition (housed in a monumental and imposing building put up by the Russians to be a Russo-Chinese Hall of Friendship and, Philippe said, quite typical of Russian contemporary architecture) was blessedly abbreviated. After the obligatory rooms of machinery and more or less precision tools (here again Chinese standards were often pathetically out of date, though what we were shown was streets ahead of what we had seen in the factories) we came into galleries of arts, crafts, and curios which were just another shop for the tourists. We managed some brief and reasonably leisured sight-seeing in the afternoon, and a visit to the Friendship Store (to which foreign visitors were led at every opportunity). This one was of special interest to me since I had read in my guide book that it was in the grounds of the former British Consulate. I wandered round to find the old building – still there, though sadly dilapidated, very reminiscent in style of the Embassy in Bangkok. For a moment the ghosts of former colleagues seemed to gather round.

The building was across the road from the Bund, the river-side dyke which was the promenade of Shanghai. Big ships were on the move on the splendid river. People clustered round us whenever we stopped, and there was always someone longing to try out their English. (How different from Beijing!) The press of people in Chinese cities was one of my unforgettable impressions. They were everywhere, including all over the streets. The motorcar was rare. But any halcyon ideas of peace and quiet were shattered the moment one arrived. Every bicyclist of the thousands that swarmed every street rang his bell, and every bus hooted its horn. The cacophony of sound made central London seem a paradise of peace. Looking back from the Bund there was a row of pre-war skyscrapers, still quite majestic though unpainted for decades. They were the foreign banks and trading houses which were the backbone of Shanghai's earlier prosperity.

I was afraid we weren't going to be allowed to see any of Shanghai's older Chinese temples and, primed by my guidebook, I asked our guide rather pointedly about some of the more interesting ones. Whether or not as a result of this tactic we were taken to a place called Yuyuan, a garden designed in Ming days which was the most frequented pleasure spot in Shanghai. To get there we had to walk through a maze of fascinating streets in the Old Quarter of the city – restaurants, booths etc, full of life and basic commercial drive. I enjoyed the garden too. It was unlike any garden I had ever seen – a riot of Gothic rockeries and grottos, with red lacquered pavilions, their roofs alive with fearsome warriors and dragons. The garden was divided into several sections by walls in the form of dragons with snorting faces and undulating backs that snaked between the grottos. Here too there were swarms of people, almost all Chinese. Everywhere there were young men with box cameras photographing their girlfriends – we got the impression that in this puritanical society, where even holding hands was generally frowned on, the photography game had a special sexual thrill. For the first time I saw people playing with their children, holding them up to the stone lion-dogs to see if they could remove the stone balls trapped in their mouths.

It was time to leave China after our long week on the galloping horse. I did so with mixed feelings, as I struggled to fathom this complex country which had revealed so little of itself. It was, I wrote, "*at the same time so sophisticated and so backward. It is difficult to see how China can ever bring an acceptable standard of living to its teeming millions, let alone make the leap into the club of advanced industrial countries.*" This seems incredibly blind and patronising now but I could not help feeling sorry for those with the responsibility of trying to achieve the transition, especially those with experience of the West – Dong, for instance, who was reading a book with a slip cover in French with advertisements for Evian-les-Bains and other resorts. "Lovely places for holidays," said Chris Croft, rather inappropriately. "Ah, holidays!" said Dong, with a world of ironic resignation on his voice. Anyhow it was with a sense of liberation that we boarded the Cathay Pacific flight for Hong Kong and ordered round after round of Buck's Fizz. Bobby Robson, always the joker, announced he had just had a nightmare: that the plane had been hijacked and was returning to Beijing.

Our return to Hong Kong was something of an anti-climax. Everyone was feeling pretty jaded, and it was time to go home. Looking around at my colleagues it was clear that even strong men were beginning to wilt. Several had had stomach problems ever since Japan. Hanno, with his bad back, had stood up in jolting buses over most of the Far East. My own fluey cold left me feeling distinctly sorry for myself for three days. As Tom Stonor pointed out to me, we hadn't had a day off for a month. So we were all pretty fed up to find an intensive programme awaiting us, beginning at 8:20 the morning after our late night arrival. There was a definite spirit of revolt among the troops as we trudged through new town, after housing development, after industrial area. Matters were made worse by the unfriendly grey clouds which swirled around the hills, periodically drenching us with unseasonal rain.

The best day was certainly our trip along the frontier, part by road, and part by helicopter. One could not have got a clearer picture of the terrain across which the illegal immigrants still chanced their luck at getting into Hong Kong – the watery flats in the North-East (fish and duck ponds mostly, instead of the rice I remembered 15 years ago), and further inland the rugged country across which the border snaked with its high wire fence festooned with coils of barbed wire. The road which we followed wound in and out of the fence between fields where the Hakka women worked, wearing strange hats with black curtains hanging all round the brim. Many of them had fields the other side of the border from their homes and there were innumerable controlled gates. The frontier was under observation for most of its length from a series of little forts and look-out posts (largely manned by Gurkhas) and it was of course patrolled. Armed frontier fences always seem an affront to human liberty, but as they go this was quite a friendly one. Hanno commented that it was very different from what we would see in Berlin where people were shot down like rats. Here the "illegals," as they were called, simply got put back across the border if caught. Until the "reach base" policy was abolished after negotiations with the Chinese those who got in undetected had full rights in Hong Kong. The HK Government was still considering what to do about the so-called "legals" – the people who came across the border openly with two-way visas from the Chinese – of whom only 4% actually went back.

One of the oddest places on the border was a village called Sha Tau Kok, the only place where, for reasons I didn't fathom, citizens of both sides mingled freely. This had been a dangerous place, with Triads, but now it was one of the few remaining picturesque villages of the New Territories. Its long wharf stretching out into the sea was lined by junks and house-boats. In theory the Chinese boats were supposed to be on one side and the HK ones the other, but in practice they mingled, and we were told that one could recognize the Chinese boats by their lack of paint.

From Sha Tau Kok we climbed back into our helicopters for the trip to Tai Po. (As a digression I might mention that in a fit of enthusiasm I got up early that morning to wash my hair, still sticky with the dust of China. I had reckoned without the gale created by the helicopter's whirling blades which gave me the most intensive blow-dry I have ever had.) Tai Po in the 1960s was a country creek with fishing boats. Now it was a new town with skyscrapers sprouting all round. One of the few spots of old Hong Kong which still survived was Island House, the residence of the District Commissioner for the New Territories. It was here that the helicopters landed and it would be difficult to imagine a more dramatic setting. The small circular pad was quite surrounded by water except for the narrow path leading to the island with its pretty white colonial house. The smaller helicopter with the Commandant landed first and then the Wessex with the rest of us came in – with considerable difficulty because of the very strong wind.

The new towns and housing estates which we saw (rather too many of them in the circumstances) were immensely impressive. Armies of skyscrapers now marched in places that were open fields a short time before, or even open sea because there had been a great deal of reclamation. But I was struck by the ruthlessness with which areas of land had been cleared of their former irregular inhabitants. The former peasant landowners of the New Territories had often become very rich but the multitude of newcomers, mostly squatters, got short shrift. This strong-arm aspect of life in Hong Kong seemed to be generally accepted, and indeed it was probably the only way to cope with the appalling population pressures.

We were taken into several flats in buildings built at various periods and for different sections of the community. The original H-blocks of the 1950s and 60s were being renovated by adding individual plumbing, improving the lay-out of rooms and allowing a little more space per head. New paint helped too and openwork concrete screens gave a little privacy. We also saw an area of temporary housing where several blocks were reserved for old people under the supervision of some nuns. I talked briefly to one very old lady who invited me into the room she shared with another old woman. They said they were happy there, but what else could they say? It seemed incredibly cramped and lacking in privacy, but presumably these things are simply accepted as facts of life. One thing about this old lady fascinated me: she had tiny deformed feet clad in slippers about five inches long. Her feet had clearly been bound and one could still see how the toes were jammed back against the heel which was creased underneath. It was the only time I saw bound feet. She must have been about 80, though it was difficult to say.

We were taken to see camps where "boat people" fleeing Communist Vietnam were interned in former British barracks on first arrival. The big rooms had layer upon layer of cubicles not much bigger than a double bed and only some four feet high; they reminded me of the scaffolding beds in the tube stations in London during the bombing in the 1940s. Each family had their pathetic few possessions gathered in their hutch. But it did not feel an unhappy place. There were children playing, and the adults looked well and healthy. Of course these were the ones who had survived the terrible journeys in which so many died and no doubt they were simply thankful to be there. Hong Kong with its problems of immigration from China did not want to give these refugees permanent asylum but they were still arriving, though in decreasing numbers, and it was getting more and more difficult to persuade other countries to take them. One of the immigration officers said that after the victory of the Left in France refugees were reluctant to accept resettlement there anyway because they took it for granted that it would be a Communist government like that they had left. No comment from Philippe.

Several of us were invited to a dinner party given by a very old and very rich Chinese gentleman called Mr. M.W. Lo. To my pleasure the party turned out to be in his house on Hong Kong Island above Repulse Bay. It was a fabulous position and we had a delicious European dinner with paté de foie and real caviar by the spoonful. There was a moment when our host said he wished to propose a toast and I had to avoid the eye of Hanno who I could hear muttering "*gambei*" but this time thankfully it was champagne, not *maotai*. The other guests at dinner were an interesting group. One of my neighbours at dinner was Mr. Stanley Ho, the owner of the Macao Casino. An easy dinner companion but someone I would be extremely cautious of in other circumstances. When I mentioned that I was due to go to our Embassy in Jakarta, he told me that he had gaming interests there which had just been closed down as a result of pressure from local Muslims, and that he had asked the British Embassy to intervene on his behalf. I took care not to pursue this line of conversation.

Finally, I should mention our meetings with Sir Jack Cater, the Chief Secretary – in effect the Prime Minister of Hong Kong. Sir Jack was a very attractive person with a fine face and a refreshingly direct manner. When introducing me to the leading member of the nominated executive council he made great play of the fact that she might really be called prime minister given the way power worked in the Colony. I found this uncomfortably unconvincing. He certainly looked after us well, laying on a lunch party and a reception to meet local Chinese as well as a briefing. His glamorous daughter – a member of the Hong Kong Stock Exchange – was in evidence at the drinks party.

Then it was time to go back to England. Our arrival at Gatwick sparked off the first real personal ill feeling of the whole trip – about going through customs. Ordinary mortals once more, each fighting for their own luggage amongst the sea of incoming passengers, we were faced with the usual choice of red channel or green. All of us had of course bought goodies in Hong Kong, and I like many others decided that this was an occasion when my smuggler's instincts had better be suppressed. It soon became clear that everyone in the red line was being charged a flat percentage of whatever value they declared. Not very serious for me because I was entitled to the status of a resident abroad, and most of what I had bought would be going to Jakarta with me. But some of the others found themselves writing out substantial cheques. Imagine their fury at finding that those who had walked through the green had all got away scot-free – and, worse, that our sharp-operating escort had actually asked some of the foreign students to carry some things through for him. It was just as well that the moment for our tight-knit group to disperse had arrived. When we regathered at the college the following week tempers had cooled, and everyone was busy swapping travellers' tales with the rest of the College returning from their five different areas of experience.

There was an excellent tradition in the College that the first week after the world tours was devoted to presentations by each team of their own stories and conclusions. As the last group back to the UK we had to work hard to get ourselves ready in the time. Each presentation was to last about 50 minutes followed by a similar period for questions. How to cover our kaleidoscopic experiences of four different countries in such a short time? Godfrey, as Deputy Tour Leader, decreed that he would introduce the presentation, then Hanno should talk on Japan, David Swinburn on Korea, myself on China, and Philippe Legrain on Hong Kong. Bobby Robson and

Tom Stonor would finish it off with some of the funnier moments of the trip. The whole was to be built round the photos we had taken, formatted as slides, bringing in our video from the Chinese Defence Academy and a recording of Shanghai street noise that Keith Lyon and I had made at great peril to our lives (by standing in the middle of the road as the buses and bicycles came at us!).

It was generally agreed that China might have the longest time but even so I was asked to compress my thoughts into 10 minutes. Not much for a nation with a quarter of the world's population! And I wanted to try to give our audience something of the atmosphere of our experience as well as the bare facts of what we saw and learned about defence, which was to be the common theme for the whole presentation. The week passed quickly as we watched other presentations in the morning (and they got better and better as the week progressed, ending with an excellent morning given by the Middle East party who had been received by King Hussein as well as by President Sadat 10 days before his murder). Each afternoon we worked on our own piece, rehearsing for timekeeping and comments, and endlessly sifting through the available collections of slides to find the images that best illustrated the points we wanted to make.

At last it was done and our day arrived. I felt distinctly nervous but with that slightly paralyzed calm that has seen me through many difficult moments. I had been told in rehearsal that I spoke too slowly. Could I speed it up and yet keep myself from a monotonous reading of my prepared text? And would I manage to control the button for the slides so that the right one arrived at the right moment and I didn't go into reverse by mistake? There was also the tape recorder to manage, with my street noise.

It started off well – Godfrey eruditely set us in the footsteps of Marco Polo. Hanno admitted that contrary to expectation he found Japan, not China, the most difficult to understand of all the places we visited, summing up with a photo of the enigmatic smile on the face of one of our ever-courteous hosts. David was good on Korea, bringing out the tension of Seoul, so close to that jumpy frontier, and the incredible vitality that had created the biggest shipyard in the world from scratch in under 10 years. Then it was my turn and I climbed onto the rostrum wearing my People's Liberation Army hat with its red star. (Hanno's actually – a useful prop.) The auditorium seemed very dark beyond the tiny pool of light illuminating my text on the rostrum, and I felt people were waiting to see what the only girl student could do. All went well and I felt that communion with the audience that carries the speaker along. Then it was Philippe's turn. He was determined to end on a lighter note, while also bringing out the essential points about Hong Kong. His joke about the definition of a queer in Hong Kong (a man who prefers women to money) went down very well. So on to Bobby and Tom's double act with some very funny photos. I figured notably on my dromedary striking a very Beau Geste pose as I waved to those on the wall above, and also in an extraordinary photograph sitting beside the Commandant on a plane – he mopping his face with an air of desperation, while I looked aside with a wry smile for all the world as if I had been turning down an unacceptable proposition.

***

Rereading this account after 40 years I am struck by our high-powered treatment in China, where we met very senior generals close to Deng Xiaoping. I am not sure we fully took in the political implications of this at the time; the programme was agreed at the last moment and we had little opportunity to brief ourselves on who we were meeting. The Chinese Government must have been sending a message about the importance it attached to relations with Britain as the country opened up to the outside world. I have no doubt that the signals were picked up by Sir Percy Craddock, our shrewd Ambassador in Beijing.

Chapter 16

SO FAR FROM HOME
Jakarta (1982–1983)

I set off for Jakarta with mixed feelings. I really didn't want to go so far away. My avowed reason was that my parents were both in their 80s and getting frailer; my mother suffered from tachycardia and had had several mini-strokes. When I put this to the FCO Personnel Department I was told that aged parents were a problem for all of us of a certain age. The unavowed reason for my reluctance was that my relationship with Alec Campbell had reached an interesting stage and I didn't know if it would survive a long separation. But, as always, I was excited by the prospect of a new world to explore.

Indonesia is a fascinating country, but then little known about in the UK. I remember one friend, on being told of my posting, apologizing for ignorance – "One can't keep up with all these small countries." It is in fact one of the biggest and most populous in the world, stretching over 13,000 islands and 3,000 miles of sea. Britain left its mark on Indonesian history at three crucial stages: during the Napoleonic wars when Sir Stamford Raffles occupied Java in the name of the East India Company; immediately after World War II when Britain briefly took over from the Japanese occupiers until the Dutch were ready to resume their rule; and during the 1960s when Sukarno challenged Britain's ally Malaysia in the war the Indonesians know as Konfrontasi. Apart from Foreign Office telegrams, my own ideas of the country came mainly from my time in the Netherlands where memories of the colonial past were still vivid. The current Indonesian government was headed by General Suharto who had come to power in 1965 in a murky coup which overthrew Sukarno and reversed the policy of non-alignment in favour of closer relations with the West. Suharto's Indonesia had the trappings of democracy including lively elections and some civilian ministers (notably a US-educated group running the economy, known as the Berkeley Mafia) but the army were the power behind the throne. It was a corrupt regime though not, I think, to the same extent that it became in later years.

My job in Jakarta was Head of Chancery, Political Counsellor, and deputy to the Ambassador, Robert Brash. Somewhere along the way I also acquired the title of Consul General and handsome documents signed by the Queen and President Suharto to go with it. It was quite a big Embassy with an emphasis on commercial and aid work. We worked in a rather horrid building which had been put up by the Indonesians to replace the identical one that they sacked during Konfrontasi. I inherited from my predecessor a pleasant high-ceilinged house in the nearby Dutch-built suburb of Menteng, and was later told by an Indonesian journalist that it had been occupied by Laurens van der Post when he was part of the brief British post-war government. The grander house opposite had been the Ambassador's Residence but was given up after a campaign by Adam Malik, then Mayor of Jakarta, to turn it into a museum of independence. During my time in Jakarta it stood largely empty while Robert Brash had a house in a new suburb a good hour away through Jakarta's choked traffic. The plus was that we could still use its swimming pool.

Lord Carrington was due to visit Indonesia, the first time in living memory that a Foreign Secretary had been there. The Ambassador thoughtfully suggested that I should arrive before the visit so that I could see some of the major players at first hand. He also agreed that soon after my arrival I could take a month of full-time language training in Jogjakarta. I was and am a great believer in learning as much of the local language as one can in any posting. It helps one get about more easily and sheds a useful light on local culture.

I decided to break the long flight to Jakarta in Delhi and Singapore. India had always fascinated me and I had friends there. Singapore was more of a working visit because the High Commission acted for certain purposes as a regional hub for other posts in South-East Asia. I also very much wanted to meet a man called John Villiers who was said to be very knowledgeable about Indonesian culture. He lived up to his reputation and was most hospitable too. By coincidence he turned out to have been one of Alec's first students at Cambridge, and told me what an inspiring teacher of history Alec had been.

Phone calls were prohibitively expensive though they were now possible in emergencies. As in Bangkok, letters were the main method of keeping in touch with family and friends, and the schedule of the Diplomatic bags became a matter of great concern with a three-week gap between letters sent and answers received. I wrote every week to Alec, so the arrival of the weekly bag took on an exciting new significance. I also quickly reverted to my routine of the weekly letter home, and the letters to my parents form the basis of this chapter.

Jakarta, 20 January 1982

Well, here I am. I arrived... the day before yesterday to find a friendly deputation from the Embassy waiting for me... Then I was brought back to a house full of orchids, or so it seemed at first glance, because several kind people had sent bouquets to greet me. All told I really couldn't have had a more welcoming reception, and a number of people are giving parties to introduce me which will help me to get off to a good start. So far so good, and it really couldn't have been better.

My house... is a very pleasant, though not beautiful, house with enormous high ceilings (18 ft was quite a fair estimate) and ceiling fans which obviously predate the air conditioning. Inevitably it all looks pretty bare at the moment – there will be no shortage of space for the Staffordshire and the accumulated maps and prints. (I acquired one or two extra colourful goodies in India too.) The really charming corner is the terrace at the back which reaches round three sides of the back garden, itself ablaze with tropical flowers – some old friends and some which I don't know. This is where I have decided to breakfast regularly and will no doubt sit when here in the day-time – so far it has been getting dark when I get home at night and then, as I have discovered all too soon, the mosquitos drive one in. Upstairs, my own bedroom is very pleasant... I have yet to explore the guest wing! Furnishing is not too bad though not my choice of colour. I am promised a choice of various other items that have recently arrived, and no doubt will be able to negotiate various other improvements.

Then there are Anni and Susi. Anni is the cook, a small saronged figure – very friendly – with whom I try to converse in a mixture of my few words of Indonesian and her few words of English. With good will on both sides and the help of a dictionary we aren't doing too badly... Susi, you will no doubt remember, is the dog... She barked at me franticly to start with, but is slowly warming to me, and I to her. Eventually I think we will rub along together quite nicely.

Yesterday was my first day at the Office – and a very long one too. The office works 2 long days a week (8–5) and by ill-luck I arrived in time to catch them both immediately!...Anyhow a pleasant colleague,

Michael Gregg, collected me from home and by prior agreement took me immediately all round the office to meet all the staff...I had already met the Ambassador who had asked me and a small group of the senior members of the Embassy to supper the night before – a pleasant and friendly evening which promises quite well. Rumour has it that Mrs. Brash can be very difficult and bullies him into being difficult too, but we will have to see about that. Otherwise, I get the impression on the whole of a cheerful and friendly bunch of people – though inevitably with a few grumblers here and there. We are needless to say in the throes of preparing for the arrival of Lord Carrington and party. They arrive a week tomorrow (i.e. Thursday 27th) staying until the following Sunday morning. I am obviously going to be thoroughly involved, which is all to the good. The press conference will be in my house because it is the most convenient place – it will feel quite like old times!

So much for first impressions of Jakarta. Except perhaps for the weather. Much cooler than I expected and not too desperately humid, but endless rain. Or rather tropical down-pours that succeed each other with brief intermissions. I gather this will last for another month or so. Fortunately with houses designed with covered car ports adjoining, and official transport to collect me from home, the elements don't bother me too much...

This letter will be finished in good time for the bag which closes on Friday morning early...It should be posted in London on Monday morning and be with you on Tuesday, or Wednesday at the latest. Just time I hope for an answer from you to reach the FCO by next Friday morning. It will be a great plus if the timing does make it possible to answer the latest letter rather than the one before. This end the timing will be easier because our bag arrives on Monday morning, and I will of course have my letters straight away.

My first week was busy with preparations for the Foreign Secretary's visit, and parties to introduce me each evening. The visit itself went smoothly. Politically there were no real problems between Britain and Indonesia, so the talks took place in an easy atmosphere, and it was clear that the Indonesians set a lot of store by having Lord Carrington as their guest. For me it was a splendid opportunity to meet people and sit in on discussions about the area. Lord Carrington himself remembered me from the RCDS. There were a number of entertaining social occasions. The Indonesian

Minister of Foreign Affairs, Dr. Mochtar, gave a dinner in a lovely building which used to be the Parliament of the Dutch East Indies – a splendidly staged affair with waitresses in traditional batik costume deployed in pairs almost like a ballet. The delicious meal was followed by a display of dancing from Sumatra and various parts of Java. Another evening there was a dinner party at the Ambassador's Residence, more intimate this time, for a mere 24, including three Indonesian ministers at the very last minute (par for the course in Jakarta).

My moment of glory was the press conference which took place in my sitting room with some 50 journalists crammed in. It looked quite well decked out in flowers and my Great Exhibition prints which arrived back from the framers just in time. Then we had a TV interview in the garden. Fortunately it didn't rain. My bedroom became the Secretary of State's private office, with couriers to and from the Embassy. It was very odd to watch the telegrams being sorted on my bed. I had Susi shut into a cupboard where she was sufficiently cowed by proceedings to be quiet.

The visit over, I had my first pay day: while I had breakfast each servant brought their book in which I had to note fortnightly payments. Apart from Anni, there was her husband Mahmat, the watchman/gardener; her daughter Noor, the washgirl/cleaner; and Rooseman, Noor's husband, as nightwatchman. The tribe of children was not on the pay roll. My mistake was not having enough small change to make up the sums exactly, but all was safely settled with a little give and take. I later discovered that I was in practice their banker, being expected in times of need to advance larger sums which were meticulously paid back month by month.

By a stroke of good fortune my old friends Hugh and Carol Lindsay were in Jakarta. I had known Hugh at Oxford and he was currently attached to the Bank of Indonesia as an IMF-funded advisor. Carol was at the airport to meet me, and they were my first guests as I tried out Anni's capacities for entertaining. We quickly decided to look together for somewhere to escape the crowded city at weekends. Luckily a quarter share was going in a cottage rented by other people in the Embassy in the Puncak mountains, about 80 kilometres from Jakarta. It was called the Villa Lola and had wonderful views over the garden and valley in one direction and a rather spectacular volcano in another. The cottage was in two parts linked by a covered terrace. One part had a kitchen and living room, the other three bedrooms and a bath- (or rather basin-) room. We decide to take it on the spot. Carol and Hugh felt it would make a great difference to their life: their Bank of Indonesia flat was hot and without much charm. I was thrilled too.

It was soon time for me to go to Jogjakarta for my month of intensive language training. I was to be a PG with an Indonesian family called Goenawan who had hosted previous language students. Determined to work hard I also planned to leave myself time to see what people called the nicest town in Java.

Jalan Cendrawasih No 10, Jogjakarta, 16 February 1982

I am writing this at a little marble-topped table in my room in Jogja where I have been installed for the last 48 hours. It is afternoon and I have just woken up after an hour or so's zizz induced by 4 hours of Indonesian followed by Ibu Goenawan's copious lunch. Outside through the rather high window I can see various sorts of bamboo and other tropical trees – including one hanging with a fruit which I cannot identify. There is a sound of sweeping, and villagey noises from the neighbouring houses in this shady backstreet. Happily there is a breeze because an electricity cut seems to have cut off the fan. It is in fact the lazy time of the day, and the shops will not reopen till 5 pm. Then I propose to go and negotiate with a betjak (3 wheel bicycle rickshaw) to take me to explore the main street some 3 kilometres away, which rejoices in the name of Jalan Malioboro, though I have yet to discover how the Duke made his mark here.

I arrived at the airport on Sunday with some trepidation. People who have trodden the same route before me were anxious to impress on me the rigours of life Indonesian style. I have no doubt profited from their advice – for instance the 4 hour's daily Indonesian lesson is made easier for the posterior at least by a cushion – and I believe the fan is a fairly new acquisition. But I do not find this simple life much hardship. My hosts the Goenawans are relatively prosperous middle class people. He is a building contractor, a quiet little man old enough to be schooled in Dutch, who wanders around in the evenings in pyjamas. I think it is his wife who wears the metaphorical trousers – a pleasant plain-faced woman of probably about my own age who speaks English in a slow deliberate voice… She speaks French as well and though she has never travelled she is obviously very interested in the outside world. Apparently the Dean of the Language Faculty at IKIP, *the teacher training college where I have my classes, first suggested that since she had a spare room*

> *she should take in foreign students and it has now become something of a tradition.*

The days followed a pattern. Early to bed (the light was not good enough to tempt one to linger) and an early breakfast at 7am accompanied by the BBC. Then a 10-minute walk to IKIP, on the campus of Gajah Mada University. The teaching – two successive lessons *tête à tête* of two hours each – left me feeling wrung out. Then back to lunch which I ate by myself with Ibu Goenawan there to talk to. The food was Indonesian and very good: typically, a soup, followed by rice with an assortment of meat and vegetable dishes, some in sauce and some dry, and fruit. The afternoon collapse on my spartan bed (a kapok mattress on board, just like Thailand) brought me back to life for a cup of tea at 4pm, then I would read or go out till supper at 7pm which I took with my host (not yet in his pyjamas) – a bit of a tester conversationally. I set myself at least two hours' homework a day. Memorizing vocabulary seemed an endless task but Indonesian is rather a good language which continually offers surprises. I was delighted to discover that "Matahari" meant the sun – or literally the Eye of the Day, originally Shiva's third eye which burned everything up. I also discovered that I was "duta wakil," which sounded very dubious but only meant "deputy Ambassador."

My main trouble was mosquitoes because the windows were unscreened, so I bathed myself in Dettol. To wash one scooped water over oneself from a big stone tank in the corner of the bathroom. This contained eight toothbrushes though nobody ever seemed to be there when I wanted to use it. The children, ranging in age from 8 to 22, were banished to the back quarters while I had a very welcome privacy in the front of the house. The population was made up by a colony of cats, one of whom was very cross and often said so in a particularly raucous voice, and various birds including an elegant white cockatoo in a cage in the backyard.

My lodgings were some way out of the centre but I borrowed a bike from one of the teachers which made it much easier to explore. Jogja was a pleasant old-fashioned town where the car was not yet king, the shops were single-storey buildings and open to the street, and there were few tourists. The main street, Jalan Malioboro, led temptingly to the Kraton, the Sultan's palace. But my first priority was to find the post office and to establish two-way communication with home. The Embassy had promised to forward letters for me *kilat khusus*, literally "by special lightning," in fact by registered express.

After the first week time began to fly. I took off on my bicycle most afternoons to the nearby Hotel Ambarrukmo whose pool was the closest thing to Paradise in Jogja on a hot afternoon. It charged a lot for a swim but by the time I had a cool afternoon, washed my hair under their warm showers, used a loo with a seat – oh what joy! – and had a look at the local paper I certainly got value for money. I had introductions from the Embassy to the small British community who were mostly aid personnel. A kind couple invited me out one afternoon to a meeting of a running club called the Hash. It was my first excursion into the countryside. The meet was by a little ruined temple, 8th-century and reminiscent of the temples at Angkhor. While the run was taking place I followed a kiddies' trail which made a very pleasant walk through rice fields and a tidy village of plaited bamboo houses with Mount Merapi, the beautiful volcano that broods over Jogja, appearing every now and then among the clouds above.

My teachers were a very nice bunch, mostly quite elderly. One day Ibu Moelono, the only woman of the four, a delightful old girl in a sarong, offered to take me shopping in the evening. I gratefully accepted, glad of local advice, and also of company for shopping after dark. We were escorted in their old car by her husband, a frail figure whose ancestors had all been servants of the Sultan. My chief purchase was a very pretty wrap-around batik skirt in the traditional Jogja colours of indigo and brown combining a number of the traditional patterns.

Sunday was the only day when I didn't go to school, and I was determined to see some of the more glamorous bits of the town. By chance it happened to be Labuan, the celebration of the Sultan's birthday, and I was told that there would be a ceremony at the beach some 20 miles away when some of his old clothes and various other goodies would be cast upon the waves as an offering to the Sea Goddess whom one of his ancestors married in a moment of aberration. (She sounded very irritable and got cross if anybody on the beach wore green, her colour.) The beach seemed too far, but by getting up early I could get to the Kraton in time to see the procession depart. There I found an extraordinary rite in progress which illustrated the curious blend of ancient and modern that pervaded Jogja. A series of Kraton officials were coming out of the Palace all in uniform (sarong, tight fitted jacket, and squat turban with a bun at the back) and with gold ribbons of office round their necks. They were carrying packages wrapped in white muslin – some obviously trays of food, something that looked like a pillow which could have been the clothes, and two clearly identifiable as umbrellas.

All these were loaded officiously into the two buses. When all was done the senior officials took off the ribbons, packed into the front of the buses and drove off waving cheerily to those left behind. Nobody who glanced at the modern-looking buses would ever have guessed the strange ritual on which they were embarked.

Later I looked around the Kraton itself – very provincial and plain compared with the palaces of Thailand – courtyards of beaten mud and single-storeyed pavilions with carved and gilded pillars, and curly snakes much in evidence. It was still very much a living court, however, with its elderly retainers and traditional school of dancing – the slowest form of entertainment I had ever seen. The Sultan of Jogjakarta, an interesting figure, had played an important role in the war against the Dutch. When Indonesian independence was declared in 1945, he immediately came out in support and for a couple of years Jogjakarta was the capital of the new republic. It then became a Special Administrative Region with the Sultan as Governor, in effect a semi-monarchy within a republic. His immense prestige was a combination of the political and the semi-mystical. During my time in Indonesia he was a shadowy presence who didn't appear much in public and to my regret I never saw him.

As I reached the halfway stage of my stay in Jogja my social life was hotting up. I was quickly drawn into the expatriate community of some 200 people. A new face was no doubt welcome because boredom was an obvious problem, especially for the wives for whom opportunities for employment were few. However attractive, Jogja was not a hive of activity, and after a couple of weeks I knew most of the faces I was likely to meet. I went out again with the Hash, who met this time on the slopes of Mount Merapi. The other centre of ex-pat life was a church group of which I was a bit wary after being lectured at length about the evils of government policy on nuclear disarmament. I was glad to be invited out to dinner and to escape the long dimly-lit evenings *chez* Goenawan.

Britain's aid programme to Indonesia was relatively modest because there were so few traditional ties, but I took the opportunity to visit some projects in the area, and what I saw impressed me. There was a technical training centre providing workshops for trainees; its primary aim was to raise the standard of the teachers, whose own education was often rudimentary. This was apparently a British idea, though the World Bank provided much of the funding, and there were nine such colleges in Indonesia with a British engineer in each. Another afternoon I was taken out by an engaging young

Scottish engineer with a Javanese wife. He was involved in a number of schemes to provide water to villages in a very poor limestone area called the Gunung Kidul. It must have been very satisfying to put in wells which pumped ground water from deep below and visibly changed the fertility of the land. Difficult though it was to believe in the heavy rains I was experiencing, later in the year the villagers had to walk for miles to get water which they carried back in tin cans suspended from their shoulders at either end of a long stick. In other areas the project helped to build or repair village ponds, lining them with clay to conserve rainwater. There were huge numbers of people despite the poor land, and villages of red-roofed, palm-thatched houses were tucked over every hill. My engineer friend wanted to explore a new track down to the sea, so the Land Rover backed its way down a couple of thousand feet only to get stuck firmly in the mud close to the shore. It needed all hands to push, including me and a local farmer, ankle-deep in mud.

One Sunday I was taken to Solo, another old Javanese town with a court tradition of its own, by Pak and Ibu Moelono (the elderly couple who took me shopping) and Pak Noer (another of my teachers whom I particularly liked). They were a hard-working bunch and it was very good of them to devote their day off to taking me sight-seeing – typical of the friendliness that I met with during my stay. We visited another Kraton, shabbier than Jogja but given added charm by a watchtower and a courtyard full of trees. It had a very attractive museum full of oddities, such as a collection of 18th-century carriages from Europe, one with leather springs, bearing the arms of the Netherlands East Indies Co. There was also a complete *wayang kulit* (set of shadow puppets) and my hosts explained some of the ritual of their use. The puppets are placed with good on the right, bad on the left. The *dhalang*, who manipulates the puppets from behind a screen, marks the stages of the play with a beautiful fan-shaped implement decorated with trees and animals representing the primitive world. Only when the world-fan is removed is the veil of the former world metaphorically lifted, and one can see the stories unfold.

As I reached the end of my stay in Jogja Pak Goenawan complimented me by saying that I had learned much more than my predecessors did in the time. I did feel that I was at the point of being able to break through and say what I meant over quite a wide range of topics. The trouble was that Indonesian often has several words for each meaning, so when people answered I was lost. I made good resolutions to start lessons promptly when

I got back to Jakarta for fear that this easy come knowledge would also be easy go.

By a stroke of luck an old FCO acquaintance turned up – Justin Staples, who was now Ambassador in Bangkok. After a round of formal calls in Jakarta, he was dispatched down to Jogja for the weekend. I was delighted to have someone to do the sights with, especially as he was determined to do them in style with hired cars. We went in comfort to visit some 8th- and 9th-century temples, notably Borobodur (Buddhist) and Prambanan (Hindu). Both had marvellous carved reliefs and were of the holy mountain type of construction. Borobodur is huge, tier upon tier of symbolic meaning rising to a series of circular terraces on which are seated dozens of inscrutable Buddhas, each in a pierced stone stupa. The site is marvellous, with views of mountains close around. Prambanan is much smaller and more like some of the Cambodian temples, though its phallic outline was not like anything I remembered there. The main temple contained four cell-like shrines in which huge statues loomed – Siva and Ganesha, and Durga, a wickedly beautiful goddess who still obviously struck fear into the hearts of the local villagers: there were offerings of flowers at her feet.

***

The news that awaited me back in Jakarta was of the worst kind. My mother had had a massive stroke. She had been far from well since January but my parents decided not to tell me the full extent of the problem while I was in Jogjakarta. I flew straight back to England and on to Guernsey and was at home for about three weeks. The Foreign Office, like my Ambassador, could not have been more understanding and helpful.

My mother was in the King Edward VII hospital in St Peter Port. She had lost the power of speech but still seemed compos mentis as far as one could tell. I tried as best I could to arrange speech and other sorts of therapy and to rally her friends to help. I was concerned about my father who was in his late 80s and had begun to show his age. In fact he rallied in a most remarkable way and I later came to the slightly sad conclusion that having a real task, making all the arrangements for his incapacitated wife, gave him a new lease of active life.

Back in Jakarta I soon decided to organize my weekly letters home into chatty ones describing the events of my daily life for reading aloud to my mother and separate notes for my father about her condition and medical arrangements. The private letters were full of my worries, made much worse by the long delays in mail and near-absence of phone contact. My father went on keeping my letters but some got lost in what must have been a very difficult time for him.

My right-hand man in the Embassy was Clive Almond, the information officer, and through him I met a cross-section of the local press. An Indonesian journalist called Sabam Siagian, who wanted to educate me, lent me a couple of novels: Christopher Koch's *The Year of Living Dangerously*, a gripping read about the culmination of the Sukarno period, and *A Gentle Occupation* by the actor Dirk Bogarde, who was in Jakarta as a junior officer in 1945. This was the bloody period when the British were left holding the ring after the sudden surrender of the Japanese and the Indonesians didn't want the Dutch back at any price.

The Argentinian invasion of the Falkland Islands had repercussions on Embassies even as far away as ours. Three times during one weekend I was summoned into the Office to read immediate telegrams – twice when I was comfortably ensconced in bed, to add insult to injury. I found myself making representations about Indonesia's position in the Non-Aligned Group to a previously unknown official – not that it made any difference to the Indonesians who, seeing the issue in anti-colonial terms, were firmly pro-Argentinian. Later we were instructed with the utmost urgency to explain why a British submarine sank the Argentinian cruiser *Belgrano* in international waters. The demarche was intended to pre-empt criticism but Robert Brash decided that if we woke up senior Indonesians with this message late at night it wouldn't improve our case. I was pleased to discover that our Ambassador had common sense and didn't flap.

As I settled down to life in Jakarta I was ever more ready to grasp at opportunities to get away. The next letter is about an excursion to a small and largely uninhabited island in the Sunda Straits which separate Java from Sumatra.

Jakarta, 27 May 1982

As it became increasingly clear that British forces were about to invade the Falkland Islands... I had duty qualms about disappearing from contact, especially as I couldn't be quite sure that the fishing boat would return to rescue us on time on Sunday. And apart from that, I began to wonder whether I was going to enjoy 3 days under canvas on a hot and sandy beach with no fresh water and no comforts or civilization. But I had talked about the excursion so much in advance and made such a fuss about borrowing a tent – eventually obtained from the U.S. Embassy – that I felt it would be a terrible anti-climax to cry off.

So it was that I was there, if barely awake, to be collected along with a mountain of gear, at 3 am on Friday morning. A low point, as you will appreciate. The very early start was to enable us to get out of the swarming sleeping suburbs of Jakarta before too much traffic was about. We drove 3 hours to the coast and at a place called Anjer opposite Sumatra we negotiated with a fishing boat to take the 10 of us and our by now many mountains of kit across to the island of Sangian which lies between Java and Sumatra. Fortunately it was calm because we were a full load and everything had to be on deck with us on top. It was an hour and a bit's trip before we were deposited on a deserted beach that looked just as hot and sandy as I had feared. But at that point there was nothing to do except help unload the gear and set up camp, and then dive into the sea to cool off. That was the turning point, especially when I was introduced to the pleasures of swimming with mask and snorkel. This means you can swim along with your eyes open looking at a framed view of the underwater world and breathing all the while through a tube. And it really is a marvellous world to see. There are mountains and valleys covered with all shapes of coral and weed. The colours are fantastic, particularly of the fish who defy any thought of prudent camouflage. Midnight blue, electric blue with orange fins, black and white striped, and countless other varieties swim right by one as if one was just another and larger fish, and harmless at that. I can see how people get hooked on this pastime.

By the time evening came I was very ready for a campfire, barbecue and early bed, and slept most soundly in my borrowed American tent. Our 48 hours there passed very quickly. We were lucky in the weather – no rain, though one night I thought the wind would surely blow our tent away even with me in it – and in the absence of mosquitos. Also to see a variety of wildlife and particularly a school of dolphins playing and leaping clean out of the water.

I came back bronzed and fit, feeling confident enough to wear bikinis again after having lost ½ stone since my return to Jakarta. But my narcissism was in for a shock. Coral watching in my bikini had let my exposed rump get an overdose of sun, and to make matters worse I missed my balance at one point and sat on a poisonous weed which brought the afflicted part out in a painful rash. I didn't feel much comforted when one of my companions suggested I had better turn the other cheek!

I began Indonesian lessons again. My conversations with Anni took a pretty limited vocabulary, and there were few other occasions requiring me to use the language in Jakarta because my official contacts all spoke very much better English than I ever hoped to speak Indonesian. But nonetheless I was determined to press on. My teacher, recommended to me by someone in the Dutch Embassy, was called Ibu (meaning Mrs. or Mother) Suleiman and was a hideous woman, poor dear, with a lump on her forehead and a throat swelling that I thought was goitre, but she had handsome eyes and the sort of personality that compelled one's attention. I enjoyed her lessons.

The arrival of the flower man, usually on Tuesday morning, was one of the nicest moments of my week. He and I and Anni would all haggle ceremoniously together. He would pick out an armful of brilliant flowers from among the red arums, purple orchids and spikey spider flowers which filled his baskets. I then protested that it was too much and urged him to put some back. He marginally reduced his price whereupon, honour satisfied and will weakened, I agreed. Then Anni would pounce on an extra bunch or two which she claimed as a present to the household and we all ended up smiling at each other. As a result, for a couple of pounds a week my house was full of beautiful flowers which Anni's husband Mahmat arranged with great taste. It helped to make the big downstairs rooms seem lived in.

Anni and Susi made a very friendly home base. Despite a phantom pregnancy, Susi remained entirely her predictable self, affectionate, insidious, and ecstatic whenever a walk was in prospect. Our regular stint was three times round the neighbourhood pond – probably about a mile there and back. I was lucky to have one of Jakarta's few little parks relatively close – a peaceful place where little boys fished and young couples sat together rather primly on the stone benches. Indonesian society is strait-laced, and when a girl rode behind her boyfriend on a motorbike she sat sidewise without holding on to him. It looked terribly precarious!

I began to entertain at home with some trepidation. There was always room for the unexpected. At my first lunch party I noticed halfway through that the price labels were still on all the peppers and salts. Another time the coffee arrived in tea-cups. But I knew the food would taste good and the family silver candle sticks looked very well marching down the long table with one of Mahmat's orchid arrangements in the middle.

Whenever I thought I was getting on top with my work at the Embassy another wave seemed to come in and I felt it was definitely getting on top of me. But I gradually managed to get out of the office and meet more Indonesians. I was particularly interested by a lawyer called Buyung Nasution, a leading liberal campaigner who had founded the Legal Aid Institute. I was rather surprised to find myself having lunch with him because many of my attempts to call on people had run into the sand. It became clear that he was something of a folk hero when the waiters in the hotel where we ate all rushed round with obvious admiration, and one later asked for some legal advice. Nasution had spent two years in prison when the authorities got jumpy about student riots and told me that the Javanese tended to refer to it as time spent strengthening the soul! This was very much in the pattern of Javanese mysticism where leaders withdraw from time to time to strengthen their spirit through meditation. The Legal Aid Institute under Nasution was one of the few outspoken critics of Suharto's authoritarian rule. It defended people accused of subversion and other political crimes as well as providing legal aid for the poor. He was a brave man as well as rather a nice one. That he was allowed to do what he did was an interesting example of how the regime operated. Some criticism was allowed as part of a veneer of democracy, but there were strict if unpredictable limits. The same was true of the press.

***

On the evening of 1 July I put through a call to La Verdure. Within three minutes I was talking to my father and a minute later to my mother. Suddenly feeling so close to my parents brought on a wave of self-analysis. I had worried about going back to the tropics and the rather strange colonial-style life that Westerners still lived there. I had moments of loneliness and missed my friends. And I had moments of frustration at the work with its heavy content of admin-cum-management which I never enjoyed and made rather heavy weather of. But there were good things too, notably an Ambassador whom I liked and respected increasingly and who was unfailingly good to me. I had met a number of agreeable people who were at least potential friends and my furry friend with four feet was a surprising comfort. All told the bad patch I always went through after arriving at a new post seemed to be more or less over.

Weekend excursions were one of the great pleasures. I went with Hugh Lindsay and a very pleasant pair called Colin and Tricia Bacon to a fishing village on the south coast called Pelabuhan Ratu. We stayed in a most agreeable hotel consisting of small cottages dotted around a restaurant, basically a series of tables under little thatched umbrellas on a promontory over the sea. Our cottage had a lovely view across a bay with a backdrop of mountains. At night the fishing boats went out with lights in their sterns to attract the fish, just as they used to in Beirut. There was a lovely long beach where we swam in the surf, being careful not to go too far out because of a treacherous current. The only drawback to this idyllic weekend was a thick grey coating of volcanic dust which covered the countryside, getting into one's clothes, even one's mouth. It really was a case of darkness at noon. We discovered later that a grumbling volcano called Galunggung had erupted violently well over 100 miles away. Fortunately the dust was feather light and most of it blew away over the weekend. A British Airways plane had an incredibly lucky escape: at 35,000ft it flew straight into a cloud of dust and grit, which choked all four engines. Miraculously the pilot got the plane down safely at Jakarta and nobody was hurt. One of those appalling disasters that Embassies sometimes have to deal with was escaped by a hair's breadth.

I very much looked forward to my weekends in the cottage in the mountains. One of the main activities up there was going for walks in the tea plantations, which Susi thought absolutely marvellous. They provided an opportunity to get away from Java's ribbon development. The tea bushes were punctuated by scarlet poinsettias and had flowers like small camellias. One met people picking tea, women carrying down large bundles of it wrapped in cloths on their heads, and men balancing twin loads at either end of a pole, moving with a strange gliding run which presumably lessened the jarring on the shoulder. One Sunday we came across a little Dutch cemetery, a couple of dozen graves with two or three recurring surnames of people buried over 100 years earlier. Some of the more recent ones were in Indonesian, and outside the plot were a few more graves, mostly Muslim. The little graveyard was beautifully kept and on some of the graves there were fresh flowers. I couldn't help wondering what ramifications of a tiny expatriate society were represented there.

***

Robert Brash was a great traveller, and in July he went for two weeks to Irian Jaya (former West New Guinea) taking the Defence Attaché for a companion. It was my first experience of being in practical charge of the

Embassy. Fortunately it was Ramadan when the general level of activity was very much slowed down. Though far from strict Muslims in many ways, most Indonesians seemed to fast. At Lebaran, the end of Ramadan, there were ceremonial calls to be made and VIPs kept open house. I took the opportunity to call at Suharto's home which was not far from mine, and to sign his book. There were lots of people milling about but we did not see the President.

People sometimes ask what it was like to work as a woman in a largely Muslim country. Indonesia, with its religious tolerance and wide variety of faiths and cultures, was far from typically Islamic. The distinction between Sunni and Shia seemed irrelevant in daily life and the religious tensions of the Middle East were remote. I wondered at first whether Indonesians would expect a woman to travel alone but I never had any difficulties and felt perfectly safe. I never had problems of access either though the members of the government were as far as I remember all men, many of them generals. The great majority of the civil servants were men too but I met some impressive and influential women, often from Christianized areas such as Sulawesi. Robert Brash sometimes mused that I might return to Jakarta as Ambassador. I believe that a woman could indeed have done the job comfortably.

In July I had a visit from Alec who was on his way to see his sister in Australia. We had been writing to each other regularly while I had been in Indonesia and had seen each other while I was in England after my mother's stroke. The correspondence had helped us understand each other better and our relationship was getting closer. As I confessed to my parents, "*I am looking forward very much to Alec's arrival. He is a nice, gentle, clever, witty man – too modest to make much of his academic distinction. I should have talked to you more about him before, but I am afraid once a clam, always a clam.*"

I took advantage of a bag run to join Alec in Singapore. He had been in Kathmandu staying with John Denson, whom I had worked with in Laos and who was now Ambassador to Nepal. Singapore had changed a great deal since the 60s. The broad streets with their shaded pavements, cheap taxis and reliable buses were all very orderly and the shopping more enticing than ever but to me it had become a bit sterile. One had to look very hard to find traces of its exotic past. The old Raffles Hotel where we had dinner one night was one of the few places where the modern world was still held at bay. Thanks to some Dutch friends, the de Vos van Steenwijks, we witnessed a spectacular parade – merely the dress rehearsal, in fact – for

Singapore's national day. We watched lots of gaily coloured marchers with flags from construction companies, police, Shell, etc. while a platoon of Singapore Airlines air hostesses got a special cheer. There was a relatively small contingent from the armed forces but a nice fly-past with fighters and helicopters trailing coloured smoke. All remarkable for the precise timing. We had privileged seats in the Singapore Cricket Club which had one of the prime sites in the city.

My goddaughter Amanda Ramsay, daughter of my Oxford friend Prue Pedder, arrived in Jakarta during Alec's visit. I took the two of them on a weekend excursion to Pelabuhan Ratu, the fishing port on the south coast which I first visited when the whole place was covered by volcanic ash. It was quite a drive to get there: three hours of windy road across the spine of Java and down to the south coast, a real cross-section of Java with spectacular views of perched villages and terraces cultivated with rice. We stayed as before at a cottage belonging to the fish restaurant. I succeeded in negotiating unaided for a fishing boat to take us out for a couple of hours and felt very smug that my Indonesian was at last beginning to show some modest practical results. It was a fascinating trip, letting us see the variety of boats and fishing methods in use, including a dozen men hauling in a huge net full of seething, glinting fish: a quite Biblical scene.

Another day we made an excursion to some hot springs half an hour's walk from where we had to leave the car, something we could not have managed without my embryo Indonesian. I got someone to guide us (paying far too much, I am sure) and we had a lovely walk up a jungly valley to a place where the river boiled. At one point there was a spout of sulphurous water about 10 feet high with clouds of evil-smelling steam. One comic element of the trip was that apart from our official guide we were escorted by a guard of three small boys, trailing along behind as we started off, but moving forward as they gained in confidence, until they led us triumphantly back to the village where we had left our car. There we were surrounded by a crowd of not very friendly people who had blocked our exit with a pile of stones. I remembered the Ambassador saying that there were nasty people in that village and had a brief qualm, but fortunately they let us go as soon as we paid up.

We also went to Bali. Alec and I stayed in a very nice hotel in Sanur run by Stanley Allison, the Honorary British Consul. It made a comfortable base to come back to and most days we set off either by hired car or by *bemo* (the local equivalent of a service taxi) to see different parts of the island.

Amanda had quickly made friends with Fenella, the daughter of my friends the Bacons, and the two of them were staying in Kuta, a beach resort created by and for young foreign tourists. Accommodation there was simple and cheap and they were obviously having a great time but they were very ready for a good meal in Sanur.

Bali was a fascinating place despite the tourists who populated its southern beaches. It reminded me of Nepal, probably because of the Hindu influence with its proliferation of temples and little offerings laid in the most unexpected places. Every bridge was guarded by stone statues at either end, most of them wearing a check cloth as an apron and some with a flower, usually red hibiscus, fresh behind the ear. The more holy temples were in fabulous spots – on the slopes of a volcano, on an islet eroded by the sea – and had multi-tiered roofs, some eleven tiers high. It was a very friendly place too, and if the phrase "for you very special price" rang in one's ears a bit too often, it was usually said in a spirit of optimism rather than pertinacity.

My house seemed very empty when Alec went on to Australia and Amanda back to England. I decided it was time that I invited the Ambassador and his wife to dinner. I also asked some rather high-powered Indonesians – their former Ambassador in London, an Air Chief Marshal who was tipped for future preferment, an agreeable man who was a personal adviser to the Vice-President, and – perhaps the most interesting of the lot – a man called Fouad Hassan, the Director of Research at the Foreign Ministry. I was rather pleased that they all accepted, along with an assorted bunch of diplomats and British community. Disaster nearly struck because we had set the tables up prettily on the terrace when the sky began to cloud over. Fortunately all was safely rearranged in a rather more cramped way inside before the heavens opened for the most prolonged and dramatic thunderstorm. The former Indonesian Ambassador insisted on putting a frangipani flower behind my ear in what he informed me was Balinese style as an expression of appreciation for an enjoyable evening.

The Embassy had property problems in Medan. The British government wanted to sell the former Consulate building while local officials were using all sorts of bogus arguments about property law to hold us to ransom. Things took a bad turn when we received a summons to appear in court in Medan for non-completion of the sale of the building which we had been longing to get off our hands if only someone would cut through the red tape. Our elderly legal adviser in Jakarta, a charming Indonesian lady whose first language was Dutch, said we were on firm ground, but that everyone in Medan was so corrupt that there was no knowing how the judgment would go. I decided to visit the authorities in Medan myself. It felt rather like Daniel putting his head in the lion's den, what with the complications of Indonesian law and the difficulty of language. Even when people spoke English one was never sure one had understood them properly, or even whether they wished to be unambiguously clear.

I arrived in Medan on a Thursday to call on a formidable lady lawyer from Sulawesi whom I had engaged to defend us. Anni Abbas, one of the most impressive people I met in Indonesia, was outraged by the behaviour of the authorities in Medan and our case was clearly in excellent hands. I stayed with the Honorary Consul and his wife who were very friendly. His main job was as an English language teacher for Mobil Oil while she taught at the International School. I also paid courtesy calls on various resident Consuls (US and Malaysian) and looked at the property which all the trouble was about. On the Friday morning the Consul and I called on the Governor and the Mayor's office. We were clearly not going to get any help from them.

But on Friday afternoon offices were closed and Alec joined me in Medan on his return journey from Australia. We took off into the country, complete with Land Rover, George Ekanayake (the Embassy clerk) and Supit (the driver) and a chest full of provisions. It was all great fun. We stayed in guest houses, the first belonging to London/Sumatra (one of the big plantations) in a hill resort called Berastagi, a lovely place quite high on the slopes of a volcano where one could grow strawberries or even rhubarb. It reminded me a little of Kashmir, with its pine woods and pony riding. Then from there a lovely drive along Lake Toba, a superb lake ringed with steep hills and containing a huge island called Samosir. We stopped from time to time to visit Batak villages (really primitive, with wooden saddle-backed houses and many peculiar customs) or simply to admire the view. So on to Prapat, a tourist centre on the lake which was a bit like some resorts in the South of France but on a much more modest scale. Here again we were lucky enough to stay in a guest house, this time belonging to a company called Sipef. It was right down by the water with a lovely view along the lake and I went water-skiing. The pattern at these guest houses was that one ate out or brought one's own food but there was someone there to cook it. Very agreeable, particularly if one had someone to make the arrangements as did George, the clerk, a character straight out of one of Paul Scott's Indian novels.

Medan still had a provincial feel and retained a number of pleasing houses from colonial days, and the expatriate community was small enough for everyone to know each other. The British were mostly involved with oil companies, some with cement, and some with Sir William Halcrow who were acting as consultants to the port extension. Then there were the plantation managers whose comfortable if isolated lifestyle had probably not changed much for decades. It was most interesting to see the large areas of rubber, palm oil, etc, and Alec asked useful questions. My visit apparently made the local papers, one of which promoted me to Ambassador!

The anti-climax of the trip was an attempt to visit a World Wildlife Fund project for the rehabilitation of orangutans. The orangutan had become an endangered species because so many little ones were taken for pets and their mothers killed. The World Wildlife Fund offered to help, provided that it was made illegal to keep orangutans. So people were shamed into giving up their pets, which had often been brought up like human babies, with nappies and rattles. But then a problem arose over teaching the baby orangutans to readapt to the wild and fend for themselves. Mrs. Plant, the Consul's wife, recounted how an English couple involved with the project would turn up to stay complete with newly-rescued orangutan. I really wanted to visit the project. But when we arrived after a 2½-hour Land Rover drive, followed by half an hour through the jungle on foot, we found we needed a permit, so were turned away. Alas, I never got a chance to go back.

Shortly after my return to Jakarta, the UN called a meeting about the eruption of Mount Galunggung, the volcano near Bandung which had darkened the sun when I first went to Pelabuhan Ratu. Some 30,000 people had already been evacuated. The Indonesian Government had refused to declare a "national emergency", apparently because to do so would suggest an inability to cope, but they had launched an international appeal for help.

The next development was that they organized a "workshop" in Bandung to discuss what to do about the problem. I decided to appoint myself Embassy Volcano Attaché and went to have a look. We were taken on a tour of the close surroundings of the volcano and a very dramatic sight it was too. Behind a great ridge of grey ash one could see smoke-rings of steam coming out of the mountain and every now and then the wind whipped up sinister clouds of ash. The area covered by lava was like a moonscape. Houses were buried up to the eaves, and whole villages had been evacuated to huge camps run by the Red Cross. One of the oddest sights was the coconut palms which seemed to collapse around their long trunks when the ash landed on them. The experts thought that the volcano, which had last erupted in the 1920s, was gradually calming down but the worry was what would happen when the rains came and brought down that threatening wall of ash. It seemed sure to wash away fields, houses, dams and everything else over a much wider area.

We were told there was a risk to health from inhaling ash over long periods, and among the list of requests for international aid was a machine to monitor the effect on the lungs. The best machine was said to be British – apparently it was used to check the health of coal miners – and not exorbitantly expensive, so when I got back I put together a proposal for the British Government to give a few. It was an exciting day when the machines arrived and I handed them over to the Ministry concerned. To my chagrin, I learned later from a disaffected senior civil servant that they were never even taken out of their boxes. He explained that they had only appeared on the list because each Ministry wanted its own share of whatever was going. I felt very naïve.

The workshop itself was something of a jamboree – far too many participants, most of them with nothing much to contribute. I was impressed by how the Indonesian Government coped with the numbers, providing transport and food. We were even issued with tee-shirts by the Red Cross with *Galunggung* written on the back. Alas, I left mine in the bus. It was all in rather bad taste when the refugees in the camps had barely enough to eat. Nonetheless I enjoyed my visit to Bandung, in country which would be lovely when not covered by dust. As it was I had a hot train ride back and came home filthy, with grit in hair and eyes, thankful for a nice cool bath.

I spent most of October 1982 in the UK taking accumulated leave. We were entitled to paid home leave once a year from tropical posts and I was of course anxious to spend time with my parents in Guernsey. I also visited Alec in Oxford and invited him to stay at La Verdure where he met my father for the first time. He had met my mother before her stroke at a lunch party I gave in my garden in Islington and they got on famously. Now, though I think she remembered him, she was unable to communicate verbally. Nonetheless I went back to Jakarta feeling that an important connection had been made. Looking back, I wonder how I found time to write long letters to my parents as well as to Alec. They became a sort of stream of consciousness; much later I remember Alec marvelling at how quickly I could write.

November saw me back in Jakarta. It felt odd at first: things were just as I had left them but somehow they shouldn't be there. It should have been one of Guernsey's autumnal gales I heard outside and perhaps the occasional foghorn – not the surge of Jakarta traffic deadened by the hum of air conditioning.

I found my household in a state of some drama. Anni's pretty 17-year-old daughter Leili had disappeared the previous weekend. Anni was convinced she was dead and didn't eat or drink for three days. Anyhow the little minx reappeared the day before my return looking rather pleased with herself, having been all the time with a boyfriend. Anni, still rather upset, greeted me by flinging both arms round my middle and burying her face somewhere close to my navel. I clucked as sympathetically as I could, rallying my forgotten Indonesian. Not surprisingly, local custom decreed that they should get married, and quite quickly at that. Anni was cross because Leili was still at school and wouldn't be able to stay on if she married. But Leili was quite a bright girl as well as pretty, and the young man, a hairdresser, was quite acceptable so things weren't too bad.

It was a pleasant time of year to come back to. The major deluges were still ahead, but there had been enough rain to bring green to the parched lawns and the flowers were at their best. My bedroom window looked over a combination of scarlet flowering raintrees and pink-and-white bougainvillea which gave me much pleasure. Back at the Office, I dazedly read up on what had been going on during my absence and pulled myself together to go to a dinner the Ambassador was giving for the former Labour Minister, Frank Judd. I had seen quite a lot of Judd in the FCO when he took over the junior minister's job covering Europe from David Owen and thought him a nice man, though regrettably anti-EEC. I also had to go to the airport to attend the departure of President Zia of Pakistan. This was a chore because the diplomatic corps were tarmac decoration, nothing more, but it was also a useful chance to nobble Indonesian ministers who all had to turn out too. The immediate excitement was a conference organized by a City of London body called the Committee of Invisible Exports – a name which gave rise to a number of jokes! In fact the conference was about how various aspects of the City – banking, insurance, and so on – could help a developing country like Indonesia. The visit served as a rehearsal for the visit of a House of Commons Select Committee a couple of weeks later. By then the Ambassador had gone on leave and I was formally in charge.

Jakarta, 18 November 1982

Well, it has really happened: I am now Her Britannic Majesty's Chargé d'Affaires!... I have moved into the Ambassador's large office (complete with private loo). The vast desk is equipped with one of those chairs which leans back as you sit in it and when I first threw myself luxuriously into it I thought I was going to go right over backwards! No hazards at all in the Daimler which is a marvellously comfortable car with acres of room inside, complete with extra bucket seats... and an electronically controlled sliding panel between driver and passengers. You have no idea what a wow I feel being driven around in all this state – particularly this morning when I went to call on the Secretary General of ASEAN and we flew a flag on the front! The diplomatic flag of course (I've just looked it up!) which has an emblem surrounded with green leaves in the middle of the Union Jack.

There is a change at home too because I have borrowed one of the Ambassador's houseboys – a very superior young man called Dedi who is clever and educated and a very different cup of tea from my nice Anni. I took soundings first of course, and hope that all will get on well together. So far things are going very smoothly, and I hear sounds of cheerful and animated discussion from behind the scenes.

Our visiting MPs arrived on a Monday evening and stayed until the Thursday morning leaving behind one exhausted Chargé d'Affaires. There were nine of them, led by Sir Donald Kaberry and including Ian Mikardo, Tom McNally, and Robin Maxwell Hyslop. As David Mackilligin (my opposite number on the Commercial side of the Embassy) said after we had seen them off at the airport, it felt rather like having successfully passed on a stick of gelignite which one had been left holding for a couple of days! After they had safely gone on their way I sent my impressions to my parents.

Jakarta, 26 November 1982

They were of course a bunch of prima donnas, and we had one or two minor incidents – one was rude to the Greek Consul, another got drunk and had a row with the British Aerospace Rep – but by and large the mood was sunny and they seemed pleased with what we had laid on for them here and picked up no serious points of criticism. We are lucky in having a friendly British business community here and its doyen, a man called Ken Mount who has known Indonesia since the late 40s, is both knowledgeable and helpful. The MPs were obviously very pleased with their contacts... and I have no doubt that the good relations between the latter and the Embassy stood us in good stead.

As Chargé I was responsible for it all in a way, but the session which really put me on the spot was the briefing we gave them on first arrival which I had to introduce and run. I was of course very aware that the tolerance of the average MP to be talked at is strictly limited, but was determined that they should get a short introductory view of this country before they went off after their own individual hares. Fortunately I think I managed to hold their attention reasonably well for 5 or 10 minutes – though Ian Mikardo in particular has an unnerving habit of shutting his eyes so that he could easily be asleep! There followed a lively, not to say inquisitorial question session – indeed I think that must be a reflex action of the breed because it turned out afterwards that they were all very tired and longing for their supper! The next night I had a vast cocktail party here – we invited about 250 and about half that number must have come though I still don't know who most of them were! Anyhow it went swimmingly, which was an intense relief.

All told I picked up some nice compliments along the way and the Embassy as a whole did its stuff very well. So now I can sit back with the relief of anti-climax! One of the friendlier MPs, Peter Emery (a former junior Minister of Trade – suave and agreeable if a touch pompous), commented that as I sat back on the comfortable seat of the Ambassador's Daimler I looked as if I was pinching myself to see if it was really me!

With the Select Committee's visit safely behind me there seemed nothing much to worry about, so I could simply make the most of the advantages of the situation. I loved riding in state in my vast black Daimler, driven by the nicest chauffeur who wore a black velvet hat with the Royal coat of arms pinned on as a brooch. Some of the more disrespectful MPs referred to the car as my hearse. I retorted that I was only rehearsing!

I enjoyed my first spell as Chargé d'Affaires much more than I expected. Being in charge with three months ahead felt very different from the odd days before when the Ambassador had been away. No need to wait to know his views: I could decide. I was glad that the experience had come after I had been in the country long enough to have a feeling for how the place worked. I became increasingly aware of the figurehead aspect of my role as Christmas approached. To my horror I was invited to contribute a Christmas message to the local St. George's Society bulletin. I failed to have any brilliantly witty ideas and ended up sending them something that could suitably have been signed by the vicar!

The next excitement was a trip to Bangkok to attend a Heads of Mission Conference in the Embassy there. I could scarcely credit that it was the same place that I used to know. There were new roads and glistening multi-storey blocks everywhere and a great feeling of prosperity. My four days' stay seemed all too short, especially as I spent several hours reading briefs and trying to prepare the rather jumbled thoughts which I had brought with me from Jakarta. But I also did some very satisfactory shopping, gawping at the new supermarkets and banks. There were of course still some familiar sights – particularly the Embassy compound with its lovely balconied houses, the grounds still presided over by the ample statue of Queen Victoria and an enormous flagpole, the gates still manned by Gurkhas. A spanking new office block had been put up to house the Chancery, and the building where I worked had been converted into flats. Soi Asoke where I used to live had become a major highway and my old house was said to be a garage. I wished I had time to go in search of Boona (my cook) but my Thai would have been quite inadequate to the task even if I had found her.

The Conference itself was a bigger affair than I had expected, with some 24 people gathered round the long table and me tucked away at one end as befitted a mere Chargé. The others came from all over South-East Asia, as far afield as Beijing and Tokyo. There was also a team from London led by the Minister, Lord Belstead, who took the chair – a pleasant and intelligent man with the long skull, slightly over-nosed and slightly under-chinned, of so many of the British aristocracy. Proceedings were opened by a round of statements in which each head of mission was invited briefly to describe the view of the region from their capital. My turn came sixth or seventh. I was a bit nervous and didn't do it as well as I might have – my predecessor went on too long, and I was so determined not to follow suit that I cut my presentation down to the bone, and a slightly dry and quavery bone at that. It was fascinating listening to the variety of accounts, from the Communist regimes where the simplest requirements of life involved continual hassle to the glittering cities of unbelievable wealth like Hong Kong and Tokyo. Overall I think I defended Jakarta's corner reasonably well though I doubt if I could really claim the "distinction" which one speaker so kindly forecast for me. Some of the participants were of course outstanding, notably Sir Percy Craddock, our man in Beijing, who had as clear a mind as I ever came across.

One anecdote I cannot resist. A dinner was given in honour of our party by the Thai Foreign Minister, which was followed by the usual speeches. Lord Belstead introduced his team saying that we were a varied group, some vastly experienced like Sir Percy Craddock, some new to the area like himself – "and some, like Juliet Collings, just very young!" I simpered – what else could I do? But too many of those gathered round the table had known me far too long for me to get away without a certain amount of ribbing afterwards.

I got back from Bangkok just in time to brace myself for my Christmas party. I had decided to get in early with a supper party cum dance for the Embassy staff. Once grown-up children and British Council were included there were about 70 guests. I was determined to make the party go with a swing. Decorating the house was quite an operation since the rooms were high and large but it looked rather good with festoons of scarlet and silver streamers, and Christmas cards pinned on scarlet ribbons. We also got a tree – not quite a proper Christmas tree, but good enough – and hung it with assorted baubles which I had bought in Bangkok. Dredging my memory, I decided to start the party with games we used to play at parties in Beirut. Anyhow it all went very successfully, with excellent food too, and by good fortune it was a fine night so people could dance on the terrace.

Later in the week I was invited along with the rest of the Diplomatic Corps to a wedding ceremony.

Jakarta, 23 December 1982

The groom was the son of the Political Director General in the Foreign Ministry, and the occasion was very much a society one. Not knowing what would happen I got there a bit early and found myself seated beside the Pakistani Ambassador who was also playing safe, in a block of seats reserved for diplomats in a vast hall. Gradually we were joined by others, each being given a small package as we entered – it turned out to contain a small earthenware pot embossed with the initials of bride and groom – just the thing for primroses if we had any! After a while a procession entered slowly, bringing bride, groom, and their parents to a row of seats like thrones looking over the hall. Bride and groom both wore jewelled sarongs down to their ankles, and heavily embroidered black velvet jackets of different cut. But it was the bride's headgear that I couldn't take my eyes off: it was as if black hair had been lacquered on in a series of petal-shaped points coming forward onto her face, and on the back of her head was a spray of wire antennae each with a quivering jewel on top. All very sumptuous, and since she was a beautiful girl, attractive too. The family apparently come from Solo near Jogja so this was the tradition of Central Java.

Anyhow after we had all sat in our respective places for some time doing nothing but listen to some twanging music, the President and his wife arrived and took up station in some large square chairs in front of us. The bride and groom then removed their shoes and came over barefoot to pay their respects which they did by kneeling in front of the President and kissing his knees and exchanging hand stroking gestures. Later all the guests of whom there must have been thousands filed past the wedding party to present their congratulations in more Western style.

During the four days off over Christmas the Embassy staff saw more of each other socially than in the rest of the year put together, very pleasantly on the whole. On Christmas Day itself I decided to go to a family carol service. The day wouldn't have seemed right without a few heralds harked. (I told my parents that the parody "Hark the Harrod's cash points ting" was very apt in Jakarta where the supermarkets had been belching out Christmas schmaltz for weeks – anything from "Rudolf the Red-nosed Reindeer" to "I'll have a Blue Christmas Without You".) The Almonds came to drink champagne before lunch, bearing a lovely bouquet of orchids constructed around a miniature rattan cart. Christmas dinner I ate with a gathering of Embassy "singles" organized by my enterprising secretary. I tottered home stuffed to the gills to telephone my parents and crawl to a rather early bed.

When I got back to the office I had a nice surprise. A rather dull-looking letter to which at first I paid no attention contained a summons to attend the inauguration of a power scheme on Bali in which British aid had played a major part – in two days' time! They never gave one much notice in Indonesia; indeed it was not uncommon to receive an invitation after the occasion was past. I easily convinced myself that this was an occasion I should grace with my presence. The inauguration of a pair of British generators worth £3½ million was a very considerable part of Britain's aid programme in Indonesia. I flew to Bali, and as I made my way by local taxi clutching the letter which was all I knew about the affair it suddenly occurred to me that I might be called upon to make a speech; I remembered my father's advice for impromptu speeches – think past, present and future – and realised just how little I knew about the electrification of Bali! Fortunately I was not put to the test, and had a pretty relaxed time sitting in a row of places of honour under an awning decorated with palm-leaf dangles and ceremonial cones of fruit and flowers, and listening to speeches by others, of which I understood about one word in four.

I decided to spend the weekend in Bali. I mostly read or sunned myself by the hotel pool, or sheltered from the rain which seemed to start at lunchtime each day and continue till dusk. But Stanley Allison, the hotel manager, swept me up into a very lively New Year's Eve party which was fun. And on Monday morning I paid some official calls – on the Governor of Bali and on the Regional Military Commander, a dark and virile-looking man who had wide responsibilities covering the islands east from Bali as far as East Timor, the disputed territory which Indonesia took over when the Portuguese left in the 70s. (The Indonesian army exploited the territory with great violence but in the early 80s Suharto was trying to defuse the problem by appointing a Timorese governor.) I had to drive myself a bit at these calls, because one often wondered what to talk about, but it seemed to be accepted as a courtesy, and was indeed an excellent way of learning about the preoccupations of the country outside Jakarta. I hoped to get better at it with practice.

From Bali I went to Surabaya, Indonesia's second biggest city, with some 4 million people, which despite its romantic name turned out to be a vast urban sprawl of little distinction. The Battle of Surabaya was one of the key episodes of Indonesia's struggle for Independence and rather surprisingly it was a battle against the British, not the Dutch – one of the events of those ill-considered months at the end of WWII when British forces took the Japanese surrender. I was curious to see it, but I was going to Surabaya to meet Mike Sumner, our Honorary Consul there, of whom I had heard slightly odd tales.

He turned out to be a Hemingway character, large and solid with a full curly black beard. He met me at the airport and as we drove along in his small coughing car he was continually replying with an airy wave of the hand to salutations from the local populace. He introduced me to a number of the small British community and took me to call on the Mayor's office. He also took me back to his house for a cup of tea – a house with an elegant brass plaque outside, and an incredibly ramshackle establishment inside dominated by vast cages full of brilliantly coloured birds. Of the teacups, only one had a handle, and flies were so thick that I quickly decided to cover my cup with a newspaper, an idea my host clearly thought entirely acceptable. Mike had lived in Surabaya for 30 years on and off, and had recently retired having worked for BAT (tobacco). When the Foreign Office, rather meanly, refused his request for a big Union Jack to hang outside his house he had one made locally in batik. I found him rather a tragic figure: it was probably the fact of being Consul which largely kept him going.

I was back in Surabaya a week later for Mike's funeral. He had died suddenly of a heart attack. It was a considerable shock, as he had been in Jakarta during the intervening weekend and came to lunch. Anni's reaction was, "You mean the man who ate the soufflé is dead?" The heavens opened as we took the body to the crematorium and we had to push it up a muddy track on a kind of trolley, while after the cremation service some touts tried to sell me back the white lilies that I had sent on behalf of the Embassy. I like to think that Mike would have appreciated the black humour. We went back to the house afterwards where a local woman presided who seemed to be his mistress. I got called on to make a very short speech – which I did adequately, if not especially well. Whatever his quirks, Mike Sumner was obviously a great personage locally, and I was very glad that the Embassy did him what honour we could.

I spent most of the morning of 6 January 1983 in the Parliament building listening to President Suharto read his annual budget speech – enough to bring anyone down to earth with a bump! A sober speech, because Indonesia like so many other countries was beginning to shiver in the chill wind of world recession, but also a very dignified one. A large section of Parliament was appointed and Suharto was listened to with great deference. The biggest cheer came when he said that civil servants would get no pay rise and would be deprived of official cars. Nobody loves us poor bureaucrats!

The following letter was prefaced by a note for my father: "Daddy – This is a letter with major news or at least advance warning. You may like to read it yourself first before deciding how to break it to Mother."

Surabaya Airport, 13 January 1983

Still no sign of my aeroplane so I will risk making a start on the serious news I want to give you. It is beginning to look increasingly as if I am going to marry Alec Campbell. This is no sudden development. Indeed the matter has been under debate at close or long range over the last 18 months. You may have guessed as much when he came to Guernsey, and if I wasn't such a clam I would have talked to you about it then. Indeed I haven't been asked the question in so many words yet, but the letter I received this week seemed to put it beyond all reasonable doubt that I will be. And I am also pretty clear in my own mind and heart that I am going to say yes. Since I don't want to present you with the news completely out of the blue, I felt it was time now to tell you how the wind was blowing.

I realize that you had very little opportunity to get to know Alec, but I hope very much that you liked him and will approve of my choice. It has not been at all easy to sort out our feelings for each other at such a distance – though in fact we managed to see quite a lot of each other during the year what with his visit here in the summer and my own to the UK in October. Nor is it easy at our age and each with established lives of our own, to know what is the best thing to do, especially as we are both highly reserved people more inclined to caution than impetuosity. But we both realized early on that we could only have any happy future together if we could learn to communicate with each other, and gradually we have succeeded to an extent which is quite new to me in my life – and I think also to Alec in his. Possibly realizing that we had many of the same inhibitions helped. Possibly having to write so many letters has helped too – Alec writes a marvellous letter, warm and articulate, and over the months I have gradually learned to do the same, or at least to discover unsuspected talents in that direction.

I hope this letter does not take your breath away too much. As always when I start on a subject I have been suppressing, the flood gates open and I find myself saying more than I really intended. I would ask you please to keep all of this to the two of you for the time being. Even after the major decision has been taken there are many other important questions to be settled. – How could our life be organized to bring us closer together? Does he leave Birmingham University? Do I leave the FCO? All very difficult questions to deal with by the rhythm of the weekly bag. I am very much hoping that Alec will be able to come out here for another visit at Easter because we really need to be able to talk things out together.

Waiting for me when I got home from Surabaya were Hugo Tobias and his wife Marianne whom I had known in Paris; they were on their way to visit their son Peter in Manila. They had spent much of the previous night at Singapore airport, and arrived alas without their luggage though this soon caught up with them. Hugo, who suffered from Parkinson's disease,

24. RCDS visit to China: in the Great Hall of the People, Beijing, 1981.
Front row centre: Chief of General Staff Yang Dheje between
Air Chief Marshal Sir Robert Freer (left) and Defence Attaché (right).
Back row far left: Dong Ledong.

25. RCDS visit to China:
welcome by the East China Sea Fleet on the Huangpu River near Shanghai, 1981

26. The weekly visit of the flower seller to my house in Jakarta, 1982

27. Simone Roell, JC and Celia Hensman with Susi, Jakarta, 1983

28. The Water Palace in Jogjakarta

29. Bromo: with Paul and Ursula Mallorie on the lip of the smoking volcano at dawn, 1983

30. Bromo: Ursula leads the ride back for breakfast, 1983

31. With Alec at Lake Toba, Sumatra, 1983

Wedding Day, Guernsey, 28 July 1983

32. Top: At the Town Church with my father.

33. Below: Sharing a joke with Alec in the garden at la Verdure while his son John made the best man's speech

34. At the Palace in Luxembourg with Court officials and Embassy staff after presenting my credentials to the Grand Duke. Don Farr is extreme right, April 1988.

35. The Irish Guards presenting their mascot to the Grand Duke who was their Colonel, 1991

36. Boat trip on the Moselle to celebrate the Luxembourg Presidency of the EC. Sidney Palmer, my then Deputy, is extreme left, 1991.

37. Interior of the Ambassador's Residence in Luxembourg, c1990

38. Mrs Thatcher's visit to SES at Betsdorf, Luxembourg, 1988

39. Girton College, Cambridge

40. The Vice-Chancellor,
Sir Alec Broers, at the Ceremony
marking 50 years of women receiving
their degrees in person, 1998

41. With the Queen Mother and Fellows at Girton, 1998

42. La Chapelle-sous-Brancion from the terrace of my house in Burgundy. Watercolour by JC.

43. Valley of the Petrusse near the British Embassy in Luxembourg. Watercolour by JC after Sosthène Weiss.

was not surprisingly exhausted. But Marianne with energy for ten had set her heart on going to Jogja to see Borobodur and went off on her own, leaving Hugo to have a rest in Jakarta. When she got back I decided to tell her all about Alec. I had not so far taken anyone into my confidence and I needed someone to talk to. To have the subject going round and round in my head for a couple of months without a word to anybody had created a slight feeling of unreality. Marianne had never met Alec and asked some searching questions. Meanwhile I waited anxiously for a reply to my letter home, longing to know my parents' reactions, though I knew they would only want what was best for me.

Anyhow for the time being I put the matter aside. I greatly enjoyed having the Tobiases to stay but it was most distressing to find that Hugo was far from well. One of the objects of his trip to Manila was to visit a faith healer by whom he set much store. We went to the Puncak for a day and had lunch at the cottage, Villa Lola, where they marvelled at the deliciously cool air, so different from Jakarta. On Sunday, when the traffic was at its lightest, I took them into the old town to see some of the remaining buildings from the Portuguese and Dutch eras. We also went to the schooner port with its wonderful wooden sailing boats that brought timber, flour, etc from all over Indonesia. It was my favourite spot in Jakarta.

The next official visitor was Lord Jellicoe who was soon to take over as Chairman of the British Overseas Trade Board. He was a pleasant, easy-going man but obviously very shrewd, and had a marvellous Punch-like profile which would have been a credit to any Admiral. I organized a dinner party for him at home which went quite well. We waited for some Indonesians who didn't come which was a mild bore, but it was a lovely evening and we were able to eat out under the stars. I borrowed the Residence cook to make eclairs and was left with two vast trays full which I put into the deep freeze.

One of the guests, a mysterious Chinese millionaire called Mr. Poo (pronounced to rhyme with Oh!), sent me the most magnificent basket of roses. Mr. Poo was an important figure in British business circles in Jakarta. Foreign companies were required to have an Indonesian partner and for British companies this was Mr. Poo. The Chinese occupied a special place in Indonesian life, keeping a low profile but controlling much of the country's wealth. Many Chinese took Indonesian names, but not Mr. Poo who was proud to tell how he started his career selling pencils and worked his way up. Now he was reputedly close to the President and acted as intermediary for all British trade deals, benefiting accordingly. The system had the incidental advantage for British firms: they could leave their local partner to deal with the necessary bribes and did not get their hands dirty. This sort of corruption was endemic in Indonesia and I accepted it as a fact of life, a sort of tax on business deals. Years later, when the whole issue of bribery in big foreign contracts became such a live issue, I wondered guiltily whether I didn't gloss over the moral aspects a bit too easily. But back to 1983 and Lord Jellicoe's visit.

Jakarta, 2 February 1983

Last week was Jellicoe week... They were great fun (not what one expects to say about an official visitor!) and I found him a considerable loss to British politics. (You may remember he resigned in the wake of the scandal about Lord Lambton some years ago – apparently it was a bit of bad luck, because Lord L, who was indiscreet in all ways, kept a diary in which the name Lord Jellicoe kept appearing. In fact, according to the on-dit, the reference was to a well-known London pub used as a rendezvous, but when Lord J was faced with the story, there was just enough truth in his involvement for him to feel obliged to resign. True or false, it makes a good story!) I accompanied him to call on several Indonesian ministers and was impressed how well he had absorbed his briefing and used the key points to good effect. We also all attended a rather splendid dinner party given by a Chinese multi-millionaire [Mr Poo] *at the best restaurant in town – delicious food, good music with lots of gimmicks like a singer who kept on putting a second mike in front of poor unsuspecting guests (like me, who could never remember the words of any song) and a marvellously ill-assorted group of guests whose terms of reference were so far apart that every now and again the conversation took on a quite surrealist turn.*

Quite some time later, a totally unexpected and extremely heavy parcel arrived, which turned out to contain a thank you present from Lord Jellicoe: an illustrated catalogue of the Tate's modern paintings. It came with a very friendly note and pleased me very much. After the Jellicoes had gone I had a good weekend in the Puncak with the Bacons who had taken over the Lindsays' share of Villa Lola. I spent a fair amount of the time reading the Franks Report: the enquiry into the handling of the Falklands Affair. I was relieved that the Foreign Office came out of it so well. The main problem highlighted, it seemed to me, was the inability of ministers to give full attention to all the multitudinous subjects coming before them for decision in the circumstances of modern government. It was a great juggling act and every now and again a ball crashed to the ground. Buried away in the middle of the report was a nugget of humour: as the crisis before the invasion reached its height the Argentine Government presented a formal protest to the British Embassy in Buenos Aires: the Argentine flag had been insulted in Port Stanley when someone broke into the Argentine Airways office there and wrote upon a desk in toothpaste the memorable words: "Tit for tat, you buggers!"

The Tobiases had gone on to Manila, and Hugo sent me a most remarkable letter about his experiences with the faith healer who was called Rev. Bro. Alex. Apparently great crowds gathered at the Rev. Bro.'s house, and he went about among them removing growths with his bare hands. Hugo said that Bro. Alex had opened up two places on his head and one in his neck from which he had removed something described (by Marianne) as looking like sweetbreads. There was apparently no blood, and no mark left on the skin afterwards. Bro. Alex told Hugo to walk straight and be strong, and Hugo walked without his stick. There was nothing about faith as such in Hugo's account. It sounded to me more akin to the sort of prowess that fakirs have, the ability to stick pins in themselves and leave no scar or to walk on nails.

After Lord Jellicoe came Sir Philip Shelbourne, the Chairman of Britoil. Lunch with him after dinner out the night before was one of those times when eating abroad for one's country became rather a strain. I chewed some milk of magnesia tablets and looked forward to a weekend of plain fare in the Puncak. Shelbourne turned out to be a slightly auntish bachelor who talked non-stop, interestingly and at times amusingly too, but rather exhausting. He recounted with glee that he had commissioned a portrait in the style of Tintoretto of his late dog Montaigne, rising to heaven on a cloud and illuminated by a shaft of light while angels played admiringly around! The current dog was called Brit (after Britoil) and visitors were apparently expected to shake its paw. It obviously takes all sorts to build up successful companies. Anyhow we clearly hit it off because he wrote a very complimentary letter about me to the head of the FCO.

We were in the run-up to a special session of the enlarged Parliament which would without a doubt re-elect President Suharto, as well as formally adopting a document called *The Broad Outlines of State Policy for the Next Five Years*. I decided to launch myself on a series of political calls. So, accompanied by our young third secretary, I set out, flag flying, to call on the leaders of the three main political groups. I am not sure that I learned a great deal, but then Indonesian politics were a particularly obfuscating business. All three refused to admit that Indonesia could be facing any serious economic difficulties, so I felt that it was almost bad form to have mentioned it. Far the jolliest of the three was the leader of the Muslim party, who despite the need for an interpreter, and despite his black nationalist cap, had a thoroughly infectious laugh. The basic problem was that while all were keen to present themselves as serious politicians with valid political objectives, they were all equally keen to present themselves as loyal supporters of the current government and all its works. I tried to explain that British politics were rather different.

One of the things which I had omitted to do on arrival was to get myself an Indonesian driving licence. I decided that I had better remedy the situation. This entailed sitting an examination consisting of choosing from four answers to a series of questions. The supervising policemen told one which answer was correct, but even so I managed to get one wrong! Then one had to have one's photo taken against a huge yardstick designed to show one's height. Ordinary mortals were also expected to donate some blood, but luckily I was let off that. I was intrigued to learn that to get a licence to drive lorries or bigger vehicles it was necessary to attend a week's course in "Pancasila upgrading." Pancasila, the five foundational principles of the Indonesian Republic, might be summarised as nationalism, humanism, democracy, social prosperity, and belief in one God. Though extremely elastic they had a semi-mythical status.

The dinner for Philip Shelbourne was quickly followed by one for Lord Kindersley, the Chairman of the Commonwealth Development Corporation. The CDC was a British Government-owned bank offering subsidised finance to suitable projects which could be expected in due course to become profitable and pay back the loans. It was very active in Indonesia where access to finance was a major problem, and I considered it a very useful form of development aid.

I was expecting Kathy Kaser of the FCO Research Dept to stay as well as Clare Agnew, the enterprising daughter of a friend from Guernsey. Yet another expected visitor was Ceridwen Legge, another Guernsey connection, who rather startled me by announcing that she was arriving with not only a daughter in a wheelchair but a cousin as well! All could just be fitted in, but I had eight houseguests in five days. Anni said I must be opening an *ashrama* (a sort of Muslim hostel for women). She rose to the occasion marvellously, her family all rallied round and there was no suggestion at all that it was too much work. But it seemed verging on the ludicrous when Clare Agnew rang up beforehand and said diffidently that she was travelling with a Swedish girl whom she had met at Perth airport. I offered them camp beds and sleeping bags, and they stayed three nights. They were nice girls and very self-reliant but I was rather alarmed to hear that they were planning to go on by local steamer – notoriously unsafe in a country where there were no safety regulations to speak of and passengers were crammed on like sardines. I was particularly concerned that they should not set off separately on their two to three days' journey which at one stage seemed likely. I felt middle-aged as I listened to myself retailing some of the more horrible stories I had heard about what could happen.

When Clare wrote recounting her experiences on the boat they sounded horrific enough to vindicate my most alarmist stories. She vividly described the fight to board, with people in every spare centimetre where "crowds sprawled, camped, ate, spat, played cards and practiced basic survival." The boat didn't take them the whole way and she ended up chartering a plane with a group of other young English and Australians who were similarly stranded. As she said, it would probably have been cheaper to fly from Jakarta in the first place, but then she would have missed the experience. Sooner her than me!

***

The Ambassador came back in late February. There was a sense of release in giving up my responsibilities as Chargé – I wouldn't need to be quite so conscientious about all the cocktail parties given by British firms, for one thing. But I had enjoyed my three months running the Embassy and the experience gave me a new confidence, as well as teaching me a lot. I felt pleased with myself. We had had a range of prestigious visitors one after another and all seemed to have gone away satisfied. There were, however, a couple of bombshells on the last day. We lost our case in Medan with £½ million at stake, though we could of course appeal, and the appeal court was said to be less liable to be bought. Then a visit to Kalimantan, organized as we thought for a group of visiting British tycoons from the oil world, was suddenly vetoed by the authorities without explanation. This might have been because of jumpiness connected with the special parliamentary session to re-elect the President or it could be retaliation for a British cut in North

Sea oil prices – Indonesia at that time depended for 70% of her revenue on oil exports and had been hoping against hope that the international price would hold. Anyhow I was quite glad to have the Ambassador back to consult about these last-minute problems.

My last day in charge was splendid because it coincided with the official reopening of Borobodur after a mammoth restoration largely funded by UNESCO. The diplomatic corps were taken en masse to witness the event like a sort of glorified school outing. It was an early start, since we had to be at Jakarta airport at 6am to catch the special plane to Jogja. Then there was a long bus ride to Borobodur itself – notable for the fact that the Sri Lankan Ambassador fell asleep on my shoulder! I enjoyed describing the event for my parents.

Jakarta, 24 February 1983

It was a marvellous clear day with the volcanos more vivid than I had ever seen them – a blessed comparison with my time in Jogja last year when clouds lowered ceaselessly and the rain was relentless. At Borobodur itself the dip corps were seated in a big pavilion newly built and corner-wise on to the monument – in protocol order of course. Obviously Protocol Dept were expecting the Ambassador because when they saw me they waved me to the back where there was no place reserved for the UK at all. I sat meekly, but when the officials had gone went on a prowl, and there sure enough were two desirable seats marked Great Britain right near the front. So I quickly moved forward (with full approval of my neighbours) and had an excellent view of proceedings. There were lots of speeches of course, and the President signed a vast stone to commemorate the day. Then there was a great parade of people from all the provinces of Indonesia in their various costumes... what a colourful and varied country this is. We began to wonder if we would be allowed any time at all to visit the temple itself: we were, but only just time to scamper up to the top and down again. Marvellous to see it complete and without the cranes which have crowded round like vultures on my previous visits.

The Ambassador's return should have made me less busy, but I didn't notice it. Indeed, bringing him up to date and talking developments over took a certain amount of time in itself. And other things had piled up considerably so it was a relief to see glimpses of sky again as I cleared away the thickets of accumulated paper. Meanwhile there was a new Government in Jakarta, which looked remarkably like the last one. However, it put an end to a period of much speculation and a little tension. Now Suharto, who had got himself re-elected as President at the same time, was all set for another five years.

My next visitor was Alec who arrived in late March taking advantage of the Easter vacation at Birmingham. I got some amusement from my father's reaction when I rang up bursting with my news that Alec and I had decided to get married. "Well, I can't say I am surprised…" I still had some difficulty in believing that it was true. It took some adjusting to get used to looking at the future in terms of "us" rather than "me." We both felt that the right thing was to get married as soon as we reasonably could but how we organized ourselves from there on did not depend entirely on ourselves because we both had commitments which could not simply be abandoned. The further future was even more difficult to envisage. Alec had already decided to opt for early retirement from his Professorship at Birmingham where he was beginning to feel a bit bored and was casting around for various other occupations, since he clearly needed an employment. It did not seem the moment for me too to quit my established career. All this I explained in lengthy letters to my parents.

But there was another immediate excitement too. I had long planned to meet my Bangkok friends Paul and Ursula Mallorie in Bali and to make the thousand-mile drive back to Jakarta together. To travel the length of Java, Indonesia's most populous island, was a great opportunity to learn about new areas of the huge country and to make some semi-official visits. When Alec suggested visiting me during his Easter break I asked him to join us though he couldn't stay for the full trip. The plan was for Alec and me to fly to Bali where one of the Embassy drivers would deliver my car and the Mallories would join us. They knew about all these arrangements though not about our engagement. The next couple of letters describe our memorable trip.

Tretes in E. Java, 8 April 1983

Our trip has been a great success so far, both as a journey of adventure, and as what is in fact for Alec and me a first venture into public as an acknowledged couple. Because we of course decided to tell the Mallories straight away of our engagement (unfamiliar word which I still find strange to use!). I also before leaving Jakarta wrote a letter to the Ambassador (who was himself away the week before Easter) to tell him the news. He rang us up here last night and invited us to dinner on Saturday night. I have arranged to fly back to Jakarta with Alec on Sat a.m. to see him off and will return on Monday to join up with the Mallories for the rest of the trip back. All rather confusing, but there are moments for special arrangements! Anyhow I am glad that we will have the chance of a discussion together with the Ambassador before Alec departs and we are once again thrown back on the weekly bag, with its frustrating gap of 3 weeks between question asked and answer received, for discussing our future plans. The Ambassador, poor man, must be suffering from mild shock since he thought he had tidily arranged the main problems of Embassy staffing up until his own retirement in a year's time.

In the meantime let me tell you something more of our trip which is turning out splendidly. Bali was of course familiar ground to Alec and myself, but having a car made it possible to see new parts of this beautiful island, well away from the tourist beat. I must say it was a great relief to find my car waiting for me on arrival at the airport there. I had entrusted it to one of the Embassy drivers in whom I had confidence, but even so I had a lurking worry that something might go wrong on such a long journey. As it was, we were able to stay inland in a pretty village well away from the tourist hotels.

But the real adventure started on Tuesday when we set off on the journey home – an early start for a three-hour drive along the S.W. coast to the ferry over from Banyuwani to Java. A half hour trip we were told. We made very good time only to find ourselves faced by a long wait for and then on a very leisured ferry boat which made us late for our appointment the other side. From that point on we were taken over for 48 hours by staff of different plantations run by the Indonesian Government. All this was arranged through a nice man from the Sugar Council whom I met in Jakarta some months ago – I thought I was simply taking him up on an offer to stay in one of the plantation guest houses, but Javanese hospitality is such that we were all four taken over, organized, transported, lodged and indeed fed.

At the ferry terminal we were met by a nice man called Mr. Effendi who had been deputed to look after us while we were on the territory of Plantation no 26, which seems to operate over wide expanses of East Java. He led us first to Situbondo [names on map on page viii] *where we had an excellent lunch and garaged the car, then in plantation high-clearance transport up a beautiful mountainous road to Sempol, a coffee plantation at some 1500 metres where we were lodged in a guest house built by the Dutch managers immediately before the war. It was a lovely spot, cool, and surrounded by the broken peaks of an extinct volcano (Mt Ijen) in whose crater the plantation lies. The following morning another lovely drive in a pack of jeeps, accompanied by the senior staff of the plantation (all Indonesians now of course) to see a coffee processing factory and view the scenery. It was a marvellous spot and our hosts could not have been kinder or more hospitable.*

Mr. Effendi insisted on coming with us as far as Probolinggo where we were handed over to the staff of Plantation no 24/25; more precisely to the Manager of a sugar factory there. This was our jumping off point for Mount Bromo, another marvellous volcano. This was perhaps the most adventurous part, the highlight, of the whole trip. We all spent the night at a very simple hotel at Ngadisari, right on the crater's rim and reached again by jeeps provided by the plantation. Or perhaps I should say we spent the first part of the night, because we rose at 3:30 am for an hour's horse-ride to the summit of Bromo itself, a newer and still active volcano within the crater of the old one. It was a fabulous moon-landscape and looking down into the pit of the seething smoking volcano in the dark from the narrow surrounding rim was an experience I will never forget. It rumbled ominously, and red patches came and went, while the sulphurous smoke when blown in our direction (fortunately the wind was mostly the other way) made our eyes smart. The inhabitants of the surrounding villages blackmail the volcano to stay quiet by throwing in offerings from time to time. Standing there looking into the cauldron and thinking how easy it would be to slip one hoped that the angry gods within had received enough tribute recently to keep them quiet. Then, after dawn, a ride back across the sand sea to the hotel, the ponies by now distinctly anxious for their breakfast and pushing the pace. I found myself remembering Daddy's riding instructions of long ago – heels down, toes up, grip with the knees!

Back to the hotel – still very early – then we were taken down to the Manager's home at Probolinggo and given a hearty breakfast – rice, fried eggs and a variety of other veg and meat dishes – which we all ate with great gusto, and which gave us the strength for a conducted tour of the sugar factory – a bit difficult to understand this, since there were linguistic problems and nothing much was actually happening.

And then on to Tretes, where we are now staying in a lovely bungalow belonging to the Tootal's Rep in Surabaya whom I met during one of my visits there earlier this year. Tretes is the mountain resort for Surabaya, and this house – also Dutch built between the wars – is a paradise of comfort after the rigours of the last few days with their hard beds, cold scoops for washing, and early starts. So today is a gloriously idle day all round...

Alec and I flew back to Jakarta and had dinner with the Brashes as planned. They couldn't have been nicer about it and broke out some champagne. I explained that we would prefer if possible to start our married life living in the same place, and that I therefore proposed to sound out the FCO about posting me back to London. The Ambassador didn't know any more than I did how this would be received. The basic rule was that officers were free to marry, but that marriage made no difference to the obligation to serve where posted. After seeing Alec off on the long flight back to England I flew back to Surabaya, where the Mallories were at the airport to meet me. It seemed rather sad to be continuing the journey without Alec, but I decided to stick to my original plan. I had already negotiated the necessary leave and there was no point in moping around in Jakarta on my own.

Jogjakarta, 17 April 1983

Here we are on the last leg of the Great Trans-Java Trek, with only a fairly easy day's drive to get us back to Jakarta. Everything has gone surprisingly well, and from my own point of view the trip has achieved its purpose, which was to give me a better idea of how the 90 million odd Javanese who don't live in Jakarta actually pass their existence. Out of the jumble of impressions two in particular. First, the mountains which form Java's rocky spine always seem to be there: there can be few Javanese who are not familiar with one or other of the great volcanoes which tend to explode once every century or so. Second, the teeming, industrious people tilling every available centimetre of land, making use of everything that comes to hand, plucking grasses, leaves, making use of the volcanic ash. They never seem to be idle.

[On leaving Surabaya] *we did one of our longer, duller day's drives South-West and back into the mountains, spending the night at another little resort town high on Mt. Lawu called Sarangan. It was a lovely spot with a little lake surrounded by peaks. Searching for accommodation at Indonesian towns which are off the foreign tourist beat can be quite an experience, but here we were lucky, following up a tip given me by our Air Attaché, and we found ourselves in a hotel run by the Indonesian Air Force appropriately called the Cyrro-Stratus. Hotel wasn't quite the word, because what we had was a 3 room bungalow with its own terrace and catering facilities, clean and pleasant if my bed was hard. The next day's road took us right over Mt. Lawu itself, a breathtaking road with stupendous views. It was here that we had our only drama – and thank goodness Paul was driving: after coming down some vertiginous bends for several miles, suddenly the brakes went soft, presumably from over-heating as a result of over-use at high altitude. We stopped and Paul removed the front wheels and flung buckets of water at the hubs, and fortunately they recovered of their own accord so we could continue our journey. Next stop Jogja where we decided to stay in the best hotel for a change – ironically it is just opposite the house where I spent my one month's hard, doing language training.*

The rest of our trip…went very smoothly, the highlight – after Jogja and its temples – being a day in an extraordinary isolated crater called the Dieng Plateau, where multicoloured sulphurous lakes steam, and wild fuchsias bloom, and cloud drifts to and fro between a row of small Hindu temples which are some of the earliest in Java. Here too there is a cave where President Suharto is reputed to go to meditate at critical junctures of his career – it is reputed to be a place of great mystic strength: we found several, without being sure which was the right one, and I must say I wouldn't care to spend the night in any of them. To get to Dieng, we spent a couple of nights at a little town called Wonosobo where we found ourselves in the most extraordinary hotel – a relic from pre-World-War I when the Dutch planters from the area used to come and spend their weekends there in splendour. Now it is virtually deserted, its vast public rooms with their crested glass gradually going to rack and ruin. We were the only 3 guests in a hotel which still claims a hundred beds!

From there on to Bandung, and then on Sunday back to Jakarta where we were all very ready to appreciate the comforts of Jalan Iman Bonjol No 2.

Among the letters waiting for me – no less than three from my father – I found one from Alec's mother in answer to one I had written her.

It could not have been nicer or warmer, and encouraged me very much. It looked as if among my many strokes of good fortune I might be able to count a welcoming mother-in-law.

Things seemed to be very busy at the Office which was perhaps just as well because it helped the time go faster in that odd period of waiting for a new pattern of life to begin. Being engaged must always be like that to some extent, but it seemed particularly odd to be going about my normal work and behaving as if nothing had happened, when my head was full of my own private excitements. I went to the St. George's Ball, a huge and well-organized affair which was one of the folk occasions of the British community. I was invited to join a party arranged by one of the big British companies, Balfour Beatty, and moderately enjoyed it. I dug out for the occasion a dress originally made for me when I was in Bangkok which I had resurrected for Jakarta. It was a long white tube of heavy lace, in three tiers. I poured myself into it with ease and it created a minor sensation among the assembled diplomats at the Dutch National Day to which I went en route to the Ball. There however the scene was definitely stolen by a lady wearing a dress of most ingenious design which contrived to have a picture window opening in front revealing most of an extremely ample bosom. Even I found my eyes riveted by the mountainous view.

One day the Embassy had an open house for a party of British community wives. It was the Ambassador's idea as a way of bringing home to the community what the Embassy really did. An excellent idea and it went well. We had two groups who visited various sections of the Embassy where each explained their jobs. As Head of Chancery it fell to me to do most of the coordination. I also sat my Indonesian exam. I didn't have much time for revision and there were far too many words I didn't know. It seemed unfair to be expected to recognise a "tidal swamp" at the lower level of exam! I told myself that I would not hear the results for months by which time I probably wouldn't care. I am glad to say that I eventually heard that I had passed.

About this time a small tabby cat joined my household. Uninvited by me, I should add. At first I thought Susi might eat him, but though no larger than my hand he had no qualms about telling her where to get off. Susi was surprisingly tolerant and would have clearly welcomed a playmate if only the small ball of fur would stop hissing at her. My breakfast on the back garden terrace was livened by the kitten's discovery that it could watch proceedings from under the glass table. He was not my cat, you understand, but Anni's. Either way, the kitten was there to stay.

In May I made a week's trip to the Sultanate of Brunei which was still a British colony and due to become fully independent the following year. Brunei shared the island of Borneo with Indonesia as well as Malaysia but I had to travel via Singapore and Kuala Lumpur to get there. The Indonesian Government was very interested in developments but direct contact was minimal or non-existent. This was no doubt a hang-over from the bitter war of Konfrontasi of the 60s in which Borneo was the major battle-ground. I wanted to inform myself of what was happening in the hopes of being able in some minor way to ease Brunei's relations with the Indonesians. The British Government hoped Brunei would join ASEAN which would only be possible with Indonesian agreement.

The FCO approved my plan and I was accompanied on my visit by a member of the South East Asian Department as well as our own Defence Attaché. We paid official calls on the embryo Ministry of Foreign Affairs and the oil company (Shell in some form) which in practical terms ran the economy. Oil rich, Brunei was still largely undeveloped with a jungly interior. The capital, Bandar Seri Begawan, was a large village with houses on ramshackle jetties around a little harbour which contrasted strangely with the gleaming dome of the Sultan's new palace. One afternoon the military took us upriver in a longboat with outboard motor and we saw how soon any pretence at modernity petered out among the mangrove swamps. My official report of the visit must be lurking somewhere among the FCO records at Kew.

The Ambassador was away on another of his trips leaving me the major chore of preparation for the Queen's Birthday Party. This was to be much bigger than previous years because the he was due to retire and wanted to have a splash for his last year. I was finding it difficult to concentrate on routine business with so much on my mind so it came as a relief when Robert, or to be exact Mrs. Brash, suggested that the party would be a good time to announce my coming marriage to the staff. I had hoped to know what the FCO planned to do with me before having to face the inevitable barrage of questions but it seemed better to have a clear announcement than let rumours start spreading.

The party took place on 7 June. The Ambassador had informed people in advance in slightly ominous terms that he wished them all to remain after the guests had left to have a glass of champagne and hear an announcement. When the moment came I began to feel a bit sheepish and self-conscious. Barbara Brash, who came to stand beside me, suddenly whispered that her husband didn't know how to say it and I saw that she was right. He said something about "in loco parentis" and "a romance budding in our midst" and then went on "The Head of Chancery is to marry Professor Alec..." tailing off a bit so I hastily chipped in "Campbell" in case he wished me off on the wrong man! There was much drinking of healths and many kind words were said. I was inevitably faced with lots of questions about the future which I had no way of answering.

I sent an impassioned letter to the FCO pointing out that I had been waiting over two months for a reply to my original request and that I was on the point of leaving on mid-tour leave. If I was to leave Jakarta for good, I should be getting the packers in. I had some funny moments as my news spread. People were mostly taken by surprise and didn't for a second know what to say. The usual lead-in question was: "What are you doing with your holiday?" – a typical diplomatic ice-breaker with people one doesn't know very well. "Getting married!" I would reply, and pause while the other party regrouped before going on to ask the obvious questions: "Are you coming back? Is your husband coming too?" – all good questions to which I found it difficult to reply.

I decided to get my dress for the wedding made in Jakarta where there were plenty of good dress makers. At 46 I felt definitely too old for a white wedding but I found some pretty navy blue and white silk on a trip to Singapore and chose a pattern with a triple shawl collar of creamy white organza trimmed with a narrow edging of lace. The wedding was set for 28 July in Guernsey and my father took over making the preliminary arrangements. There was also to be a major family gathering for his 90th birthday on 8 August. In true military style he referred to the two celebrations as "Operation Matrimony" and "Operation 90th."

Then, with three or four days left before my planned departure, a telegram arrived from the Personnel Department telling me that they had arranged a direct job swap with Meg Rothwell, Head of the FCO Training Department. They said I should start in September without returning to Jakarta. The Embassy would pack up my things and send them after me. I was horrified. I did not want to leave a post where I thought I had done well and where people had been kind to me without the courtesy of saying my goodbyes. Nor did I fancy semi-strangers supervising my packing. The Ambassador supported my protest and it was agreed that I could return to Jakarta for three months in the autumn. Not an ideal arrangement but it seemed the best possible at that stage.

Our wedding took place on a lovely summer's day in Guernsey. After a major dither about hypocrisy and my lack of faith, I opted to be married in the Town Church where memorial plaques to my grandfather and uncle mark the long family connection. There followed a lunch party on the lawn at La Verdure and a brief honeymoon in France. Ten days later the Collings family gathered at full strength to celebrate my father's 90th birthday. Alec's children, John and Ann, each joined us for a few days too, John with his soon-to-be fiancée Susanna. We made a brief start on married life in Oxford and my father hosted a big reception at the Army and Navy Club in London for our wider circle of friends. All too soon it was time for me to go back. Those final three months were more difficult than I had naively expected. More than ever I had the feeling of life suspended. To make matters much worse my mother died in the middle of November and I was not there to say goodbye to her or to help my father.

***

I can't leave Jakarta without a last word about Susi. When the packers came she clearly knew I was going. It is the fate of Embassy dogs to be left behind and she recognized the signs. Retreating to the back porch she rolled up into a tight ball and would not budge. She would not even look at me when the car came to pick me up for the airport and I went to say goodbye. "*Ia menangis*," said Anni, and I knew that meant she was crying. It felt like betrayal though common sense told me that a dog from the tropics wouldn't have enjoyed England even if I could have sorted out the practical arrangements. But I am glad to report that she had a happy life and a devoted new owner in Meg Rothwell. She even had that longed-for litter of puppies.

Personal considerations apart, I would have liked to stay longer in Indonesia, a country I found fascinating in its beauty and variety, and I leapt at chances to return. When I went back in 2013 with a group from the Royal Society for Asian Affairs I took my granddaughter Naomi, then in her early 20s. What struck me most was the huge explosion of population in Java – from 90 million to around 150 million – and the consequences for traffic and congestion. I wrote a detailed account of our trip for the journal *Asian Affairs* under the heading "Indonesia 30 Years On."

Chapter 17

WHAT COULD WE DO BETTER?
FCO Training Department, London (1984–1987)

Back in England at last I spent my first Christmas in my new Oxford home. My father came to stay and for the first time met Alec's mother Oma. Despite their very different backgrounds – she from a rather severe German missionary background, he the soldier son of a Guernsey doctor – they hit it off very well. I enjoyed the peaceful opportunity to spend time with my father after the anguish of the last year. But, alas, his health soon began to fail. We talked often on the phone and I visited Guernsey every few weeks. But at the end of March he died in the all-too-familiar hospital in St Peter Port and this time I was there. Here is the last letter I wrote to him from my little house in Islington which I had reclaimed from the tenants.

26 Sudeley Street, 30 January 1984

I thought it might also amuse you to hear a little more of my first impressions of the FCO Training Dept than I could easily give you over the phone. The premises, despite the fact they are just across the road from the Houses of Parliament, are dingy in the extreme – condemned for redevelopment years ago, so that nobody has been prepared to spend any money on them since. The floors are covered with chipped lavatorial tiling, and many of the offices including my own bear a notice on the door to the effect that no heavy weights should be placed on the floor. Alec has suggested that would-be Heads of Training Dept are weighed before they are allowed to take up their appointment! But the premises are so universally recognized as awful that it is agreed that we should move as soon as something else suitable can be found, and with any luck a building in Lower Regent Street may be on offer in the not too distant future.

The content of the job is more immediately promising. Indeed I think it will turn out to be rather interesting. There is such a wide range of training done in the FCO, ranging from the traditional hard language training (and there are lots of echoes of MECAS crossing my desk) to preparing ordinary diplomats for the computer age, that I won't have much chance to be dull. And I also seem to have a finger as of right in a number of outside pies. For instance I am to be on a working party reviewing extramural studies at the School of Oriental and African Studies of London University. You may well ask what I know about the matter, and of course I do too, but one can't let oneself be put off by a little matter like that! The fact that the FCO is an important user of such facilities gives us the right to a voice.

I've run into a number of old friends in my first week back in the Office too, which has been pleasant. I was summoned as a new Head of Department to pay a formal call on the Permanent Undersecretary – none other than my old friend Antony Acland! I found it difficult to be altogether serious!

The only disadvantage of my new way of life looks like being that the weekends are too short and the weeks too long. Alec went back to Oxford by the early train this morning and I will join him there on Friday night.

The premises were indeed awful and shortly after I took over surveyors discovered that there was nothing much in the way of structural support to stop them falling into Westminster Tube Station. We were very hastily moved to a temporary home near Marlborough House in a suite of rooms which had recently been the press centre for a Commonwealth conference. Then started an urgent search for something more suitable and more permanent. Apart from space for teaching and offices the main requirement was to be in easy walking distance of the main FCO so that people working in busy departments could get there quickly for classes. Mike Hodge, my deputy, and I inspected several possibilities including a building in Lower Regent Street which came complete with a huge mainframe computer filling one of the biggest rooms. In the end we moved into Cromwell House, a handsome corner building on the Embankment. Once again I had an office with a wonderful view, this time of the river and the Houses of Parliament. It was time to get down to the job.

When Personnel Department proposed back in Jakarta that I should do a direct swap with Meg Rothwell as Head of Training Department it was with an apology that nothing more interesting could be found. Training did not have a high status in the Office where the general culture assumed that members of the Service were clever enough to pick up most things on the job. But it turned out to be one of the most satisfying jobs I did in my

DS career. I had enough experience to know what I thought the Service did badly (staff management for a start – too many clever policy wonks rose to the top with little idea of how to run a team) and with no one breathing down my neck I could do something about it. The department had a full-time staff of about 30 divided into two separate wings, one responsible for language training and the other for all the rest. My key assistants were the two men who headed these sections and I was very lucky in both of them.

Of course we were not working in a vacuum. The Training Department came under the Chief Clerk who had overall responsibility for the running of the Service at home and abroad. His weekly meetings gathered the heads of all the departments dealing with personnel, communications, security and so on. There was also a wider "training community" which included all my opposite numbers in Whitehall departments as well as the Civil Service College. The Thatcher government of the mid 80s had an ideological commitment to management by defined and measurable objectives which faced the Civil Service with deep changes of culture and implications for training. Being separate from the Home Civil Service, the Diplomatic Service was not obliged to follow the many initiatives wholesale but there was an expectation that we would do so to the extent that our different circumstances warranted. There was a good deal of resistance to much of this in the Foreign Office. My own view was that spelling out clearly what one was trying to do was a thoroughly good idea though diplomacy did not lend itself to easy measurement and a lot of what we were asked to do was unnecessarily bureaucratic. Coming totally fresh to training I found the meetings of more experienced experts a stimulating source of ideas and I enjoyed sampling courses offered by the Civil Service College or elsewhere if they sounded useful.

A new head of the Diplomatic Service Language Centre, John Moore, arrived shortly after I did. He was a linguist from the British Council who knew exactly what he was doing so I gave him his head. He soon convinced me that the system of language exams which drove all our teaching and served as the basis for the elaborate system of language allowances was out of date. We sent out a questionnaire to all members of the Diplomatic Service to find out how they used languages in practice and what skills they most needed. The replies made it very clear that spoken language was key: diplomats wanted to be able to make themselves understood and to get the general gist of what was said. Only at the very highest levels did they ever need to write polished prose of the kind that the traditional exams had tested. A complete overhaul of the exam system followed, with input from the Institute of Linguists. My role was basically to get the reforms approved by the hierarchy in the FCO and then explain them to the Service. But there was one change in the system for which I take full credit – introducing a system of rewards for spouses who passed the various exams. I knew all too well how isolated wives could be in a distant country when they could not speak the language – and what a help those who did learn about local languages and culture could be.

The Diplomatic Language Centre was really a small language school and employed a range of teachers in French, German, Spanish etc. Teaching in other languages was commissioned as necessary. Many diplomats liked to get a start on a language before posting, as I myself had done, and once in post one was entitled to 100 hours' local teaching. Training in "hard" languages was a much more serious business. New entrants to the Service were tested for aptitude and after a year or so in London a number of them would be chosen to learn the languages needed to fill whatever posts were likely to be required later on. Initial training was in London followed by a period in the country concerned. In my day our students learning Chinese went to Taiwan for a year while the Japanologists went to a small FCO-run school outside Tokyo. But there was a problem about the Arabists: MECAS had been abandoned during the civil war in Lebanon so where should they go for their final in-country training? We settled on Jordan for a while but I don't believe a wholly satisfactory answer was ever found.

Meanwhile there was a question mark over the future of African and Asian language training generally in the UK. As the generation who had served in the colonies died off a gap in the country's language skills was becoming apparent. This fed into particular concern about the future of SOAS (the School of Oriental and African Studies which is part of London University) on which the FCO depended for a range of languages. A number of the people at the top of the Foreign Office took a personal interest in all this – in particular John Whitehead, the then Chief Clerk, who was a Japanese specialist – and they put together a proposal for a Royal Commission, only to have it vetoed by Mrs Thatcher. No quangos, she said. The problem was then put in the hands of a most interesting and charismatic man, Sir Peter Parker, the former Head of British Rail, who had himself learned Japanese in his youth. He got together a group of interested people including someone from SOAS, a Professor of French from Reading, a retired Arabist Ambassador (Sir Michael Weir) and me, as mentioned in the letter to my father. It was a most interesting exercise, made fun by Peter Parker's enthusiasm and generosity; amongst other things he was Chairman of the National Theatre and one day after a long meeting he took us all to dine at the Garrick. First there was a national appeal for written evidence from interested parties, and when all this had been digested there was a day or two of oral evidence, all rather as if we really had been a Royal Commission. The idea was to find out what universities, government, banks, businesses etc thought their requirement of linguists would be over the next decade and then to work out how many extra teaching posts would be needed to provide them. The FCO Planning Staff provided some excellent think pieces. (Manned by some of the Service's brightest and best, this department inevitably included some loyal Arabists.) Some of our witnesses were very helpful but I remember grinding my teeth when a banker blithely said that if he needed linguists he would simply buy in people who had been trained by the Foreign Office!

The Committee agreed to put forward a series of recommendations for new teaching posts in British universities focusing on three main languages – Chinese, Japanese and Arabic. The Secretary to the Committee who was provided by SOAS dutifully amassed a great deal of information to support all this. It included all the evidence and was quite a tome. Then one weekend Peter Parker rang me up at home at his most persuasive – "Nobody will read all this. What are we going to do about it, Juliet?" I can still hear myself offering to write an introduction summarizing it all to which the evidence could be attached as a detailed annex. That was the end of that weekend! The Report was finally published under a title of my inspiration – "Speaking for the Future." It was one of those times when I did feel I had made a small difference and I am glad to say that the posts we recommended were eventually funded, a number – but not all – going to SOAS.

So much for the language side of things. The other wing of the department was headed by Mike Hodge. It provided a range of courses preparing staff for specific types of work such as commercial or consular as well as courses of more general interest to the Service such as economics and TV training all of which seemed to do very well without any input from me.

And then there was management training, which interested me greatly. This consisted of short residential courses run by an admirable outside consultant called Gerry England. I made a point of taking one of these courses as soon as I could and many of the skills dealt with seemed immensely relevant to a diplomat's life whether at home or abroad.

How should one best organize one's time when under pressure? How does one delegate work to people who are unlikely to do it as well as one can oneself? How can one help people unburden themselves by becoming a good listener to their troubles? These two- or three-day courses were residential and usually took place in the agreeable surroundings of Wilton Park, the Foreign Office-sponsored conference centre. They were only available to staff when they were in London where pressures were great and there was an almost competitive culture of long hours and indispensability. Many people took the suggestion that they should go on a management course as an implied personal criticism, but those who did one were very appreciative.

One of the axioms about training that I took on board was the importance of having the support of those at the top. I was very lucky that another old friend from Beirut, Patrick Wright, took over as Permanent Under-Secretary when Antony Acland moved on. By then I had sorted out my ideas, and I persuaded Patrick to let me have half an hour of one of his daily meetings with all the top brass of the Office so I could give them a whizzy presentation of what Training Department could offer. It went very well. I got it agreed that all staff should do some management training at the appropriate stage of their career. I repeated the same presentation to the staff of my department a few days later, so they had a clear idea of where the Department was going.

Of the new initiatives we introduced there are two of which I am particularly proud. The first was a two-day course to be taken before becoming an Ambassador for the first time. After an introduction from the Chief Clerk this included sessions with a Minister, senior businessmen, etc to explore what they expected of an Embassy. But we also included sessions with the Diplomatic Service Wives Association and the FCO's Finance Department. An Ambassador can be hauled before the House of Commons if anything goes seriously wrong with his Embassy's accounts. It is useful to know something about the sorts of fraud to look out for. He (or she – or his wife if he had one) also had to account for the spending of his special allowances down to the soap used by visitors and the flowers bought to decorate the Residence. Having listened to the briefing on all this I asked the very helpful Deputy Head of Finance Department if he could not produce some handy check list to help with this chore. The result was a multipage questionnaire covering all the information that had to be provided. When I became an Ambassador myself I regularly blessed him.

The other innovation was called "A Day in Parliament", and Tristan Garel-Jones, then an FCO Minister of State, was instrumental in launching it. Members of the Diplomatic Service often reached mid-career without having any experience of dealing with Parliament, partly because the FCO has so little legislation, and partly because of long spells abroad. The course took place in the Houses of Parliament and consisted of sessions with a Minister, a leading Opposition MP, a member of the House of Lords, the Clerks from both Houses, etc. For this course there was no need to dragoon people. It was oversubscribed.

I mentioned Computer Training in my letter to my father. It did not loom as large as I had expected because of the failure of a big scheme to computerize the whole Office, putting consoles on each desk and connecting them with No 10 and other key Ministries. The security problems proved insoluble and the firm involved went bust. It was, however, clear that the computer age was here to stay and there was a widespread worry in the Office, especially among the older generation, that they would find it difficult to learn to type. I signed up for a course which promised one could learn the basics of touch typing in a couple of days and convinced myself that this was indeed possible. I regret to say I didn't keep this up and now use four fingers. I didn't possess a computer of my own for another ten years.

I was proud of my time in Training Department and thoroughly enjoyed doing such a practical job which played to my strengths. I got golden reports and to my surprise and slight dismay was awarded a special bonus of £1,000 under one of the Government's trendy individual initiative schemes of which I thoroughly disapproved. The scheme seemed to me to distort people's motivation for doing their best. Most surveys of motivation that I had seen suggested that, once people felt they had received a fair reward for their work, factors like pride and satisfaction in the job were more important than money. I also was and still am a believer in team work rather than too much individualism. But after thinking it over I decided to accept the money, keeping half of it for myself and using the rest of it to pay for a champagne party for the whole of the Department which had helped me win it.

Chapter 18

HER EXCELLENCY
Luxembourg (1988 – 1991)

I was sitting at my desk in Cromwell House having just returned from a spell of leave when the phone rang. It was the Head of Personnel Operations Department. "We have posted you during your absence," he said. "You are to be Ambassador to Luxembourg. It's gone through all the Boards and been approved by the Secretary of State... Oh, but it has still to go to No 10..." Then a pause. "Have you met Mrs Thatcher?" I said that I had but she was most unlikely to remember me. "Oh, that's all right then!"

This was immensely exciting news and it came as a complete surprise. When I first joined the Western Department all those years earlier Ambassadors seemed like a different species and of course they were all men. There was the tragic story of Barbara Salt who after a wartime career in SOE joined the Service on a temporary basis in 1946. She was appointed as Ambassador to Israel in the 1960s, only to fall gravely ill, lose both legs and never take up her post. It was not until 1976 that Anne Warburton became the first woman to become an Ambassador, in Copenhagen. By the late 80s there had still only been a handful of women Heads of Mission. I was beginning to hope that I might get there myself eventually but had no idea that moves were afoot.

Luxembourg was an ideal posting in many ways. It was not too far from England. My own parents were, alas, both dead but Alec's mother was still very much alive, though very old, and it was important to us both to keep in touch with her. I looked forward greatly to my first posting as a couple. Moreover, in Luxembourg I would be back at the heart of European politics, my primary interest. I had never been to the Grand Duchy but had vivid memories of Luxembourg colleagues stumping into the Brussels conference in the early 60s and shaking the snow off their boots. There was also *Call me Madam*, a famous film from my youth in which Ethel Merman was the US Ambassador to Luxembourg: "the Hostess with the Mostest", as the song put it. So it seemed vaguely romantic. By a lucky chance my predecessor, Oliver

Miles, was a friend and neighbour in Oxford and his very helpful briefings gave me a more up-to-date picture of what to expect.

There was a rather frustrating period when we were not allowed to tell anybody about my posting. At first it was a total ban; the appointment had to be put to No 10 and the Palace, but then they agreed and more people seemed to know but the Luxembourgers had still to be asked. Our control broke at Christmas when we told the family who were all there for the biggest family Christmas we had had yet. It was nearly a month later before all was settled and the announcement made. And then it all became a great rush to get through the briefing and the administrative chores and to get ourselves there by 24 February.

We drove down that day from Brussels to arrive in a Luxembourg dusted by snow. Tension mounted as we followed the route advised by Don Farr, the acting Chargé, who came and joined us for a cup of tea. Then a quick round of the office to shake everyone there by the hand.

The Luxembourgers had been most obliging in arranging an audience with the Grand Duke for me on 4 March – only a 10-day wait in that limbo of non fully-fledged Ambassadors which sometimes drags on for so long. By chance it was on the morning of the ceremony that Pickfords decided to deliver my heavy luggage. I had of course fussed about what to wear. Diplomatic uniform was still *de rigueur* for men on such occasions but there was no such uniform for women. But a long dress at 10 o'clock in the morning? I opted for a military style red silk jacket which I had bought at Jaegers with a long black skirt and a black silk sombrero with a sweeping brim. The whole effect was faintly military and it must have been a surprise to the men from Pickfords.

It was snowing as the Palace Rolls-Royce drove up the drive to collect Alec and myself. I don't know why, but the credentials ceremony was the one point at which I had a mild fit of nerves. For me it was one of the big occasions and I described it in my diary in some detail while the picture was still clear in my mind.

Easter Monday, Luxembourg, 4 April 1988

We had been briefed in advance... to be ready for the fleet of cars to come to collect us and take us to the Palace. Apart from Alec and me, there were the resident diplomatic staff here – Don Farr, Chris Poole and Alice Lewzey – and the supporting extras from Brussels – Defence Attaché, Commercial Counsellor, Cultural and Labour Attachés. So we were quite a party. A nice young aide de camp came to collect us and we drove in procession to the Palace – all of 500 yards as the crow flies. There we were greeted by the Marshal, the Chamberlain, a Lady in Waiting and various flunkies, all dressed in suitably splendid formal attire. After a brief wait in a waiting room (we must have got there too quickly!) we were summoned and conducted upstairs in a little procession with the Marshal and myself leading. It is an impressive stair leading up out of a wide, low, vaulted hall which must be in the oldest part of the building. Upstairs we were led into the State apartments, grandly furnished in French (18 cent?) style. Not that I was taking in the details of the décor. I was nervously clutching my two large envelopes with their crisp red seals (I had ditched protective outer envelopes in the car) and saying over to myself the few sentences I had prepared to say to the Grand Duke. No speeches, I was told, but it is usual for new Ambassadors to say a few words. So say a few words I did, in my high pitched voice, expressing a few high flown banalities about Anglo-Luxembourg relations. I became aware that the slight, pleasant man before me was smiling gently and holding out his hand as if to prompt me. So I hastily handed over the two envelopes which appeared to go on in the same movement to the Marshal, Roger Hastert. Did the Grand Duke ever read the letters, I wonder, with their splendid wording informing him that the Queen ("Your Royal Highness's Good Sister and Cousin Elizabeth R") had "need elsewhere for the services of My Trusty and Well-beloved Richard Oliver Miles, Esquire" and had selected "My Trusty and Well-beloved Juliet Jeanne d'Auvergne Campbell to proceed to the Court of Your Royal Highness" in his place?

Anyhow when the letters were safely handed over Alec was ushered in and we followed the Grand Duke into an adjoining room where the three of us sat down on some of those spikey French chairs and conversed. ("Talked" doesn't seem the right word!) The Grand Duke is rather a charmer and is reputed to have been shy. He is obviously very conscious of shyness in others. The result is a conversational style of questions leaving little time for reply. Just as well since the questions were of the "what does the future hold for Britain" variety, to which one can only reply by a banality or a quarter hour discussion. I remembered one or two things I had planned to raise – eg about the Irish Guards of which he is Colonel in Chief. He obviously takes great pleasure in this connection and as he referred to plans for St Patrick's Day his face lit up. He told us he would be there as host for the Queen Mother to distribute shamrock to the regiment. "We look on her as our Fairy Godmother," he said.

After a quarter hour or so our private audience was over. Silent signals must have passed but I did not see them. Without interrupting our conversation the doors opened smoothly and "the suite" was ushered in. I introduced them all to the Grand Duke and fortunately regained my savoir faire sufficiently to get all the names right. There was 5 minutes or so of general chat, hogged I am a bit sorry to say by the Defence Attaché – I had tried to give Don a push by identifying him as the senior member of my staff who lived in Luxembourg.

Then effortlessly it was made plain that it was all over... The Grand Duke shook our hands, we all bowed/curtseyed again, and he withdrew. We were all then escorted downstairs back to the waiting room where, to my amusement, we were shut in while the next new Ambassador arrived. There were in fact four of us that day - myself first, then Australia, São Tomé...

Even at the time I couldn't remember who the fourth one was! The return journey to the Residence took longer than the outward trip because of the one-way system. I was glad to get my money's worth of being driven in such state. I invited the ADC who escorted me to join us for a glass of champagne. There were also photos which caused him some confusion about whether to remove his sword. By this time I was relaxing and could easily have become flippant about this. The whole Embassy staff came in and joined us for the celebration. And then, still only noon or so, we all dispersed to put on ordinary clothes and go back to an ordinary day.

Once again the date of my arrival had been dictated by the visit of a Foreign Secretary, this time Sir Geoffrey Howe who was our first overnight visitor. He had been invited to deliver The Churchill Memorial Lecture which was one of the highlights of Luxembourg's political year, attended by Grand Duke, Prime Minister, Foreign Minister, etc. As I wrote to my mother-in-law "*It was my task to introduce proceedings, so I found myself on the platform facing the audience with two or three minutes to fill. Fortunately I didn't forget my lines – written with Alec's help and carefully memorized – and it passed off pretty well... Afterwards we hosted a "vin d'honneur" at home – a reception for 100 or so people. I was jolly glad when it was time to get to bed.*"

On the evening of Howe's arrival Don Farr, who had done all the work preparing for the visit, briefed us on the programme. Apart from the Lecture itself the social highlight of the visit was to be a luncheon at the historic Abbey of Echternach on the Moselle. When this event was mentioned Geoffrey Howe as an experienced politician immediately spotted that it was likely to be an occasion for speeches. Don checked and yes, the Foreign Minister Jacques Poos (name rhymes with close not loose) would be making a speech. We had hastily to put something together for a response. The subject of the moment was Yugoslavia and Alec came into his own when Howe began asking questions about the historical background to the civil war which had just broken out there. All went very well and when Howe made his speech he introduced me saying how nice it was to have a new Ambassador, especially when she came gift wrapped with a Professor of History! The visit was an excellent start from my point of view because it meant that I met most of the key Luxembourgers straight away. By happy chance Jacques Poos had been in Brussels for Britain's first negotiations with the EEC and vaguely remembered me.

In the normal course of such events I should have called on the Queen before I left London to "kiss hands" but she was away. It was therefore arranged that Alec and I should call on her – "be received" is the proper term – on a return visit to London a few months later. This time we were in more ordinary clothes and took a taxi to the Palace. However I cannot go into details of the half hour I spent with the Queen because, although I left the Diplomatic Service over 30 years ago, I am still bound to follow the rules: what is discussed in audiences with the Monarch must remain private. Suffice it to say that the Queen was charming, putting us at ease, and revealing herself to be an excellent mimic.

But it is time to get to my work. What of the Embassy in Luxembourg and why does Britain have one there anyhow? It was established immediately after WWII when Luxembourg was put back on the map having been swallowed up by Nazi Germany as part of what they called Gau Moselland. The Grand Duchy then became a founder member of the post-war international organisations such as NATO, WEU, OEEC and the UN. When the EEC was established it was a founder member of that too. Its vote in these fora could make a difference to whether Britain got what it wanted on all sorts of subjects. The UK was also interested in sectors of the Luxembourg economy such as telecommunications and banking. It might be only the size of a small English county with a population to match but Luxembourg had the highest per capita income of any country in the EEC.

The Embassy offices were conveniently next door to the Ambassador's Residence which occupied a prime position overlooking the deep valley of the Petrusse. I enjoyed taking unsuspecting visitors to the end of the garden and watching as they looked over the cliff to the stream hundreds of feet below. The house had been built in one of Vauban's bastions after Luxembourg's fortifications were dismantled in the 19th century. The Residence was a big establishment for the two of us but it came into its own in the three months of each year when EEC ministers held their meetings in Luxembourg. This rather absurd arrangement was the result of the Community's historic inability to decide on a permanent seat for its institutions. For me it meant that during April, June and October I was running a hotel for visiting UK ministers and their entourages.

The Residence staff could be difficult. There was a running dispute between Leonor, the feisty Portuguese maid, and Fernand the cook, who had been engaged by Oliver Miles shortly before my arrival. The history between them went back to Antony Acland's time as Ambassador when Fernand had been the Embassy chef for the first time. The story went that when Antony started to carve the chicken at some dinner party the bird was still frozen and the knife bounced off it. Fernand, though an excellent cook, had a fondness for the bottle. To start with all went very well, but there came a day when I had a dinner planned and Fernand failed to show up. Leonor and the others saved the day and produced a perfectly acceptable meal but they were furious. When a shamefaced Fernand turned up the next day something had to be done. Summoning my fiercest demeanour I gave him a letter of formal warning that if it ever happened again he would be out on his ear. Imagine my surprise when I was at my desk doing the Residence accounts a few weeks later and Fernand suddenly appeared and, saying "Look, Madame," he raised his shirt to reveal a small scar. He had had an implant to make him feel sick if he took any alcohol. It seemed to work because we had no further problems. Fernand decided that I had been his saviour and became a devoted fan. Later on he came to visit me in Oxford, staying a full and slightly taxing week, and cooked a fabulous dinner for 10 at which I acted as serving maid. As long as he lived he rang up each Christmas to check I was well.

I also had a bodyguard, hired from Securicor. The deal was that whenever I was doing anything that had been announced in advance, he came too. I felt rather embarrassed when paying my introductory calls on diplomatic colleagues accompanied by my bodyguard because nobody else seemed to have one. But, as I told myself, they hadn't got the IRA either. My official car, a Jaguar, was armour plated making it slow on the hills and cramped inside. Poor Geoffrey Howe, who was a plump man, looked very uncomfortable in it.

Britain's relations with Luxembourg were conditioned by what was happening in the European Community. Like Britain, Luxembourg was touchy about threats to its independence but unlike Britain it regarded the Community as its guarantee against being overwhelmed by its larger neighbours. The most recent big step in European integration had been the Single European Act which abolished non-tariff barriers to trade, thus establishing the Single Market, and reintroduced some majority voting to help get common standards agreed. The Commissioner responsible for steering this package through was Lord Cockfield, a protégé of Mrs Thatcher's, and she herself claimed much of the credit. Thus when the Grand Duke asked me if Britain was now fully committed to membership I felt able to assure him that our problems were behind us at last. How wrong I was!

But the serious troubles were still hidden in the future. Back then our work on Community issues followed the rhythm of the monthly meetings of the Council of Ministers. Before each meeting of Foreign Ministers (or sometimes other more specialized meetings) a telegram would come round all EC posts setting out the expected agenda and what the British delegation hoped to achieve. My role was to see the appropriate senior official or Minister, to drum up support and to report back the expected Luxembourg line. With this and similar reports from other Embassies our negotiating team would with any luck know in advance where they could expect support and where the difficulties lay. I paid visits to our missions in Brussels and Strasbourg to get myself up to speed and felt myself part of a well-oiled machine.

The wide diffusion of telegrams from all over the world kept me very well informed. Other instructions from London might be specific to Luxembourg or part of a wider exercise such as lobbying on issues coming up in the UN. For the rest of the time I could make up my own mind as to what I and the Embassy should be doing. We had a framework – a Mission Statement approved by London which I had a hand in drafting. It included obvious broad aims like supporting British trade and winning hearts and minds, as well as specific plans such as organizing visits and staging exhibitions of British goods in the Residence.

There was no lack of interesting subjects to get my teeth into. One of the first was satellites, a subject on which I had been briefed before leaving

London. The ideal spot for a communications satellite, I learned, was in geostationary orbit over the equator, and an international convention gave each member country their own spot. A Luxembourg company called SES (Société Européenne des Satellites) was planning to launch a communications satellite into this orbit as was the UK government-backed company BSB (British Satellite Broadcasting) and there was acute rivalry between the two. Once in Luxembourg I invited myself to visit SES at their base in Betzdorf and was given a friendly welcome there. I was struck by the field of giant dishes pointing towards different parts of the sky and also by the confidence of the Luxembourgers that they had made the right decision to go for the smaller, cheaper Astra satellite rather than the much more ambitious model being developed in the UK. The battle was decided when Rupert Murdoch's Sky Television bought out BSB, abandoned its satellite and backed SES instead. When Mrs Thatcher paid a flying visit to Luxembourg a few months later she was very interested in all this so I took her to visit SES which pleased them no end. Another episode in the Astra story came a year or two later when I was invited to a grand party in the presence of the Grand Duke to watch the first satellite being launched from its base in French Guyana. Listening to the count-down was a tense shared experience; the counting stopped and started again with the passage of distant clouds – only to come to a complete stop with seconds to go. The limited window in which a launch was possible that day was over. We all sadly went home. I was not invited back the next evening when the satellite finally went on its way. Google tells me that the first Astra, my satellite, is now in a "graveyard orbit" but its 16 successors now broadcast Sky TV to households across the world.

Another commercial story in which I dipped my toe concerned Luxair, the national airline, which was looking to buy a new short-haul plane. Britain had a horse in this race too but we lost out to the Dutch company Fokker. Looking back I can't think my involving myself in this made the slightest difference to anybody and I remember my French colleague telling me with slight disdain that French Ambassadors were not expected to cover commercial matters. But we very much were, and it added interest to the job.

Another quite different aspect of the work concerned the British community of which the Ambassador was ex officio head. There were about 3,000 Britishers living in Luxembourg, many of them working for the European Community institutions there – Court of Justice, Investment Bank, Court of Auditors and sections of the Commission and Parliament.

One of my first official calls was on the President of the European Court of Justice, Sir Jack Mackenzie Stuart. He had already dropped into the Embassy to say a friendly hullo. I was therefore not particularly apprehensive as I was driven in my armoured Jaguar across the ravine that cuts through Luxembourg City to the Court's elegant building on the Kirchberg Plateau. (The Court has grown hugely since then with the accession of so many new members to the EC and there is a new building wrapped around the one I knew and admired. The Kirchberg now boasts a dazzling display of modern architecture.) I was shown up to Jack's office for a friendly chat after which he announced he would introduce me to the other judges. So in we went to a large chamber with men sitting in big square chairs down each side and a couple of empty chairs across the top. It reminded me of nothing so much as the Great Hall of the People in Beijing but this time with me in the hot seat. Scrabbling back to my memories from the European Integration Department I asked about judge-made law and whether the Court in making its decisions deliberately extended Community competence. Whatever they said in reply it clearly has and does. Trying to hold my own with the judges was a formidable experience and I was immensely relieved when Jack told me afterwards that I had acquitted myself better than most new Ambassadors.

Shortly after my arrival I was invited to a lunch given by the British Chamber of Commerce. I was preparing to be bored or baffled when I heard that the speaker would talk about a recent EC Directive introducing UCITS (Undertakings for Collective Investment in Transferable Securities). But as he talked my ears pricked up because it became clear that Luxembourg was stealing a march on London and other financial centres in setting itself up as the easiest place to establish investment funds which could be sold throughout the EC. This was a turning point in the City of London's interest in Luxembourg about which it had hitherto been rather dismissive. During my time in the Grand Duchy I watched a succession of British investment funds being established there, and often gave a party in the Residence to mark their inauguration.

The Luxembourg financial centre concentrated on fields where light regulation and a reputation for honesty and efficiency could capture a niche market. The tax system was geared to support this strategy and banking secrecy was regarded as sacrosanct. The strategy was severely tested when a major scandal broke over the BCCI, a Luxembourg-registered bank that operated in many countries and was, it turned out, involved in massive money-laundering and other crimes. It was owned by a shady Pakistani and had its headquarters in London but the finger was pointed at Luxembourg for poor regulation. The Head of the Luxembourg Monetary Authority, a clever man called Pierre Jaans whom I used to see regularly, complained to me of the hypocrisy of the Bank of England which he argued should have kept themselves informed of what was happening on their doorstep. I had considerable sympathy but the scandal did call into question Luxembourg's ability to regulate on an international scale.

It was of course part of my job to get to know the members of the Luxembourg government, not difficult in such a small place where everybody knew everybody. Jacques Poos, the Foreign Minister, was my obvious first point of contact. I also frequently met the Prime Minister, Jacques Santer, an amiable and shrewd operator, but the rising star was Jean-Claude Juncker, then Minister of Finance, Labour and various other things. Because I followed financial and monetary issues I used to call on him from time to time and always found him stimulating. One winter day he was involved in a bad car crash driving back from Brussels. It was touch and go whether he survived but after a few months he returned to his office. I have always wondered if it left him with pain. Certainly he had a reputation for a short fuse. He went on to become Prime Minister and then President of the European Commission. In the light of how he was portrayed by the British press during the Brexit debate – almost as if he delighted in doing Britain down – I should record that I found him unfailingly helpful. When I moved on to Cambridge I invited him to lecture there. "I promised you I would come," he said, and he did.

Another person I liked to call on from time to time was the former Prime Minister, Pierre Werner, who was widely credited as the father of the financial centre and thus of Luxembourg's rise to prosperity. The Grand Duchy had been the poorest of the six member states when the EEC was formed but now had the highest income per capita of them all. Werner was a charming old man, rather stately, and always ready to talk about European affairs. My interest in him was piqued by his role in earlier discussions of Economic and Monetary Union which I had followed when I was in The Hague in the early 70s.

The single currency issue was again under active discussion in the Community, to the embarrassment of the UK government. As it became clear that some sort of agreement was likely to emerge, Britain came up with a new proposal – for a common currency which would circulate alongside existing national currencies rather than replacing them. The argument was that if it was useful it would increasingly be used and would grow in strength. It seemed a sensible proposal and Pierre Jaans thought it might well have been adopted had we put it forward sooner. But as so often our positive move came too late and was seen as a wrecking tactic.

One of Luxembourg's problems was that its population (about a third of a million when I was there) was just too small. There were large numbers of *frontaliers* – people who came in to work daily but lived across the borders in France, Belgium or Germany. Earlier in the 20th century many Italian immigrants came to man the steel mills in the south of the country but as Italy became more prosperous fewer Italians wanted to come. Luxembourg then turned to Portugal as a source of good Catholic immigrants but as time went on there were increasingly vocal fears that Luxembourgers might become a minority in some areas of their own country. One village was in the news as a place where the Portuguese were already in the majority. Alec and I decided to investigate, calling on the mayor as I had done in other places. It was a sticky visit but conversation warmed as it became clear we were not out to criticize. I remember the mayor telling us that he had nightmares of becoming an exhibit at the entrance to the village with a notice hung round his neck reading "The last of the Mohicans." As he said this he flung out his arms as if pinned to a cross.

It was fun getting to know this tiny country and calling on mayors was one way of doing it. We also explored at weekends. Some kind person gave us an excellent book of *auto-pédestres* covering the whole country. There are some lovely walks in the mountainous north, and one Sunday we found ourselves having lunch at a small hotel in Clairvaux which had on the wall a framed letter from Ethel Merman. We particularly enjoyed walking in the vineyards along the Moselle. It was there one All Saints Day that we rounded a corner to find ourselves faced by a group of people in a small cemetery honouring their dead, including the Prime Minister. Everybody was a bit startled but nothing was ever said. Sometimes we went further afield into Germany or France. Theoretically an Ambassador is supposed to send a telegram to the Foreign Office if they leave the country to which they are accredited, formally handing over responsibility to a deputy. But this seemed nonsense with borders half an hour away, so I simply made sure that the Embassy duty officer knew where I was spending the night.

The Grand Duke's birthday fell on 23 June and was a national holiday. As I told my mother-in-law "*It had touches of Luxembourg at its most Ruritanian – the whole army/police and gendarmerie paraded in the main square – flags flew everywhere and brass bands played – Luxembourg town staged a firework display of which we had a splendid view from our garden on the ramparts – and a 101 cannon salute seemed to last most of the morning... Alec and I and the rest of the dip corps were involved in a good deal of the festivities. Most impressive was the Te Deum held in the Cathedral...”*

The day ended with an evening reception given at the Palace by the Grand Duke himself. This event was enlivened by the presence of our diplomat colleagues from Brussels, many of them in national dress. And a very colourful bunch they were too – Japanese in kimono, a Korean lady in spectacular peacock silk gliding across the floor like a doll, the Indonesian in batik, the Fijian Ambassador (grandson of Queen Salote) in skirt and sandals. The most comfortable person there must have been the Sudanese whose long galabia dress ended in a pair of leopard skin sandals – just the thing for standing around. Alec, forced to wear white tie with its stiff shirt, was very jealous of Jack Mackenzie Stuart who had declared, with the Grand Duke’s full approval, that his national dress was a kilt with velvet jacket – and a soft shirt.

There was a very different occasion on 30 September 1988 when Mrs Thatcher came for a flying visit, fitting Luxembourg in between her famous Bruges speech one evening and Madrid the following day. She was accompanied by her husband, a string of officials and 18 British journalists, including TV. Such visits are planned to the minute and an advance team from No 10 came to look into the detailed arrangements including security, press, etc. Once again there was to be a grand lunch in Echternach, and I discovered to my horror that I was the one who would sit with her in the car for the half-hour it took to get there. Having watched her lay into more senior diplomats than me I was distinctly nervous, but I needn’t have worried. As we got into the car she said, “Do you think I should be wearing a hat?”

“No, Mrs Thatcher,“ I replied. “I am not wearing one myself.”

Pause.

“Are you sure I should not be wearing a hat?”

I calmed her down as best I could and soon became aware of silence. She had gone to sleep! I had a peaceful drive through the countryside looking at the men with guns on the rooftops as we passed. The IRA was still active and the Luxembourgers were taking no chances. This time neither Alec nor I had any hand in the speech which was a reprise of the one she had given that morning in Bruges arguing against a federal Europe.

At the time I thought it was a good and even positive speech setting out an alternative path for Europe, but it proved to be a milestone on her lurch towards Euroscepticism.

Apart from the lunch and the visit to SES mentioned above, I arranged for her to meet the leading lights of the financial centre. She clearly enjoyed lecturing them about what she saw as excessive lending. "But what do you expect us to do?" one of them cried. "We are bankers!" I am glad to say even she laughed. Meanwhile Alec accompanied Dennis Thatcher on a programme of his own. Afterwards I told my mother-in-law "*I find myself quite weak with anti-climax and sheer relief that our big visit passed off so well... The Luxembourgers were determined that the visit should be a success notwithstanding* [the Bruges speech] *and in practice want many of the same things in the Community – in the financial and tax fields as well as re broadcasting. So they were not out to pick a quarrel and she was all honey...*"

***

After a couple of years the Foreign Office began to suggest that it might be time for me to move on. Luxembourg was often regarded as a short posting on the way to other things. I was not keen to move. It was a very happy posting for us and accessible for friends and family. Alec did a bit of teaching and lecturing locally and could go back to Oxford when he wanted to. My slight misgiving about becoming an Ambassador had been that it might prove difficult to make real friends from such a lonely eminence, but having Alec to discuss everything with made it all more interesting. He was a great asset when entertaining too. I asked the Office to let me stay, arguing that with Luxembourg due to take over the Presidency of the EEC Council of Ministers the following year it would be good to make the most of my contacts. This was agreed and I found that the two-year mark made a difference to our Luxembourg friends who began to invite us to parties in their homes rather than always entertaining in restaurants.

Meanwhile we had a constant stream of visitors, official as well as family and friends. Both Alec's children came to stay and my eldest grandson, Graham, took his first steps in the Residence. Alas, Alec's mother died in October 1988. Once again there was the heartache of not being there when the moment came.

In July 1989 Geoffrey Howe was replaced as Foreign Secretary by John Major, a man I liked from the start. At our one and only pre-Council dinner party for him he was totally unruffled as officials told him how incredibly difficult it was going to be to achieve the desired agreement on some complicated subject of the moment. The following day he seemed effortlessly to get what he wanted in the Council with good will on all sides. But these were the last throes of the Thatcher Government. SES had kindly provided the Embassy with satellite TV and I remember watching in fascination as that amiable man Geoffrey Howe, goaded beyond endurance, attacked the Prime Minister in one of the most memorable speeches the House of Commons has ever heard. It became clear that Thatcher's support was ebbing away, and I watched again as Thatcher stood on the familiar steps of the British Embassy in Paris, taking in the results of the leadership challenge that followed. In no time she was gone, and to general surprise it was John Major who emerged as the new Prime Minister.

The new Foreign Secretary was Douglas Hurd, whom I had known a little when he was a budding diplomat. When he returned to the Foreign Office in 1979 as Minister of State the Permanent Under-Secretary sent a circular round the Service advising us not to treat him as an old chum! Hurd was a slightly aloof character, often too deep in thought for small talk, but I always liked him and I suggested that he might bring his new wife Judy to Luxembourg some time. One day she came and, rather than going to the British delegation offices to pick up the political gossip as I normally did during Council meetings, I took the day off to show her around. We had great fun walking round the old town, in and out of the sun-lit battlements and visiting the splendid Bentinck-Thyssen picture collection that was then in the national museum. She was good company and I was sorry that I never met her again.

It must have been just before Thatcher fell that I received an invitation from the local British Conservative Association to a dinner in honour of a junior British Minister. I reluctantly decided that I ought to go, and remember arguing about the merits of the Poll Tax, which I thought a disastrous idea and the Minister valiantly defended. (The Poll Tax was second only to Europe as the issue which brought Thatcher down.) A photo of the event appeared in some magazine in Strasbourg and was spotted by Glenys Kinnock who, apart from being the wife of the leader of the Opposition, was a Member of the European Parliament. As a result I received a letter of reprimand from Douglas Hurd saying that Ambassadors should not go to political meetings. I protested of course, saying I only went out of a sense of duty, however misplaced. But I got brownie points when a young man trying to get in touch with his MEP turned up in Luxembourg by mistake.

He had a tent and the weather was fine so I invited him to camp in the Embassy garden and this somehow got into the British press.

There were no resident British correspondents in Luxembourg but whenever there were important meetings the Brussels correspondents would turn up *en masse*. Douglas Hurd liked to brief them over breakfast at the Residence. My one and only brush with Boris Johnson, then a junior correspondent for the *Telegraph*, was when he shambled in to one of these breakfast meetings half an hour late to the ribald laughter of his colleagues. Another time Douglas Hurd wanted to have a private meeting with the President of the European Commission, Jacques Delors, and I laid on a small dinner party. I greatly admired Delors who was putting forward ideas on Europe that made a lot of sense to me – that a core should move towards closer union with looser relationships for those who couldn't or wouldn't join in. For Britain of course the problem was that we wanted to have it both ways: maximum say in Community policy without being sucked into moves towards further union.

Meanwhile great things were happening in Eastern Europe. We watched our TV astonished as the Wall fell in Berlin and one by one the former satellites threw off Soviet domination. Being in the centre of Europe it all felt very close, and one day Alec and I decided to get in the car and drive east to see for ourselves. I felt a slight shiver as we drove through what had been the border between East and West and saw the threatening guard towers that had until so recently kept people apart. We drove to Weimar for a couple of nights at a hotel of faded grandeur called The Elephant. It all seemed very peaceful as we visited Goethe's house and bought a lovely blue jug in a pottery fair beside the Cathedral – but there were still Soviet troops goose-stepping across the main square. Then on to the walled city of Bautzen in the extreme east of Germany where we turned south into Czechoslovakia. Here we stopped for petrol to find a huge queue of agitated people trying to fill up. With the help of my radio we learned that a coup was underway in Moscow and we followed developments avidly as we made our way to Prague.

There we had accommodation arranged in a university hostel in the suburbs but that left the problem of getting something to eat. Restaurants were few and we quickly discovered it was essential to book whatever was offered which usually meant dinner at 5pm. I was determined to go to a restaurant called the Three Ostriches which had been recommended by a knowledgeable friend. It was in a prime position beside the great river and when the day came for our meal we went with high expectations. We were quickly given a table but then all the waiters disappeared for a good hour. Eventually we realized they were all huddled round a radio. When a waiter at last arrived he explained that they were listening to the news from Russia where hardliners critical of President Gorbachev's reforms had imprisoned him in his holiday estate. The hero of the hour was Yeltsin who faced down the rebels sitting on a tank. As the waiter smilingly served our delicious dinner we joined in deep relief at the outcome.

In the EEC itself pressures were increasing for another major move towards further integration. Despite British delaying tactics a constitutional conference was called to amend the Treaty of Rome, the Community's founding document. This fell during the Luxembourg Presidency of the Council of Ministers in the first half of 1992 which promised to be a very busy period for our Embassy. I made a case to the FCO for reinforcements and they sent a very bright young man called Julian King. Having the Presidency meant chairing a multitude of committees on all sorts of subjects and Luxembourg harnessed all its talent regardless of age. Some very young and inexperienced people rose to a challenge that would never have been given to a British diplomat of the same age. Julian did a great job of cultivating them. Much later he became our Ambassador in Paris, only to be sent abruptly to Brussels after the Brexit referendum as Britain's last European Commissioner. Poor man. It must have been a most uncomfortable job after the plum of Paris.

The negotiations for what turned into the Treaty of Maastricht were intensely complicated and we needed to follow them in detail. At one point a conference was called in London of all British Ambassadors in EC countries and I found myself being asked to start discussion of each item with a description of the Presidency's intentions. The Luxembourgers very much hoped to complete negotiation of the new Treaty on their watch but as the summer wore on – and my own time in Luxembourg drew to a close – it was clear that they would have to hand over to the Dutch whose Presidency came next. Jumping the gun, the Dutch who were fervent integrationists tabled a draft treaty which went much further than anything proposed so far. To Britain's intense relief the Luxembourgers saw this off. It was their own draft with its separate "pillars" – making a clear distinction between fields in which Community law applied and those on which there would be intergovernmental cooperation – that became the basis of the Treaty of Maastricht. The wily John Major negotiated opt-outs for the UK from two of the Treaty's main provisions – the common currency and the agreement on social policy – and he received much praise, only for it all to go wrong in the Commons during the debate on ratification which took place after Denmark had rejected the Treaty in a referendum and France passed it by the narrowest of margins. He faced down the right-wing rebels in his own party (whom he famously referred to as "the bastards") by tying ratification to the survival of the government in a vote of confidence, but by that time I had left Luxembourg, and the Diplomatic Service.

After the Luxembourg Presidency was over Julian organised a splendid boat trip on the Moselle for all the Luxembourgers who had been so helpful to us as well as for the Embassy staff. It was a beautiful sunny day as we sipped pinot gris, one of Luxembourg's nicest wines. The vineyards in which Alec and I liked to walk looked particularly enticing.

I had begun to wonder what the Foreign Office planned to do with me next, so on one of my trips to London I dropped into Personnel Department. I was assured that there would be another job but it became clear that they hadn't given much thought to what it would be. We went through the "grid" together, looking at what posts of my seniority might become vacant on my timescale. Malaysia was mentioned as well as New Zealand. As I discussed this with Alec he made it clear that he would not want to accompany me to such far-away places; his own interests lay in America and Europe.

About this time I was surprised to receive a letter from Girton College, Cambridge. They were looking for a new Mistress (as the Head of the College is called) and someone had mentioned my name. Would I like to visit the College to discuss the possibility, without commitment on either side? One thing led to another and I was invited to spend a couple of days meeting the Fellows in whose hands the final choice lay – always without commitment. It was an interesting visit and I learned a great deal about the College and the very different things people hoped the new Mistress would be able to bring. An interview with the whole Fellowship of some 40 people might have been a bit intimidating but I had little time to think about it and was on something of a high from all that was going on in Luxembourg. Anyhow I was not sure that I really wanted to leave the Diplomatic Service. All this helped me to be on top form and I rather enjoyed the experience. I remember telling them that different types of leadership were needed in different circumstances; I was good at leading a happy community but knocking heads together was not my forte.

Back in Luxembourg a couple of weeks later the phone rang while we were at breakfast. It was the Vice Mistress to say that, if I would accept their offer, the College would elect me as Mistress. Would I please think it over during the weekend and give them my answer? I was highly amused by this way round of putting it which Alec, as a long-time academic, found perfectly normal. It was the moment of decision. Girton offered a solution to the problem of how Alec and I should organize our lives. Cambridge would be an exciting new world for me and one in which he was at home. To become a Head of College was a job to which members of the Diplomatic Service aspired on retirement. I felt very flattered. So I said yes. I have often wondered where my final posting in the Diplomatic Service would have taken me and what life there would have been like. Probably not as good as Luxembourg where Alec and I had so many happy times together.

But it was time to leave. I hastily drafted a farewell despatch to London and prepared for the movers. My old friend Jacques Poos gave a big farewell lunch party for me, inviting all the local diplomatic corps as well as the senior Brits from the European Court and other resident institutions. It was a lovely day and we sat at round tables in the sun outside one of Luxembourg's many castles. There were of course speeches. He referred to his first meeting with Miss Collings in Brussels all those years before, while I mused on becoming an ex-Excellency. I had the brilliant idea of presenting Poos with the original of a cartoon from the Times about the draft Treaty episode, showing Luxembourg as a brave galleon sailing on while a ship labelled Holland foundered on the rocks. Back in London there were farewell calls to be made, including one on the Foreign Secretary Douglas Hurd who had sent me a particularly nice telegram as I signed off from Luxembourg. (He said "You leave the Diplomatic Service on a high point. The Luxembourg Embassy under your command has been described as the jewel in the crown: a model of efficiency and good management…"!) It felt strange to say farewell to the imposing Whitehall building in which I had spent so much of my working life, and I left it with some sadness.

Chapter 19

MISTRESS OF GIRTON
Cambridge (1992–1998)

My first impression of Girton, on that rainy day when I went for the interviews there, was of overpowering red brick. I wondered if I could ever be comfortable working in those straggling buildings, let alone become as fond of them as I later did. Alfred Waterhouse's original conception of a college suitable for women abandoned the traditional pattern of staircases opening into courtyards in favour of long corridors with rooms on one side and windows on the other. To keep the price down he used basic brick and tiles. Over a century and a half his successors have added long extra wings in much the same idiom. For my first weeks I didn't dare stray from my office without clutching a map.

Girton was the first of the Oxbridge colleges for women, founded in 1869 by Emily Davies with five students. Indeed it can claim to be Britain's first residential institution dedicated to the higher education of women. A doughty clergyman's daughter, Emily believed in the importance of education as a step towards women getting the vote and founded her college on a shoestring. A century on, Girton was a well-established institution with a high academic reputation, but by then some of Cambridge's most prestigious men's colleges had begun to take women students too, often skimming off the most adventurous ones. This faced the women's colleges with a dilemma: should they stick to their feminist principles or should they take men? For Girton the problem was made more acute by its situation on the outskirts of the city. The decision to go mixed in stages was taken well before my time. The first men Fellows arrived in 1977 and male graduate students the following year so that by the time the first men undergraduates arrived in 1979 there were already a good many male faces around. The College I inherited aspired to be a model mixed community with a roughly even balance of the sexes at all levels and it was very comfortable in its new persona.

The question immediately arose of where I should live. The earliest Mistresses lived in what is now the Mistress's office, a charming Victorian room with a hidden balcony looking out over great cedar trees. A more spacious flat for the Mistress was built in the 1960s but my predecessor Mary Warnock hated living there. She said it had three problems: it got baking hot, the picture windows meant one was on view to passers-by in College, and the only access was through undergraduate accommodation. Mary did me a great favour by drawing attention to these issues and it was agreed that work should be done to remedy them. Our architect Fellow Peter Sparks designed a circular staircase leading down to a private entrance. At my suggestion he also designed doors for the Fellows' Rooms immediately below the flat to connect them to Eliza Baker Court; spilling out into this charming little court has given much pleasure to me and many others on countless summer occasions since. All this work meant that for my first year I lived out of College. It was a relief when we could move into the renovated flat where I could entertain guests less formally than at High Table. I got home to Oxford for weekends when I could. Alec came and went; by now he was fully retired from Birmingham but still doing some teaching in Oxford.

If I initially found the buildings daunting the Fellows were most welcoming. As Alec pointed out they had a vested interest in my success. "To start with," he said, "you can do anything you want because you are not your predecessor; then you won't be able to do anything because you are you; and after that it won't matter anyway!" With this encouraging advice I set out to discover what my role should be. When I had asked for a job description during the interviews I got the answer that it wasn't quite like that: they wanted to see what I could bring to the College. Later I was told that there was no job description because the Fellows couldn't agree what they wanted the Mistress to do! The interview process had however given me a good picture of the College community,

When I took up the job one of the first things I had to get used to was being addressed as Mistress. Needless to say my brothers made bad jokes about the title. I quickly found that the Mistress had considerable influence but virtually no formal power, apart from the right to chair all meetings. This was very different from the Foreign Office (or indeed most other walks of life) where if people differ at one level the decision is referred up a chain of authority. In a College every Fellow has the equal right to stick to his or her opinion, and usually does. Heading a College depends on persuasion, a bit like it must have been to run a Greek city state. While not in itself a full-time job I needed to be pretty well constantly available. I am sure that exasperation with this way of doing things was one reason why some admirably qualified Heads of College from outside academia fell out with their Fellows in both Oxford and Cambridge. In Girton the main decisions were taken by the College Council, a largely elected body of some 16 members with student representatives coming in for certain subjects. I was immediately struck by how ill-prepared and often inconsistent its decisions were. When I mentioned this to one of our more worldly Fellows, he said that in Girton the long run was three months! I soon realized that if decisions were to be coherent I would have to do a lot of the preparation myself and that it was essential to re-establish a system of committees to predigest important issues.

I should perhaps explain that if the College felt a bit run down in various ways it was mostly because my two predecessors were for different reasons semi-absentee Mistresses. Brenda Ryman, a distinguished medic, was taken fatally ill before she got to grips with the job, while the distinguished philosopher Mary Warnock was (as she made clear in her own memoir) much happier in Oxford where her husband Geoffrey was Principal of Hertford and for some time Vice-Chancellor. Apart from dealing with the admin I set about trying to reinvigorate the College's social life. At the first suitable opportunity I invited Lord Wolfson to a College Guest Night, with the intention of persuading him to support the ongoing extension of Wolfson Court, Girton's downtown site, which had been originally endowed by his father. Another guest that night was the former Lord Chancellor, Lord Mackay, whom I had met in Luxembourg and discovered was an Honorary Fellow. I asked the Steward to ensure that both had suitable rooms in which to change and was a bit startled when Lord Wolfson came steaming into dinner saying our bathrooms were a disgrace and he expected an application for funds to modernize them to be on his desk the following week. He gave us £200,000, the first of a number of generous donations and the start of a long programme of upgrading Girton's dilapidated student accommodation. Other notable guests included the Queen Mother, who was the College Visitor and came twice during my time, arriving by helicopter, and talking at length to students. Queen Margrethe of Denmark was another. She had spent a year studying archæology at Girton as a young woman and the College, to my mind belatedly, made her an Honorary Fellow. She was excellent company, chatting late into the night.

Fundraising was an activity which took more and more of my time and energy as it became clear that the College's finances were precarious. I had been told during the interviews that there was no particular problem, but in fact costs were rising faster than the income from students and its meagre endowment. This is the moment to introduce the Bursar who is in many ways a more important figure in College life than the Head. When I arrived Girton had quite recently appointed its first male Bursar, Charles Larkum, a nice and clever man who had been a banker in the City. We both quickly realized that Girton urgently needed a new computer-based budgetary system. The pattern hitherto had been to roll over the accounts each year deciding what could be afforded and what had to be cut. Neither Charles nor I had any experience in setting up budgetary systems and it was not until Charles' successor Debbie Lowther was appointed that we acquired an off-the-shelf system which also provided a database for alumni.

Through no fault of his own Charles became unpopular with some sections of the Fellowship – his influential predecessor was strongly against the appointment of a man – and his life became very difficult. This was one of the most painful periods of my time at Girton and I still worry that I did not support him adequately as I struggled to keep things together. Fortunately Charles himself decided to leave Girton to become Bursar of one of the traditional men's Colleges where he was a better fit. He later played an important role in the University, chairing the Committee of College Bursars. The appointment of Debbie Lowther as his successor was a great day for Girton. I still remember the feeling of surprised excitement when the Selection Committee decided to appoint this young woman with her flowing red hair and glowing references. She did the College proud over many years.

I had no experience of fund-raising and started with rather haphazard begging letters. One of my first successes was £50,000 from the popular author Catherine Cookson whose books were often about women who like herself were born to lives of extreme poverty. By then old and bedridden she warmed to the story of Girton's pioneering role in providing opportunities for women. To my great regret I never met her but I much enjoyed corresponding with her devoted husband Tom. Another benefactor I remember with affection is Dr Lawrence Pilkington of the glass family. His sister, who taught music while Mary Warnock was head of the Oxford High School, had given the College a Fellowship in Music, and Dr Lawrence followed this up by the gift of a grand piano. I will never forget sitting in the Stanley Library as Martin Ennis, the Pilkington Fellow and a very fine musician, played three pianos in turn – rather like interviewing undergraduates, said Alec.

Like other Colleges we set up a Development Office but this took a while to get going. Alumni records were haphazard and asking for money was counter-cultural; many Fellows felt uncomfortable in handing over contact details of their former students and it was only after Debbie's arrival that we got a centralised computer base. Everyone whose advice I sought on academic fund-raising said it was essential to start with the support of one's own former students, and I felt as if I were thrashing around in the dark of ignorance.

About halfway through my time at Girton we organised a splendid black-tie evening at the Tower of London – dinner and the Crown Jewels followed by the atmospheric Ceremony of the Keys as the Tower was locked for the night. We charged an eye-watering sum per ticket and the occasion was a great success. It had the valuable by-product of identifying supportive alumnae with money. Some became personal friends, most notably Shirley Littler, who with her husband Geoffrey offered their London house as a base for my fund-raising activities. Their generosity is reflected in the reading room in the new archive building, of which more anon. It was at a very different occasion organised by the Oxford Region Girtonians that I first met Barbara and John Wrigley. Barbara had set her heart on endowing a prize for poetry about love. Apparently this had been offered to John's Oxford College who had replied that money for buildings would be more useful. Girton accepted the prize gratefully and the wonderfully generous Wrigleys followed up by endowing the Fellowship in Classics as well as launching the Emily Davies bursaries for students of limited means. These are all people whom I came to value very much and would never have met if I hadn't been obliged to fund-raise. But I hated the way in which the need to raise money made me assess everyone I met in terms of their wealth

So far I have hardly mentioned the students. When I became Mistress, Girton was one of the biggest colleges in Cambridge with around 400 undergraduates and some 150 graduate students. I made a point of meeting each new student briefly in their first week or so and gave regular student parties. It was, however, too big a community to hope to know them all personally and in practice I mostly came across the very good – such as members of the choir and representatives of the Junior Common Room – and the very bad, who had to appear before Council for disciplinary reasons. But teaching was central to the College's being. I never taught and did not feel qualified to do so but I kept a beady eye on exam results and arranged post-mortems in subjects where they were poor. In the days of single sex colleges Girton had been one of the top performers in Cambridge but we now bounced along the bottom of the league table. To what extent was the problem admissions, or teaching? Direct applications had fallen dramatically and a high percentage of our students now came via "the pool," the system whereby over-subscribed colleges passed on good students they couldn't take. I suspected some tutors of social engineering, ie choosing students they wanted to give a chance to rather than those with the best academic record. Perhaps they were right to do so, but I saw my duty as being to push up the quality of our intake. To put things in perspective, the differences in results between colleges were not huge and I never doubted that our students were receiving a very good education. Furthermore in some subjects Girton was very strong, notably English, and it was interesting to look at teaching methods to see if there were lessons that could be replicated. But I can't claim success in pushing up results overall and wonder if I should have made a virtue of necessity by building up Girton's reputation as being culturally inclusive. Compared to most colleges it certainly was. I wonder too if this was an area in which my lack of academic background was a hindrance.

Rather to my surprise I found no such problem chairing the committees to select our Research Fellows of whom two or three were chosen each year, funded by special endowments. These Fellowships provide the ideal foundation for an academic career and are hotly competed for. Girton in its turn was competing with other colleges for the brightest and best. The interviews were a joy as the young scholars explained their work and why it mattered to them and to society more widely. It was, however, difficult to compare candidates from different fields and some Fellows fought hard for personal protégées. On Alec's advice I introduced a system whereby each member of the committee cast two votes. That way the combined verdict of the academics came through and I was delighted to discover that my opinion usually mirrored theirs, even in the sciences where I lacked the most basic of educations. The clarity of thought which defines the very best minds came shining through.

Once Debbie had introduced a modern budgetary system, which was several years into my tenure, it became possible to plan in a more purposeful way and to prioritise expenditure. I tried my hand at a SWOT analysis (strengths, weaknesses, opportunities and threats) for discussion by the College Council. It wasn't a memorable document but it was a first step towards a long-term plan and it produced the germ of an important idea. Why not use one of Girton's strengths, the remarkable 19th century archive on women's history, to help tackle one of its weaknesses, the need to modernise and computerise the Library? The Librarian, Frances Gandy, was understandably enthusiastic and when we decided to put in an application to the National Lottery, it was her energy that produced a detailed and beautifully illustrated document to support our case. The application failed, which was a huge disappointment. The project had already attracted a number of substantial donations from alumni and others but when I left Girton in 1998 its fate was very much in the balance. I am glad to say my successor Marilyn Strathern gave it her backing and the turning point came when Alison Duke put serious money into it. Alison was an elderly Fellow and former Senior Tutor whose life revolved round Girton. We all knew that she would leave her money to the College one day. I must admit that, despite some qualms, I put pressure on her to give immediately, while she was still alive and could have the enjoyment of it. I left with her a copy of the Lottery document and it may well have been that which decided her in the end. Anyhow I am delighted to say that she survived to see the new Archive Building which bears her name and it gave her very great pleasure.

As mentioned above, the strictly college business of a head of house is not normally a full-time job. Soon after my arrival I was sounded out about taking on University roles which I was very ready to accept. Unlike Oxford, many heads of Cambridge colleges also head a busy academic department so those with spare time are in great demand for other jobs. I quickly found myself on the University's Council of the Senate and was later elected to the Council which succeeded it. (This was the only time I ever stood for public election and I can't help bragging that I got more votes than any other candidate!) This involved me in other key committees as well as chairing various appointments committees.

Another task was to stand in for the vice-Chancellor at degree ceremonies. This meant being led in a procession into the Senate House and conducted to a sort of cupboard behind the throne where my black MA's gown was replaced by a scarlet one trimmed with fur. Then I was conducted to the throne itself where I sat intoning, "*Admitto te ad gradum…*" over the graduands one by one as I clasped their hands between mine. Some were quivering with nerves while one cheeky young blade gave me a broad wink. I still remember a moment of slight panic when I spotted a stretcher coming up the aisle towards me; as I hopped off my throne to utter the magic words conveying his degree I imagined how much they must mean to the unknown invalid. Geoffrey Skelsey, the University's master of ceremonies, was always beside me feeding me the right lines but even so it was difficult to concentrate on some of the Latin tongue-twisters and on one occasion I heard myself giving someone a PhD in the wrong subject. Geoffrey gave me a stern look but the recipient seemed blissfully happy.

It was a struggle to understand the arcane ways in which the University and its participant colleges interacted. Basically it was and is a federal structure with each college responsible for selecting and tutoring its own students while exams, labs and lectures etc are provided centrally. The colleges are separate financial entities and apt to be jealous of their independence. Think EU and relations between Brussels and the member states (though fortunately there are no signs of Brexit). Old hands whom I consulted about the financial relationship usually said it was a mystery to them too and I began to suspect that it suited some senior administrators for it to remain that way. It was not to the University's advantage to look too rich, particularly in its relations with Government on which it relied heavily for research funding as well as student support; opaque accounts put off casual enquiry.

I realized after a bit that the less well-endowed colleges, such as Girton, were bearing a disproportionate share of the cost of teaching in certain subjects. The best and cheapest way for a college to ensure it had top class teaching was to get it done by University teaching officers, so whenever a new University appointment was made there would be a beauty contest between colleges looking for extra teaching in that field. I remember one young geographer telling me she had been offered Fellowships by five different colleges within her first couple of weeks. Understandably enough she chose one of the rich colleges that could offer help with a mortgage among other benefits, which Girton could not. This scenario was repeated many times and, as there were not enough University teachers to fill the requirements of the whole system, it was the poorer colleges that ended up filling much of the gap by making appointments at their own expense. These "College Fellows" made a great contribution to the whole system, as well as being valued members of their own colleges and often very distinguished, but they did not enjoy the status of "University Teaching Officers." The Vice-Chancellor asked me and Patrick Bateson, the Provost of King's, to prepare a paper on the subject which was circulated throughout the University asking for comments. These were numerous and revealed widespread unhappiness about the inequalities of the system. A year or two later the ever-generous Trinity College (the richest by far) launched a scheme of Newton Trust Fellowships to recompense College Fellows who did a lot of University teaching. I like to think that by stirring the pot I made a small contribution to this outcome but I have no evidence of this.

One of the trickiest issues to come up during my time at Cambridge was the College fee. When the government decided back in the early 60s to democratise higher education they took over the responsibility for paying for students so higher education was effectively free. In the case of Oxford and Cambridge the government also paid the fee to the student's college on top of the one to the University. I first became aware of how much this enraged other less privileged universities when I was got at on the subject by the vice-Chancellor of Bristol during an otherwise wholly enjoyable and undemanding visit to Prague as the appointed representative of Cambridge at an international conference of University heads. (Some people have all the luck!) By my time at Girton the proportion of young people going into higher education had increased massively and the government had capped numbers as well as university fees. The College fee was an obvious target in the drive for further economies. A small group of Oxbridge bursars negotiated on behalf of both universities and the colleges. They achieved a remarkably satisfactory deal which took account of the costs to the two ancient universities of maintaining so many old buildings which were part of the national heritage. I was not involved and can claim no credit. I mention it partly because it was a rare example of cooperation between Oxford and Cambridge and partly because the outcome profoundly altered the relationship between each university and its colleges. All government money was henceforth channelled through the university itself.

I was very lucky to have the opportunities I did to learn about the problems of higher education, about which I knew very little when I arrived in Cambridge, and I enjoyed my involvement in the University very much. But I wish on first arrival I had made more of my EU expertise. To make the most of Cambridge one needs an academic as well as a College identity. As it was, to my surprise I found myself missing the challenge of some of the things I had had to deal with previously. Diplomats have to be able quickly to absorb a complicated brief well enough to defend a given line. Examples in the Luxembourg context were finance and satellites. My Cambridge diet was admin heavy and I was appalled by the University's bureaucracy. Every other weekend during my years on the Council a huge pile of papers would arrive by special messenger to be digested by Monday morning. Rather than a précis of the arguments concerning the points to be decided, they would contain all the minutes of all the committees that had already discussed each issue. How I longed for those Foreign Office submissions concisely outlining the pros and cons with a clear recommendation. The Council meetings themselves sometimes took place in a medieval hall in the Old Schools. They were long mornings but whenever my attention wandered I could look up at the carved statues of bishops and other worthies who held up the roof – very different from the semi-clad beauties on the ceiling in the Embassy in Paris.

Out of the blue the vice-Chancellor asked me one day if I would like to represent Cambridge on a British Council expedition to sell British higher education to Indonesia. I jumped at the chance to revisit my old haunts but was taken aback when I discovered that what the Indonesians really wanted to know from Cambridge was how to establish a successful Science Park. The Cambridge Science Park, a model of its kind and the first in the UK, had been established by Trinity College around 1970 but that was all I knew about it. John Bradfield, the legendary Bursar who had transformed Trinity's finances and played a key role in the Park's development, responded to my plea for help. He briefed me during a visit to the Park while the Director gave me some very useful slides. Once in Jakarta I deployed this new-found wisdom to the best of my ability. I suspect my basic message was rather discouraging – one must start with the fizzing science rather than look to a science park to create it.

The British Council's main aim was to encourage more Indonesian students to look to Britain for higher education, rather than Australia (the most popular destination at that time) or the USA. Once the Jakarta meetings were over the visiting team spread out to visit universities in different parts of Indonesia. I went, with Clive Booth of Oxford Brookes University, to North Sulawesi which I had never managed to visit during my time in Jakarta. We had a fascinating trip. This area had become proudly Protestant under the Dutch who sent different types of missionary to different islands and there were churches everywhere. It was coming up for Christmas and I will never forget a long taxi ride through tropical forest with local versions of seasonal music blaring over the radio. My favourite was "For the sake of old man Syne." As well as the University of Manado we visited an institution financed by American Baptists in a beautiful spot in the nearby mountains. The contrast between the cash-strapped state institution in its dingy buildings and the glamour of the Baptists with their slick presentation could not have been more stark. Later, back in Girton, a student came to me asking for help in arranging a summer attachment in Indonesia and I wrote to both universities. Both eventually said yes but of course the Baptists got their act together first and that is where she went. In retrospect I am sorry about this because she would have had a more authentic experience – and I suspect more real kindness – in Manado. She told me on return that she had felt like a trophy to be shown off.

In paying my farewell Foreign Office calls I told the Foreign Secretary, Douglas Hurd, that I would do what I could to promote the European cause in Cambridge. Once there I discovered that the lawyers were way out ahead, with the very active Centre for European Legal Studies organizing courses on European law in the countries of Eastern Europe which were applying to join the EU. I enlisted the help of its Director Bill Cornish and a few other sympathisers to consider what else could be done across the University. At times our meetings felt a bit fruitless but looking back some very positive things did happen. On the student side I joined forces with Anil Seal, a Fellow of Trinity, who ran the Cambridge Commonwealth Trust scholarship scheme. Trinity had leapt to the rescue when the Thatcher government suddenly introduced high fees for foreign students, and now they agreed to introduce a parallel scheme for European students, from both east and west. The Cambridge European Trust lives on in name as part of a wider scheme now run by the University and called The Cambridge Commonwealth, European and International Trust. Another achievement was setting up a lecture series bringing leading European speakers to Cambridge. The lectures were very popular, particularly with graduate students doing Masters degrees. I called in contacts from my Luxembourg days, such as Tristan Garel-Jones, whom I had known as Minister for Europe, Robin Leigh-Pemberton, former Governor of the Bank of England, and Jean-Claude Juncker, now Prime Minister of Luxembourg. John Eatwell, the President of Queens, was a valuable ally in recruiting exciting speakers. I particularly remember the influential German politician Wolfgang Schäuble, not least because he came in a wheel-chair and we had to explore Queens' murkier regions to find a lift to take him to dine in the medieval College Hall.

Towards the end of my time in Cambridge an embarrassing anniversary loomed. In 1948 Cambridge was the last British university to grant women full degrees. The antennae honed in the Foreign Office News Department twitched nervously. I raised the matter in the University Council and predictably the vice-Chancellor asked me to chair a committee and to make proposals as to what to do about the problem. All of the women who had lost out had of course been to Girton or Newnham, which were the only two women's colleges in 1948. My opposite number at Newnham was the brilliant philosopher Onora O'Neill. It was she who pointed out that the pre-1948 alumnae did not regard their Cambridge experience as in any way second rate. In fact, by the time the University did the right thing by them, women students had bit by bit acquired full rights in most practical matters, apart from receiving the title to their degree through the post (vulgarly known as a BA tit) rather than getting the real thing with a ceremony. Women dons were far more discriminated against, with no right to vote on University matters or take part in events such as Honorary Degree ceremonies, while the two women's colleges did not have the status of full colleges of the University.

My committee met and different people came up with a number of ideas, all of which I think went ahead. There was a conference on women's history at Newnham, an exhibition of photographs of prominent women alumni, a special edition of the University journal *Cam*. As a member of the Honorary Degrees Committee I proposed that we should have a list of honorands with equal numbers of men and women. There was a tendency on the Committee to bewail the lack of women of sufficient stature, so with help from expert friends I tabled a list of women nominees for each of the categories usually honoured. We ended up with a splendidly balanced list including Barbara Castle and Aung San Suu Kyi. It was also agreed that the lunch which traditionally followed the Degree Ceremony should be at Girton, for the first time, I believe. What I didn't realize in proposing this was that the University would take over all the arrangements including the guest list. As it was, very few Fellows were able to share my pride in welcoming these prestigious guests to the College. It felt unreal to be sitting at High Table with the Duke of Edinburgh (as Chancellor of the University) on my left and the Queen Mother (as College Visitor) on my right. Prince Philip produced a laugh when he started his speech by saying he did not expect to be up staged by his mother-in-law in his own university. This induced the Queen Mum to make an impromptu speech of her own. She was then in her late 90s and we had not expected her to come at all, but that was to reckon without her indominable spirit. She arrived by helicopter on the hockey pitch and insisted on meeting students before she left.

But the centrepiece of what became the year of women had to be a Senate House ceremony for those pre-1948 women graduates who had been deprived of one long ago. This was the main focus of my own efforts. When

I put my proposal to the University Council, the vice-Chancellor asked me how many women I expected to come. Don't know, I said; perhaps 300. In the event 900 women came back for their great day – far more than the Senate House could contain.

The University pulled out all the stops to celebrate them and all they had achieved. Everyone in the University seemed happy to join in, from vice-Chancellor Alec Broers down. I must again mention Geoffrey Skelsey who had the wonderful gift of making things happen. We had to run the Senate ceremony three times, with processions in scarlet gowns and speeches by the vice-Chancellor and the University Orator. Onora and I settled on three remarkable women to reply on behalf of their contemporaries. For the oldest group it was Baroness Nora David (a sprightly Labour peer in her mid-80s), for the middle group Dame Beryl Platt (an aeronautical engineer and Conservative politician) and for the youngest group Dame Margaret Anstee (who had a stellar career at the UN). They all spoke well and from the heart. After each ceremony there was a champagne reception on the Senate House lawn. The sun shone, the bells of Great St Mary's pealed, and the crowds who had gathered to watch spontaneously cheered. There were lunches for the returning alumnae in their respective Colleges and fleets of buses with police escorts carrying them to and fro. I saw hardly any of what happened in Girton itself because I was busy at the University end so I had to leave the college arrangements in the capable hands of my secretary Judy Stone. She did a marvellous job corresponding with our old ladies and looking after their differing requirements.

I don't know who had the brilliant idea of making a film of the day. It is called *As is Your Due* and is very moving. I watched it a couple of years ago, sitting next to Marilyn Strathern, who succeeded me at Girton. She suddenly gasped: she had no idea that her 90-year-old mother was on film talking about her time at Cambridge. Twenty-five years on I still occasionally meet someone who participated in the day; one told me, without realizing my involvement, that it was one of the best days of her life. It is certainly one of the achievements of which I am most proud and it was a splendid climax to my own Cambridge years.

Whenever I go back to Girton, which I do with pleasure, I find it a bit disconcerting to be looked down on by my own portrait in the College Hall. There is a tradition that Mistresses are painted and there we all are in our own period styles. My portrait was painted by Andrew Festing, a fine painter who later became President of the Royal Society of Portrait Painters.

He was a nice and interesting man but I found the process of being painted much more taxing than I expected. Being stared at so intensively for about a week felt intrusive and to my mind the Juliet of the portrait looks a bit defensive. Alec never liked her.

Girton has gone from strength to strength under my successors. Wanting to give something back a few years ago I pump primed endowment of a Fellowship in International Relations. Since Brexit I see it as more important than ever that our country understands and works with the wider world. It has been a thrill to meet the first Juliet Campbell Fellow and I am most grateful to all the generous people who helped make my dream a reality. For me personally it seems to complete the circle of my professional life.

AFTERWORD

My adult life has been lived (until very recently) in a period of peace and prosperity, for most of the world at least. Technological change has been astonishing and it has been a time of great advances in health and longevity. In many ways we have had it too good, relying unthinkingly on the investments of the past and assuming that the natural world would keep on giving. It is only recently that I have fully realised this and started to have a sense of guilt about the legacy my generation has left to those who follow us. I dread to think how many air miles I personally have clocked up for work and probably more for pleasure.

As I have worked on this book, now in my 80s and reliving my own past, I have often thought how lucky I am to have lived in such interesting places, met such interesting people and had such interesting jobs. For women in particular, opportunities have opened out spectacularly during my lifetime and I have certainly benefited. I was lucky in my parents who supported me in wanting a career at a time when marriage was still considered the main object for girls of my class. After university I was able to sit the Foreign Office exams along with the men which would have been impossible ten years earlier. As I progressed up the diplomatic tree possibilities opened up before me. Being a woman in a man's world was fun though it also had its problems. In my early career being a woman ruled one out from consideration for some jobs. By the time I was appointed as Ambassador to Luxembourg the Office was actively looking for women to promote. Today many of our senior ambassadorial posts are held by women.

The Diplomatic Service changed in other ways too. Life was certainly much more leisurely when I joined the Western Department in the late 50s. Even the most urgent of telegrams had to be decoded, typed and circulated by hand and I seldom got to my desk in the Foreign Office before 10am when "the distribution" reached the department. My seniors had lunch at their clubs and dropped into my shared office in the afternoon for a cup of tea and discussion of world events. In Bangkok and Jakarta my working and private lives were largely governed by the rhythm of the weekly bag with its all-important letters. Instant communications have changed all that in the same way that computers on every desk have made typists obsolete. Perhaps staffing levels were on the lavish side in Embassies like Bangkok but they reflected the situation in many other fields. It was a less pressured world.

Today's Service sounds in many ways a less enjoyable place to work in. But many of the seeds of change were planted during my time. The tendency of successive Prime Ministers to side-line the Foreign Office was already evident under Mrs Thatcher who despised diplomats and liked to call the shots from No 10. Since then the traditional role of diplomats and civil servants to give impartial advice has increasingly been called into question by Ministers impatient to get things done their way. The trend towards politicisation of the Civil Service is to my mind a disaster. The Diplomatic Service has suffered more than its share of budget cuts which translate directly into cuts in personnel. Here again I think this is profoundly unwise, particularly at a time when Britain is having to rethink its post-Brexit place in the world. In one area of particular interest to me the abolition of its own language training school by Margaret Beckett (though reversed to some extent by William Hague) must have damaged area expertise. I don't believe the Service has lost its own sense of dedicated mission – the young diplomats I meet are very like the people I worked alongside – but it has suffered a loss of public esteem.

If the Service has changed, did it change me? The answer must be yes because I was pretty green when I joined. My role models were almost all men and very clever ones too. I learned from them to look at problems from all sides – and today irritate some of my family by my dispassionate approach to issues they see as simply right and wrong. I find it difficult to be as appalled by stories of individual human misery as I think one should be. (To myself I call this "the Mountolive syndrome" after the disengaged diplomat who figured in Lawrence Durrell's *Alexandria Quartet*.) At a very different level the quality of the writing in the despatches that regularly crossed my desk inspired me to self-conscious efforts at fine writing in my own letters and diaries. As is clear from this book I was prone to agonising lapses of self-confidence. I didn't suffer more than the usual bouts of shyness as a girl and I don't remember suffering this way at Girton. I certainly don't now. It may have had something to do with my years in the Diplomatic Service. Perhaps it was the result of feeling I always had to struggle to be good enough, a feeling that was probably accentuated by being a woman in a man's world. In the early days I felt very much on trial, as myself and as a pioneer of sorts, with a duty to prove a woman could do the job as well as anybody. It was a privilege to belong to such an elite Service; I was and still am immensely proud of having done so.

I sometimes ask myself whether I would have got married earlier if it wasn't for being in the Diplomatic Service. I was in my late 30s when the requirement for women to leave the Service on marriage was dropped. I was 47 when I got married: my life plan as I was growing up was to marry at about 24 and live in the country with lots of dogs, horses and children. Things turned out very differently! The pattern of frequent postings to far places was certainly disruptive to slow-burning relationships and I might never have married at all if Alec and I had not been devoted letter writers. But I do not think it was commitment to my career which stopped me from marrying earlier so much as reticence about committing myself to any particular man.

And what of politics? The problem of the Palestinian refugees was the background music to my teenage years in Beirut which planted a life-long interest in the Middle East. Like other students of my time I was stirred and outraged by the very different invasions of Hungary and Suez. But it was during my time in the Foreign Office that the seed of political interest grew into a fascination. Though I never wanted to be a politician myself I was increasingly absorbed by the personalities involved and the problems they faced. From my ring-side seat at Britain's first attempt to join the Common Market in the early 60s I watched many of the leading politicians of Britain and of Europe. I greatly admired the young Edward Heath (though not the bitter old man he tragically became). I became convinced that Britain's future lay in Europe and played my small part in helping defeat the anti-marketeers at the time of the first referendum on membership in the early 70s. I remain horrified by the casual way our recent leaders threw away the benefits of membership with scarcely a thought to the damage done to the structure of the UK or to the historic project of building peace in Europe.

Watching politicians at close quarters during my time in the European Integration Department gave me a sympathy for the pressures they face. Few problems that reach them are simple and problems seem to come in droves; it is difficult to focus fully on more than one or two major crises at a time. Most of those whom I came across were doing their best for the good of the country as they saw it, though party interests could never be completely absent. Old people are all too apt to think that things were better in their young days but I wish that today we had more men in active politics of the calibre of Heath, Heseltine, Hurd or Howe – and that is only to name Tories beginning with H!

My years in Cambridge were a coda to my main career – seven years as opposed to 35 in the Diplomatic Service. I would never have been elected Mistress of Girton if I had not previously been a successful woman diplomat. They were enjoyable years spent among highly intelligent people. I loved the fizz of bright young minds and the opportunity to meet so many people at the cutting edge of research. I may have found the admin indigestible but my years on the University Council involved me closely in the life of Cambridge and brought me into contact with many remarkable people. It was an exhilarating period. I remember walking through Kings to attend a Council meeting one morning with the spring flowers around my feet and wondering how I had earned the right to work in such a beautiful place. Girton's red brick grew on me too and I relished the fellowship of the College community. It was an honour to head Girton for a while and I greatly enjoy going back there when I can. I much approve of my successors and rejoice to see the flourishing College it is today.

But ultimately the greatest pride of my life is to have represented Queen and country.

INDEX

Notes

1. Abbreviations used in the index
   AC (Alec Campbell)
   EID (European Integration Dept, FCO)
   JC (Juliet Campbell)
   NC (Nancy Collings) (JC's mother)
   WC (Wilfred d'Auvergne Collings (JC's father))
   WD (Western Dept, FO)
2. Titles where shown are normally those held at the time of the events being described.

Planting trees to catch carbon • Planting trees to catch carbon
Printed on Carbon Captured paper
Holywell Press
14039900282